# Autistic Masking

## Understanding Identity Management and the Role of Stigma

Amy Pearson and Kieran Rose

Pavilion
PUBLISHING

# Autistic Masking: Understanding Identity Management and the Role of Stigma

© Pavilion Publishing & Media

The authors have asserted their rights in accordance with the Copyright, Designs and Patents Act (1988) to be identified as the authors of this work.

**Published by:**

Pavilion Publishing and Media Ltd
Blue Sky Offices
25 Cecil Pashley Way
Shoreham by Sea
West Sussex
BN43 5FF

Tel: 01273 434 943
Email: info@pavpub.com
Web: www.pavpub.com

Published 2023

A catalogue record for this book is available from the British Library.

**ISBN:** 978-1-803882-11-6

*Pavilion Publishing and Media is a leading publisher of books, training materials and digital content in mental health, social care and allied fields. Pavilion and its imprints offer must-have knowledge and innovative learning solutions underpinned by sound research and professional values.*

**Authors:** Amy Pearson and Kieran Rose
**Editor:** Mike Benge
**Cover design:** Emma Dawe, Pavilion Publishing and Media Ltd
**Page layout and typesetting:** Tony Pitt, Pavilion Publishing and Media Ltd

Dedicated to the members of the Autistic community who are no longer with us, and to a better future for those that remain, and for those still to come.

"We don't have to fall into the same category to be of equal value."

Becky Chambers,
A Psalm for the Wild-Built (Monk & Robot, #1)

# About the authors

Dr Amy Pearson is a Developmental Psychologist and Senior Lecturer at the University of Sunderland. Her research focuses on understanding factors that impact on wellbeing among autistic and other neurodivergent people across the lifespan, such as interpersonal relationships and victimisation, social identity and stigma, and increasing accessibility for neurodivergent people in higher education. She lives on the North East coast with her partner, Andrew, and their Alaskan Malamute, Ragnar.

Kieran Rose is a trainer and consultant to organisations across the world, with a career background in education. His academic work and publications focus on autistic masking, identity and interpersonal victimisation. A passionate advocate for the rights of autistic people, he was diagnosed as autistic in 2003. Kieran lives on a windy hilltop in the North-east of England with his Neurodivergent wife, three Autistic children and two enormous Maine-coon cats. His work can be found at theautisticadvocate.com.

# Acknowledgements

Though it is a bit of a cop-out to thank everyone (to try and manage the risk of forgetting someone important), I would like to extend my deepest gratitude to all of my family, friends, colleagues, collaborators, and frankly, vague acquaintances, who have listened to my ramblings about this book and supported me in getting to the point of writing it. Monique, especially you, for always being a brief message away and inspiring me always. To the Narratives of Neurodiversity Network and all of the wonderful people within, to the members of CAPTAP pushing for the recognition of the impact of stigma among autistic people.

I would also like to acknowledge those who paved the way for us to write this, for the scholars and activists (and scholar-activists) who have been working for many, many years to improve the lives of autistic people, and to whom I feel deeply indebted for the knowledge that you have shared and how you have shaped, and continue to shape, my thinking. I will never feel well-read enough and know that everything I write is laid over the foundations you built.

To Andrew: I cannot put into words how much I appreciate your unwavering support in all things and your encouragement to be my authentically weird self (and thank you especially for the oat milk lattes that have kept me going throughout writing this book). And to Ragnar, who cannot read, but deserves a mention for being the biggest fluff and the softest muffin.

To Kieran: You are the most phenomenal collaborator, and an even better friend. Who would have thought that meeting someone from Twitter for a coffee would lead to so many adventures. I cannot thank you enough for your support, for helping me to unpack my *own* identity, and for the tireless work that you do for our community.

**Amy**

This book is a culmination of a decade of autistic masking being unashamedly the primary work and personal focus of my passionate monotropic mind, but to say that writing it has been easy would be an enormous lie. Beyond the difficulty of honing in on a topic that could essentially be endless and that I could endlessly talk about (and do), the

12 months during which it has been written have coincided with one of the most distressing periods of my life. Without the specific support of two people this book simply would not exist.

The first of those is my co-author Amy, the most incredible friend and colleague who has simultaneously furiously pounded at the keyboard, offered the most supportive shoulder I could ever ask for, and gently steered me through some pretty extreme demand avoidance. I also have to point out that a book mostly written via Whatsapp messages and GIFs is so very quintessentially us.

The second person is my wife, Michelle, who is ever and will always be: my love, rock, partner, confidante, advisor and strategic guru, without whom I wouldn't even have been alive to write this.

Shelly Rose: forget the world now, we won't let them see.

The path to this book's existence is paved with countless conversations and debates indirectly and directly related to masking from over the last ten years and prior. I am thankful to my community, from whom I learn in perpetuity; and the conversations within it which I have been privileged to be a part of and observe, along with those conversations that came before me: we stand on the shoulders of giants. I am particularly grateful to the members of the autistic community and the wider autism community, who have patiently and enthusiastically answered my questions or calls for responses over the last decade. While there are specific people I would like to thank, I'm also terrified that I will leave someone out unintentionally; it is inevitable. So, to cop-out like my writing partner, thank you to everyone: family, friends, colleagues, who have wittingly and unwittingly shaped my work, thinking and practice. You know who you are and how grateful I am.

It has truly taken a village to write a book. I hope we have done you justice.

I couldn't possibly write an acknowledgement without acknowledging the three people whom I am most proud of and who have done their very best to do what all good children should do, which is to distract me every step of the way ("Every time I sit down...!"): Quinn, Albie and Livvy.

Lastly to the late Dr William Edward Burghardt Du Bois, a pioneer, an inspiration and my hero, whose work I had no idea I was paraphrasing with my own words and thoughts for so long, and whom I will forever be indebted to.

**Kieran**

Collectively we could not have achieved this without the support of our publishing team:

Louisa, Mike and Caitlin from Pavilion. Thank you for everything.

We would also like to thank:

The logistical and editorial support of Danni Woodhams.

The powerhouse and incredible mind (and human that houses it) that is Dr Monique Botha-Kite.

We want to thank and acknowledge the following people for their groundbreaking work, conceptualisations and meaningful conversations around masking and all things autism/autistic (and apologise for anyone who we have missed, we currently have the collective brain power of a sack of mashed potato): Dr Damian Milton, Dr Robert Chapman, Dr Steven Kapp, Dr Wenn Lawson, Dr Nick Walker, Dr M. Remi Yergeau, Tanya Adkin, Dr Chloe Farahar, Jodie Smitten, Dr Louise Chapman, Dr Virginia Spielmann, Kristy Forbes, Ira Kraemer, Dr Georgia Pavlopoulou, Dr Roslyn Law, Alexis Roberts, Danny Whitty, Lindsey Bruce, Hannah Molesworth, Dr Jon Rees, Marie Manalili, Mariah Person, Lyric Rivera, Damon Kirsebom, Meghan Ashburn, Dr Kristen Bottema-Beutel, Dr Amy Laurent, Dr Jacquelyn Fede, Dr Erin Bulliss, Dr Morénike Giwa Onaiwu, Nic King, Elaine McGreevy, Christine Stephenson, Melanie Sykes, Dr Meng-Chuan Lai, Dr Becky Wood, Richard Woods, Jodie Issitt, Julia Bascom, Shannon Des Roches Rosa, Julie Roberts, Mandy Chivers, Waleska Watkins, Professor Sara Ryan, Kerrie Highcock, Dr Luke Beardon, John Greally, Professor Morton-Ann Gernsbacher, Laurence Cobb, Dr Dora Raymaker, Autistic Parents UK, David Gray-Hammond, Dr Anna Stenning, Dr Hanna Bertisldotter Rosqvist, Sarinah O'Donoghue, Fergus Murray, Cos Michael, Ann Memmott, Carol Black, Ray Winter, Alex Mitchell, Wendy Joseph, Dr Noah Sasson, Professor Sue Fletcher-Watson, Dr Laura Crane, Pete Wharmby, Dr Felicity Sedgewick, Ryan Boren, Dr Elliott Spaeth, Dr Laura Hull, Dr Catherine Crompton, Joanne Limburg, Dr Gareth Farmer, Holly Smale and the late Dr Dinah Murray.

Dr Christina Nicolaidis for taking a chance on our paper for 'Autism in Adulthood'.

And to our Autistic community.

# Contents

Please follow the link below, or scan the QR code using a mobile device, to access a variety of resources about autistic masking and other related themes.

**www.theautisticadvocate.com/bookresources/**

# Prologue

The primary aim of this book is to act as an academic touchstone, detailing the current research landscape on the phenomenon known as 'autistic masking'. At the time of writing there are already multiple books on this subject, aimed at autistic people and others with a more general interest in this area. We hope that this book too will be accessible to a broader, non-academic audience and that a general reader may be able to pick it up and follow along with us as we explore what is arguably an incredibly complex topic.

The journey to writing this book is probably not as long as it feels. We are a late-identified autistic psychologist (Amy) and a vaguely earlier-identified autistic consultant, trainer and researcher (Kieran). We met in 2019 after a Twitter discussion, which led us to realise that we were living in the same local area. We met to discuss the possibility of working together about five months before the UK went into the first COVID-19 lockdown, at a small cafe in Durham city centre (which serves the most delicious stilton scones!). Almost three hours passed in an instant while we discussed our views on the current narratives surrounding autistic people and our frustrations with the direction that discussions around masking were taking, for example the focus on gender. We continued our discussions, deciding early during lockdown to turn our thoughts into a conceptual paper. The journal 'Autism in Adulthood' had just launched a call for a special issue on the 'state of the science' in autism research, and it seemed like the perfect opportunity (and the pressure of a hard deadline) to put our thoughts to paper.

The idea for this book initially came about while we were working on this paper, which we called "A conceptual analysis of autistic masking: Understanding the narrative of stigma and the illusion of choice'. The word limits of academic journals can be incredibly tight, and as we ruthlessly chopped down the manuscript we kept coming back to the idea of writing something much, much longer on the topic. The idea remained on the backburner until Pavilion contacted us and asked if we'd ever thought of writing a book related to the ideas we discussed in the paper, and again we were presented with what seemed like the perfect opportunity to explore this area in more depth. At the time of writing this book, our original article has 162 citations and is one of the most read papers in the journal to date. There were so many aspects though that we felt we wanted to explore in more depth, and since writing it some of our thinking has evolved (particularly with regards to framing masking as purely suppressive, which we will discuss in chapter 11). This book has provided us with the opportunity to take a deep dive into the area and given us the means to (hopefully) convince the reader of the importance of understanding the way that social context shapes masking among autistic people.

Amy and Kieran

# Chapter 1: Introduction

## Defining masking

We will use the term 'masking' throughout this book to refer to the conscious or unconscious suppression or projection of aspects of self and identity, and the use of non-native cognitive or social strategies.

We choose to use the term masking as this is the term that has most commonly been used by the autistic community to refer to their own experiences (Milton & Sims, 2016; Willey, 2014), however other researchers have used terms such as 'camouflaging' (Hull et al., 2017), 'adaptive morphing' (Lawson, 2020), 'compensation' (Livingston & Happé, 2017), 'impression management' (Ai et al., 2022) and 'self-monitoring' (Forster & Pearson, 2020). The nuances of these terms (and their associated definitions) will be discussed further in chapter 6. However, for the sake of clarity, we are using masking as an umbrella term and not in reference to one specific aspect of the tripartite model proposed by Hull et al. (2017). At the time of writing, autistic masking is an emerging research area and the language we use to describe masking and related concepts is likely to evolve as our knowledge and operationalisation expands.

Thus, though we use masking we acknowledge that it is an imperfect and loaded term, which carries different meanings and interpretations for different groups, creates different perceptions for different groups, and doesn't go far enough in explaining the actuality of processes, mechanisms, and underlying factors involved in shaping its existence. The term masking itself is dynamic, and we do need better language to describe it and its facets in a more nuanced way.

We also need to acknowledge the importance of intersectionality in our understanding of masking, and related concepts. The process of 'masking' has heavy overlap with several related concepts (e.g. code-switching and concealment) and is not just an 'autistic thing'. In understanding the link with these concepts, we must also acknowledge that autistic people who have other marginalised identities may have a more nuanced perspective on the similarities and differences between them and be careful not to co-opt or appropriate these experiences.

# Telling complex stories - understanding complex concepts

Masking is an *incredibly* complex topic. Going beyond the sheer inadequacy of the current language we have to describe it, there are a myriad of interacting and intersecting factors that shape its existence. We have attempted to tell a story with the order of the chapters in this book, starting with exploring the historical context that has shaped our perception of what autism is, and the value of autistic people in society. We move on to explore autistic identity development (and identity development more broadly), and how being autistic intersects with other aspects of identity. Intersectionality is a particularly important concept for understanding masking and its relation to stigma, as well as the autistic experience more generally, however an intersectional approach to autism research has been vastly under-explored so far (Cascio et al., 2021).

After setting up the basic context for understanding identity, we move on to outline current theoretical approaches to masking, before then laying out what we view to be crucial factors in the development of masking: stigma, and trauma. Following this, we discuss and evaluate the research landscape to date, and our knowledge about the impact that masking has, before ending the book with a discussion of our current thoughts on how masking is constructed, and whether it is possible for autistic people to lead more authentic lives. In summation, we have aimed to explore an ecological approach to masking, understanding multi-level factors that might help us to understand the development of masking, and its maintenance. Our thinking on masking is incredibly broad, and though we subscribe to a view of masking as a form of stigma-driven impression management, we believe that the operationalisation of masking may include a multitude of methods, such as suppression *and* projecting the expectations of others, leaning into their confirmation bias.

# Positionality

As two autistic people who firmly believe that external framings shape how autistic people are perceived and treated, it is important to us that our work and writing does not contribute towards ableism (or any other 'ism' for that matter). Though preferences differ between individuals, the majority of autistic people appear to prefer identity-first language (autistic as opposed to 'has autism'), and this is indeed our own preference. Thus, we use identity-first language throughout this book and we also are mindful of how we describe other aspects of autistic experience (e.g. 'passions' as opposed to 'special interests'). Language has a tangible impact in the lives of autistic people (Botha et al., 2020; Bottema-Beutel et al., 2020), and can perpetuate dehumanising narratives and stigma. You will also note that we use the terms 'we/our' and 'they/their' interchangeably throughout the book, fluidly acknowledging our own status as autistic people alongside a more 'birds-eye' view of the literature. This is a political choice, and one that we think is important to make, as to remain situated within the paradigms that we discuss. It can be easy for the reader to distance themselves from the nebulous group of 'autistic people' while reading academic literature, however these issues impact our lives personally and we want you to remain mindful that when we (and you for that matter) are talking about autistic people, that includes us.

We also subscribe to a neurodiversity-paradigm approach to autism. We outline this approach in further detail in chapter 2, but suffice to say we view autism as a value neutral (neither a tragedy, nor a superpower) form of neurodivergence that includes both inherently disabling features (e.g. sensory distress that would be difficult to reduce without rolling back to a time without electricity) and socially-disabling factors (e.g. a lack of consideration and accessibility in the external environment) that can be reduced with a more adequate understanding of autistic needs. Beyond the classical, problematic, theoretical formulations of autism (e.g. the 'triad of impairments'), autism appears to involve shared relatable experiences among autistic people of all kinds, such as a more monotropic (singularly focused) form of cognitive processing and an overlap, or co-occurrence, with a variety of phenomena such as Attention Deficit Hyperactivity Disorder (ADHD), Ehlers Danlos syndrome and dyspraxia. We are pro self-identification with regards to neurodivergence, acknowledging that neurodivergence is more complex than discrete diagnostic categories might suggest (Astle et al., 2022); that diagnosis under the current medical model is problematic and relies on outdated conceptualisations of autism (Kapp, 2019; Waltz, 2008); and that formal diagnosis is also often inaccessible to people for a variety of reasons (Giwa Onaiwu, 2020; Lockwood Estrin et al., 2021), some of which we discuss in this book.

This book is written from the perspective of critical autism studies (CAS, Milton, 2014; Woods & Waldock, 2021), and critical neurodiversity studies (Bertilsdotter Rosqvist et al., 2020). By this, we mean that our work is situated within a paradigm that rejects deficit-focused constructions of neurodivergence, acknowledges relationality (which will be essential for understanding masking), and highlights the power imbalance often seen within the field, whereby autistic and neurodivergent researchers are simultaneously prized as participatory contributors in box-ticking exercises and also undermined for 'lacking objectivity' when we use our experience to critique prevailing narratives (Bertilsdotter Rosqvist et al., 2023).

Despite this book being written primarily with an academic audience in mind, we draw empirical support throughout from both academic literature, community contributions and autobiographical writings. There is often a sense within (psychological) research, that autobiographical accounts gain legitimacy through their re-telling and interpretation by academics, rather than in and of themselves (Yergeau, 2013). Whilst there is value in the creation of a shared narrative via the combined weight of individual stories, it is important to recognise the value in individual accounts and life writing from the autistic perspective (Stenning, 2020). Autistic narratives do not require academic or non-autistic re-tellings in order to provide a meaningful insight into autistic lives and, as we will come to discuss, non-autistic re-tellings may lack hermeneutical authority due to barriers across autistic / non-autistic interpretations. These methods are not controversial in other fields (e.g. anthropology) where (auto)ethnographic work is more widely utilised.

As such, though much of the research that we draw upon is from psychology we have also attempted to draw in theory and literature from other fields such as sociology to create a fuller picture of the myriad factors that shape and impact upon identity. As much as we have aimed to integrate work from across disciplines, we are however apprehensive to call this book *truly* interdisciplinary. Our main concern here is related to the assumptions that may foster in the reader: there may be key texts that a reader outside of psychology may deem to be 'missing' from our analysis and they would be correct – we do not, and cannot, know everything there is to know. In a sense, we hope that the book sparks this sort of discussion. The work we outline here is not exhaustive and is informed by what we have (and have not) read. There are likely readers working in other areas who may see links with theory that we have not discussed, or similarities with narratives in other research areas (e.g. the wider research generated around critical race theory or decolonisation) that we do not have the expertise or scope to discuss at this point in time.

Our aim is to generate wider discussion and interest in the broader societal constructions that lead to various forms of identity management among autistic people, which in turn we hope will generate more empirical work focused on these factors and their relation to long-term outcomes.

In summary, the aim of this book is to in some way highlight the complex factors that lead to autistic masking, and examine areas that are currently under-explored, leading towards an understanding of masking situated within an ecological framework. Whilst we feel that it would be inappropriate to say that we hope you, the reader, *enjoy* this book (given the subject matter), we hope you come away from reading it with a sense that you have a more in-depth understanding of masking and the related concepts that we discuss.

# Chapter 2: Setting the scene: Social and historical context

Our understanding of a particular phenomenon is often shaped by the historical context within which it is formulated, and how our knowledge of it evolves over time. Autism is no different. Understanding the history of autism as a discrete diagnostic category is essential for understanding the social context that autistic people inhabit and the contribution of social stigma to Autistic masking. Whilst it would be beyond the scope of this book to give a full meta discussion of the nature of autism (and any other form of neurodivergence for that matter), it is worth unpacking a little how autism is constructed, not only because the history underpins the context we exist within now, but also because Neurotribes (Silberman, 2015), an important and ground-breaking text which describes this historical narrative, came out almost a decade ago and our understanding of autism and the history behind it has changed dramatically since its publication.

Many researchers view autism as a concrete thing, something that exists in reality and is observable, possessing measurable characteristics (Fombonne, 2023). Neurodiversity, or the idea that human brains (and the thoughts and behaviour that they manifest) differ (Singer, 1999) through either developmental diversity or acquired change, is a biological fact (Armstrong, 2015). However 'autism' is a category that humans have created. Do autistic people exist? Of course. Do we have things in common? Sure. But the category of autism is not fixed, it has been shaped by the researchers and practitioners who formulated the label, and the diagnostic criteria have changed over time as knowledge has developed (Chapman, 2021). Understanding why these specific criteria came to be key, and how they were constructed within the notion of 'difference as deficit' is important for understanding *some* of the stigma that autistic people experience. Specifically, stigma applied at the group level about 'autistic people' (though conceptualisations of normality also drive stigma at the individual level). Thus, the aim of this chapter is to deconstruct this historical narrative, and set the scene for understanding how different types of stigma (e.g. group stigma at the level of 'autistic' versus individual stigma for failing to meet normative behavioural expectations) shape masking.

# The history of autism

Use of the term 'autism' in relation to supposed psychological difference had roots in the early 20th century, and is often attributed to the Swiss Psychiatrist Eugen Bleuler (Bleuler, 1924). Bleuler's work focussed primarily on Schizophrenia, which had been previously called, 'dementia praecox' due to the apparent cognitive degeneration that occurred in early adulthood. Bleuler worked to rename it Schizophrenia, and to develop distinct categories of symptoms that captured both the 'positive' symptoms such as hallucinations, and negative symptoms such as social withdrawal. It is the latter that sparked the use of the term 'autism', taken from the Greek 'autos' (self), to describe the loss of social interest and retreat into an inner life experienced by schizophrenic patients. Bleuler's work was informed by an observational method, the same psychiatric approach that would later define autism as its own diagnostic category. Bleuler's work was pioneering- he argued that schizophrenia was influenced by biological, psychological, and social factors (a bio-psycho-social approach) and advocated for evidence based treatment. However, he also advocated for the enforced sterilisation of patients on the basis that the offspring of 'mental cripples' would produce a burden on society and impact on those 'healthy stocks' (Bleuler, 1924).

The influence of this eugenic thought was foundational to the development of the academic and cultural understanding of autism that we have today, constructed in the late 1930's and early 1940's through the work of Hans Asperger and Leo Kanner. An Austrian national, Hans Asperger's career began in Vienna under the mentorship of Franz Hamburger, a renowned proponent of the Eugenicist movement, and a staunch Nazi. Hamburger was the co-founder of Graz's 'Society of Racial Hygiene' and named as Director of Vienna Children's Hospital in 1921. Under his purview, Hamburger removed Jewish staff from the hospital and appointed his own body of staff, including Hans Asperger in 1931. Despite being newly qualified and of limited experience, the relationship between Asperger and Hamburger meant that the latter was appointed as Director of the Curative Education Clinic in 1932. This clinic drew upon the work of Erwin Lazar, a Paediatrician at the University of Vienna Children's hospital. In Vienna in the 1920's and 1930's it was normative practice for children deemed as 'abnormal' to be removed from society under government purview (though things were not much different in the UK, as we will later discuss). During this time, Lazar developed what has been described as his theory of "curative education", a move away from 'Special Education' towards medical psychiatry framed around 'biological healing'. Eventually this led to Lazar founding the Curative Education Clinic at which staff rejected disorder classifications and instead focused on 'behavioural deviations', assessed by multiple practitioners through multiple tests. This methodology fit with the Austrian government's social work and practice, using a multi-practitioner model that centered the views of child-development 'experts'.

Asperger worked as a paediatrician, assessing children referred to the Curative Education clinic. During the early 1930's, as National Socialism took hold of Germany and Austria, eugenicist practices became codified into law. The law for 'the prevention of genetically diseased offspring' introduced enforced sterilisation for those considered to be mentally or physically disabled. This was shortly followed by the establishment of the 'Aktion T4' programme, under which disabled children could be removed from the family home, institutionalised, and euthanised without parental consent. At the time that Neurotribes was published, Aspergers role in assessing children destined for Am Spiegelgrund (one of the main Austrian children's inpatient clinics) was viewed through a mostly benevolent lens. Asperger appeared to differentiate a select group of children he encountered in his clinic as 'little professors', who expressed some of the same social challenges as 'feeble-minded' children, but had a greater 'intellectual capacity'. These children, deemed 'educable' and capable of contributing to the productivity of the Reich were saved from certain death, and it is this that led to Asperger being viewed as a potential Schindler-like figure, attempting to save those children that he could argue were not 'life unworthy of life'. However, more recent evidence has emerged to suggest that Aspergers motives were not so altruistic (see Czech, 2018). Though Asperger was a member of several Nazi-adjacent organisations and had joined an Austrian Nationalist and Fascist group in the early 1930's, he did not join the National Socialist Party itself and there has been considerable discussion as to how his politics and personal beliefs aligned with those of the Nazi party. Asperger certainly appeared to take a more empathic approach to his patients than those around him (e.g. Erwin Jekelius - whom Asperger spent 6 years working alongside at the Curative Education clinic), however there is little evidence to suggest that his beliefs about sterilisation were not aligned with those prevailing at the time despite his reluctance to recommend it for his patients (Czech, 2018). Regardless of the controversy and sensational context surrounding Asperger, the insidious and banal nature of eugenic thought pervaded early constructions of autism. Aspergers diagnoses were framed around who was capable of 'educating' and who wasn't, who was a worthwhile member of society and who wasn't- even if his own role was more proximal to the euthanasia of disabled children, it was still 'worth by numbers'.

Asperger's descriptions of the children he labelled as 'autistic psychopaths' focussed on behavioural, social and communicative differences in comparison to peers. Examples included lacking integration with their peer group (e.g. were bullied or lacked friends), motor difficulties ('clumsiness'), having strong interests (e.g. nature, or science), ignoring the social context when talking, and struggling to maintain attention (Hippler & Klicpera, 2003). His description shows significant similarity to a profile described by Grunya Sukhareva, a Ukrainian child psychiatrist, in a 1926 German translation of an earlier paper (Sher & Gibson, 2023). Sukhareva described 6 young boys (and later 5 girls) who she said had 'autistic tendencies', outlining their social/affective differences, stereotyped mannerisms and sensory sensitivities (Sukhareva, 1925). There has been considerable debate as to whether Asperger was aware of Sukhareva's work, and chose not to credit her because of her Jewish heritage (either due to personal risk, or antisemitism), and Kanner certainly cited her later work, though never credited her with regards to her conceptualisations of autism.

Leo Kanner was also originally an Austrian national, who worked in Germany during the 1920s as a cardiologist. It was after his emigration to the United States that he trained in psychiatry and paediatric care, followed by a move to John Hopkins University. Kanner spent some of his time at John Hopkins working with Georg Frankl and Anni Weiss, ex-colleagues of Asperger, though Kanner maintained that he had been unaware of Aspergers work when he collated his collection of 11 case studies, later published under the title 'Autistic Disturbances of Affective Contact' in 1943. Similar to Asperger, Kanner's conceptualisation of autism focussed on how the children had an 'inability' to relate to others in a 'normative way', had strong, dedicated interests, and differences in communication (e.g. had a tendency to take information literally). Kanner's description of the children (and their families) paint an empathic (and insightful) picture of their lives, echoing his general approach to those considered at the time to be 'mentally retarded', however Kanner was also an advocate for sterilisation of those who fell into the latter group which is indicative of broader eugenicist attitudes held towards to disabled people during this time period. Whilst the practices used under Nazi occupation are often spoken about as harrowing, the wider endorsement of sterilisation and institutionalisation of those considered mentally 'defective' was also prolific in both the US and the UK where Kanner and others were working on descriptions of autism.

There is no doubt that Kanner had a lasting impact on how we understand autistic people. The full accounts he gave about the children and their families provided rich data on the lives (and outcomes) of people he called 'autistic'. His formulations also aligned with similar work being conducted in the UK, and led to the later establishment of autism as a form of childhood psychosis in the Diagnostic and Statistical Manual (DSM), followed by its (remaining) categorisation as a developmental disability. However, Kanner's desperation to make a name for himself in the field of Psychiatry led to prolific misconceptions about autism, i.e. that it was a rare, childhood disorder. These misconceptions have had a lasting impact, contributing towards a lack of support for autistic adults (Lai & Baron-Cohen, 2015), and underestimations of prevalence of autism within the general population (O'Nions et al., 2023).

This supposed 'twin-history' of autism, which is focussed on the contributions of Kanner and Asperger, often neglects work that was occurring more broadly in child psychiatry. In two detailed historical accounts of how autism came to be established, Bonnie Evans (Evans, 2013, 2014) outlines work conducted in the UK during the pre- and post-war periods focussed on determining the mental status of children under the purview of the Mental Deficiency Act (1913) and Education Act (1944). Though institutionalisation of those classified as 'mentally defective' was standard practice at the time, the post-war focus on the importance of the family environment and educational opportunities led to a growth in child psychiatry as a field. Work conducted at the Maudsley Hospital sought to distinguish between 'mentally defective' and 'mentally ill' children, in particular, how children displaying 'childhood psychosis' (of which autism was thought to be a sub-category, before later becoming a classification of its own) could be rehabilitated as opposed to institutionalised. This approach very much mirrored the work of Asperger, focussing on distinguishing those children who were deemed to be 'educable' and those who were not.

## Where does 'autism' come from?

Like schizophrenia, autism was assumed to have a strong biological component, though there were disagreements as to whether this was primarily genetic, or neurological in nature. The eugenicist approach was to assume a genetic predisposition, and Asperger in particular stressed the hereditary (or 'constitutional') nature of autism and related childhood diagnoses. Later research stressed the neurobiological underpinnings, with Wing & Gould, (1979) suggesting that organic neurological differences could lead to the profile associated with 'Kanner's autism', alongside a genetic predisposition as suggested by Folstein & Rutter, (1977). However, some individuals had more controversial views about the predisposing factors involved in autism.

Similar to Kanner, Bruno Bettelheim started life in Austria. His academic background is much debated, with most agreeing that he may have had a doctorate in Art History or Philosophy (Pollak, 1998, p.49). After the annexation of Austria, Bettelheim was arrested, and spent 10 months in a concentration camp before being released as part of an amnesty (Silberman, 2015). He immediately fled to the US, where his first wife had already emigrated, and became a self-styled Psychologist, citing earlier work with Freud and Jung (whom he had never met). Bettelheim's claims at the very least misrepresented his academic background, yet this did not prevent him from becoming an incredibly influential figure in the field of child psychology and psychiatry. Bettelheim's major contribution to autism theory was that autism had a psychogenic cause, specifically, that it was a result of parenting. The 'refrigerator mother' theory that Bettelheim proposed as an explanation for autism was predicated on his belief that "the precipitating factor in infantile autism is the parents wish that the child should not exist" (Bettelheim, 1967, p.125). Bettelheim argued that this parental attitude was logical, given the "burden" of caring for an autistic child due to their behavioural demands. Kanner expressed similar beliefs, stating that parents of autistic children often appeared cold, obsessive and 'mechanical' in their response to their children (Kanner, 1949) though he later rescinded these comments. Whilst it could be argued that Bettelheim's work contributed towards an understanding that environment could impact on development, it also had a profoundly negative impact on autistic children, and their parents.

Bettelheim's theory of parents being responsible for their child 'developing' autism remained popular into the 1970's, underpinning much of the behaviourist research used to 'treat' autistic children (Kirkham, 2017). Ivar Lovaas, who developed Applied Behaviour Analysis (ABA) as an intervention for autistic children, believed that autistic people were not fully human: "You start pretty much from scratch when you work with an autistic child. You have a person in the physical sense – they have hair, a nose and a mouth – but they are not people in the psychological sense" (Chance, 1974). He used 'aversives' such as electrical shocks and physical violence to 'train' the children, asserting that they had to be taught to communicate (Lovaas et al., 1966). Lovaas claimed to be able to cure autism, with intensive ABA therapy, and whilst we know now that autism is developmental in nature and cannot be cured, ABA still remains one of the most popular forms of therapy used with autistic people despite a questionable evidence base (Reichow et al., 2018), and first-person reports of lasting trauma from autistic people who have received it (we will address this further in Chapter 8). Despite the contemporary acknowledgement that parents are not responsible for their child 'developing' autism, there remains a pressure upon parents to be the one to 'treat' it, continuing a long tradition of parent (mother) shaming and blaming in the autism industry (Waltz, 2015).

## What's in a name?

The history of autism is one shrouded in pathology. The application of statistical normality to human behaviour (i.e. where someone is placed on a bell shaped curve and how far they are from the 'average') has led to anyone who falls outside of these somewhat arbitrary values being classified as 'abnormal' and has moulded our idea of modern worth. Whilst early autism researchers were instrumental in recognising those shared characteristics that seemed to distinguish autistic people from their peers, the prevailing emphasis on the normative standards of the time and the capacity to be a functioning worker has had a lasting negative impact.

The shared observation across early conceptualisations of autism that autistic characteristics were present in both those children classified as being of 'low intellect' and in those classified as having 'normal' or 'high' intellect continues to be the subject of much debate. Asperger explicitly noted this in his descriptions of the children he encountered, stating that a small number of 'autistic psychopaths' were 'feeble-minded' or 'mentally inferior', and incapable of contributing to society (Czech, 2018). The approach to these children among western psychiatric professionals were the same- provide intervention and education to those thought capable of responding, and segregate those who were not. In a seminal study of autistic characteristics across a population of children with developmental disabilities in London, Lorna Wing and Judith Gould (1979) noted that a 'triad of impairments' in language, social interaction, and stereotyped behaviour were present in children who met the criteria for Kanner's autism, but also across other children marked as displaying 'social impairment'. Though the triad of impairments came to be the defining criteria for autism as it is still diagnosed today, Wing and Gould noted the incredible heterogeneity across the children they had identified, and questioned whether autism as a discrete diagnosis was meaningful.

The variability in profile across those identified led Lorna Wing to propose 'Asperger Syndrome' (AS) as a differential diagnosis within the same broad category of childhood disorders as autism. Wing noted that Asperger differentiated his syndrome from autism, arguing it was a personality disorder, though he noted the similarities between the two. Wing argued that a separate category that distinguished Asperger syndrome on the basis of a lack of functional speech delay, and more social-seeking behaviour might be useful for classifying those (children, and importantly adults) who displayed autistic features but had grammatically correct language and were not 'socially aloof'. Critically, Wing stated that, given the lack of empirical evidence as to a definitive underlying cause, no differential diagnosis of autism or otherwise should be based on the presence or lack of any individual feature.

Wing's intended use of AS was to provide a meaningful set of criteria by which those who demonstrated social differences, but did not quite meet the criteria for Kanner's autism (or any related diagnostic classification) might gain access to self-understanding and support. However, this was not how the criteria was operationalised. The introduction of AS to the DSM resulted in an unintended demarcation between those who displayed autistic characteristics alongside delayed language development and/or intellectual disabilities (those with both were referred to as 'low functioning autistic' and those with no intellectual disabilities referred to as 'high functioning autistic'), and those who displayed autistic characteristics but had no history of delayed language and/or intellectual disabilities. Whilst Wing's aim was not to distinguish based upon perceived intellectual functioning (indeed she noted that those with early developmental delays may later show a profile more consistent with AS), AS came to be known as synonymous with the concept of 'high-functioning autism'.

The association between higher and lower functioning autism, and Wing's idea of a 'spectrum' led to the misconception that the 'autistic spectrum' was a linear conceptualisation, with high functioning (autistic people classified as having a higher IQ) people at one end, and lower functioning people (those classified as having a lower IQ or intellectual disability) at the other. Rather, Wing's use of the term 'autism spectrum' was meant to reflect the multi-dimensional and dynamic nature of the classifications used. Wing argued that behavioural assessments were sub-optimal, and that an individual's presentation may fluctuate across the lifespan. While we have recently returned to acknowledging the richly varied nature of 'autism', the idea of a linear autistic spectrum and perceived IQ was well aligned with the original (eugenicist) observation of Asperger that 'autistic psychopathy' was present across both intellectually able, and 'feeble-minded' children. Functioning labels exist as essentialist terms based on how productive or useful someone is perceived to be in regard to their contribution to society, a notion further informed by misconceptions around intelligence and communication. The term 'High Functioning' has traditionally referred to those Autistic people who have fewer perceived 'struggles', those identifiable from an external perspective as being simply 'quirky' or 'eccentric' compared to peers. Low-functioning (or severe autism) was used to refer to those who displayed an intellectual (or learning) disability alongside autism, and was often conflated with partial or non-spoken communication (which may result from multiple factors including situational mutism, or Apraxia).

These perceptions led to the mischaracterisation of 'high functioning' autistic people as needing little support, and 'low functioning' people being denied agency through assumed lack of capacity on the basis of communicative differences (e.g. being non-speaking). 'Low functioning' autistic people in particular were the subject of much conflation around perceived verbal-IQ/language use, and the capacity to understand speech. This perception reinforced the ableist belief that people tarnished with the label of low functioning are incompetent and unreliable narrators of their own experience. Indeed, non-speaking Autistics are often denied agency through the active withholding of alternative communication methods, or the provision of only limited communication methods such as PECs, as an attempt to encourage the use of speech (Brignell et al., 2018; Heyworth et al., 2022; Peña, 2019).

Despite the pathologizing nature of Wing's descriptions of autistic people, she recognised that attempts to divide autistic people into discrete and unmoving categories likely did not represent the complex and dynamic nature of developmental differences. In her 2000 book chapter titled 'past and future of research on Asperger's Syndrome' (Wing, 2000), Wing laments on the reification of AS as a separate entity to autism. She discussed how the application of what she intended as a way to capture the multi-dimensionality of those showing socio-communicative differences, was forced into a rigid pattern of classification via the DSM. In 2013, the utility of such a divide was finally acknowledged, and AS was collapsed back into autism. Since then there has been a growing recognition that lack of speech is not necessarily an indicator of support need, and vice versa. However the spectre of a linear spectrum still haunts autistic people.

# The medical model

The approach to autism outlined thus far aligns with what is called a medical model approach to disability. The medical model views deviance from the assumed norm as something requiring remediation and intervention. Mitzi Waltz (2020) outlines how the idea of a 'normal' child became more prevalent as eugenicist ideals proliferated within academic thought, and the requirement for compliant workers and military personnel grew to meet industrial and wartime need. She discusses how the eugenics movement proposed that societal ills could be attributed to those who displayed undesirable qualities, such as low intelligence, a criminal background, and living in poverty. The medicalisation of societal difference, and the intervention-industry that sprung up around it sought to pathologise anyone who did not fit with a narrow societal ideal, and terrify caregivers into ever more unachievable standards of parenting to ensure optimal outcomes for their child. The shift towards compulsory education in the UK in particular fed into a need for conformity- provision for children needing specialist educational support was (and still is) limited and costly, thus a need for uniformity among students was a necessity. This desire for a homogenous student body has not changed in the intervening years. The parent shaming facilitated by Bettelheim is still commonplace, with parents blamed for the behaviour of children who do not meet normative expectation (or alternatively, dismissed when they suggest that their normative-passing child is struggling outside of school, which we will come to discuss). Thus therapies and interventions such as ABA have become more ubiquitous, designed to ensure that those who do not meet elusive normative standards can be regressed towards the mean.

This medicalisation of autism (or the collection of characteristics that we came to know as autism) has impacted on how we have spoken about, and treated autistic people for almost 100 years. As outlined at the start of this chapter, stigma towards autistic people has likely long preceded the label of autism, as it has for people with other forms of neurodiversity (e.g. learning disabilities, schizophrenia, etc). Katherine Quarmby's (2011) book 'Scapegoat', which outlines the history of disability hate crime, certainly demonstrates that stigma towards disabled people is no modern invention. However, with the specific categorisation of subsets of the population as 'medically disordered' reified within diagnostic manuals, a pathological approach to assumed difference became scientific.

Since the 1980s research into autism has grown exponentially, with the majority of this work focussing on the potential biological and genetic factors that underpin autism, or an attempt to understand the supposed deficits associated with autism through examining the cognitive features that contrast with those of neurotypical people. While it has been hard to determine singular neurological or genetic differences, there have been many attempts to distil the key features associated with autism down to particular cognitive 'deficits'. The most well-known of these explanations is perhaps the theory-of-mind theory of autism (Baron-Cohen et al., 1985). Baron-Cohen and colleagues conducted research with a small group of autistic children, examining their ability to predict where a character (Sally) would look for an item after (unbeknown to Sally) another character (Anne) moved it to a new location. They found that autistic children were less accurate at the task compared to non-autistic children (both neurotypical children, and children with Downs Syndrome). This study sparked a multitude of research into theory of mind deficits in both autistic children and adults, and the proliferation of the assumption that autistic social differences might be pinned on a lack of understanding of other minds (and our own). Autistic people were argued to be socially unmotivated (Chevallier et al., 2012), egocentric (Frith & Mira, 1992), mindblind (Frith, 2001), lacking in empathy (Baron-Cohen, 1997), and incapable of self-insight (Frith & Happe, 1999). Not only did these findings contribute towards pervasive misconceptions about autistic people, but they also impacted on the way that autistic phenomenology was perceived. If autistic people were mostly incapable of reflecting on their own experiences (save for a rare few, Frith & Happe, 1999), there was no pressing need to ask them, or trust that any response would provide meaningful and insightful knowledge.

## Outsider-Insider perspectives

This framing of autism through an outsider, medical lens has led to the proliferation of epistemic injustice (Fricker, 2007). Epistemic injustice refers to the creation of knowledge about a particular group or individual that marginalises and misrepresents their experiences. Fricker (2007) proposed two distinct subtypes of epistemic injustice, both of which are relevant to the historical framing of autism. Testimonial injustice refers to the dismissal or discrediting of a person's experience due to their status, i.e. believing that autistic people would not be able to reflect on their own experiences because of the difficulties we face relating to non-autistic people. Hermeneutical injustice refers to the exclusion from access to shaping the language used to describe the experiences of the group you inhabit, e.g. autism being framed as a deficit defined by perceived impairments in social communication, social imagination, and stereotypy compared to the non-autistic population. Foucault (1977) uses the term 'power/knowledge' to signify that power is constituted through accepted forms of knowledge, scientific understanding and 'truth', and this power to shape knowledge about one's own group is rarely handed over to those who are marginalised. Renowned autistic scholar Damian Milton referred to this particular form of injustice in his article 'autism from the inside out' (Milton, 2017), in which he describes how the categorisation of autism (and the behavioural criteria used to assess it) have been grounded in outsider perceptions of what autism looks like to an external observer. In this case, due to the impact of the historical autism narrative and its intersection with power dynamics in the wider world of social development and communication, the 'truth' has excluded a large amount of important context. The lack of an appropriate or accurate language to describe what it is like to be autistic, and the exclusion of autistic testimony and viewpoint in the development of 'autism' as a diagnosis has led many autistic people to internalise these deficit-based conceptualisations (Pearson & Rose, 2021). This has contributed towards the attempted suppression of autistic ways of being in order to meet societal expectations (we will return to this in detail in Chapter 7).

The social model of disability, in contrast to the medical model, frames disability as an interaction between person and environment (Oliver, 1983), and was part of an emancipatory shift driven by disabled people designed to re-frame and re-situate perceptions of 'impairment'. Autistic people experience disability through both this interaction (e.g. communicative challenges in a society that is mostly inhabited by non-autistic people), but also through some features that are innate to being autistic (e.g. sensory sensitivities) that would be difficult to relieve even through societal accommodation (though accessibility aids do go some way to remedying these issues, Ballou, 2018). Thus a social-relational model (Thomas, 2004), which takes into account individual challenges, and structural/societal barriers can be useful for framing autistic experience.

As the world has changed, so has the conceptualisation of autism, though it has struggled to move on from its initial, medicalised reference point. As Chapman, (2020, p.7) states:

> *"In recent years, historical analyses of autism have found that the concept expands and contracts in relation to the following factors: the drive for normalization and the medicalization of childhood (Nadesan, 2005); shifting economic and gender norms (Timimi et al., 2010); the multitude of industries and economic need surrounding autism (Mallett & Runswick-Cole, 2012); and passing trends in medical and scientific thinking (Silverman, 2011)."* (Chapman, 2020).

Chapman highlights how attempts to 'explain' autism provide essentialist explanations (the idea that autism can be 'distilled' to a particular biological difference or defining property e.g. theory of mind impairments). These attempts to essentialise autism reify diagnostic criteria as a distinguishing feature, rather than relying upon a socially constructed set of norms that fluctuate as society changes. To date, all attempts to essentialise 'autism' (e.g. categorise it through a specific cause, as opposed to recognising it as a constructed category) have been unsuccessful.

# Current conceptualisations of autism

Currently, we are on the precipice of a shift in autism knowledge. An important contribution towards this shift has also been the relentless work of autistic and disability advocates, who have fought for better recognition of autistic expertise in defining what it is like to be autistic, and for autistic acceptance (Kapp, 2020; Sinclair, 1993). The richly varied nature of autism means that there is not (and is never likely to be) consensus over what autism *is*, however advocates have pushed for a conceptualisation of autism that takes this into account (Hens, 2019). The neurodiversity (ND) paradigm provides such a conceptualisation.

The ND paradigm (Walker, 2021) is an emancipatory approach to framing cognitive otherness that argues for a value-neutral understanding of neurodivergence (divergence from the assumed normative standard of functioning, i.e. neurotypicality). Whilst there has been a recent move towards uptake of the neurodiversity paradigm in framing developmental differences like autism, the re-conceptualisation of autism through a non-pathological lens has garnered much controversy. There are disagreements about what the neurodiversity paradigm is or should be (see Dwyer, 2022). At the time of writing, there are factions within autism research who advocate on either side (see Collis, 2023; Natri et al., 2023; Singer et al., 2023). Those in favour of maintaining the status quo argue that a neurodiversity approach erases the experiences of those labelled as having 'severe autism', and their caregivers (Singer et al., 2023). They view the paradigm as a radical attempt to erase disability from the concept of autism and emphasise a 'strengths only' approach that they argue excludes autistic people with higher support needs. However this misrepresents many neurodiversity proponents (den Houting, 2019; Dwyer, 2022). Those in favour of a neurodiversity approach (including many autistic researchers) draw upon research into the impact of epistemic injustice to highlight the dehumanising nature of framing human diversity and difference as inherently flawed compared to an assumed ideal (Botha, 2021). The neurodiversity paradigm does not seek to erase the struggles of autistic people, or to replace it with a strengths based approach, but instead to acknowledge that diversity is an important part of society and that normative standards harm those who do not meet them. It also acknowledges that autistic 'functioning' (or flourishing) is driven by the relationship between the individual and their environment, consistent with Beardon's golden equation (autistic person + environment = outcome, Beardon, 2008).

This can also be explained through the use of an enactivist approach. An enactivist approach to neurodiversity (Jurgens, 2020) acknowledges the interaction between the social world, and our biology, cognition and behaviour in shaping who we are and how we think. This interaction is *intersubjective*, meaning that it involves a dynamic transformation through which our embodied and embedded interactions within the social world shape our development (this will be discussed in further detail in chapter 4). An enactivist approach to understanding autistic people goes beyond the medical ('fix the person') and social ('fix the world') model approach, and in line with the neurodiversity paradigm approach acknowledges how constructions of normality shape the people considered 'abnormal'. Both Chapman (2021) and Walker (2021) relate neurodiversity to the ever-shifting accounts of 'queerness' which are constructed in relation to the social norms of the time. In her book 'Neuroqueer Heresies', Walker argues that autistic people by virtue of their difference queer expectations of neuronormativity. Autistic people inhabit a world that is predominantly non-autistic, and our existence and ways of being eschew outsider schemas of how a human should think and behave. She proposes that 'neuroqueering' can provide an emancipatory platform for anyone (autistic and non-autistic alike) to reject normative social standards (including the idea of as heterosexual, cisgender, white, etc as the default and anything else as 'variations' on the norm) in order to flourish. We will return to Neuroqueering in Chapter 12.

The increasing uptake of the neurodiversity paradigm among autistic people has led to the establishment of autism as an identity. Chapman (2021) outlines how autism as a shared political identity can foster emancipation from pathologising conceptualisations and provide a sense of community/ solidarity among autistic people. However this sense of identity relies on access to accurate language and concepts about ourselves (hermeneutical justice, as discussed above) which are not available within current deficit based constructions. Thus, within an enactivist framework autistic people cannot shake off the impact of historical epistemic injustice in the development of how we consider ourselves in relation to the social world that we inhabit. This will be useful for understanding the relationship between identity, intersectionality, stigma and masking later in the book.

We take a neurodiversity approach in our own work. The perspective we draw upon throughout this book is that the label autism currently represents a value-neutral difference seen throughout the human population that manifests in multifarious ways of processing sensory and social information, and behaviour that may differ from the assumed societal majority. One useful way for characterising the cognitive and behavioural differentiations between autistic and non-autistic people is through the presence of what has been called a 'spiky profile', or a more marked pattern of strengths and challenges across these domains among autistic people in comparison to those we think of as 'neurotypical' people. The spiky profile is captured within the conceptualisation of autism as a 'spectrum'. Autistic people are not homogenous, and like all humans display individual differences across multiple domains (Milton, 2017). This suggestion was based on evidence showing that whilst there appeared to be a distinct section of the population who displayed differences across particular domains (e.g. social, sensory, behavioural), these differences were not static across or within an individual. Wing described children who were socially aloof, *and* children who were socially active but struggled to make friends due to differing social skills. Some children had language delays, or did not use spoken language to communicate, while others were incredibly verbose and had precocious speech.

Thus the concept of 'heterogeneity' has always been a part of autism, however the polarising of 'high' and 'low' functioning autistics neglected this more nuanced recognition of a fluctuating profile. It is possible that this variability that we label 'heterogeneity' can be better explained through a) understanding individual differences, and b) the lens of Walker's more recent concept of the 'neurominority'. Individual differences are characteristics that differ between people such as personality traits, but may also include things like cognitive diversity (Boogert et al., 2018). Though we expect to see individual differences among neurotypical people, there has been somewhat of a suggestion that heterogeneity (or, individual differences) among autistic people is an issue and may warrant subtyping (we address this in more depth in chapters 5 and 7) in order to 'alleviate' specific difficulties. Walkers' concept of the neurominority states that members of a neurominority 1) share a similar form of neurodivergence, which is 2) immutable and shapes who they are, and is 3) responded to by the outside world with stigma and othering. Within this broad concept, there is space to recognise that autistic people may differ from each other in a variety of ways while still being 'autistic'. Interestingly, research is starting to show that this spiky profile is also present across other discrete diagnoses/forms of neurodivergence (Astle et al., 2022), such as dyspraxia and attention deficit hyperactivity disorder (ADHD) which are often identified as co-occurring alongside autism (Caçola et al., 2017; Lai et al., 2019). Evidence of high overlap between discrete diagnoses is potentially an indicator that our understanding of developmental differences is still in its infancy. As outlined in this chapter, what we have come to call autism has been heavily influenced by historical context and the same can be said of other developmental differences. Research from Astle and colleagues (2022) suggests that over time we may move towards a transdiagnostic approach, by which a specific diagnostic label becomes less important and we focus more on identifying and supporting specific needs (e.g. support with attentional difficulties, regardless of diagnostic label). Support based on need, rather than the presence of specific 'traits' or a requirement for significant impairment, may represent a shift towards a more progressive and less impairment-focussed view of developmental diversity. However, this will not only require more empirical evidence to guide practice, but may also need to be underpinned by policy, and a societal shift in thinking.

At the time of writing, autism is diagnosed based upon the guidance provided in the DSM-V (APA, 2013) or ICD-11 (WHO, 2022). Both the DSM-V and ICD-11 define autism through 'persistent deficits in social communication' alongside the presence of 'restricted or repetitive behaviour. Both manuals specify the presence of 'significant impairment' based on the presence of these differences, however the ICD-11 contextualises these, specifying that difficulties may vary within social, educational, or other settings, and presence may be impacted by social demands exceeding capabilities. While this nuancing of diagnostic criteria is an important move towards acknowledging the importance of environment and demand upon autistic presentation (Beardon, 2008), autism is still defined by 'deficit', and socio-cultural aspects of 'impairment' are less accounted for. There is however an increasing recognition that autism is (and has been) constructed under the existence of a neurotypical hegemony. Social rules and structures are centred around the needs of the assumed majority (in this case neurotype). Instead of recognising the inherent diversity within a population and making adjustments, the minority are expected to conform (Jellett & Muggleton, 2022) and are viewed as deviant when they do not meet normative standards. Whilst this conceptualisation of what is 'normal' has contributed towards the pathologisation of those who do not meet it (e.g. autistic people), it has also meant that the 'blame' for any difficulty (e.g. in social interaction) is placed squarely on the minority party.

In addition to his work on 'autism from the inside out', autistic scholar Damian Milton proposed that 'impairments' in social interaction can be de-pathologised through the consideration that social interactions are at their very heart, social (Milton, 2012). Differing social interpretations and styles of any two people (in this case autistic and non-autistic) develop based on our experiences, with each of us gaining expertise with familiar ways of interacting (e.g. speech, or how we move). When we interact with someone who is dissimilar, there may be misalignments between us, and difficulties or a breakdown in communication. Historically, communicative difficulties between autistic and non-autistic people have been characterised through autistic deficits, rather than as a result of bi-directional misalignment. Milton's 'Double Empathy Problem' (and indeed, similar theories such as Beardon's cross-neurological theory of mind, 2008 and the Dialectical

Misattunement Hypothesis or DMH, Bolis et al., 2017) instead states that social communication between two (or more) people should consider communicative difficulties arising as a result of both parties being misaligned, providing scope for mutual learning and empathy rather than pathologising one party. Whilst empirical research into the DEP is in its infancy, evidence supports this notion showing more effective communication between one autistic person to another, which likewise is found between neurotypical people (Crompton et al., 2020; Williams et al., 2021).

Autistic-led theory appears to be paving the way for a more insightful understanding of autistic people. In addition to the Double Empathy Problem, recent work on 'monotropism' has provided a theoretical explanation for differences in aspects of autistic cognition. Murray and colleagues Murray et al., (2005) hypothesised that autistic people display a more monotropic attentional style, that is, we allocate our attention on a more singular or focussed basis in comparison to non-autistic people, who appear to be more polytropic and are able to shift attentional states more fluently. Monotropism can be used to explain multiple differences in Autistic experience in comparison to Neurotypical existence, such as attention, communication, and behaviour, to emotional and bodily responses, and more.

A very deep focus, or flow state (Csikszentmihalyi et al., 2005), focused on a particular task or topic, is often used to describe attentional states focused on what have historically been called 'special interests', which in the language of monotropism have been reframed as passions (Lawson, 2011). Moving beyond that monotropism can also be used as a method for explaining deep attentional states of focus on 'non-passion' interests, such as tasks we are intrinsically motivated to complete.

Monotropism can also be used as a medium to describe differences in sensory responses, whereby the Autistic nervous system is attempting to filter out competing (and potentially overwhelming) sources of sensory information. This in turn leads to understanding social and communication differences in Autistic people, such as the propensity to use direct communication with a heavy grounding in information exchange, as opposed to what might be described as the non-Autistic propensity to use more indirect language. Other differences in social communication can also be explained by monotropism, such as subtle and not so subtle differences in the use of body language and the different use of eye contact.

Lastly, framing autistic attention through the lens of an attempt to filter out competing sensory information also helps us understand the difficulties

Autistic people often experience in transitional shifts. Here monotropism can provide a new basis through which to frame and better understand sources of 'executive dysfunction' (difficulties starting a task, or moving between tasks) among autistic (and potentially other neurodivergent people). Monotropism highlights the sensorial and emotional dysregulation that occurs during the small movements of our attentional states such as from one task to another, and also larger transitional shifts in environment, both geographical and sensory. This theory may be particularly useful for helping us to understand the experiences of Autistic children and young people who struggle in educational environments where there are near-constant macro *and* micro transitions (we will discuss this in more depth in chapter 8).

## Conclusion

The history of autism is fraught with an early 20th century conceptualisation of normality, and grounded within a eugenicist approach to productivity and worth (no doubt compounded by capitalist ideals, though we have not touched on this in this chapter). This conceptualisation has remained fairly static despite exponential societal changes (e.g. in technology and medicine) and some advances in how we consider disability more broadly. In the following chapters we will explore how societal framings around autism contribute towards the broader stigma and dehumanisation of autistic people, and thus towards autistic identity development, impression management, self-monitoring, mental health, and masking.

# Chapter 3: Constructing the self

As can be seen from the historical framing of autism, the autistic self has been highly pathologised. In order to understand and deconstruct current theories of masking, we must first address the concept of self and identity, as understanding how they develop and are situated within a social context underpins the development of masking itself, and the impact of stigma. In this chapter we will explore the 'typical' development of the self and identity across the lifespan, drawing upon evidence from social and developmental psychology, and sociology. Though there is currently very little research with autistic people in this area (particularly young people, and older adults), we will explore how existing research may apply to autistic people in chapter 4, taking into account current conceptualisations of autism as outlined in the previous chapter. We will present evidence on both individual and group identity, and examine how outsider perceptions can influence the way in which we present ourselves to others.

## Me, Myself, and I

The self and identity are notoriously difficult concepts to define, given their multidimensional, dynamic nature. Historically, western views of the self have been shaped by the social structures that were dominant at the time, e.g. religion and the concept of the afterlife vs. the more secular focus on existentialism, industrialisation and views of the self as a 'worker'. During the advent of psychoanalysis, there arose an interest in the 'hidden' self, through the understanding of the human subconscious, and an attempt to understand who someone *really* was and how it might impact their mental wellbeing. The psychoanalytic approach underpinned much of the early psychological theorising into the self and identity, leading to the development of work still used today.

In the previous chapter, we outlined how an enactivist approach can provide a more holistic understanding of autistic identity (Jurgens, 2020) as it recognises the development of cognition and self as an embodied process that occurs in interactions with the social world (i.e. we are shaped by our environments). Though the enactivist approach is a relatively modern position used in cognitive science to understand how cognition is shaped by environment (Caracciolo, 2012), the intersubjective nature of the approach aligns with aspects of classical and recent theories of identity development.

Erikson, (1950) described the development of self and identity through a set of eight 'psychosocial phases' (see Table 3.1), drawing upon the work of Freud but incorporating the social context. He argued that identity is formed through our experiences at each stage and our attempts to resolve the conflict present at that time point, finding the middle ground between virtue and 'maldevelopment'.

| Stage | Definition | Virtue | Maldevelopment |
|---|---|---|---|
| 1. Infancy Period | Trust vs. mistrust | Hope | Withdrawal |
| 2. Early Childhood period | Autonomy vs. shame | Will | Compulsion |
| 3. Play age period | Initiative vs. guilt | Purpose | Inhibition |
| 4. School age period | Industry vs. inferiority | Competence | Inertia |
| 5. Adolescence period | Identity vs. identity confusion | Fidelity | Repudiation |
| 6. Young Adulthood period | Intimacy vs. isolation | Love | Distantiation |
| 7. Adulthood period | Generation vs. stagnation | Care | Rejectivity |
| 8. Old age period | Integrity vs. despair | Wisdom | Disdain |

**Table 3.1:** Erikson's eight stages of psychosocial development

These stages were not age-based in nature (unlike Freud's psychosexual stages), but situated within particular stages of life (e.g. adolescence, adulthood). They were also not necessarily sequential, and a person could move to the next stage regardless of resolution, which was argued to be an ongoing process which included the re-evaluation and re-integration of new information with each stage. This constant evolution provided a framework for considering our sense of self holistically, with each part contributing towards the creation of a self that was greater than the sum of its parts but never truly 'complete'. Though Erikson's work was foundational in theorising how our sense of identity might develop and transform across the lifespan, the cognitive revolution and ability to measure mental representations and their relation to behaviour have provided us with a more concrete understanding of the self. Whilst psychoanalytic approaches offer much in the way of introspection and self-reflection, a cognitive-developmental approach also seeks to integrate an embodied understanding, e.g. is the self innate? When does the 'self' emerge? Where might the self be situated in the brain?

Developmental research examining self-representation in early childhood suggests that a sense of 'self' develops during infancy through the process of self and environmental exploration, which is perceptual in nature (Butterworth, 1995). This occurs prior to the emergence of an explicit 'self-'concept' or verbalised self (Rochat & Striano, 2000), which emerges through the ability to engage in self-directed cognition. Explicit self-concept can be demonstrated in children through the 'mirror rouge test', whereby a red dot is covertly placed on the child's face and their behaviour is noted when presented with their reflection in a mirror. Children who recognise that their own face is that reflected in the mirror will reach for the mark on their own face, which occurs more reliably by around 2 years of age (Mentzou & Ross, 2023). Implicit self-concept however manifests through the child's interactions with caregivers (interpersonal self) and their environment (ecological self). The 'interpersonal self' develops through interactions with others, grounded in shared experience and a recognised distinction between self and other, whereas the ecological self develops through embodied exploration of the surrounding environment and the child's ability to display agency within it (Neisser, 1991). In addition, self-exploration provides crucial knowledge about oneself as a distinct agent. The ability to move one's body and recognise where it is in space via proprioception, whilst also seeing the movement (the perception-action link) allows an infant to recognise themselves as the pilot of their own body. (Rochat, 1998) found that infants as young as 3 months could distinguish between a familiar view of their own body and an unfamiliar view (as demonstrated via longer looking time when presented with a proprioception-violating viewpoint). Thus, here the self can be understood again through an enactivist framework, whereby our cognitive representations and 'higher order' self-awareness develops in interaction with our environment (both physical, and social).

The view of self being contingent on our external environment echoes early theorising from James, (1890), who defined the self as being composed of the 'I' (the self as the subject of experience) and the 'me' (the self as the object of experience). The 'I-self' represented the experiencing or thinking self, whereas the 'me-self' was the sum of our personal experiences (material, social and spiritual in nature). Whilst the distinction at first appears to suggest a dualist view of mind and body (and identity situated somewhere between the two) with the 'I-self' representing our thoughts, and the 'me-self' representing the more perceivable, embodied aspect of our existence, James was explaining the notion that 'I' can be aware of 'me', and how others might also perceive 'me'. Mead, (1934), and Blumer, (1986) explained this through the theory of symbolic interaction, which much like the later cognitive model used by Neisser, viewed selfhood and identity as a relational process. As we begin to interact with our environments we develop a sense of the 'I' that exists, but also of the other people that we interact with in our environment (the interpersonal self, outlined by Neisser). Blumer and Mead emphasised the use of verbal and non-verbal communication (or symbol) in our social interactions, and how our understanding of others is based upon our attempts to interpret or define each other, as opposed to simply responding. Mead proposed that we develop a sense of self through taking into account how others might interpret us, putting ourselves into the role of the 'generalised other'. By taking this role, we can better align ourselves with our interlocutors, attempt to smooth social interactions, and communicate more effectively. Interestingly, modern research into the role of movement kinematics and use of gesture (a form of symbolic communication) in social interaction supports this notion, demonstrating that humans have a greater affinity for people who have similar movement patterns to themselves. Motor resonance (activation in the motor system in response to watching another person perform a movement) increases when viewing a movement that is present in our own motor repertoire, which contributes towards a more positive evaluation of a conspecific, and can increase action imitation and prediction (Cook, 2016). We will consider how this might relate to social judgements of autistic people in chapter 4.

# Self-awareness

Morin, (2011) proposed that self-awareness develops as a result of a dynamic interplay between neurocognitive and socioecological factors. Work from Rochat and Neisser on perceptual and cognitive aspects of self-development demonstrate that the environment shapes our implicit (perceptual) and explicit (or cognitive) self-awareness, consistent with an enactivist approach to identity formation. Additionally, self-representation at the neurological level is spread across multiple areas, including the pre-frontal cortex (Saxe et al., 2006) which is linked to many aspects of self-referential cognition (e.g.

inhibition, emotional regulation, etc). Morin argued that the social world holds several sources of information that we might draw upon in order to develop a self-concept: non-verbal face to face social interactions (e.g. joint attention with caregivers), perspective taking (e.g. imagining how things may appear to others), reflected appraisals (e.g. as in symbolic interaction), and having an audience (e.g. imagining how we specifically appear to others). In addition to the social world, the physical world also provides a source of information about the self. This develops through our interaction with physical objects, and more abstract representations (such as forms of media), and can draw heavily upon our embodied sense of self (our proprioceptive mechanisms). Finally, the self itself can be a source of self-awareness, with our own inner speech and mental imagery facilitating the mental representation of 'I' or 'me'.

Duval & Wicklund's (1972) conceptualisation of the 'I' self and 'me' self, drew upon the use of internal mental representations to argue that we (the 'I') have self-awareness of ourselves (the 'me') as much like we would have awareness of an external object such as a lamp. They argued that we make attributions to ourselves based on how we are in the moment (our current self) and compare this to who we would like to be (a more ideal self). This self- awareness is activated in situations where we may consider ourselves through an objective lens, e.g. we are in front of an audience, or standing in front of a mirror. Here we are able to make an assessment of how we *are* and how we *appear* to be, and examine the two for consistency. Higgins (1987) expanded this concept through self-discrepancy theory, which proposed that in addition to our ''actual-ideal' self, we also have an 'actual-ought' self. This 'actual-ought' self is based more upon how we feel we ought to appear to others, as opposed to our ideal self-based upon our internal values, beliefs and desires. Our attempts to regulate ourselves are built around balancing these competing drives, whereby we seek to achieve our goals (ideal self) but also to fulfil duties and expectations set by others (ought self). Higgins referred to this as 'self-regulatory focus', which we use to minimise harm towards ourselves (either through engaging in a promotion mindset to attain our goals, or minimise harm from external perceivers through engaging in a prevention focus). Balancing these competing ideals through self-regulation can be positive in that it allows us to reflect on our actions, and to engage in self-development and self-improvement. However, self-reflection and regulation can also increase negative emotions, such as anxiety, and agitation (a failure to resolve an actual-ought discrepancy) and rumination and feelings of dejectedness (a failure to resolve an actual-ideal discrepancy).

In contrast to this introspective approach, Bem's (1972) self-perception theory states that we learn about ourselves and the beliefs and attitudes that we hold from observing our own behaviour in the context in which it occurs, whether this be in private or in interaction with others. He proposed that when our attitudes about a particular stimulus are weak, we will draw upon our behaviour to make inferences about them, assuming that the way we act must be consistent with our values. Bem argued that both our internal sense of self, and outsider perceptions are based upon our observable behaviour (a somewhat more simplistic assumption than symbolic interactionism). Like Mead and Blumer, Bem's theory was predicated on the assumption that our internal judgments of our own motivations would follow the same pattern of logic imposed by an outside observer. However we do not always behave in a way that is consistent with our own beliefs or value system (we will return to this again when we discuss Snyder). Bem's theory drew upon research into cognitive dissonance to examine how people respond when presented with two competing attitudes about a particular stimulus. He used an example from Festinger & Carlsmith (1959), whereby students were paid a sum of money ($1, or $20) after taking part in a laborious task to tell other students waiting to take part that it was interesting. It was expected that students in the $1 condition would display more dissonance as the compensation would not be worth a positive assessment of the task, whereas those offered $20 would feel well compensated enough to do so, and consistent with this they found that students offered the $1 compensation gave a more favourable reflection on the task than those offered $20. Festinger and Carlsmith argued that this was due to an attempt to resolve the negative feeling of dissonance by bringing the attitude (the task was fun) more in line with their behaviour (telling others that the task was fun). However, Bem argued that the resolution may be due instead to the participant assessing their behaviour as an outsider might do (e.g. 'what must their/my attitude be if I am willing to engage in this positive assessment of the task), and then aligning their attitude and behaviour accordingly.

Thus overall, our self-concept and self-awareness appears to be based upon both information we derive from our own sense of self (e.g. our values, what we think we are like as people, and how we have acted in the past), and outsider perceptions (e.g. how we think other people might perceive us and the actions that we have carried out).

# The development of Personal and Social Identity

The above approaches all draw upon the idea that we have both a private (private thoughts, feelings, and attitudes) and public self, (public image and how we are perceived by others) (Carver & Scheier, 1981), which relate to the concept of a personal and a social identity. It is difficult to disentangle personal from social identity, not only because our sense of self appears to rely heavily upon interpersonal interactions and our ability to distinguish between oneself and others, but because of the functional role that identity plays in social relationships. Personal identity characterises the self as an amalgamation of our unique personal attributes, personality traits and unique relationships, whereas social identity defines the self through our social relationships and group membership. Aspects of identity allow us to locate and align ourselves with like (or likeminded) others, whether this be based on group or collective characteristics such as gender or race, or similarities in values, personality and beliefs.

Social identity theory (SIT, Tajfel & Turner, 1986) proposes that our self-perception integrates all of these aspects, and evolves across the lifespan depending on the context surrounding us (situational factors) at a particular time point (temporal factors). As an individual we may hold membership within many different groups or collectives, for example a child could be a member of their family, a school, a football club and an after school science class (and so on). How we appear within these different settings will be driven by which aspects of our identity are most salient or relevant at the time. Being at school might activate the identity associated with being a 'pupil' (e.g. putting up a hand to ask a question, walking instead of running) compared to being in football club (e.g. wearing a particular set of clothes, running around, shouting), however even within the school itself, different identities may be activated when moving between contexts (e.g. the classroom where shouting is not appropriate, and the schoolyard where it is part of play). Turner et al. labelled this specific aspect of SIT 'social categorisation theory' or SCT, which explains the cognitive and social processes involved in making decisions about contextual social identity. The fluctuation of which aspect of identity is salient shifts with the prototypes we hold about a particular category (e.g. the defining features of a 'pupil'), which emphasise similarities within a group (e.g. children at school) and also emphasise differences between groups (e.g. teachers and pupils). Whilst this shift in salience may occur implicitly as we shift through different situations, it may also be a result of more conscious decision making to facilitate positive social judgments from others. Tanti et al., (2011) described social identity under SCT as "group-based cognitive representations of the self that differ in their level of accessibility depending on relevant social contextual cues".

Our personal and social identities are impacted by factors linked to where we are in the lifespan. Adolescence is a crucial time for both personal and social identity formation. Erikson viewed adolescence as a time to engage in personal identity exploration, and an attempt to break away from outsider expectations (e.g. caregivers) to establish one's own values and sense of self. Marcia, (1980) however argued that adolescence was not just a period for exploration, but for commitment to an identity. He outlined four stages comprising foreclosure (commitment without exploration), identity diffusion (withdrawal from identity exploration or commitment), moratorium (identity crisis and exploration), and identity achievement. In addition to identity exploration adolescence is characterised by the onset of puberty, and the hormonal and social changes associated (Sebastian et al., 2008). As maturation occurs the social world becomes more complex, due to the changing nature of social relationships and self-consciousness. These changes are not purely hormonally driven, but interact with the shifting social context (e.g. an increase in independence, a change in which outsider perceptions of identity are prioritised such as a shift from caregivers to peers, and the emergence of romantic interests).

Sebastien et al. (2008) examined how the concept of self is impacted during adolescence in neurotypical young people. The shifting social pressures in adolescence lead to a higher priority being placed on external social judgments (and the looking glass self) as young people strive to gain and maintain positive social standing. As a result, during this time, neurotypical young people become more adept at taking the perspectives of others, however there is also an increase in self-consciousness (Pfeifer & Berkman, 2018) as the generalised other becomes more salient. From adolescence into early or emerging adulthood, the clarity of self-concept generally increases as young people develop a more coherent and stable sense of who they are (Arnett, 2000; Lodi-Smith & Roberts, 2010).

Interestingly, Lodi-Smith and Roberts (2010) found that this increase in stability is not maintained across the lifespan. Whereas self-concept stabilises and becomes clearer during early-middle adulthood, in later adulthood this clarity can decrease. However, their findings also suggested that stability of self-concept was related to other important factors such as income, community involvement and physical health, which could have a negative impact on how much someone felt like they were 'themselves' in the face of changing circumstances. In their 2017 follow up (Lodi-Smith et al., 2017) they found that these results were maintained, with social role limitations dictating self-concept stability. These findings are consistent with Tajfel and Turner's suggestion that our social identity is related to our personal sense of self and can impact on self-esteem (Tajfel et al., 1979).

The idea that our different group memberships manifest in multiple identities is consistent with Gergen, (1971), who argued that we have multiple selves and display high 'self-complexity' due to the various relationships we develop and contexts that we inhabit across the lifespan (e.g. school, profession, interests, friends, and family). However, whichever social identity is most salient at the time will take precedence over other aspects and influence action accordingly. Brewer & Gardner, (1996) drew upon SIT, and Gergen's work to expand more individualised constructions of self to include multiple factors, including who we view ourselves to be as an individual (person based), who we think we are in relation to others (relational), who we are within the groups we inhabit (group based), and who we are as part of our wider collective/society (collective identity). They highlight how SIT necessitates a certain amount of depersonalisation, whereby an individual that is part of a larger collective becomes somewhat interchangeable with another, based on the existence of prototypical features. Whilst depersonalisation can foster a sense of 'sameness' within ingroup members, it can lead to stereotypes and dehumanisation from outgroup members.

Tanti (2011) outlines how group identity leads to depersonalisation in order to align more with the group (i.e. minimising differences between members) which can lead to both self-stereotyping, and favouritism of ingroup members to the detriment of outsiders. They measured how social identity related to ingroup favouritism (gender, and peer group identification) and depersonalisation in adolescents, finding that younger adolescents tended to have the strongest social identity effects (stronger ingroup identification and favouritism) compared to older adolescents. However, their ability to define themselves by the social identity of the ingroup was lower, which the authors suggested may be related to the cognitive skills needed to consider and incorporate abstract concepts into their self-definition. The ingroup effects for peer group were stronger than identity across all ages, however the magnitude of difference was stronger for both older both older and younger adolescents. The authors attributed this difference to the social context that both groups inhabit compared to mid-adolescents, which may relate to the transitional nature of these stages (e.g. younger people attempting to find their place in their peer group, and older adolescents developing more intimate peer relationships that may lead to a lower favouring of ingroup gender.

Importantly, Tajfel and Turner also posited that perceptions of the groups that we are members of, can impact positively or negatively on our own identities, and our wellbeing in general (Haslam et al., 2009). We will address this issue of outsider perceptions of group membership in more depth in chapter 5, where we explore stigma.

# Impression management and self-monitoring

In order to influence outsider perceptions of our public and a private self, or our personal and social identities, we can engage impression management (IM). IM and self-monitoring (SM) are terms used to refer to the process of attempting to control the way that other people perceive us through the way we present ourselves to them (Goffman, 1959; Snyder, 1987). Given that identity plays a key role in social cohesion, presenting ourselves in a positive manner can make or break a relationship or our position within a group. We may intentionally or unintentionally hold back information about ourselves (for example our more niche interests) unless it is relevant or of interest to our interlocutors, or monitor and modify which aspects of our personality are salient. For example, a person may show the more competitive side of themselves with their tennis table buddies, but reign it in when at their child's sports day event lest they make a negative impression on the other parents. Whilst this description may sound potentially manipulative (e.g. designed to control how others perceive us), all people engage in IM and the process is not always driven by conscious decision making. Goffman referred to this as 'dramaturgy' (Goffman, 1959), drawing upon the Shakespearian assertion in 'As you like it' that 'all the world's a stage and all the men and women merely players'. He defined our interactions with others as featuring a 'front' and 'back' element, which would impact on the 'performance' created for both the actor and the observer.

Goffman defined the 'front stage' as including features such as the setting of the interaction (e.g. a classroom), our appearance/physical characteristics (e.g. gender, race, clothing) and manner (e.g. detached and professional). Whilst some aspects of performance might be specific to the situation (e.g. a classroom would be used solely for teaching), the clothing worn within the classroom may also be present across other contexts and settings, and the manner of the wearer might vary when they moved from the classroom to dinner with friends. Goffman suggested that an *idealised* performance was based upon the recognition of the prototypical representation of a particular role, societal norms, and the ability to integrate these into socialisation. Whilst some aspects of performance might be particularly fragile to mishaps (for example wearing uncomfortable or impractical shoes because they appear more 'professional' may lead to an injury/accident that shatters the illusion of being 'well put together') they are nevertheless important for communicating that you are aware of social expectations, and are willing to 'play the game'.

Despite the mutual awareness between actor and observer of the socially constructed nature of these interactions, Goffman outlines how misrepresentation of the self can be particularly harshly judged by an observer, depending on the reason for the deception. Attempts to conceal perceived flaws and avoid stigma, or accidental/unconscious misrepresentations are judged less harshly than those that are deliberate or used for personal gain. Additionally, misrepresentation of group membership (e.g. misrepresenting oneself as a golfer) is judged less harshly than misrepresentation of a specific individual (e.g. misrepresenting oneself as being the owner of the golf course). Finally, the 'back stage' is the place where the actor can 'step out of character' and relax; the place where they can be their 'private' self.

Despite the relevance of Goffman's work to everyday social interactions, he did not intend for this theory to be applied outside of a specific framework involving a particular role (e.g. the service industry). However, Snyder (1974)'s work on self-monitoring presents a similar idea that can be applied more generally. He defined self-monitoring as engaging in self-observation and self-control, prompted by situational cues in order to assess and deliver a socially appropriate response. Snyder drew upon Goffman's theory applying it to everyday interaction, and taking into account how our non-verbal signals (akin to symbolic interactionism) can influence how we appear during social situations. He emphasised the importance of different communication 'channels' for our self-presentation, e.g. our voice, facial expression and body movements. Importantly, Snyder identified individual differences in self-monitoring across the general population. Whilst some people were high in self-monitoring, and highly sensitive to the expressions and self-presentation of others, other people were low in self-monitoring and were primarily driven by their internal states as opposed to what was most appropriate for the situation. In contrast to stigma (which we will discuss in chapter 7), Snyder asserted that the primary reason for high self-monitoring was a strategic method to project a desirable public persona, designed to impress others, whereas self-monitoring in low self-monitoring was primarily used as a means to seek validation. These findings also provided some explanation as to why some people's behaviour may be inconsistent with their attitudes, and others were not. He argued that people high in self-monitoring would vary their behaviour depending on the situation, showing a higher degree of inconsistency between attitude and behaviour in comparison to low 'self-monitorers', who would act in a way that was more aligned with their attitudes and values.

However, work by Jones & Pittman, (1982) also suggested that strategic/high SM was not just a means to impress others, but could be further delineated into 5 separate motives: self-promotion/being viewed as competent, ingratiation/being liked, intimidation/causing fear, exemplification/ appearing virtuous and supplication/fostering pity. These considerations will be relevant when we discuss autistic motivations for masking later in the book, however it is worth noting here a crucial aspect of strategic SM is not mentioned- stigma/harm avoidance.

In summary, the ability to monitor the impressions we make and how others perceive us can play a crucial role in fostering positive social judgments as people as individuals, and with relation to the social groups that we inhabit. IM and SM appear to be important tools for helping us to navigate different contexts and ensure that our interactions with others are relevant and smooth.

## Conclusion

This chapter explored how the development of the self and identity is heavily intertwined with the social world and our interactions with those around us. This enactivist approach to identity formation can help us to understand how our ideas about our identity are shaped through how others view and respond to us, whether positively or negatively. In the following chapters we explore autistic identity formation, and how stigma (directed at both autistic individuals, and autistic people as a group) may impact on autistic identity.

# Chapter 4: Autistic Social Identity

Given that the term 'autism' derives from the Greek word for 'self', we might expect to see a wealth of literature on autistic self-representation and identity. However, there is a minimal amount of research on autistic social identity, owing to historical conceptualisations of autistic people as socially unmotivated (Chevallier et al., 2012), mindblind (Baron-Cohen, 1997), and lacking in the composite meta-cognitive skills to be self-aware (Frith & Happe, 1999). Despite the suggestion that autistic people might be 'self-biased' in their interactions with the world, until recently much evidence asserted that autistic people lacked a sense of self (Zahavi, 2010). Thus, it was assumed based on this theorising that autistic people would not engage in identity management, because they were unaware of how others may perceive them (Cage et al., 2016). However, the theories outlined in this chapter and the previous one, and an emerging body of research can help us to understand how autistic identity is both constructed and masked/monitored in order to traverse the social world, and alongside that support us to unpick how trauma influences the relationship between social identity and the whole self. In this chapter we will explore the development of the autistic self and identity, drawing upon historical literature, and the theory that we outlined in the previous chapter.

## Development of autistic self-awareness

Early conceptualisations of autism as a form of childhood psychosis (Evans, 2014) listed difficulties differentiating between self and other as a core feature, which led to the assumption that autistic people lacked a coherent sense of self, or had no sense of self at all (Zahavi, 2010).

Research *does* suggest that autistic social development does not follow the same trajectory demonstrated in non-autistic people. Autistic people display differential patterns of development across multiple domains that manifest in both externally visible differences (e.g. facial expression and body movements, Brewer et al., 2016; Cook, 2016; Keating et al., 2022), and internal, non-visible differences (such as divergent cognitive performance in areas such as memory and attention). An enactivist approach fosters the consideration of how complex internal and external factors interact to produce these differences. Despite there being no identified consistent biological differences among autistic people (e.g. neurological or genetic factors) despite years of research into this, it is assumed that they play a role in neurodivergence due to familial prevalence (Thapar & Rutter, 2021). However, it is also difficult to disentangle the interaction between genetic input and social environment. Whilst there is a wealth of (inconsistent) literature on the neurological and genetic contributions to autistic differences, there is little exploration of the role of family environment and parenting on the development of autistic self and identity. However, as more people receive a diagnosis in adulthood, spurred on by the identification of their own children it is important to acknowledge the interaction between caregiver and child and consider how this might shape both self-perception, and skills. Here we do not mean that autism is a result of parenting (an argument which in itself derives from conceptualising autism as pathology that requires an essence of 'blame'), but that we know very little about how socio-cognitive skills in autistic people are shaped through implicit early modelling (e.g. mirroring the movement kinematics of a parent, Schröer et al., 2022).

Autistic people show differential patterns of eye contact (Senju & Johnson, 2009), facial expressiveness (Brewer et al., 2016), tone of voice and prosody (Paul et al., 2005), and movement kinematics (Cook, 2016). Thus many of the typical indicators that neurotypical people use to signal 'social competence' are often not in the native social communicative repertoire of autistic people. It is assumed that this divergence emerges early in infancy, however as outlined above, the role of biological factors and social environment is currently unclear. Following the discussion of implicit and explicit self-concept development in chapter 3, it is worth noting that there is very little exploration of early development of a variety of different skills in autistic infants for a very obvious reason. Autism is behaviourally diagnosed, and the majority of children are identified from ages 2 and above - there is currently no scientific or diagnostic way of determining whether an infant is autistic.

Research into emerging self-awareness in autistic people has provided inconsistent findings. Some studies exploring self-awareness via the mirror-self recognition in older autistic children have demonstrated no difficulty (Lind & Bowler, 2009), whilst others have demonstrated an inability to recognise oneself (Spiker & Ricks, 1984). Grisdale (2014) suggests that this hallmark of explicit self-awareness simply develops across a different trajectory in autistic people. Indeed, other cognitive-developmental skills involved in self-other representation and argued to be foundational to self-awareness (Morin, 2011) such as eye gaze detection (Nation & Penny,

2008) and following (Riby et al., 2013), joint attention (Gernsbacher et al., 2008) and perspective taking (Pearson et al., 2013) are sometimes shown to develop in a way that diverges from what we see in neurotypical children. Some researchers have used this as evidence that autistic people may have an extreme self-bias (egocentrism), which they argue could account for the lack of social interest found in some autistic people (Frith & De Vignemont, 2005). However others have found reduced self-bias (e.g. not responding to self-related information such as someone calling your name), which could be argued to indicate a lack of egocentrism. Lombardo & Baron-Cohen (2010) argued that it was difficult to ascertain whether reduced self-bias was truly a difficulty in self-reference, or related to other socio-cognitive differences (e.g. not knowing that a name call was an indicator that someone wants you to turn and look at them). They proposed that autistic people might exhibit both extreme self-bias, and reduced self-bias simultaneously, through a reduced ability to distinguish between self and other. They argued that the neural systems involved in self-other coding may be impaired leading to difficulties across a variety of socio-cognitive abilities. This was supported by research showing that some autistic people have difficulties with the use of personal pronouns (Lee et al., 1994) and recognising one's own emotions (Gaigg & Bowler, 2008). However more recent research into the latter suggests that difficulties with representing one's own mental and emotional states may be more attributable to alexithymia (we will discuss this more in Chapter 8), which appears to have a prevalence of over 50% in the autistic population (Kinnaird et al., 2019). Difficulties with distinguishing self from other might also manifest during implicit self-awareness development. Many autistic display differences in proprioception (Paton et al., 2012) and motor intentionality (Gernsbacher et al., 2008) which might lead to problems in identifying oneself as a distinct agent at an earlier point in infancy. However, given the lack of research into early self-awareness in autistic people, it is impossible to assess such claims.

Given the nature of the term 'autism' and historical beliefs about autistic self-awareness it is perhaps no surprise that there is a wealth of literature exploring whether autistic people display one of the hallmarks of cognition that supposedly make humans unique (Gallup, 1979). However, there are two key issues to consider regarding research into a lack of autistic self-awareness. The first issue is how such research contributes towards the dehumanisation of autistic people (by fundamentally placing them outside of the category of 'truly human'). The second issue is that this research has (unsurprisingly, given the first issue) not been informed by the insight of autistic people themselves.

We will consider the dehumanisation of autistic people in more depth in the chapter 8, but it is important to note here that the denial of agency (e.g. to what extent is this person capable of distinguishing themselves from others) and downplaying of uniquely human traits (e.g. lack the capacity for self-awareness) are two key failings of research which aims to explore whether particular groups demonstrate hallmarks of 'humanity' (Kteily & Landry, 2022). As outlined in chapter 2, dehumanisation feeds epistemic injustice; in this particular instance testimonial injustice, whereby the testimony of autistic people is viewed as neither a necessary nor reliable way to learn about the development of autistic self. Thus, until recently conceptualisations of autistic selfhood and identity have been through an outsider lens. Autistic people were assumed to lack insight into their own experiences, and where autistic first-hand accounts were present (e.g. autobiographical writings) these were assumed to be a rare exception. As a result, the autistic voice was minimised, and autistic reflections on self were eschewed in favour of evidence from experimental tasks developed to measure skills in other populations.

More recently, there has been a shift towards recognising that differences in the development of various neural and cognitive processes might manifest in distinct profiles of self-representation between autistic and non-autistic people. The double empathy problem provides a foundation for understanding how this might manifest and what it means for how we conceptualise autistic self-awareness. The double empathy problem considers the role of context in development, exploring how different experiences and ways of thinking shape who we are and how our socio-cognitive skills develop. A similar approach has already been applied to understanding mentalising, proposed by Conway et al., (2019) who argues that our understanding of other minds is shaped by our developmental experiences. Our ability to infer how others may be feeling, or what they may be thinking draws upon a multidimensional representation of a mind separate from our own, not just the representation of a particular mental state. The more dissimilar the mind (or the person behind it), the more difficult we might find it to make inferences about their mental states. This theory considers the complex interaction between individual minds that might make it easier for people to estimate the mental states of people who think and behave more like themselves.

This approach aligns well with a double empathy problem approach whereby we might consider the misalignment, or even cultural differences, between two individuals as the source of social difficulty, rather than impairment on behalf of one party. It also allows us to consider the development of a particular skill in and of itself, as opposed to situating a skill or lack thereof within a value-laden normative/disordered framework, for example exploring autistic development within its own set of norms (e.g. whereby eye contact may not be the signal that someone is paying attention). By taking these differential developmental trajectories between autistic and non-autistic people and framing components and outcomes through a lens of divergent rather than disordered, we can start to develop a more meaningful understanding of how autistic self-concept develops and how this relates to the formation of identity.

One example of applying this perspective to autistic self-processing comes from Gernsbacher et al. (2008). They explored how different patterns of attentional expression may be interpreted as difficulty with self-referential processing (e.g. joint attention) due to the lack of overt typical attentional cues such as establishing eye contact. The authors argue that autistic movement differences may manifest in these different social cues, which when interpreted through a normative lens may lead to the assumption of impaired socio-cognitive development. They draw upon evidence from a range of studies on attention, intentionality understanding, perception, and action to support their argument. They suggest that instead of forming uncharitable interpretations of autistic agency based on atypical responses to self-referential cues, researchers should instead work to understand autistic social development as distinct. One example they draw upon is from research that demonstrates that autistic people have a more monotropic (Murray et al., 2005) attentional focus, and are both less likely to disengage their attention from a particular interest *and* become distressed if required to do so. The authors suggest here that interlocutors might instead join their attention in a reciprocal manner instead of demanding that the autistic person switch what they are doing. Here autistic ways of being are not interpreted through the lens of 'faulty', but links are made between how skills manifest and what this might mean for building bridges in social interaction. Similarly, Nijhof & Bird, (2019) have suggested that future research should explore similarities and differences in self-referential processing among autistic and non-autistic people, and take into account the different pathways that autistic people might use (in line with research into cognitive compensation from Livingston & Happé, 2017).

We suggest taking this a step further in considering autistic representations of self, whereby embodied differences are not taken as evidence of a 'lack of' self-awareness (or compensatory), but instead acknowledged as evidence that measures of self-awareness designed for neurotypical people may not have the same utility for other populations.

Overall, our understanding of the development of autistic self-awareness is, for want of a better phrase, still in infancy itself. In the following sections we move past these initial self-perceptions to explore social self-awareness, and how our identity and conceptualisations of self are shaped by the social world.

## The development of social self-awareness

Whilst the aforementioned research has focussed on neurocognitive aspects of self-awareness, there has been somewhat less of a focus on socio-ecological aspects of self-awareness among autistic people prior to the emergence of research into masking and identity management in autistic people. However, drawing together research from autistic social identity, and theoretical work on the double empathy problem and minority identity representation can help us to understand how current theory may apply to autistic people (and where there may be scope to develop new theory).

Symbolic interactionism takes into account the role of both the environment and interpersonal interactions in shaping self-development. Mead and Blumer's work position the generalised other as the lens through which we consider how others might view us. However, when it comes to autistic self-representation, a discrepancy exists between the 'I' self, and the 'me' self. Autistic people exist in a primarily non-autistic world, which means that the generalised other that we draw upon in order to assess how others may view us may be fundamentally misaligned with our internal sense of self, based upon the non-autistic viewpoint. As outlined, autistic and non-autistic people display differential developmental pathways and skill development across a variety of domains. The visible domains, such as differences in action kinematics may contribute to some of this misalignment. Here we explain how.

Throughout development we develop expertise (and preference) for our own movements, and those which are similar, fostering an increased sense of motor resonance. As outlined in chapter 3, this leads to an increase in positive social judgement, and social affiliation. Autistic people display differences in movement kinematics across both modalities compared to our non-autistic counterparts, characterised by greater jerk, acceleration and velocity (Cook, 2016).Thus the use of symbolic communication (e.g. gesture) may differ between autistic and non-autistic people, fostering greater difficulty in symbolic interpretation during social interaction. If interactions between autistic people and non-autistic people are inherently lower in quality due to lower resonance, and increased communicative misalignment, it is likely that autistic people will come to view themselves as flawed in comparison to their peers (and develop ways to cope with this perceived negative judgement, as we will explore).

Whilst research has suggested that we are in fact imagining how we *think* others perceive us, not how they *actually* perceive us (Shrauger & Schoeneman, 1999; Tice, 1992), studies have shown that autistic people *are* more likely to be perceived negatively by their non-autistic peers (Belcher et al., 2022). Multiple studies (DeBrabander et al., 2019; Sasson et al., 2017) have shown that autistic people are judged more negatively by non-autistic observers, who display lower interest in future interactions based on thin-slice video clips including speech and movement, but not speech content in isolation. These findings suggest that there is something about autistic movement and audio content of speech that non-autistic people find negative. Likewise, non-autistic people display some difficulty with interpreting the facial expressions of autistic people, which is related to them making less favourable social judgements about autistic people compared to those they make about non-autistic peers (Alkhaldi et al., 2019).

The development of social self-awareness in the face of negative social perceptions can have an impact on how we balance how we see ourselves, and how others might perceive us (we will discuss this with specific relation to stigma in chapter 9). Duval and Wickland's work on self-awareness specifies that self-awareness is activated when we are forced to consider ourselves through an objective lens, for example when we are in front of other people. These situations activate consideration of that generalised other, whereby we think about how other people might perceive us. For autistic people, the generalised other may be likely to reflect the non-autistic perspective, rather than an autistic one given their minority status. Both Duval and Wickland (1972) and Higgins (1988), explore how this self-awareness relates to our current (or actual) self, our ideal self, and the self we think others want us to be (our ought-self). For autistic people, the discrepancy between their current, ideal (or 'aught') and their ought selves is likely to be larger given that their ought self is dictated by outgroup norms. The standards and expectations set by a majority non-autistic society devalues autistic ways of being, seeing autistic ways of thinking, being and doing as impaired. Autistic identity expression can thus be heavily impacted by the expectations of outgroup members, meaning that autistic people cannot meaningfully express themselves whilst feeling that it is safe to do so.

This discrepancy can lead to a sense of dissonance and a difficulty in regulating who we *are*, who we *want* to be, and who we feel like we *should* be in order to satisfy society. Higgins, (1998) argues that when we strive to balance the two we engage in either a promotional mindset (e.g.

maximising pleasurable outcomes) or prevention mindset (i.e. minimising harm that we might experience from others). Oyserman et al., (2007) outline how unfair treatment (e.g. from being part of a marginalised and stigmatised group) can lead to a bias in regulatory self-focus being allocated towards harm reduction. People who have experienced unfair treatment in response to aspects of their identity become vigilant to threats of harm and as a result develop avoidance strategies, e.g. minimisation of 'aught' self-promotion strategies, and engagement in stigma-reduction focussed identity management (we will return to this in chapter 7). Autistic people show higher levels of social anxiety (Linden et al., 2023) compared to the non-autistic population, which may be in part driven by their social status and perceived difference in comparison to the social majority, in addition to differing social motivations and social needs.

## Personal vs. social identity

Proponents of 'identity first' approaches to autism often argue that autism is situated within the individual, and cannot be removed. Whilst this can be read as an essentialist approach (whereby autism is viewed as a concrete 'thing' within the person), it is not necessary to essentialise autism to see it as an important aspect of an individual's identity. Autistic people experience 'othering' (being treated as different) regardless of whether they are formally identified, on the basis of perceived differences in social style and neurocognitive functioning (Pearson et al., 2023). Additionally, autistic people often experience a sense of relational similarity to other autistic people through sensory experiences, aspects of embodied self, such as movement, and shared experiences (e.g. interpersonal trauma). Thus even if we consider the thing that is 'autism' to be constructed as a result of the interaction between where a person is perceived to be in regards to 'normality', and the environment that they inhabit, this has a material impact on autistic people as they are currently conceptualised. Ellis (2023) has defined this as 'strategic essentialism', which provides a "strategically adopted response to current realities". Laying claim to essentialist narratives is argued to provide a basis to reclaim them and advocate for change through developing a shared political identity, with a long term goal of dismantling these narratives and replacing them. Recent work has suggested that strategic essentialism may be useful for autistic people until society is a more equitable place (Crawshaw, 2023).

Autism can contribute to both a personal and a social identity (Tajfel & Turner, 1986), whereby a person may define themselves personally through characteristics that they have which may be associated with autistic people, and also through the relational aspect of being part of the wider label of 'autistic people' as a group or community.

An autistic personal identity may arise through a person viewing aspects of being autistic as inherently related to their personality, e.g. thinking of themselves as 'blunt' or 'detail oriented'. Here characteristics associated with autism may be integrated more broadly into one's own sense of self, regardless of whether that is named or not (e.g. one might associate with particular characteristics which are usually linked to autism without having a formal diagnosis, such as people who are late identified). Interestingly, the ability to integrate aspects of autistic personal identity without an awareness of being autistic is due to the ubiquitous nature of 'autistic traits'. Many people who grow up without a diagnosis are labelled as 'picky', 'blunt' or 'resistant to change' long before they are identified as autistic. This perspective on 'autistic characteristics' is one associated with the concept that 'autistic traits' are simply human traits. Whilst some researchers characterise these as 'extreme ends' of a distribution (e.g. autistic social skills being viewed as extreme social incompetence, and no suggestion of what lies at the other end), others acknowledge that our current conceptualisations rely more upon the relationship between skills (i.e. the spiky profile) than a binary distinction. Recent research suggests that many autistic people experience 'othering' because of their differences long before they are identified as being autistic (Pearson et al., 2023). We will explore this issue with specific relation to trauma in chapter 9, however it is worth noting here that outsider perceptions of 'difference' shape the development of an othered identity, regardless of whether that identity has a label.

In addition to constructing ourselves through our perceived personal characteristics, autistic personal identity can be shaped by (outsider) conceptualisations of both 'autism' and of individual 'otherness', that is through whether a person fits with pre-ordained expectations for what is normal (and sometimes, what is 'normal for an autistic person', or whether you meet their expectations of what autistic *should* look like). In this regard, the interaction between autistic personal identity and outsider perceptions is complex. The role of the generalised other may drive how autistic people consider themselves in relation to perceived external attitudes about the self. But personal identity is also impacted through knowledge about what autism is, what it isn't, and how autistic people are expected to be. Bertilsdotter Rosqvist & Jackson-Perry (2021) refer to this as an 'epistemic struggle' whereby autistic people attempt to understand their own experiences in the face of outsider conceptualisations dominating autism knowledge. As a result autistic first-hand accounts can undergo 'epistemic infection', making it difficult to disentangle views of self and first-hand experiences from the outsider lens through which they are predominantly framed. Here it becomes difficult to distinguish autistic perceptions of their own strengths and difficulties from those outlined in the literature about autism and the internalisation of clinical perspectives and deficit narratives about autistic people. Hermeneutical injustice has a role to play here. Many people do not realise that they are autistic because they do not 'see' themselves in mainstream descriptions of autism (Cage et al., 2022). However, some autistic people (who are aware that they are autistic) may come to internalise these descriptions into their self-concept, even if they are not necessarily accurate. We will discuss this epistemic infection in more detail in the chapter on Stigma. There is currently very little work on autistic personal identity.

By contrast, a small body of work has started to develop on autistic social identity examining how autistic people position themselves in relation to their label or diagnosis, how it helps or hinders their sense of self, and how they connect to other autistic people. Given the growing body of research in this area we will unpack it further in the following section, where we explore the development of the autistic self across the lifespan, examining how they view themselves, their diagnosis, and their relationships to other autistic and non-autistic people.

# Development of autistic self

As outlined in chapter 3, adolescence is a period of intense social change for many young people, in which social pressures can increase. These social pressures may be particularly stressful for autistic young people, who are already disadvantaged by attempting to keep up with non-native, normative social practices. Thus in addition to self-identity exploration and crises within emerging social hierarchies, autistic young people must also decipher the hierarchies themselves as they strive to balance their individual identity with a social identity and find their place within the group. The increase in self-consciousness here can be particularly difficult for autistic young people, as the generalised other, or outsider lens that responds to them socially, is often reflecting the perception of the more dominant group.

As autistic people progress into adulthood, the social world can become even more complex with a need to navigate a variety of different social environments and balance the demands of different aspects of life (e.g. family, romantic relationships and friendships, a career) whilst managing a (stigmatised) identity in a world that has normative expectations of what success and flourishing looks like (Chapman & Carel, 2022).

Erikson emphasised how the stage-like progression of identity was linear but also iterative, and though there has been little exploration of autistic identity formation, theorists have suggested that autistic autobiographical integration and identity development may follow a particularly non-linear trajectory. Pyne (2021) relates this to the concept of chrononormativity, or the expectation that people will progress through a set of life stages at a particular time (e.g. joint attention will develop with caregivers in infancy marked by use of eye contact) following a particular set of expectations (that is, a normative developmental trajectory). He outlines how autistic people disrupt these expected temporalities, demonstrating an alternative trajectory and the possibility of new narratives of development. Not only does Pyne's work provide space to consider what 'normative' identity development looks like and how this might be interrogated, but he also provides space to explore non-linear autistic identity narratives from a non-pathologising perspective. Milton (2018) has outlined how autistic identity may be shaped by what he refers to as 'rhizomatic' memory, that is, memory in which connections may be seemingly random and non-linear. Both Milton and Pyne question the construct of normative identity development as one that results in an 'efficient' and 'productive' adult, whose worth is judged through their contributions within a neoliberal framing (in contrast with the historical approach to autism outlined in chapter 2). Milton highlights the concept of an 'aut-ethnography', through which constructions of self and identity may follow a more fragmented and rhizomatic "model of becoming". He outlines how conceptualisations of continuum models such as Erikson's as linear and static do not take into account how our self-concept is under constant construction and revision (as stated by Erikson himself). Milton draws upon Kelly's Personal Construct theory (Kelly, 1955) to explore the idea of a fragmented personal construct, which, as opposed to being centred around a core construct as outlined by Kelly, might be composed of "endless connections" which vary in their relevance and coherence. This work may be particularly helpful in considering how autistic identity shifts across the lifespan, and whereby various narratives, events, and social demands interact to produce an embodied sense of self within a society that expects linearity, coherence, and above all else, productivity.

The concept of chrononormativity may be particularly important for understanding autistic identity across the lifespan. In addition to autistic self-narratives transgressing the expected developmental trajectory and coherence, they can also be impacted by when a person is identified as autistic (either by a caregiver, or through self-identification). Autistic people can undergo momentous shifts in identity as they re-integrate autobiographical information and reconceptualise themselves as autistic.

As such, though we attempt to present extant research in the following sections in chronological order (from adolescence to adulthood) it is worth considering that this pathway is not linear, and many of the issues discussed will be pertinent across both timepoints as people revise their autobiographical narratives to integrate new information.

## Autistic self in adolescence

Much of the research into autistic identity in adolescence has focussed on two distinct issues: identity specifically related to being autistic (e.g. views on the autism label, and disclosure), and social relationships. Research on reflections about being autistic among young people are reliant on parental disclosure to the young person (McLeod et al., 2019). Many autistic people grow up knowing that they are different but not knowing that they are autistic, either through a lack of identification, or a lack of parental disclosure. With regards to the latter, literature on parental disclosure has suggested that it can be a difficult decision for parents to disclose (Crane et al., 2019), and the decision to do so is often based on situational complexity (e.g. the age of the child and their level of understanding, parental confidence in explaining, attempts not to make disclosure a 'defining moment'). Parents believed that disclosure was important for empowerment of the young person, but also expressed wanting to 'get it right'. Interestingly, research with *autistic* parents of autistic children (Crane et al., 2021) showed similar concerns, with parents wanting to ensure their child was old enough to understand. However they also spoke about the importance of being able to use their own lived experience to validate their children's concerns, and of helping their children to develop a positive self-concept whilst advocating for their own needs. Riccio et al., (2021) found that young people whose parents had voluntarily disclosed to them tended to have a more positive conceptualisation of autism and themselves compared to people whose parents had not disclosed, or had disclosed involuntarily. Their findings suggested that voluntary disclosure could be important in helping autistic young people to develop self-understanding and a more positive sense of self later in life.

In contrast, a lack of disclosure might deny autistic young people the self-determination and agency to learn about themselves, what autism might mean for them as an individual, and the possibilities that exist in regards to their own identity. Multiple studies have shown that young people vary in regards to whether they regard a diagnostic label as a positive (Humphrey & Lewis, 2008; Mesa & Hamilton, 2022). Some autistic young people value a label for their difference, and find that knowing they are autistic helps them to achieve self-understanding and self-advocacy (e.g. being able to share their accessibility needs in their school environment). However, some young people find the label highly stigmatising and attempt to distance themselves from it for fear of being further marked out as different by their peers. Despite knowing that others find them different, they feel that the label of autism comes with particular stereotypes (see chapter 7) that might cause their peers and teachers to make negative social judgments about them. These concerns are often grounded in prior experiences. For example Humphrey and Lewis (2008) explored the experiences of autistic young people at school and found that they felt singled out as 'different' in comparison to their peers, and treated as less capable as a result. This led the young people to view being autistic as a negative thing, internalising outside attitudes into their self-concept and desiring to be seen as 'normal'. These findings were echoed by Mesa and Hamilton (2021) who found that autistic young people drew upon societal discourse (medical versus neurodiversity framings of autism) when speaking about their own identities, with neurodiversity framings leading to a more positive sense of self. However, all students still viewed normal and 'different' as dichotomous, with even the students who did not view autism as a negative aspect of themselves reporting that they engaged in masking whilst in school. These findings suggest that autistic young people can develop a positive autistic personal and social identity, but that the expression of this identity may be moderated by social pressure and a felt need to 'fit in' within their social environments. Importantly, in Mesa and Hamilton's study both parents and young people outlined how teachers treated autistic young people as homogenous, often underestimating them or expecting them to all have the same needs. These findings emphasise a) how external (and stigmatising) perceptions of autism impact on autistic people, and b) how the pervasive nature of dehumanising notions around autistic uniqueness has a tangible impact on how people are treated by those who aim to support them.

A small amount of research has focussed more broadly upon self-concept in autistic young people, and their engagement in impression management. Cage et al., (2016) interviewed autistic adolescents about their experiences of IM and relationships in a school setting. They found that some autistic young people described modifying the way they acted to fit in, e.g. trying to find out about other's interests and learn about these to facilitate relationships, though some also spoke about realising they were attempting to fit in without trying to do so. Some spoke about not caring about fitting in and wanted to be themselves. Regardless of whether students identified themselves as engaging in IM, they struggled to understand what made other people popular or 'cool', and were not interested in learning about why people would act in this way. These findings suggested that whilst some autistic young people had a desire to blend in with the social groups they identified with, they did not see themselves aligning with those who were attributed as having a higher social status. This is consistent with Sedgewick et al., (2016, 2019) who found that autistic adolescent girls in particular struggled with peer conflict and wanting to fit in at school, however were unaware of the social hierarchies that neurotypical girls referred to (e.g. competing with others).

In regards to their self-concept, the young people in Cage's (2016) study described themselves using mostly physical traits and some features of their personality, however when asked to describe themselves from an outside perspective they more frequently used personality and behavioural descriptors. These findings suggested that the young people had considered how they might appear to other people, and the personal features that other people might perceive them to have. This study, alongside others on autistic identity, provided an important insight into how autistic people feel about how others perceive them, and how they see themselves within the social hierarchy. It was long assumed that autistic people would not display insight into external social judgements due to the suggestion that autism was characterised primarily by a deficit in performing mental state inferences and understanding the thoughts, beliefs and desires of other people. Studies into autistic identity and impression management fundamentally undermine such accounts by demonstrating that autistic people can and do consider outsider perceptions of themselves and attempt to shape their behaviour accordingly.

More recently, Morgan (2023) has explored both self-concept and social identity in autistic adolescent girls. She found that a diagnostic label served to help them make sense of their own narratives and situate their struggles growing as more than just 'problem behaviour'. However the author acknowledges that in this study it was the experience of a formal diagnosis that acted as the catalyst to provide this meaning. Consequently those who are denied formal diagnosis, or those who self-identify may struggle to be afforded legitimacy for their identity and are beholden to gatekeepers (e.g. professionals involved in the diagnostic process) who hold the power to shape their self-concept. With regards to balancing autistic personal with social identity, the young people stressed their own sense of uniqueness within the overarching category of 'autistic', resisting stigmatising and dehumanising narratives of homogeneity in order to establish themselves as an individual. They viewed themselves as being in the process of 'becoming their best self', but also conceptualised being autistic as something that could hold them back within a neoliberal society. Their future self-narratives were centered around employment and 'being behind', emphasising how they saw themselves in relation to the expected trajectories a young person is meant to process through. Finally, the young people outlined how normativity impacted on their self-concept and development, impacting on where they saw themselves fitting (e.g. not fitting in with expected norms, but also sometimes not fitting in with other autistic people). This led to a sense that authentic identity expression could only be achieved in safe environments, which the "normative world" did not provide.

Going beyond self-concept, Cooper et al. have conducted multiple studies to explore how autistic identity (both personal and social) might relate to mental health outcomes. In Cooper et al., (2021) they explored how an autistic social identity might contribute towards self-esteem in autistic young people. They were interested in the factors that might influence how closely autistic young people identified with a broader autistic social identity (e.g. stigma and negative social perceptions), and how this might moderate self-esteem. The authors found that autistic people who associated autism with more positive character attributes tended to have improved collective self-esteem and a stronger affiliation with their autistic identity. Participants identified autism as having both intrinsic (e.g. emotional dysregulation) and external (e.g. social rejection) challenges, and acknowledged the need to adapt and develop self-acceptance, manifesting in a sense of pride around being 'different'. In Cooper et al., (2017) they found that an autistic social identity was related to self-esteem, and that collective self-esteem (a positive perception of being autistic) mediated this relationship. A positive autistic social identity also appeared to indirectly lower anxiety and depression through increasing both personal and social self-esteem. This work highlights how important positive social comparisons among in-group members can be in fostering a positive sense of self.

In a related extension of this work (Cooper et al., 2023) Cooper and colleagues explored whether a positive autistic social identity and feelings of solidarity with the autistic community could also improve psychological wellbeing and lower social anxiety. They found that higher satisfaction with being autistic and autistic solidarity were related to increased psychological wellbeing, however only a positive autistic social identity was related to lower social anxiety. Interestingly, the authors also found that young people who viewed autism as a more core component of their identity also tended to have higher social anxiety. These findings may indicate a complex relationship between fear of negative social judgements and social challenges within a neuro-normative world. It is also likely that these findings highlight the role of stigma (e.g. viewing something that is negatively judged as a core component of oneself creates a prevention focus, and vigilance around negative social perceptions). Indeed, Cresswell

& Cage, (2019) explored personal identity, and acculturation (psychological change as a result of moving between cultures, in this example autistic and non-autistic cultures) in relation to mental health outcomes in autistic young people. Autistic acculturation was here defined as a sense of similarity to other autistic people, and desire to be around them (e.g. with items asking participants to rate statements like "Being autistic is an important part of who I am" on a scale of 1-5). They found no relationship between personal identity and mental health outcomes, and no relationship between acculturation (i.e. whether the person viewed themselves as marginalised, bicultural, assimilated or separated) and mental health outcomes. They did find that young people who viewed themselves as marginalised made fewer positive statements about their own identity, and that those who aligned themselves more with non-autistic culture tended to generate more positive statements about themselves. Their findings may reflect a desire to fit in with the dominant group among some autistic young people, however not many people who took part had a strong alignment to autistic culture, making it difficult to make any strong claims about this finding.

Emerging research into the importance of autistic community connectedness (ACC, Botha, 2020) has suggested that a connection to a wider 'ingroup' of autistic people can both facilitate a sense of belonging and moderate the impact of stigma. However, there are aspects of connectedness that appear more helpful than others. Identifying strongly with a stigmatised community can result in more psychological distress, but engaging in political action with your chosen community can increase wellbeing and reduce internalised stigma. This itself is a radical act in a world where survival as an 'other' is so frequently hostile that it can leave disabled people with little energy to fight oppressive systems (Watermeyer & Swartz, 2016). Indeed, there are several community driven movements that aim to foster a positive identity at both the individual and social level, such as weird pride, and autistic pride which both emphasise the importance of authentic self-expression, celebrating difference, and connecting to like-minded others. Autistic pride events such as Autscape have taken place online and in person, leading to a sense of physical connection, with people often travelling long distances to access them. These events provide the opportunity for social connectivity with a focus on both support and positive identity, allowing a geographically disparate group of people to find solace, connection and education among a community of others who support each other's self-exploration and identity expression. They enable autistic people from different cultures to cross connect.

Importantly, these movements also specifically facilitate political community connectedness, providing shared spaces for advocacy both online and in-person. Online platforms like Aucademy, provide bridges between communities and research, focussing on making research accessible, and framing discussions and platforming community discussions through a lens of identity focused insight, as opposed to observation and misinterpretation. Similarly, online campaigns such as #TakeTheMaskOff (which reached 5,000,000 people across 4 social media platforms in 2019) provide a space to discuss identity and social injustice, develop advocacy tools, which in turn underpins the development of academic and public understanding (Mandy, 2019).

The studies in this section highlight the importance of considering the wider social environment on autistic identity formation in young people. Autistic people grow up in a primarily non-autistic world, where their social communication style does not necessarily align with those around them. This can lead to difficulties developing and maintaining relationships with others whilst being able to express their authentic selves. Research into autistic relationships during adolescence have suggested that whilst autistic people value relationships founded upon shared interests and like-mindedness, relationships can be difficult to navigate and maintain due to social differences with the dominant group (Cresswell et al., 2019). Thus the development of a positive autistic social identity and the opportunity to interact with ingroup members provides the opportunity to align oneself with more similar others, and to express oneself authentically. Indeed (Keates, 2022) argues that there are benefits to socialising with those who have an insider identity due to the lack of normative expectations around communication. Interestingly, a recent study exploring the efficacy of a social skills intervention (Afsharnejad et al., 2022) highlighted this issue. Whilst the study focussed on an intervention designed to 'reduce autistic traits' and increasing normative social communication skills, the young people enrolled spent time in groups with other autistic young people. Both the young people and their parents emphasised how important this had been, fostering a sense of belonging amongst the autistic young people and giving them a chance to thrive with people who were 'like them'. Overall it can be seen that the development of identity in autistic young people is complex, and impacted by myriad internal (e.g. personal characteristics and experiences) and external (e.g. stigma, societal structures, etc) factors that shape and re-shape who we consider ourselves to be, and where we view ourselves in relation to ingroup and outgroup peers.

## Autistic self in adulthood

Much of the research on autistic identity in adulthood has focussed on the impact of diagnosis on the shaping of identity. For those who are identified late in life, many go through another period of moratorium, or identity crisis, needing to re-integrate new information about themselves into their self-concept. Many autistic people identified later in life have experienced periods of significant difficulty and report feeling like they are 'broken' compared to their peers (Leedham et al., 2020). The realisation that they are autistic can foster feelings of self-understanding and meaning making (Kelly et al., 2022), self-compassion (Harmens et al., 2022; Lilley et al., 2022), and a sense of belonging, realising they have a broader autistic social identity (Lilley et al., 2023). However, these realisations can also be a double edged sword, raising negative emotions and requiring people to undergo what can be a traumatic period of reframing their life experiences through a new lens, with some describing their experiences as akin to 'grief' (Huang et al., 2023; Leedham et al., 2020). These realisations are often related to a sense of gaining new knowledge and insight into oneself, and the terminology to accurately describe one's own experiences (Pearson et al., 2023). However, many people experience significant barriers to reaching this stage, including from professionals within the diagnostic system, but also as a result of hermeneutical justice, that is, not being able to 'see' themselves in descriptions of autism due to stereotyped and overtly negative public conceptualisations (Cage et al., 2022). These people are often referred to as the 'lost generation' (McDonald, 2020) (though as we will discuss in the chapter on intersectionality, there is a difference between being lost/ missing, and being overlooked), with efforts being made to address current barriers within the diagnosis and identification process that might prevent access to self-realisation and potential support. As Morgan demonstrated, a formal diagnosis is often viewed as the step needed to legitimise identity and need, and a lack of access to identification can result in multiple negative outcomes, including a risk of anxiety and depression (Lewis, 2016).

There has been less of a focus on the impact of self-identifying as autistic, despite the notion that to seek formal diagnosis one must first identify themselves as autistic. Huang et al., (2020) completed a scoping review of the literature around self-identification, highlighting the impact of self-identification on self-understanding and helping to facilitate understanding in others (e.g. family members). They found that self-ID had an overwhelmingly positive impact on self and identity, despite usually resulting from immense challenges across the lifespan. Lewis (2016) found that those who had started to identify themselves as autistic reported feeling othered throughout their lives, and struggling to understand themselves. Realising they were autistic provided a sense of self-understanding and the ability to find others 'like them', which fostered feelings of belonging. However, their participants also reported the experience of self-doubt around their autistic identity. Many had developed a strong focus on autism after learning about it, feeling an "immediate fit", but initially struggled to move past a lifetime of "writing off" their struggles, indicative of the internalisation of their othered status and outsider ableism (e.g. 'I can't be autistic because I don't fit with [stereotype]').

In regards to formal diagnosis, Milton & Sims, (2016) explored autistic identity through the online posts of participants on the Asperger United forum. They found that adults who had been diagnosed as autistic referred to the diagnosis as a process of self-discovery. It helped participants to make sense of their own lives and the experiences that they had had so far. Many spoke about the experience of living as 'other', knowing that they were different from other people, and how diagnosis had led to a period of "self-discovery" through which they were able to learn more about themselves and how they needed to navigate the world in order to help them thrive. Developing an autistic social identity and spending time around other autistic people (whether online, or at autistic-led events such as 'Autscape') had a positive contribution to wellbeing, leading to feelings of inclusion and belonging that had been difficult to find elsewhere. Likewise, Lilley et al., (2022) explored the experiences of late diagnosed (post 35 years) autistic adults in Australia. They also found that participants had experiences of stigma, being othered and social isolation growing up. The trauma from these experiences contributed towards the development of masking, and a lack of authenticity whereby people felt like they didn't know who they really were. Realising they were autistic allowed them to make sense of their experiences, and develop self-compassion and a more authentic self-expression.

Corden et al., (2021) examined autistic identity and mental wellbeing outcomes in late identified autistic adults using a mixed methods approach. They found that those who had known that they were autistic for longer felt more positive about it, whereas those newly identified had a less positive attitude towards their autistic identity. Their findings suggested that people need time to make sense of their new identity after that crisis point, and having more time to process the information leads to greater pride in being autistic, and increased self-esteem. These findings provide important insights into how identity may evolve after receiving an autism diagnosis, and the role that time may play in that reassessment and re-integration of autobiographical information about oneself. Though the realisation that a person is autistic may provide them with information to help them make sense of their lives and experiences, this requires an intense period of re-processing this information through a new lens. It can be difficult to disentangle an autistic sense of self without epistemic infection/

outsider lens, and who people *really* are. Autistic people have described the identity crisis they experience post-diagnosis, often realising that they aren't sure of their 'true' selves due to masking for such long periods of time (we will discuss the impact of this further in chapter 10). Here there can be an insidious relationship between how outsider perceptions (e.g. the generalised other) interact with the double empathy gap to promote autistic self-suppression. Instead, identity becomes 'infected' with the views of the dominant group, and the true self pathologised and distanced. In addition, the liminal nature of the time/space that people inhabit during/just after a diagnosis/identification may be distressing in itself for autistic people, who find comfort in certainty and predictability. Identity at this point has a certain transience as people try to make meaning out of their experiences. Thus it is unsurprising that people at the start of this process are less satisfied than those who have been through it, and have had more time to unpack their experiences and develop a more authentic sense of self.

In regards to personal and social identity, there is a small body of research among autistic adults. Botha et al., (2022) explored how autistic people made sense of their own identity, finding that autistic adults generally referred to being autistic as an immutable aspect of who they are, drawing upon essentialist framings in order to distinguish themselves from neurotypicals. This finding is consistent with Ellis's suggestion that strategic essentialism can be used as an attempt to establish legitimacy in a society which devalues and questions the testimony of autistic people. Similar to research with adolescents, autistic adults view autism as an important part of their identity, but are also aware of the pathologising narratives surrounding them. Bury et al., (2023) found that autistic adults conceptualised being autistic as something they *were* as opposed to something that they *have*, and highlighted how outside perceptions could sometimes seek to minimise individual differences among autistic people. Their participants rejected the notion that they were 'disordered' and called for a more humanising approach to autistic people that de-pathologised their identity.

Autistic social identity was explored by Maitland et al., (2021) who found that autistic adults identify socially with multiple groups (e.g. other autistic people, people of the same gender, family), and that a stronger autistic social identity was related to lower levels of depression and better mental health. A positive autistic social identity is likely shaped by whether an individual has access to a broader community of autistic people, and whether they view the people within this collective (and themselves) positively. Likewise Botha's work on ACC suggests that an autistic social identity and alignment with the broader autistic community can foster a sense of belonging, friendship, and shared advocacy, which again supports Ellis's notion that a shared political identity is beneficial to improving society for neurodivergent people. However, a strong ingroup identification is also likely to have potential negative impacts, as discussed in the previous chapter. The process of depersonalisation can lead to engaging in ingroup stereotyping. For autistic people this is likely confounded by stigma. We will discuss this in chapter 8 with relation to the internalisation of stereotypes about autistic people, and how despite being used as a coping strategy by some may propagate stigma about other autistic people.

It is important to note that despite autistic people being classified as a social group more broadly, there exist many communities within the 'autistic community'. Community is often viewed as a way to connote shared values and interests, however as with any broad identity label, there will be immense variation among the individuals within these groups. Here Chapman's work on autistic people as a serial collective, and Walkers concept of the neurominority is useful for helping us to conceptualise how entitative autistic people need to be (i.e. how unified, coherent, etc) in order to align ourselves with each other as a 'group'. Autism is the label we currently give to people who display a collection of characteristics that are devalued within the current economic and social context according to the existing norms and structures (Chapman, 2020). Thus what we refer to as the 'autistic community' includes an incredibly diverse set of people, with individuals sharing the label of autistic alongside some other potentially overlapping or distinct aspects of identity (identity features such as gender, race, values etc).

This distinction can help us to understand why we might see variation among both adolescents and adults in regards to a broader autistic social identity and how they align themselves with autistic culture. In addition to the stigma of being part of a widener marginalised group and an attempt to distance oneself from that stigma, we must acknowledge that social distancing may also be related to the nebulous nature of the autistic community and how people see that as aligning and intersecting with other aspects of their identity.

# Impression management and self-monitoring

As can be seen from the evidence presented from both adolescence and adulthood, autistic personal and social identity across the lifespan is currently an emerging but relatively under-researched area. The majority of work has focussed on how autistic people view being *autistic*, rather than providing a broader insight into how autistic people conceptualise themselves across a broader range of personal and interpersonal domains. There is also a lack of exploration as to how autistic identity shifts with context. Whilst there is now a growing body of literature on masking and camouflaging, there has been less of a focus on general IM strategies used by autistic people, and how this might overlap or differ from those used for masking.

Snyder proposed that we may use IM strategically, in order to influence how other people think about us, or expressively in order to demonstrate values and seek validation. Given the devalued and stigmatised status of autistic people, it is possible that their use of IM across these domains interacts with a need to minimise stigma. Cage & Troxell-Whitman (2019) explored the use of masking within different environments in relation to what they classified as 'conventional' reasons (akin to Snyder's strategic axis) or 'relational' reasons (akin to Snyder's value expressive axis). They found that autistic people endorsed the use of masking and IM for both, but that autistic women endorsed using conventional reasons more frequently, suggesting an intersectional pressure to manage outsider impressions of being both autistic and a woman (we will discuss this in more detail in chapter 5). Schneid & Raz, (2020) found that autistic adults viewed IM as a social asset, yet distinct from the descriptions of IM in the broader social literature, autistic IM was very much focussed on a need to 'pass for normal' and hide 'flaws' from potential interlocutors as opposed to self-promotion and value expression. It is possible that some of the distress caused by autistic masking is related to the discrepancy between how others use IM (e.g. for strategic promotion and value expression) and how autistic people use it (e.g. to minimise stigma). Research has suggested that autistic people may hold particularly strong values, which can be an important aspect of personal identity (Stenning, 2020). Here, some autistic people may be suppressing an important aspect of themselves (i.e. their value expression) in order to maintain social standing, as opposed to being able to express these in alignment with like-minded others (e.g. for fear of being negatively judged by others not necessarily for the value itself, but for being 'too much', see Forster & Pearson, 2020). Thus self-monitoring may not be used in the same way in autistic people (or other stigmatised groups for that matter) due to particular concerns about how external perceivers may respond to aspects of authenticity.

As we will discuss in chapter 10, research to date suggests that masking has an incredibly negative impact on the health and wellbeing of autistic people. However, a lack of research into general IM and self-monitoring among autistic people makes it very difficult to unpick specifically which aspects of masking are harmful. Whilst we hypothesise that the negative impact of masking is related to stigma and stigma-related processes (see chapter 8), it is also possible that IM and self-monitoring in general are more difficult for autistic people due to the double empathy problem. That is, trying to work out how to make a good impression on people who do not think like you creates an additional layer of difficulty. We will discuss this in more detail in relation to Ai et al., (2022)'s work on transactional IM in Chapter 6.

It is also possible that in addition to the double empathy problem, certain aspects of autistic cognition might make aspects of impression management and self-monitoring more difficult for autistic people. The ability to track different parts of identity within social situations may be shaped by monotropic cognition. Impression management is to some degree a more polytropic function, as an individual needs to keep track of several competing streams of information at a single time (e.g. who you are interacting with, what they know about you, which context you are in) in order to work out which aspects of your identity are most relevant for the situation. Choosing the correct aspects of identity may rely on integrating information from these streams, and then seamlessly choosing the appropriate response. Here there may be an interaction with the DEP, by which an autistic person not only has to manage competing streams of information, but do it in a way that is relevant to understanding and responding to an interlocutor with a different social style. As discussed in chapter 3, self-categorisation is dependent on a certain amount of cognitive flexibility, by which an individual is able to balance both prototypical information about group members, and individual information about themselves. This may be more difficult for autistic people due to their monotropic cognitive style, and we may naturally lean towards a model of identity that favours low self-monitoring that is centered more around our core values (putting masking particularly at odds with a preferred self-representation). However, there is currently a lack of research in this area to make strong claims either way.

## Conclusion

In this chapter we explored the development of autistic self-concept, personal identity, and social identity across the lifespan. Despite only a small body of research so far, there is growing evidence to suggest that the identities of autistic people are shaped by the label of autism, external perceptions of other conspecifics, and the (often hostile) social context that we exist in. However there are many other features and social group memberships that shape our identities and impact upon who we consider ourselves to be. In the next chapter, we will explore some crucial intersecting aspects of identity that have been somewhat neglected in research up until fairly recently.

# Chapter 5: Understanding intersectionality and the importance of multiplicious identities

## What is intersectionality and why is it important?

Intersectionality is a term that was first used by Crenshaw (Crenshaw, 1990; Crenshaw, 2017) to describe a theoretical approach to understanding (legal) discrimination that takes into account the multidimensionality of identity. In this seminal work, Crenshaw argued that a tendency to view discrimination as sex based (e.g. sexism) or race based (racism) ignores how these features intersect to produce the unique experiences of multiply-marginalised people. Here Crenshaw focussed on the experiences of Black women, who were often excluded from feminist or sex based theorising (e.g. not being included in voting rights legislation alongside white women) on the basis of their race, and antiracist theorising and politicising (e.g. employment equity focussing on black men) on the basis of their gender. Crenshaw's work built upon that of other Black feminist scholars (e.g. King, 1988) who explored how the devaluation and oppression of Black women and their identities should be conceptualised as multiplicious (e.g. an interaction between race, gender, socio-economic status, etc). Importantly, both Crenshaw and King argued that the discrimination and oppression that Black women experience was not simply additive (i.e. the sum of racial and sex based discrimination) but is sometimes unique to existing as a Black woman in the world (Crenshaw, page 149; King 1988). Since Crenshaw's original work, the concept of intersectionality has been applied more broadly to understanding the impact of marginalising power structures upon individuals and groups, and the importance of identity across multiple social justice movements and their members.

Both intra and intergroup differences are important aspects of intersectionality. Whilst intersectionality recognises different aspects of our identities that may be impacted by our experiences, the point here is not to infinitely reduce group members by splitting hairs until we reach an individual (Strand, 2017). Crenshaw emphasised the importance of recognising intragroup differences in emancipatory action (e.g. not assuming that white and Black women, and Black women and men will experience the same barriers and oppression), lest we take the same approach as those who perpetrate stigma and oppression: reducing the individual distinctiveness of group members and ignoring the multifaceted impact of power on individuals. Likewise, a focus on intersectionality can be corrupted by this splitting down to individual characteristics resulting in the 'oppression Olympics', whereby an attempt is made to attach weight to each aspect of marginalisation in order to ascertain who is the 'most oppressed' and thus the most worthy of listening to. Martinez (Davis & Martínez, 1993) stated that it was important for intersectional communities to reject a hierarchical approach to understanding need, and instead groups should work together to advocate for each other and recognise shared goals. This will be an important consideration later in this chapter, when we discuss intersectional issues across autistic people with multiple-marginalised identities. Though we will discuss these within an 'autistic and' frame work (e.g. autistic and Black), people within these groups may also be a member of other communities (e.g. autistic, Black and queer). The point here is not to divide and subtype on the basis of the number of marginalised identities, but to acknowledge that complex interactions between aspects of identity will shape experience, and as such, will shape the ways in which people manage their identity(ies) across different settings.

# Why has autism research lacked an intersectional approach?

The lack of focus on intersectionality within autism research has two distinct main contributors. The first can be understood via the historical context that we outlined in chapter 2, whereby a particular presentation (e.g. white, male, young) became associated with autism due to the limited sample characteristics of those who were described in early case studies. As discussed in the introductory chapter, historical perceptions of autism being associated with a particular profile led to underdiagnosis in anyone who did not meet these narrow, biased perceptions, e.g. women, non-binary people, Black people - anyone who was not a white, male child with a particular (externally visible) presentation. In recent years, attempts to remedy these diagnostic disparities have led to discussions about *why* these people went unrecognised for so long. The initial categorisation of autism by Kanner and Asperger had an incredibly limited sample. Though Aspergers children have been described as more 'diverse' (Baron-Cohen, 2015) than those included in Kanners first case study (Kanner, 1944) there were three girls in total among both samples of children, all of whom were white and the majority from middle class families (Silberman, 2015). Thus, this limited data led to assumptions about what autism 'looks' like. This was further compounded by sampling bias in autism research. As discussed in Chapter 2, Wing acknowledged that 'autism' was a broad category, and included people of varying presentations. However, autism research has generally included an incredibly homogenous sample (i.e. white, middle class, mostly male). Like Kanner's case studies, the explanation for this is likely to be partially driven by bias around who engages in autism research (families with enough time and resources to take part, links to the wider academic community to hear about studies), and where research samples are drawn from (e.g. communities within which academics have good links, e.g. particular schools and charities).

The limited scope of early research samples was likely compounded by racial segregation in the earlier party of the 20th century in Austria and the US; in Austria owing to the political environment at the time and hostility towards those who did not fit the Aryan profile, and in the US due to racial segregation and systemic racism that prevented Black people from accessing the same healthcare supports, education, and opportunities as white people. Indeed, in his 2015 book Neurotribes, Steve Silberman outlines how many of the children that Kanner initially encountered heard of him through shared social circles (i.e. that included white, middle class professionals). The exclusion of people who are racialised on the basis of their skin colour or ethnicity cannot be overstated within Western perceptions of autism and who is autistic. It has led to a self-propelling system under which those initial barriers led to the reification of autistic stereotypes (e.g. 'autism looks like a white, male child who makes no eye contact, flaps his hands, and has no interest in social interaction), which were further propagated by those who gained a diagnosis going forward (i.e. people who fit with this particular profile), creating a vicious cycle. We will discuss in further detail the specificities of how white supremacy manifests in diagnostic disparities later in this chapter.

The second (but related) contributor is how autism has primarily been the focus of psychology, which has led to multiple further issues in the broader consideration of intersectionality. Western psychological research has typically assumed that population samples derived from their cultures are broadly representative of human cognition and behaviour, and that the researchers conducting these studies are also unbiased and objective (Dupree & Kraus, 2022). Thus, western psychology has primarily been shaped by middle-upper class white men, who have relied on university students as research participants which are often particularly homogenous samples; primarily white (Cheon et al., 2020), and primarily from WEIRD (western, educated, industrialised, rich and democratic) societies (Henrich et al., 2010; Schulz et al., 2018). Henrich et al., (2010) highlight how the majority of studies have WEIRD samples, despite evidence to suggest that the way that people from these societies think and behave does not generalise more broadly to those from other cultures. Of course this speaks to a broader issue around civil rights and access to these spaces (e.g. changing laws around gender and race in regards to higher education), particularly in a US context. Whilst the majority of autism research participants have not been university students (up until very recently autism research with adults was fairly sparse, Pellicano et al., 2014) the majority of autism research has been conducted in WEIRD settings, and impacted by the people who are more likely to self-select or be recruited into research studies (Maye et al., 2022) - white middle or upper class parents of autistic young boys.

Another issue that has arisen from autism being the remit of psychology, is the psychological approach itself. Psychologists seek to find explanations for phenomena, which in the latter half of the 20th century led to the development of a focus on the scientific method (i.e. experimental psychology) and a mechanistic approach to understanding human mind and behaviour. The majority of Autism research historically has drawn upon a developmental perspective, exploring the deviations between autistic and non-autistic development and trajectories. Forbes et al., (2022) outline how issues of generalisability in developmental research transcend the usual discussions of replicability and emphasise the importance of contextualising developmental differences, and how the concept of 'normative' development has been misused, not taking into account cultural differences and the majority of developmental research originating in WEIRD countries (Singh et al., 2021). Whilst Forbes' article focuses on the myth of normative developmental standards in regards to cultural diversity, similar arguments have been made about neurodiversity (Bertilsdotter Rosqvist et al., 2022; Pearson et al., 2021). Hens & Van Goidsenhoven, (2023) highlight the importance of understanding developmental *diversity* as opposed to categorical difference, and how this can support a neurodiversity affirming approach. Neurodiversity is a concept that provides space to explore all variations in human development (including normativity, or neurotypicality) without attaching virtue to the most prevalent pathway (i.e. the assumed norm). The assumption that a normative pathway exists has led to issues in how complex phenomena are understood. Some key components of diversity have been reduced to a particular binary, whereby aspects of identity such as gender or culture have been considered 'individual differences' rather than factors that shape our development (in line with an enactivist framework).

Instead of recognising that this diversity can and should be accounted for even in the cognitive sciences (Manalili et al., 2023), there has been an attempt to instead to regress more inclusive approaches for the purpose of facilitating a more granular research approach to autism in particular (Frith, 2021). An intersectional approach to autism prompts researchers to acknowledge autistic experience as multifaceted and our identity composed of more than just autism (Botha & Gillespie-Lynch, 2022), which can be difficult for researchers who are used to having a high degree of control of the characteristics of their research population. Recent advances in autism research have failed to replicate historically key theories that have been used to explain autistic differences (e.g. Theory of Mind), leading some researchers to suggest that autism as a label has become too broad to be meaningful (see Frith, 2021). This argument rests upon the idea of autistic people as 'heterogeneous', i.e. that autistic people differ in how their autistic characteristics are expressed (e.g. as outlined in Chapter 2 in relation to Wing's work, that some people might be socially seeking whilst others might be socially ambivalent or avoidant) and that for the purpose of research and potentially support, it might be more effective to subtype them.

This argument is problematic for multiple reasons. The first is that many more people are being recognised as autistic due to our shifting understanding of what neurodivergence is and looks like across a broader range of people (Woods et al., 2023). Whilst it is possible that we may shift to a more transdiagnostic approach in future (a system based on need rather than labelling), our current system being more inclusive is a positive shift towards recognition that bias has impacted who is identified as neurodivergent (e.g. women, Black people) and how these people gain access to support and community. We will come back to this later in this chapter. A second reason is that the labelling of autistic people as 'heterogeneous' is dehumanising. Whilst people assumed to be neurotypical are labelled as having 'individual differences' that impact on their similarity to each other (e.g. differences in attention or memory), autistic people are often assumed to be a monolith, despite early research highlighting the variation across the population (Wing & Gould, 1979). The emphasis on similarity, and minimisation of individual uniqueness implicitly suggests that whilst humans in general are complex and differ from each other in many ways, autistic people are expected to show more similarities. These assumptions are often applied to incredibly rudimentary features of identity, such as shared interests (e.g. that a defining feature of being autistic is a specific interest in trains or dinosaurs, rather having a strong passion in and of itself that might be directed at any number of interests), creating rigid stereotypes with limited clinical utility.

In addition to the impact that intersectionality can have on identification, Cascio et al., (2021) highlight the importance of taking intersectionality into account to create a more stringent ethical environment for autism research. They argue that many of the factors that can impact participants, for example uneven power dynamics, and risk of marginalisation or harm through the research that they take part in, are particularly pertinent for people who are marginalised across multiple aspects of identity. The inequalities that research can drive can contribute towards unique intersectional barriers for multiply-marginalised people, e.g. gatekeeping of transition for autistic transgender people due to a patronising assumption that being autistic means that they cannot fully understand their own gender (Smilges, 2022). It is important to respect the participant as a whole, taking an individualised and unique approach, building a good researcher-participant relationship, providing empowerment to inform decision-making, and acknowledging the complexity of the lifeworld of the participant. This theory is also echoed in  Pavlopoulou's life world theory (Pavlopoulou, 2020), which emphasises a humanising and experience-sensitive approach to working with autistic people to enable them to flourish. Cascio and colleagues also draw upon intersectionality to argue that quite often disability is considered the core aspect of the person in disability focused research. In chapter 2 we discussed how this is important for situating disability as something that exists as an interaction between person and environment, however, Casio and colleagues argue that an intersectional lens stresses the importance of considering disability in relation to other aspects of identity, a person cannot be reduced to their disability alone, and their experiences are the sum of the interaction between their disability, their race, their sex, their gender, et cetera. Whilst we have discussed the development of autistic identity in chapter 4, it is important that we recognise that many autistic people are marginalised in multiple ways and that this will shape not only their identity and their experience of the world, but their access to societal participation.

Autistic masking as a concept was initially explored in the psychological literature in relation to the idea that some people may appear 'less autistic' or 'pass' for neurotypical when interacting with others (e.g. see Hull et al., 2017). This work was groundbreaking in explaining why some people were less likely to be diagnosed as autistic, leading to clinical consideration that measuring external indicators of 'autism' (e.g. lack of eye contact) may not always be reliable. Whilst this was an incredibly important advancement in knowledge, there very quickly emerged a conflation between the concept of masking, and 'atypical' presentations of autism (Pearson & Rose, 2021). Instead of recognising that autistic people may present in varied, unexpected ways that did not necessarily fit with the clinical stereotype, theorising on masking suggested instead that some autistic people had become more adept at hiding these stereotyped behaviours. As this work was emerging, so too was interest into gender disparity in autism diagnosis whereby men were diagnosed as autistic at a rate of 7:1 compared to women (Loomes et al., 2017). Unsurprisingly, it was suggested that masking may help to explain this disparity. Thus, the emerging notion that intersectional issues might impact on autistic experiences and outcomes has been somewhat eschewed by narratives around masking and visibility, as opposed to an acknowledgement that autistic presentation is multidimensional. However researchers *have* begun to focus on how key intersecting aspects of identity might impact on opportunities and outcomes for autistic people, which drives the need for us to consider the interaction between intersectionality and masking.

Intersectionality is an incredibly important concept in understanding a) the structures that lead to the development of masking, and b) the way that masking may develop in relation to, and interacting with other aspects of our selfhood. It is also crucial for helping us to understand the unique forms of oppression that various autistic people experience that might relate to both masking, and under-recognition within the diagnostic system. Our aim for this chapter is to explore different intersecting aspects of identity in relation to autism, and how these may shape the experience of masking. It is worth us pointing out here that, though we discuss race in relation to autism, this is still from a western (and mostly UK/US) perspective. We currently know very little about masking discourse outside of a western context, though academic research is starting to emerge (Hongo et al., 2022; Keating et al., 2021; Oshima et al., 2023).

In the following sections we explore some key intersections in autism research that have recently started to garner interest, and consider the impact the overlooking them has had so far on understanding diverse presentations of autistic people, and masking.

# Key Intersections in Autism Research: Race, Gender and Intersecting Disability

## Autism and Race

As we have established, autism research is an overwhelmingly white field (Giwa Onaiwu, 2020), with the experiences of Black autistic people, and autistic people who are racialised as minorities having been overlooked and excluded in both academic research and clinical practice. This issue has a variety of underlying factors involved, from the historical contextualisation of autism being based on data from white children, to racist stereotypes concerning interpretations from practitioners of behaviour among different racial groups (Jones & Mandell, 2020). It is worth noting here that we are both white authors, and as such we have a limited perspective on this area and it is likely that our discussions will not capture to true level of nuance in this area. Thus we defer to, and highlight the work of Black scholars and scholars from other racialised communities[1] as the key texts for those who want to develop a deeper understanding of the issues that people from racialised communities experience, and acknowledge that there are likely limitations to our discussion.

Whilst the aim of this section is to focus on racialised experiences of autism, it is also important to acknowledge the distinction and intersection between cultural experiences and racialised experiences. The majority of autism research thus far has emerged within WEIRD settings (particularly the US and Europe), where white supremacy has underpinned many of the disparities that autistic people from racialised minorities face. However there is a growing body of autism research conducted by scholars from the global South (Kassous, 2023) which highlights the role that culture might play in how autism is conceptualised and identified, and how this might impact on access to support for people who occupy minority status within *these* cultures (Hoekstra, 2022). Whilst some cultures view autism through a highly medical or culturally pathologized (Kassous, 2023) lens, others have a different approach (e.g. the Maori concept of takiwātanga). As such, one should note that cultural differences will also play a role in how autism is conceptualised and identified across people with similar racial, but dissimilar cultural backgrounds (e.g. a Black person living in America may have a different racialised experience compared to a Black person living in

---

1    Multiple terms are used to refer to people racialised as minorities in different sections of the world, e.g. Black, Indigenous People of Colour (BIPoC), People of Colour (PoC), racialised minorities, people of the global majority, Black, Asian and Minority Ethnic (BAME) people. Preferences differ across different societies, and many people find these terms to homogenise a diverse group of people in comparison to those who are racialised as white. We use Black, and racialised minorities/global majority throughout

Nigeria, indeed two Black people from different cultures living in the same country may have completely different racialised experiences). Here our focus is upon racialised autism in the European and American setting, and we draw primarily upon work from the Black autistic community due to the growing body of literature emerging in this area. There is currently limited work on autism among other racialised minorities (Brown et al., 2017; Mallipeddi & VanDaalen, 2022), and moving forward it is essential that we engage with wider racial and cultural considerations within a global autism/ neurodiversity research framework (see Cheng et al., 2023).

Giwa Onaiwu ( 2020) highlights the inequalities that Black and indigenous, autistic people of colour face in the US (autistic BIPoC). She discusses how wider representations of autistic people in the media, and in the public consciousness default to an overwhelmingly white male profile, leaving room for little else. She argues that the lack of representation and inclusion is known to professionals working with autistic people, yet we still see marked diagnostic disparities, lack of access to support, and poorer outcomes for autistic BIPoC. Similar issues were highlighted by Jones and colleagues (2020) in a roundtable discussion on structural racism in autism research and practice. The authors highlight how for many BIPoC autistic adults, autism has been another layer of bias in their experiences. Difficulties accessing healthcare, or equitable education (Maye et al., 2022) are compounded by external perceptions and a lack of recognition of the different ways that autistic people may present. Morgan et al., (2022) put out a call to arms  for researchers to focus on the experiences of Black autistic people and other people of colour in research going forward, she argues that the lack of an intersectional focus thus far has led to health disparities, particularly among Black people in the US. Jones and Mandell highlight how these disparities have also arisen out of the exclusion of Black scholars, and that  moving forward we must ensure opportunities for Black academics in shaping research and priorities (Jones and Mandell, 2020).

These assertions are supported by empirical evidence, showing that Black children and young people are less likely to be diagnosed with autism compared to their white peers despite displaying similar levels of autistic features in clinical assessment (Fombonne & Zuckerman, 2022). Multiple studies have shown how diagnostic services display a racialised bias during assessment of children and young people (CYP). Obeid et al., (2021) provided clinicians with profiles of children displaying autistic characteristics and labelled the profiles as coming from either a Black, or a white child. They found that Black children were more likely to be associated with a conduct disorder compared to white peers, who were more likely to be associated with being autistic. This disparity is endemic of systemic racism, whereby implicit perceptions of Black people are driven by racist stereotypes of Black people as more aggressive and dangerous (Epstein et al., 2017).

Spence, (2020) discussed how these racist stereotypes can impact perceptions of autistic Black CYP in the education system, with a particular focus on the experience of Black boys. Black autistic boys are more likely to experience school exclusion in comparison to their peers, with their behaviour labelled as 'challenging' and 'defiant' and their anxiety overlooked. These labels have an impact on both access to diagnosis, and support within the school environment. Racist interpretations of behaviour mean that Black children are less likely to be referred for disability assessment, and instead experience punitive measures aimed at 'reducing behaviour' as opposed to exploring whether the child's needs are being met.

Similar issues have been highlighted among Black autistic women and girls (BAWG). Lovelace et al., (2022) examined how the experiences of BAWG are severely underrepresented in the autism literature. Their paper explored access to early intervention, but from a non-deficit based, harm-reduction perspective grounded in critical disability and critical race studies. Lovelace emphasises how, like black men and boys, the identity of Black women and girls is shaped through a racialised lens and based heavily upon negative stereotypes created to dehumanise and devalue them; e.g. that Black girls are expected to be hypersexual, aggressive, and more independent than their white peers (Epstein et al., 2017). These stereotypes are grounded in historical mistreatment and dehumanisation of Black people (including children) during slavery, and continue to have a tangible impact today where Black children and young people are more likely to experience punitive treatment for their behaviour (Epstein et al., 2017), as highlighted by Spence. The adultification and racialisation of BAWG can intersect to create particularly harmful practices in regards to how they are treated by practitioners, for example, a heightened risk of psychopharmacological intervention as opposed to behavioural support. In addition, Bobb (2019) highlights how stereotypes can intersect with other stigmatised aspects of identity (e.g. family background, socio-economic status) which results in misinterpretation of needs and invalidation of experiences. Both of her daughters were diagnosed later than her son due to not fitting with clinical stereotypes, which was compounded by cultural perceptions of how Black girls should behave, and cultural approaches to fostering safety outside of the home (e.g. self-reliance, within community social conformity). Indeed, the intersection of racism and autistic experience can manifest in particularly harrowing outcomes for Black autistic people. In both the UK and the US there have been a number of high profile cases of Black autistic adults and children experiencing arrest, beatings, deportation attempts, unwarranted detentions at immigration centres and being murdered as a result of racism and white supremacy within law enforcement (Dababnah et al., 2022; Hutson et al., 2022).

Like Lovelace, Malone et al., (2022) draw upon Dis/ability Studies and Critical Race Theory (DisCrit) and intersectionality to explore how the interaction between systemic barriers and methodological issues has led to the scholarly neglect of Black autistic people in autism research, and as such have contributed towards poor outcomes for Black autistic people. As outlined in at the start of this chapter, racial disparities arising from systemic barriers (e.g. anti-Black practices in healthcare) have contributed towards the reification and maintenance of autism as a white diagnosis. Malone et al. highlight how a lack of multicultural competence in modern research (e.g. an inability for researchers to engage with and centre the voices and experiences of Black autistic people) to maintain the exclusion of Black autistic people. They recommend that researchers learn how to engage in cultural reciprocity, and construct more inclusive designs that acknowledge the intersectional lived experiences of their participants, and adopt anti-racist practices which acknowledge the impact of structural and systemic barriers to meaningful societal participation.

These suggestions call back to the issue we outlined early in this chapter. There has been an assumption among many psychologists that psychology is 'race neutral' (Dupree & Kraus, 2022). Dupree and Kraus outline how white researchers are generally ignorant to the ways in which race shapes development (e.g. through the experience of racism), and how racial privilege is often denied leading to the minimisation of the impact of racial inequality.

Finally, we want to end this section with a brief discussion of racism within the autistic community itself, and the harm it enacts on Black and racially minoritised autistic people. The wider autistic community is composed of many different people, and is far from being homogenous. Many Black and racially minoritised autistic people have highlighted racism within the community (Giwa Onaiwu et al., 2021; Smith, 2020), both overt (people using racial slurs and stereotypes), covert (microaggressions such as false equivalences, which we will return to in a moment), and systemic (e.g. upholding systems and narratives that benefit white autistic people and disadvantage Black people, and other autistic people of colour, such as inferring that autistic people who are being racist 'don't understand' their own actions). This racism pushes Black autistic people out of the broader community making them feel unwelcome and excluded (Smith, 2020). In addition, the use of false equivalence by white autistic people in order to establish minoritised status (arguing that there are consequences for racism that are not applied to ableism) ignores a) both the prevalence of, and lack of action taken to minimise, racism, and b) evidence that Black and other racially minoritised autistic people are disproportionately likely to experience both the negative impact of systemic ableism (e.g. higher likelihood of incarceration, restraint, unnecessary medication, etc) due to the way this intersects with racism (Botha & Gillespie-Lynch, 2022).

It can be difficult for white autistic people to recognise their privilege. In 2018 Kieran Rose and Hannah Molesworth created a campaign to bring attention to autistic masking (Rose, 2018b). #TakeTheMaskOff was designed to 'take the mask off of autistic masking', inviting autistic people to share their experiences across a number of weeks and reaching a global around 5,000,000 people across various social media platforms. However, the hashtag alienated autistic people from racialised and ethnic minorities, who felt excluded from these supposed shared narratives due to the lack of safety for them to be or act more authentically, and the lack of understanding in white autistic spaces. This is one of many ways in which white autistic people unwittingly engage in activism which excludes non-white experiences, or doesn't recognise and centre the narratives experienced by autistic people who aren't white (Giwa Onaiwu et al., 2021).

In summary, autism research needs to be more mindful of racialised experiences and the exclusion of race from the autism narrative so far. Researchers and practitioners need to work to try and ensure representation of a more diverse group of autistic people, and take into account how race intersects with the experience of being autistic. In addition, the autistic community needs to recognise that it has a problem with racism which in turn exacerbates stigma and the associated outcomes for Black autistic people. We will discuss this issue specifically in chapter 8.

## Autism and Gender: unseen and unheard

The current gender disparity in autism diagnosis between males and females is highly debated, with some studies putting it at around 4:1 (Lord et al., 2020), and others suggesting the global median is closer to 2:1 (Zeidan et al., 2022) with girls who do not have a co-occurring intellectual disability more likely to experience misdiagnosis, and later diagnosis of autism, compared to male peers (Belcher, Morein-Zamir, Mandy, et al., 2022; Gesi et al., 2021). As outlined earlier in this chapter, the original research that fed into the labelling of autism led to a limited conceptualisation of what autism 'looked' like, including an association with males despite Kanner's original sample including 3 females.

In this section, we will explore potential reasons as to why there remains a pervasive gap in diagnosis amongst women and girls (before we move on to acknowledge and address gaps among non-binary, and transgender autistic people in the following section, for whom there has been much less of a focus thus far).

## An extremely male brain?

Despite the historical lack of investigation into how gender might impact on how autistic people 'present' in a clinical setting, gender did play a role in defining features of autism, albeit indirectly. One of the key theories instrumental in reinforcing autism's association with maleness, is the Extreme Male Brain theory (or EMB), proposed by Professor Simon Baron-Cohen (Baron-Cohen, 2002). EMB posits that the features (or 'autistic traits') that we commonly see used to identify autistic people, for example a desire to engage in 'systemising' and difficulties with understanding the mental states of others (Frith, 2001) are extreme manifestations of traits associated with a 'male brain type'. The argument for gendered neurotype expression was based upon evidence showing that, on average, men tended to be drawn to and excel more in areas more related to systemising (e.g. attention to detail by way of embedded figure recognition, Almeida et al., 2010), whereas women tended to be drawn to, and excel in areas related to empathising (e.g. making inferences about the mental states of others, Baron-Cohen, 2002). Baron-Cohen posited that these sex differences were likely underpinned by variations at the neurological level, though he recognised that culture and socialisation may play a part. He suggests that there may be 5 distinct neurotypes associated with his theorising: the male, and female brain, the extreme male, and extreme female brain, and the 'balanced' brain. Importantly he also suggested that, despite the terminology, women may have a 'male' neurotype, and vice versa (we will return to this point later), hinting that these neurotypes were less related to sex and gender stereotyping than to literal neurological differences.

Baron-Cohen argued that features of autism such as heightened attention to detail, being drawn to mechanistic interests, and a difficulty with understanding the minds of others were indicative of the 'extreme male' neurotype (Baron-Cohen, 2002).

Evidence for the EMB theory of autism was drawn from the literature on sexually dimorphic characteristics. Baron-Cohen posited that if autism was a form of 'extreme male brain', we may see an increase in the hormones associated with the development of characteristics associated with sexual dimorphism in males (e.g. foetal androgens, and post-natal indicators such as 2nd and 4th digit, or 2D:4D ratio). Early empirical evidence to support this hypothesis came from work showing that autistic people were more likely to have a lower 2D:4D ratio than neurotypical people (Manning et al., 2001). However, overall research in this area has been inconsistent. Whilst some studies have suggested that 2D:4D is lower in autistic samples (see Teatero & Netley, 2013), others have found no significant differences between autistic and non-autistic people (Kyselicová et al., 2021). Likewise no consistent relationship between foetal androgens and increased likelihood of being autistic has been found (Kung et al., 2021) and indeed, recent research from Baron-Cohen et al., 2020) has suggested that prenatal oestrogens are also related to likelihood of autism diagnosis positing the role of prenatal steroids more generally in the expression of neurodivergence.

It is important here that we draw a distinction between a tendency towards systemising, and the gendering of brains. The cognitive phenotype associated with autism (e.g. detail focussed, systematic) is not indicative of a particular sex or gender, but may be more reflective of a particular cognitive processing style seen among autistic (and potentially other neurodivergent people). Recent evidence suggests that a dimorphic approach to sex and gender, particularly with regards to neurological and cognitive differences, cannot be simplified to 'male brain vs. female brain' (Hodgetts & Hausmann, 2022). More recently, Baron-Cohen has conceded that it may have been better to refer to the differences between people who are primarily 'systems driven' and those who aren't (Baron-Cohen, in Offord, n.d.). However, the naming of the theory had a lasting impact on the consideration of autism and gender and Baron-Cohen's work further cemented the association between autism and maleness. While the original samples from Kanner and Asperger focused, mostly on white male, middle-class, children, Wing and colleagues acknowledged that autism was prevalent across a much wider population. With the extreme male brain theory of autism, Baron-Cohen, not only essentialised autism as something that could be reduced to sexually dimorphic characteristics, but also implicitly suggested that diagnostic disparities were likely due to these essentialised differences between males and females. He maintains that sex-ratio diagnostic disparities persist after taking into account missed/misdiagnosis and masking (Baron-Cohen et al., 2020). However there are multiple reasons that these figures may not accurately represent autism across the broader population. One issue is that current diagnostic disparities may be reflective of the time taken for academic advances in understanding around autistic presentation to filter down into practice. Whilst we may be more aware of diagnostic barriers and the impact that these have on autistic women, men, and non-binary people who transcend stereotypical profiles, there is evidence to suggest that this knowledge has not yet proliferated across services and still has a tangible impact on those seeking recognition (Cage et al., 2022). Relatedly, diagnostic disparities reflect the number of autistic people *currently* diagnosed. UK NHS data from 2014 (NHS, 2016) suggests that in adult services, higher numbers of women are seeking diagnosis than men (which may be related to boys being more likely to be identified in childhood). However these figures are almost a decade out of date. More data on who seeks diagnosis, who gets diagnosis, and factors that might bias this process are needed. In addition, aforementioned issues around hermeneutical injustice suggest that many autistic people may not recognise themselves as such due to not fitting with current stereotypes about autism. Similarly to the issues raised around autism and race, autistic people who do not see themselves represented in information about autism will not seek diagnosis and thus remain underrepresented, driving the continuation of confirmation bias among professionals.

Not only did these theories apply sexist ideology to the 'cause' of autism, they overlooked the multifarious ways in which autistic people (and autistic characteristics) may present, leading to the proliferation of stereotypes. Indeed, Diemer et al., (2022) highlight how the 'male brain' profile is based upon WEIRD perceptions of masculinity, enshrining racism within the theoretical approach to understanding autism. Though many autistic people are indeed drawn to careers where a strong detail oriented focus and propensity for systemising is beneficial (e.g. software development, engineering), there are many autistic authors, artists and creatives who also benefit from a passionate approach to their interests (Betts et al., 2022). Thus as a result of the EMB theory, there occurred somewhat of a narrowing of the diagnostic criteria for autism, meaning that autism came to be associated with what is often viewed as the stereotypical autistic archetype: white, male, geeky, and uninterested in social interactions (Wood & Freeth, 2016). Where autistic women were identified, they were expected to also fit these narrow criteria.

These stereotypes left little space for the consideration that autistic people might not only not fit this narrow representation, but that the representation itself might be self-perpetuating- that women were going underdiagnosed due to conceptualisations of autism as extreme maleness, and that in turn this reinforced the idea that women were less likely to be autistic.

Thus, autistic women were viewed as somewhat 'rarer' than autistic men. This led to speculation as to what may be driving this effect. EMB theory provided its own explanation in the form of foetal androgens, with women 'naturally' less likely to have higher levels of foetal testosterone assumed to shape autistic biology and cognition (Baron-Cohen, 2002). However, the weak evidence implicating foetal androgens as an underlying cause of autism led to the development of alternative theories, the most enduring of which have been the female protective effect (FPE), and the female autism phenotype (FAP).

## The Female Protective Effect

The Female Protective Effect, or FPE, states that genetic expression may account for the differences we see between males and females in regards to autism diagnosis, with women requiring an increased genetic likelihood of autism compared to men in order to 'express' behavioural characteristics. Polygenic risk score refers to the propensity for an individual to develop or express a particular characteristic based on evidence of increased heritability, i.e. comparing the genomes of people with and without a particular characteristic, and looking at how the variation in their genetic material relates to its expression.

Evidence to support this theory comes from studies showing that whilst females are more likely to display more de novo mutations (a mutation seen for the first time within an individual family member) associated with autism, they display similar levels of autistic characteristics to males (Hull et al., 2020). Whilst researchers have argued that this may be evidence that females require a greater genetic impact in order to "meet diagnostic thresholds", Hull and colleagues argue that these data are based on differences between those autistic people who are a) currently diagnosed, and b) the assumption that current diagnostic rates are accurate, which, as we outline above, is unlikely to be the case. They posit that there may be autistic women who currently do not meet the threshold for diagnosis who *are* autistic and who may display higher or lower genetic load, or genetic variations not yet explored with relation to autism. Thus, no strong claims can be made regarding the likelihood of the FPE being an accurate account for diagnostic disparities between males and females.

## Female Autism Phenotype

An alternative explanation for the underdiagnosis of women is the Female Autism Phenotype, or the FAP (yes, we know). The FAP hypothesis states that women are likely underrepresented in autism diagnostic cases due to a) a lack of recognition of the way in which the expression of autistic traits may occur in women, and b) the diagnostic criteria being biased against recognising the expression of these traits in this manner (i.e. they are based upon how autism is perceived to look in males). Research has shown that despite there being little difference between the levels of autistic characteristics between diagnosed autistic males and females, females are less likely to receive a diagnosis unless they also experience co-occurring intellectual disabilities (for a full discussion, see Hull et al. 2020). It is posited that there are key differences in how autistic women appear which make them less likely to receive a diagnosis, including a higher propensity for social relationships (Sedgewick et al., 2018), more 'normative' repetitive and restricted interests, a higher likelihood of 'internalising' difficulties (e.g. anxiety), and finally their aptitude at masking which allows them to 'fly under the radar' (we will explore the research around masking in relation to gender in more detail in the chapter 9), known as the 'female compensation hypothesis'.

## A different kind of prejudice

Of course neither of these arguments are particularly parsimonious, as proponents of Occam's razor dictate 'when you hear hoofbeats, think of horses'. Both the FPE and FAP rely upon essentialist conceptualisations of sex and gender, portraying underdiagnosis as either a biological consequence of being female, or as a potentially 'less noticeable' form of autism that manifests as a result of being female. Of the two explanations, the FAP at least takes into account how autism is *perceived* in women, but it still does not quite hit the nail on the head. To quote Rose, (2018) what we are seeing in the underdiagnosis of autistic women (and other underdiagnosed populations) is "not a different kind of autism, but a different kind of prejudice". Indeed, Fombonne (2020) points out that gender differences across other diagnoses (e.g. depression) that have shown to manifest in gender differences have not led to the proposal of gendered criteria. This exploration of autism and gender through an intersectional lens prevents the additive approach Crenshaw warned about, by which autistic women are 'autism + female', and instead explores the way in which the gendered experience of growing up autistic (and importantly, external perceptions of what this looks like to others) shapes our identity and behaviour. This is important because the labelling of this particular presentation as 'the female autism phenotype' has a negative impact on autistic people of all genders.

Firstly, as we outline in Pearson & Rose, (2021), distinguishing 'autism' from 'female autism' suggests that there is a 'true' autism and that women and girls present a variation on this. As discussed earlier in this chapter, a granular approach to intersectionality could see a reductionist move towards subtyping on the basis of each aspect of identity (e.g. female autism, Black female autism, ad infinitum). This essentialised approach detracts from other intersecting factors which are likely to shape our experiences as autistic people (e.g. our upbringing, or socio-economic status, our culture). It attempts to binarise autism, viewing everyone who is not a white cis male as a variation of the default, rather than recognising the diversity of the autistic people manifesting as a result of us being part of the human race. The recognition of intersectionality within addressing gender disparities is essential for ensuring that we do not simply reify another limited conceptualisation of autism. The majority of research on the female autism phenotype thus far has been based on the experiences of white autistic women (Diemer et al., 2022). Lovelace and colleagues highlight the importance of the inclusion of black autistic women and girls in research designed to highlight support needs and future directions. The exclusion of black autistic women and girls from the research narrative to date means that our conceptualisation of the female autism phenotype is yet another understanding of autism that is seen through the lens of whiteness (Mallipeddi & VanDaalen, 2022). There is an issue with conceptualising the under diagnosis and missed diagnosis of autistic women and girls being caused by internalisation and subtlety, not least that it blames autistic women for their own lack of recognition. However, this profile may interact with racist perceptions of 'behaviour' to drive further racial inequalities. Black girls already experience pressure to internalise emotions due to racist stereotypes of characteristics that outsiders associate with blackness in women and girls, such as aggression and independence (Lovelace et al., 2022) in order to avoid racist stigma. Black autistic girls will experience these pressures in addition to the pressure to mask autistic characteristics. This multi-layered experience of masking may lead to worse outcomes overall due to the impact of increased minority stress, as we will explore in chapter 10.

Secondly, (and related to our previous point) it minimises and excludes the experiences of anyone who does not fit either narrow category, that is, autism and *female* autism. This dichotomous subtyping could lead to autistic cisgender men who may not fit with traditional stereotypes of autism being labelled as expressing 'female autism', and given that autistic people have been found less likely to identify strongly with gender norms (Cooper et al., 2018) centering phenotypes on gender is unlikely to accurately represent the experiences of autistic people. These subtypes also completely ignore the experiences of autistic non-binary people (who we will discuss in the following section). There has been some suggestion that we might instead consider such differences in whether autism appears externally visible to an observer as a difference in internalising versus externalising profiles however this may be equally as problematic.

Internalising is associated with inwardly orienting emotional responses, which can manifest in rumination, and secondary mental health disorders such as anxiety. By contrast, externalising is associated with an outward facing, more visible response, such as aggression. Internalising of difficulties experienced across the lifespan may manifest in a higher likelihood of being diagnosed with mental health conditions such as anxiety while autism is overlooked due to the lack of associated visible indicators (i.e. shutting down as opposed to melting down). Externalising is more likely to be labelled as 'challenging', is more externally perceptible, and is more likely to lead to consideration of autism (in white males). Whilst recognising that there are individual differences in how autistic people may respond to stressors is useful in formulating support for an individual, or cueing professionals that anxiety may be related to unconsidered issues (e.g. sensory distress), we must again avoid a binary categorisation.

The psychological focus on the individual as opposed to society means that we often reduce humans into simplistic categories. Whilst this approach might have utility for experimental work. It oversimplifies the complex interactions that shape who we are and how we think (i.e. an enactivist approach), and ignores that one single individual may fit either, or both of these proposed profiles at different timepoints, depending on context. For example they might internalise a sensory response to something that causes them anxiety in a school setting, such as certain sounds or smells, but externalise a response in a home environment around family.

Judith Butler (Butler, 1988) drew upon symbolic interactionism to describe how gender expression is constructed at any given time using gesture, movement and other forms of stylisation. Thus, the outward portrayal of gender is a *performance*, as opposed to an innate or concrete identity. The understanding of gender as a constructed identity rather than a concrete one can help us to understand how autistic women might appear to fit within a more normative expectation of what 'neurotypical' looks like. The discussion in the literature around autistic women displaying more interest in social relationships and more relational or normative interests can be argued to result from the socialisation of gender norms and the performance of gender, rather than a specific expression of autism. Of course, discussions around masking complicate this discussion further (Radulski, 2022, has applied Butler's theory directly to masking, which we will discuss in chapter 6). It can become difficult to disentangle what is masking (e.g. the development of interests that align with those of peers to avoid derision and to foster peer relationships) versus what is simply individual variation that we see across the population in general. For example, you do not tend to see arguments about whether someone is neurotypical centred on whether they are more interested in football or cars for example, but you *do* see discussions around what constitutes an acceptable feminine versus masculine interest. Within the category of autistic, we also see gendered discussions around what constitutes a 'normal' interest versus a 'circumscribed' interest, e.g. a girl who is interested in a particular band and a boy who has an interest in printer ink cartridges, versus a girl who has a stamp collection and a boy who collects football memorabilia.

This is where EMB theory has likely caused more damage to how we apply a particular diagnostic criteria, i.e. moving from 'an incredibly strong interest' to 'an incredibly strong interest in systems' to 'an incredibly strong interest in systems associated with masculine pursuits'. The solution to this problem is not to create additional subtypes, but to recognise the multifarious ways that autistic people may appear, and to apply diagnostic criteria accordingly. Interestingly, it may be that this issue is particularly pertinent in childhood due to the tools used to assess autism relying on particular behavioural presentations, whereas in adulthood there is scope for a more relational and holistic consideration of the person with the introduction of more nuanced tools, though this will also be entirely dependent on the experience and approach of the diagnostician.

Importantly, our perceptions of what is 'normal' behaviour may also shape how we view autistic characteristics and how 'severe' they are across the lifespan. Mandy et al., (2018) found that autistic characteristics (as measured by parent report) increased in adolescent girls compared to boys (who showed a decrease between ages 7 and 16). Whilst Asperger posited that autism may show 'later onset' in some individuals, it is more likely that (as we discussed in chapter 4) autistic characteristics (particularly those related to difficulties in social communication) become more apparent as the (majority neurotypical) social world becomes more complex, demanding, and subject to a different set of rules than those present prior to adolescence. This may be particularly apparent for girls, for whom there is a particular expectation around social relationships and the performance of femininity. Additionally, puberty brings the onset of additional sensory challenges (such as menstruation) as well as hormonal fluctuations that may lead to more apparent changes in mood and forms of dysregulation that are associated with autism (e.g. 'meltdowns').

In summary, the idea of 'female autism' does little to capture the complex intersection between being autistic, and being female. In the following section we will expand this discussion to consider people who may be entirely excluded in the binary discussion of autism and gender.

## Autism and a trans and/or non-binary identity

Discussions of the gender disparity in diagnosis often exclude transgender autistic people, and those who do not fall into a binary gender category. Research suggests that autistic people are more likely to be trans and/or non-binary (TNB + ) and part of the LGBTQIA + community (Dewinter et al., 2017) compared to the non-autistic population, and there are many crucial issues related to these intersecting identities (Strang et al., 2018, 2019, 2020). At the time of writing, there is a rising hostility towards TNB + people in Western society, with the codifying of anti-trans legislation proposed in both the UK and the US. Whilst we will discuss stigma in the next chapter, it is important to note that many of the intersecting issues that TNB + people experience are *directly* related to stigma.

Like many autistic women (and autistic men who do not fit with an expected profile), autistic TNB + people may be likely to face barriers in the diagnostic process due to not meeting stereotypical expectations of what 'autism' looks like. The emphasis on distinguishing gendered phenotypes in order to remedy diagnostic disparities not only excludes TNB + people, but can also invalidate experiences and expressions of gender in TNB + autistic people by forcing them to engage with binary conceptions of themselves (e.g. the labelling of autistic trans men and non-binary people who were assigned female at birth as having 'female autism', or lumping every autistic person who is a not a cisgender man into one group). Timely identification of autistic TNB + people can also have an impact on mental health and sense of self. Cooper et al., (2022) explored gender dysphoria in a sample of autistic TNB + adults, finding that meaning making in relation to identity, and balancing needs around both gender and autism were key aspects of their experiences. The participants described trying to work out who they were whilst feeling estranged from their own body, and trying to find labels that accurately described their experiences. They spoke about how this could be particularly impacted by the intersection of gender and autism, e.g. trying to dress a certain way to minimise dysphoria but finding affirming clothing difficult due to sensory distress. They had also experienced negative social judgements and treatment from others, and had struggled to access gender affirming healthcare.

Barriers to accessing gender affirmative healthcare appear to be common across the autistic TNB + population, relating to both inaccessible environments, and ableist misconceptions about autistic capacity for agency impacting on how gender non-conforming presentations are perceived. Autistic young people in particular have been derided as 'not understanding' their gender or how their decisions may impact them in future (Smilges, 2022), with their gender identity invalidated and patronisingly written off as being related to them being autistic, rather than the two being viewed as interrelated but distinct aspects of their identity. Additionally, Koffer Miller et al., (2022) found that general healthcare needs for those who self-identified as a gender 'other' than male or female were more likely to go unmet, with difficulties accessing services like counselling therapies.

Conversely, some autistic people *have* described how their transgression of expected gender norms is inherently tied to their autistic identity because of how it interacts with gender performance and socially normative gender expectations (Cooper et al., 2022). The distinction between 'not understanding because they are autistic' and 'being autistic interacts with other modes of identity and self-expression' is an important one. The concept of 'autgender' has been used to describe how one's own gender can be inherently intertwined with the experience of being autistic, due to embodied autistic ways of being impacting on how the experience of gender is personally interpreted and constructed (Botha & Gillespie-Lynch, 2022). Likewise, Neuroqueer theory provides a basis upon which transgression of expected societal norms through the lens of neurological otherness can provide an emancipatory platform for eschewing dominant (and binary) narratives of what gender, sexuality, etc. can and should look like (Walker, 2021). These narratives provide an alternative standpoint from which to advocate for an intersectional approach to understanding autism and gender divergence, and to push back against ableist perceptions of autistic capabilities of understanding our own identities. Given that human identity can be conceptualised as a set of performances, it might be expected that sometimes the performances will be internally 'smooth' (e.g. consistent across different aspects of self), and sometimes they may interact (e.g. performing gender as an autistic person may include some sort of fluidity between the autism and the gender as seen in the concept of autgender). Given the performative aspect of masking, and the performative aspects of other aspects of our identity, a neuroqueer lens to how identity is constructed can provide the means to understand our co-existing and fluctuating identities as embodied expressions of our internal worlds, and a reflection of external social norms (which we can reject if we so choose).

Currently understanding the intersection of autism and TNB+ identity is an emerging area, but we hope that this research continues to grow exponentially to meet the needs of the significant number of TNB+ autistic people in the broader autistic community.

## Autism and intersecting disabilities

Whilst evidence suggests that autistic people are more likely to experience a range of physical and cognitive disabilities (Jadav & Bal, 2022; Lai et al., 2019), here we are going to focus on autism alongside intellectual or learning disability. A learning disability is defined as a difficulty with learning or understanding certain kinds of information, learning particular skills, or needing help with various aspects of daily living (NHS, 2018). We will focus on the intersection between autism and learning disability here due to a) the large number of people who are autistic *and* have a learning disability, b) the frequent conflation of the two, and c) the existing narratives around autistic people with a learning disability in relation to masking. We will discuss the intersection between autism, being multiply disabled, and masking in chapter 7 when we explore the impact of stigma on autistic people and their IM engagement.

There are debates around the number of autistic people who also have a learning disability. Whilst some studies indicate numbers as high as 40% (Fombonne, 1999), other population studies have stated that this may be as low as 18% (Roman-Urrestarazu et al., 2021). Ascertaining an accurate representation of prevalence is important as this information forms the basis for understanding the needs of autistic people more broadly, and informs diagnostic expectations, and the services available afterwards. Additionally, research suggests that autistic people with a learning disability are frequently excluded from research about autistic people (Russell et al., 2019). Ironically, this has contributed to a situation where autism and learning disabilities have become somewhat synonymous, but people with a learning disability left out of research which underpins our understanding about autistic lives.

The historical narrative around learning disability is (as one might expect given the social context outlined in chapter 2) incredibly ableist. This is evident in the evolution of language used to describe learning disabilities at various points in modern history: mentally defective, idiots, imbeciles, feeble-minded, subnormal, retarded....These terms, once used as the official medical language to describe people with learning disabilities have each eventually entered the public vocabulary as insults, become labelled as offensive, and replaced with a new term which then follows the same pattern (known as the euphemism treadmill). As outlined in chapter 2, the historical narrative around the utility of people with a learning disability was one that devalued them on the basis of labelling them as lacking in functional contribution to society. This led to the institutionalisation, sterilisation, and state sanctioned murder of many disabled people. Early descriptions of autism from Asperger made clear that the characteristics that came to be associated with an autistic profile were present in children both with and without a learning disability (referred to at the time as 'feeble-minded' or 'useless eaters'). Later research from Wing and Gould suggested that over 50% of children with a learning disability also met the criteria for autism, however it was suggested that the two were difficult to disentangle due to overlapping characteristics (e.g. social difficulties). O'Brien & Pearson

(2004) argue that a diagnosis of autism could be impeded in people with a learning disability due to diagnostic overshadowing, that is, attributing autistic characteristics to their learning disability rather than exploring the existence of both. Likewise, it has been suggested that a diagnosis of a learning disability holds more utility for gaining support, compared to a diagnosis of autism. Interestingly, recent research has suggested that the diagnostic overshadowing that can sometimes be seen in autistic people with a learning disability may actually intersect with other aspects of identity. For example, girls, and Black autistic people are more likely to get an autism diagnosis if they also have a learning disability. This is despite previous suggestions that it could be more difficult to identify autism in people with a learning disability due to the overlapping characteristics present in both (e.g. delayed speech).

Recent discussions have emerged about the classification of autistic people based on the presence of co-occurring learning disabilities. As discussed in chapter 2, historically autistic people who were classified as having a 'low IQ' or developmental delay were viewed as 'low functioning'. There was often a conflation here between factors that could potentially indicate a learning disability (e.g. needing more support with daily living) and the reliable development of expressive language, whereby it was assumed that people with little to no spoken language would also have high support needs. Whilst this is the case for some people, it is certainly not the case for all. Regardless, assumptions should not be made about the capacity of autistic people who are non-speaking, and those with learning disabilities because of their lack of expressive verbal speech, or IQ. After the collapsing of Aspergers and Autism back into one classification in the DSM-V, some argued that the diagnosis had become too broad, and that grouping people together regardless of factors like IQ lacked utility for assessing how much support people might need (despite the fact that within the classification there was a shift towards 'levels', designed to indicate this). As such, there has been an argument that the category of 'profound autism' should be introduced in order to ensure that those with the highest need have access to support (Lord et al., 2022; Singer et al., 2023) based upon the presence of autism, alongside significant intellectual disability (as measured by IQ testing) and very limited use of language. Lord et al. (2022) argue that the use of profound autism may not apply broadly to all who experience the intersection of both autism and learning disabilities and does not have to be used, but should be available to individuals, families and services for the purpose of specificity and advocacy. Though the authors specify that the term is not appropriate for young children, they do suggest that it could be useful in later childhood (e.g. ages 8 and up) to identify potential suitable behavioural 'interventions' that take into account the level of understanding of the individual, via a 'personalised approach'. However, other researchers have argued that the category of profound autism lacks specificity to indicate the actual needs of an individual (which are assumed on the basis of communication differences or IQ tests) (Natri et al., 2023), and may further propagate stigma against non-speaking autistic people and those with learning disabilities (Collis, 2023).

Assumptions about the capacity of autistic people with learning disabilities and those who are non-speaking are often used to advocate for this splitting of the diagnosis and a demarcation between those who should be 'included' within the more emancipatory conceptualisation that is the neurodiversity paradigm (Baron-Cohen, 2017). Some researchers have suggested that whilst it is reasonable for 'high functioning' autistic people to consider themselves outside of a pathology paradigm, the same cannot be said for those who experience 'significant impairment' as a result of their differences (Hughes, 2021). However, as Botha & Gillespie-Lynch, (2022) argue, all autistic people should be "afforded dignity despite neuronormative ideas of functioning and traditional constructions of independence and productivity". A neurodiversity approach does not mean ignoring significant difficulties, but as we outlined in chapter 2, a value neutral approach under experiencing difficulties does not warrant the devaluation of a person, or the revoking of their rights and personhood.

We will focus explicitly on stigma, and the impact of trauma on autistic people in chapters 8 and 9, however it is worth acknowledging here there are specific aspects of stigma that have contributed towards a) higher likelihood of certain forms of trauma for autistic people with learning disabilities, and a narrative around masking that excludes autistic people with learning disabilities, higher support needs, and who may have unreliable speech or be non-speaking. Part of this is grounded in the assumption that autistic people with learning disabilities lack the capacity for understanding due to a lack of access to appropriate communicative tools (Zimmerman, 2022). Autistic people with learning disabilities and those who are non-speaking are assumed to lack the ability to advocate for themselves, but often are not given the tools to do so (e.g. access to alternative forms of communication such as augmentative and alternative communication, or AAC). Zimmerman (an AAC user who was labelled as 'severely' and 'profoundly' autistic) states "When we do not have access to effective and reliable forms of communication, people in power make destructive decisions about our lives". Historically support of autistic people, and particularly those with learning disabilities, was focussed on normalisation (Waldock, 2019). Despite this, a narrative has emerged suggesting that masking is a skill of 'high functioning' autistic people, mainly due to the link with later diagnosis and 'flying under the radar'. Here communication from autistic people with learning disabilities or those who are non-speaking is taken at face value, with assumptions made about the communication of internal states (e.g. interpreting expressions of distress as 'challenging behaviour') as opposed to recognising the immense energy that often goes into suppressing distress in hostile environments (Zimmerman, 2022).

Non-speaking autistics, and those with learning disabilities also face barriers accessing services and navigating healthcare and educational systems, sometimes due to the lack of appropriate communicative tools such as AAC, information not being presented in an accessible format (e.g. an 'easy read' version of an information leaflet), a lack of knowledge about how motor apraxia affects speech, or assumptions about the capacity of the individual to understand and advocate for their own needs. Adults with learning disabilities have stated how healthcare providers often attribute mental health difficulties to their learning disability (Paul et al., 2020), rather than taking into account psycho-social factors that contribute towards poor mental health (e.g. social isolation, stigma, lack of access to employment).

Overall, the paternalistic approach to autistic people who are non-speaking, and autistic people with learning disabilities has impacted understanding, general quality of life, and access to appropriate support. We will explicitly discuss this as it relates to trauma in chapter 9. Thus, it is important that instead of conflating autism with learning disabilities, we consider the needs of autistic people who experience the intersection of both with more care and respect.

# Problems arising from intersectional disparities

Recently debates have raged over whether autism has become 'so broad that it is meaningless'. Theories proposed to explain the supposed deficits in autistic people have not been replicated across wider groups of autistic people (Pearson et al., 2021), prompting researchers to suggest that sub-grouping autistic people may solve this issue (Frith, 2021). These arguments have neglected to consider whether researchers were correctly applying Wing's initial criteria in their own conceptualisation, issues around transdiagnostic overlap, and the tangible impact that an autistic identity has had on the lives of people who have been late identified due to an 'atypical' autistic profile. By narrowing autism to try and ensure that theory still fits, researchers unintentionally alienate and marginalise a wider group of people who have already spent most of their lives unrecognised and invalidated (Pearson et al., 2021), many of whom are marginalised in other ways (as this chapter explores). Many late identified autistic people (particularly women and Black autistic people of all genders) experience misidentification prior to a formal diagnosis of autism, most commonly being diagnosed with a personality disorder, Bipolar, or 'just' anxiety (Belcher, Morein-Zamir, Stagg, et al., 2022). The external expectations that are attached to these labels, and the lack of appropriate support based on their presence can lead to increased risk of secondary mental health difficulties and heightened risk of suicide. It is time that researchers and practitioners acknowledged our own biases and privileges that have impacted upon identification, instead of looking for ways to regress criteria to uphold traditional conceptualisations.

It is worth considering the role of diagnostic assessments in the outcomes across the groups we have discussed. Diagnosis relies upon the presence of externally visible, or *observable*, characteristics that we associate with autism, often called 'autistic traits'. Various tools and measures are used to diagnose autism, however the current gold standard measures for children are the Autism Diagnostic Observation Schedule II (ADOS) and the Autism Diagnostic Interview Revised Version (ADI-R). For adults, the ADOS may also be used in addition to psychometric measures (e.g. the Ritvo Autism Asperger Diagnostic Scale or RAADS, and the Autism Quotient or AQ), clinical observation, and a developmental history. It is acknowledged that the ADOS is not always appropriate for use with adults (Milton, 2016; Timimi et al., 2019), thus clinical uptake varies, however there have been wider discussions as to the utility of these measures in regards to what they are actually assessing (Timimi et al., 2019). Early researchers questioned the utility of behavioural assessments during the autism diagnostic process, stating a need for a multidimensional approach (e.g. developmental background, etc). However, more recent critique of the diagnostic process has centred on the lack of experiential expertise used to shape the identification criteria and assessments used to diagnose autism. Milton describes this as a lack of insight into 'autism from the inside out'. The history of autism research is grounded in external perceptions of what autism *looks like* to predominantly non-autistic people. Despite the internal worlds of autistic people being assumed to differ significantly from non-autistic people (e.g. in sensory processing, memory, attentional allocation, etc) there was up until recently a dearth of literature on the subject (for reasons that we outline in chapter 5). Autistic people have reported feeling a sense of resonance with other autistic people when discussing these shared internal experiences, however these features are mostly absent or a tangential part of the identification process (e.g. the presence of repetitive and restricted behaviours are more important than sensory processing differences). These issues hearken back to general arguments around the identification of autism, and the necessity of formal diagnosis versus informal identification.

With regards to the evidence we have discussed here, it is difficult to truly estimate the prevalence of autism across the groups we have discussed. Whilst we are aware of diagnostic disparities pertaining to race and gender, our current conceptualisations of autism limit any access to true numbers. That is, there are likely many more autistic people within the population who go un-identified due to a) other intersecting issues that contribute disparities (e.g. socio-economic status and access to healthcare), and b) not meeting the criteria for 'significant impairment' (Jellett & Muggleton, 2022). As outlined in chapter 2, our current (medicalised) approach to autism means that we consider it for the most part, something that must be identified and diagnosed by a professional. Whilst there are plenty of people who self-identify as autistic (Lewis, 2016), access to services and support is usually predicated on the presence of a formal diagnosis. This dilemma can lead to rather circular arguments about prevalence, for example that autistic people who are thriving will never need to self-identify *or* seek diagnosis because they have a good person-environment fit and have never considered that they might be autistic. However, this does not mean that they *are* not autistic. Discussions around the necessity of diagnosis have been made by people who simultaneously believe that autism can be essentialised, but also predicated on requiring significant impairment to be diagnosed (Baron-Cohen, in Offord, n.d.). This gatekeeping of the label accentuates the impact of hermeneutical injustice, in that if we say that a diagnosis requires significant impairment, and people cannot see themselves in that statement (and cannot be seen by others to reflect it either), they are less likely to identify themselves and gain the potential self-insight and understanding that comes with this. Relatedly, this also means that we are (perhaps unintentionally) pushing autistic people towards poor mental health outcomes by suggesting that they need to reach crisis point before they can have access to this label, and such we return to the point that one could self-identify, but if they did reach difficulty further down the line, would have no evidence with which to seek access to specific support services because they are gatekept by the need for labels.

In addition to understanding the way that conceptualisations of autism are constructed and then identified, an intersectional lens can also facilitate the recognition of the multifaceted impact that marginalisation can have upon autistic people (Botha & Gillespie-Lynch, 2022). In chapter 7 we will explore how stigma impacts on neurodivergent people, and how this stigma may intersect with, and be impacted by, marginalisation across other aspects of identity.

# Conclusion

In this chapter we have examined why intersectionality has been absent from discussions about autism, and how this has impacted the recognition of autistic people who fit with a more diverse representation than a white, cisgender young boy. Racism and white supremacy has impacted on the identification of Black autistics, and autistics who are racialised as a minority, leading to disparities in education, healthcare, and a lack of representation in research about autistic lives. Sexism and cis-heteronormativity has impacted on the recognition that gender disparities in diagnosis may be related to factors beyond gender essentialism, and have fuelled unhelpful narratives around masking and identity. Autistic people who are non-speaking, and/or have a learning disability have both simultaneously held up as the 'face' of autism whilst being devalued, dehumanised, and excluded from both research and societal inclusion. In order to rectify these issues we need to consider our own biases in both research and practice, and listen to autistic people rather than assume we know what is best: many of us are not aware of our own ignorance, and it leads to the (mostly unintentional) overlooking of important intersectional issues, which are then compounded systemically.

Overall, the key takeaway message from this chapter is clear: there is a difference between hiding, and not being seen.

# Chapter 6: Deconstructing theories of masking

Throughout this book so far we have explored the history of autism to provide a context for understanding current issues around autistic identification and the treatment of autistic people in society, the development of identity, and intersectional aspects of identity that shape autistic experience. The aim of these chapters was to contextualise the discussion of masking, and critical reflection on our understanding of masking thus far. The aim of chapter 6 and chapter 7 is to provide a critical overview of current theories of masking, deconstructing both theory and evidence in order to examine how we currently conceptualise masking, followed by an overview of research to date. It is important to recognise that though the exploration of masking in academic research is a new focus, the wider autistic community have been talking about masking for many years, and the narratives around masking found in academia and wider community discussions do not necessarily align. To date research has focussed on two main approaches to understanding masking; delineating the components that comprise or are involved in masking, and theorising the underlying conceptual factors that drive masking whereas community discussions (e.g. Rose, 2018) have focussed on the impact (which we discuss in Chapter 10). In the current chapter we will discuss both component approaches and conceptual factors, in addition to attempts to reconcile them in order to contextualise the evidence presented in chapter 9.

## Component approaches

### The tripartite model of camouflaging (masking, assimilation, compensation)

One of the earliest studies that attempted to examine the components involved in autistic masking was that of Hull et al., (2017). The research emerged following on from Bargiela et al., (2016), who found that women identified as autistic later in life reported masking or 'camouflaging' being autistic as an attempt to cope in the neurotypical world. Hull and colleagues used the term camouflaging to describe multiple facets of autistic self-monitoring and the attempt to 'hide' or 'fit in' within social situations. They developed their theory of camouflaging based on qualitative research conducted with autistic adults, which explored their experiences of self-suppression and masking within social interactions. They found that their participants highlighted several distinct aspects to their experiences and based on their data, proposing that camouflaging comprised three key features: masking, assimilation, and compensation. They define masking as hiding autistic characteristics and instead implementing socially palatable personas in social interaction. This might involve actions such as minimising stimming in front of others, and instead engaging in effortful mimicry of the actions and behaviours of others. Assimilation was defined as the act of blending in with others, or 'pretending to be normal' in order to avoid negative social consequences, and might involve trying not to stand out through not sharing unique interests with others. Finally, compensation was defined as engaging in non-native social behaviours in order to minimise social challenges, such as forcing eye contact. This model provided a lens through which to further explore the prevalence of these features among autistic (and non-autistic) people, to determine whether camouflaging was a unique experience that may lead to some autistic people 'flying under the radar' when it came to diagnostic identification.

The operationalisation of these features was further attempted by Hull et al., (2019) through the development of the Camouflaging Autistic traits Questionnaire (or CAT-Q), which was designed to examine self-reported features of masking in autistic people across all three components. The development of this model, and the associated tool had important clinical implications. Given that it is based on the self-reported experiences of autistic people, it captured features of everyday self-monitoring that are likely to impact on how 'autistic' a person appears to a clinician. Thus, the tool provided the ability to gather empirical evidence that behavioural traits stereotypically associated with (and used to diagnose) autism may not always be visible to an external observer, and to develop a measure that could assess and quantify the degree to which someone engaged in these behaviours quickly and accurately

These developments would prove to be crucial for clinicians, in understanding that camouflaging may impact on the appearance of someone who is being assessed for autism, and being able to quickly gauge the degree to which they might be engaging in camouflaging both in their diagnostic assessment, and everyday life. The CAT-Q has since been validated for use with children and young people, and parent report (Hannon et al., 2023), and provides one avenue for the application of masking in clinical identification.

However, it is also important to recognise that early advances in research often do not tell the full story, and may not be clinically universal. The development of this model focussed very much on the 'visible' aspects of masking; how autistic people may change or minimise their behaviour, how they may dress, and how they may mimic others in order to fit in. These visible aspects are more superficial or 'surface' in nature, akin to the perceptual aspects of self-representation that can be used by others to make a judgement. Whilst self-report can be limited in terms delineating conscious/unconscious strategies, Hull et al. (2017) took autistic people's testimony and attempted to explain the different aspects of self-monitoring through the development of key themes within their experiences. As such, though the tripartite model of masking may not have captured the full complexity of autistic self-monitoring, it provided the basis to begin to delineate more superficial or surface strategies from deeper/unconscious aspects in addition to sparking a wider interest in masking among autism researchers. Hull's study was crucial in bringing masking to the forefront of autism research. A quick (read: not systematic) Pubmed search for autis* AND camouflag* from 2001 to 2017 (the year that the article was published) reveals a total of 15 academic papers (and a further 3 that mention masking). Between 2018 and 2023, a Pubmed search brings up 88 articles under autis* AND camouflag*, and 39 articles under autis* AND masking, with the area developing exponentially.

However, one issue that has arisen from the early development of the CAT-Q is that it was based upon limited theorising, and limited empirical data (Fombonne, 2020). Whilst the tripartite model provides a framework through which to examine the presence of these SM features, it did not provide a theoretical grounding for the presence of masking, thus the development and subsequent use of the CAT-Q ended up reifying certain aspects of the model (e.g. what 'masking' is compared to 'assimilation') instead of providing a basis from which to explore. This resulted in a lack of consideration of other factors that may be involved, or play a part in masking, e.g. intersectional aspects of identity and other socio-contextual mechanisms. As will be seen in the discussion of stigma and social identity, IM and SM is a situated (and somewhat universal) process. The discussion of autistic people attempting to appear 'normal' decontextualises the power relations and oppressive systems that lead stigmatised people to try and blend in with majority norms, beyond the desire for a favourable social judgement.

Overall, this model provides an important contribution to understanding some of the more 'visible' or perceptual aspects of IM and SM that autistic people engage in in social situations in order to facilitate favourable evaluations, or to avoid stigma.

# Compensation

In addition to the use of the term *compensation* as part of the tripartite model of masking, compensation has also been used to describe the process of appearing socially competent (or more neurotypical) despite lower scores on classic socio-cognitive tasks, e.g. those measuring theory of mind. Researchers have suggested that some autistic people attempt to bypass socio-cognitive challenges through the development of alternative routes or mechanisms for task completion, for example using rule-based strategies to determine the difference between a lie and a joke (Livingston et al., 2019). Livingston et al. argue that this compensatory mechanism might account for supposed changes in a behavioural profile of social behaviour across the lifespan whereby someone may appear to have fewer 'autistic symptoms' in adulthood, or no longer meet the criteria for a diagnosis. Evidence to support this hypothesis has been found in both discrepancy approaches (e.g. studies which examine the difference between behavioural assessment of autism, and scores on socio-cognitive tasks), and reflective approaches (which often use self-report from autistic people).

## Discrepancy approaches to compensation

Livingston et al., (2019) explored whether performance on a theory of mind task and scores on the Autism Diagnostic Observation Schedule (ADOS) were discrepant across a sample of autistic young people, and compared these to their non-autistic twins. Results distinguished several sub-groups within their study- those who had worse performance on ToM and showed fewer autistic traits via the ADOS, those with lower ToM scores who showed higher autistic traits via the ADOS, those who had good ToM scores and fewer autistic traits, and those with good ToM scores who had higher autistic traits. Those in the group with good ToM performance and lower ADOS scores were labelled 'deep compensators', as they appeared to show fewer behavioural characteristics of autism, alongside the ability to pass the ToM task used. Interestingly, a high number of participants in the 'unaffected twins' group showed low performance on ToM, alongside low ADOS scores, putting them in the 'high compensators' group alongside their formally diagnosed autistic twins. Similarly, Corbett et al., (2021) also examined compensation in autistic young people through comparing ADOS scores to performance on the contextual assessment of social skills, and a battery of neuropsychological measures including theory of mind. They found that autistic girls showed fewer repetitive behaviours (RRBs) but similar social affect compared to autistic boys, positing that this may be evidence of masking of RRBs in autistic girls. However, the authors acknowledge that this is speculative due to the lack of additional RRB measures in the study.

They used scores on the theory of mind and ADOS tasks to split the young people into groups akin to those used by Livingston. The deep compensation group (lower ADOS and higher ToM) had stronger vocal communication scores and use of gesture compared to 'high compensators' (lower ADOS and lower ToM), however both showed better use of 'subtle language skills' compared to low and unknown compensators. There were no effects of gender on group membership for high compensators, suggesting that conceptualising compensation (or masking) as a female trait is misleading.

## Reflective Measures of compensation

Livingston et al., (2020) explored self-reported compensatory methods in a sample of 117 autistic adults using a qualitative approach. They identified 4 distinct categories of compensation, which they called 'masking' (increasing or suppressing existing social behaviour, such as mimicking the speech of a group you are part of), 'shallow compensation' (strategies to appear neurotypical, such as appearing to make eye contact), 'deep compensation' (using alternative routes to social cognitive, such as drawing from complex sets of information about tone of voice, facial expression etc) and 'accommodation' (seeking out accommodation as opposed to making any alterations, such as working in an environment which values difference).

The compensatory approach to understanding the relationship between autistic social cognition and social style acknowledges that behaviour is not necessarily the best representation of cognitive mechanisms (e.g. different routes to the same endpoint). It also aligns well with evidence showing that performance on socio-cognitive tasks do not necessarily reflect real-world social skill. Sasson et al., (2020) found that performance on socio-cognitive tasks did relate to functional and social skills, but that this relationship was weaker than previously assumed and somewhat indirect. Relatedly, Morrison et al., (2020) found that performance on socio-cognitive tasks was not predictive of in-person social interaction success in autistic adults.

These findings present initial evidence that tasks used to assess social cognition (e.g. emotion recognition, ToM) may not accurately predict functional social skill. It is important to note that many of the tasks used to assess ToM are incredibly abstract, and do not necessarily align with the demands of real world social interaction. One example is the Frith-Happé triangles task (Livingston et al., 2021), which requires the participant to decide whether a moving triangle is displaying a mental state (e.g. is trying to trick another triangle), a purely physical state (dancing), or moving randomly. Putting aside the anthropomorphic aspect of the task, a lack of accuracy does not necessarily mean that the participant lacks a ToM, but that their interpretations may differ from that of the researcher (Conway et al., 2019). Another example is the 'mind in the eyes' task, which isolates emotional information to the eye region, using static images. In real life interactions there are few examples of only having access to the eye region as a source of emotional information (e.g. your interlocutor is wearing a niqab), and emotions are much more dynamic in appearance.

A further strength of this model is the use of a mixed methods approach to explore the link between social cognition, in person social skill, and lived experience of learning how to interact with non-autistic people. Livingston et al. (2020) used first person accounts of compensatory processes to develop a compensation 'checklist', which allows for a more in-depth examination of differences between 'superficial' strategies (such as mimicking someone's way of dressing to fit in), and deeper processing (such as using contextual information and prior experience to infer how someone may be feeling) across a larger group of autistic people. The use of such a measure in conjunction with the approach used by Ai et al., (2022) (discussed later in this chapter) can provide important and contextually-situated insight into the interaction between the different components of SM and IM, and cognition, in autistic people.

At its heart, the compensation hypothesis can be used to acknowledge that autistic people may be socially 'skilled', desire social interaction, and find ways to build bridges with non-autistic people. It recognises that there are many routes to effective social cognition and understanding others, which lends support to the double empathy problem. Two interlocutors may not always be drawing upon the same information in order to understand or align themselves with each other, but the ability to find workarounds can help to increase social cohesion (though arguably more pressure is placed on the autistic person, as the minority in a majority non-autistic society). However, there are also some fundamental issues with the framing of compensation, one of which is the term itself, which infers that neurotypicality is the 'gold standard' in social style and cognitive performance, with autistic equivalents inherently deficient by comparison. Whilst the core assumptions of the model may be accurate (that some autistic people may appear to interact more easily with non-autistic people, and may also appear skilled at more abstract tests of social cognition), there has been less of a focus on whether this may simply reflect variation in the autistic social repertoire. The defining of autism as an impairment in social interaction appears to have led to a reductionist approach to autistic sociality by which a deficit is assumed by default, and any appearance of skill viewed as 'making up' for this deficit, rather than sheer heterogeneity in presentation. This framing of autistic social skills through neurotypical hegemony perpetuates ableist assumptions that there is a correct way to 'do' social cognition, and social interaction. A shift in thinking around compensation (e.g. moving to framing compensation in terms of the use of non-native social skills, or social strategy) can provide a valuable contribution to our knowledge about within and cross-neurotype interactions.

# Theoretical approaches

## Adaptive morphing

Adaptive Morphing is a term used by autistic scholar Wenn Lawson (Lawson, 2020) to describe the process of identity monitoring in autistic people. Lawson argues that the terms 'masking' and 'camouflaging' can infer an intention to deliberately and consciously deceive others to 'fit in', and may ignore the role of trauma and safety as a mechanism that underpins increased self-monitoring. Lawson compares this safety-driven adaptation to the colour-changing response of chameleons, who adapt to their surroundings based on the presence of threat, a mate, or changes in environment such as temperature. This conceptualisation acknowledges the role that trauma can play in heightened self-monitoring (which we will address in detail in Chapter 9), and importantly emphasises the role that societal stigma plays in promoting self-monitoring as a survival strategy. Support for this framing is provided through personal correspondence between Lawson and community members in the 2020 paper, however it is also supported by work on the relationship between interpersonal victimisation and masking (Gibbs & Pellicano, 2023; Pearson et al., 2023).

## Impression management as a minority group

More recently, researchers have started to take into account how identity and impression management strategies through a minority group framework may help us to frame autistic masking within a socially situated context. Though earlier studies on masking found that autistic people felt that they had to hide their true selves, there was very little research exploring how this may be driven by social context. A key empirical study from Cage & Troxell-Whitman, (2019) drew upon disconnect theory to argue that autistic self-monitoring may be driven by the potential risk of stigma related to both environment and intersecting aspects of identity (in this case gender). They explored the different contexts in which autistic men and women reported masking, finding that while both groups reported masing for relational (e.g. to maintain relationships) and conventional (e.g. to appear competent at work) reasons, women more frequently reported masking for conventional reasons compared to men. These findings suggested that both being a woman and being autistic may affect masking, with autistic women trying to avoid negative stereotypes associated with being a woman, and being autistic, consistent with Cage & Burton, (2019). Both groups also reported the avoidance of bullying from others as a key factor in masking, suggesting that masking was not just a social strategy to 'fit in', but to avoid harm.

The focus on masking as a) driven by social context, and b) as a complex interplay of both conscious strategies and an unconscious survival mechanism was one of the key takeaways from our 2021 conceptual paper, published in the journal 'Autism in Adulthood'. Though there had been an attempt to discern the components involved in masking on both a social and a cognitive level, these components had been explored in a rather detached manner from the social context that fostered their development. We drew upon Cage's work on Disconnect Theory in addition to work on social identity to examine the relationship between social context, stigma and self-monitoring. We argued that the historical framing of autism, alongside modern accounts of autistic people as a stigmatised minority group (Botha & Frost, 2020) made stigma a crucial factor in autistic masking, due to the internal and external pressure for autistic people to suppress aspects of their selfhood to avoid bullying, abuse and othering. We identified a lack of focus on the relationship between identity and self-concept in autistic people, and how this may interact with stigma.

Radulski, (2022) further highlighted the importance of an interdisciplinary approach to understanding autistic experiences as a function of a minority identity. She drew upon the work of Sara Ahmed, Franz Fanon, and Judith Butler to embed further sociological understandings of masking as a function of existing as a minority neurotype (or 'neurominority, Walker, 2021) in a majority neurotypical society. Crucially, Radulski suggests that autistic people defy the notion of an 'invisible disability' due to patholigisation of the way we move (e.g. stimming), which renders autistic people as 'visible' in a society where neurotypicals can blend in by virtue of being the norm. Radulski situates masking within this neurotypical hegemony, arguing that non-autistic people have shaped society in a way that makes it inherently accessible to them, negating the need to engage in masking for the sake of safety and 'blending in' as autistic people do. The notion that autism is not an invisible disability is consistent with the work of Sasson and colleagues (Sasson et al., 2017), which suggests that there are differences in the movement and speech of autistic people that render them 'visibly' different, whether this is named or not.

Radulski also acknowledges the importance of an intersectional lens (see Chapter X for further discussion) in masking research, given that autistic people may experience minoritisation in multiple ways (e.g. through racialised experiences, gendered experiences, etc) that may lead to IM and SM across complex, interacting aspects of self. This theorising provides an important framework through which to understand varying experiences with, and opinions of masking across autistic people, accounting for the societal contribution to the ability to live authentically when marginalised.

## Transactional Impression Management

Further theorising on the social mechanisms underpinning autistic masking has been provided by Ai et al., (2022) who situated masking within a cognitive model of self-monitoring and impression management. Ai and colleagues integrate evidence from the DEP to explore IM as a transactional process, integrating an understanding of autistic people as a marginalised social group whose socio-communicative style differs to that of the societal majority. They drew upon Goffman's use of dramaturgy to propose that autistic people engaging in SM must monitor 'front-stage' presentations, whilst suppressing any 'backstage' expression that may interfere with the success of the social interaction (i.e. an inability to 'switch off' even when not interacting with others due to the internalised need to meet normative expectations). To this end, autistic people are attempting to 'play the role' of a non-autistic person, or pass for neurotypical by suppressing their autistic characteristics, and drawing upon the expected social norms used by non-autistic people to facilitate effective social interaction. Whereas non-autistic (or non-marginalised people more broadly as discussed in the previous chapter) use IM to strategic or expressive means to increase social favourability, Ai et al. argue that the social favourability of autistic people is already skewed negative, falling below baseline. Thus the motivation of autistic people engaging in SM and IM is not only to increase social favourability, but also to minimise the risk associated with falling into such a stigmatised group (i.e. as a survival mechanism) such as victimisation (Gibbs & Pellicano, 2023; Pearson et al., 2023), and discrimination.

In addition to exploring masking as IM, Ai et al. provide a computational model of transactional IM, drawing upon Bayesian ToM and predictive coding. They argue that during social interaction, the actor takes into account their own internal beliefs, expectations and desires, and those of their interlocutor in addition to external factors such as the social and situational norms of the current environment. During the interaction, the actor seeks to balance the cost of engaging in effortful processing (drawing upon current, and past contextual information, or priors) and selecting the correct response to successfully manage the situation. Importantly this process is iterative, with the actor learning over time which responses may apply more broadly, and which may be more specific to particular situations contributing towards a more efficient and less cognitively effortful outcome.

For autistic people, this form of computational IM may be best understood through the DEP/DMH, given that the social styles/norms of autistic people and their non-autistic interlocutors may not align. Ai et al. argue that this divergence can lead autistic people to develop attenuated priors and thus struggle to predict the 'appropriate' social response when interacting with non-autistic people. Though this will also be the case for non-autistic people in cross-neurotype interactions, neurotypical people as the majority group are less likely to encounter these difficulties (fewer opportunities to interact with autistic people). They may also be less likely to be motivated to seek favourable social assessments from their autistic counterparts due to their minority status- in terms of cognitive trade-off, the lower chance of encounter may not be worth the initial IM effort.

This theory provides a solid framework for generating empirical data on IM and stigma in autistic people, accounting for the different strategies (both perceptual, and expressive) that autistic people may use when masking. We believe that this framework, in conjunction with wider theoretical considerations (e.g. minority stress) can provide a more operationalisable definition of masking through which to explore (conscious and unconscious) strategies, and outcomes.

## Conclusion

The theoretical work discussed in this chapter focuses on two distinct aspects of masking; understanding the components involved in masking, and understanding the underlying mechanisms which drive the development of these components. A thorough understanding of masking will integrate these approaches to provide a bottom-up understanding of how/why masking occurs, how it feels, the processes involved, and how it might look or manifest as an externalised strategy.

# Chapter 7: Stigma

In chapters 3 and 4 we explored the development of social identity and the strategies used to socially affiliate ourselves with other individuals or groups of people. The aim of this chapter is to delve a little deeper into the influence of stigma on identity management. Whilst the primary reasons provided for engaging in self-monitoring and impression management were to strategically influence the way people perceive you, or to express yourself in an attempt to seek validation, one factor that was given little consideration is the role of stigma.

Stigma is defined as the presence of a characteristic or attribute that renders a person 'discreditable' or 'disgraced' through the perceived negativity of its presence (Goffman, 1963). Goffman posited that a negative response to the presence of the stigmatised attribute arose through the association of the particular characteristic with a negative stereotype, leading those marked by stigma to having a 'spoiled' identity. He proposed that some stigmas are visible (rendering the person discredited), and others invisible (rendering the person discreditable), and that as a result, people might engage in particular strategies in order to either conceal their stigmatised attributes or identity, or attempt to pass as 'normal' through IM.

Following Goffman's seminal work, research on stigma explored how the construction of stereotyped identities may contribute towards perpetration (e.g. through the dehumanisation that occurs from minimising the uniqueness of an outgroup group member in favour of associated stereotypes). Link & Phelan, (2001) argue that as stigma became the remit of social psychology, research focussed less upon the relational aspect of stigma (e.g. how the person is viewed in relation to the norms that exist around them) and stigma became an essentialised aspect of the person (e.g. a disability itself being the stigma, rather than outsider perceptions of it). Likewise, Coleman-Brown, (2013, p. 148) stated that "Stigmas reflect the value judgements of the dominant group" and Herek has argued that the definition of stigma should be framed around the actions of the perpetrator, i.e. "the negative regard, inferior status, and relative powerlessness that a society collectively affords to people who possess a particular characteristic, or belong to a particular group or category" (Herek, 2009, p.66).This acknowledgement of the importance of conceptualising stigma as relational highlights the need to view stigma through an interdisciplinary lens, integrating sociological, societal level contextualising of stigma as a relational process with psychological processes and mechanisms to ensure a multidimensional understanding. The acknowledgement of relational aspects led to crucial contributions from Link and Phelan (2001), and Herek (2009), who identified the role that power plays in understanding the perpetration of stigma. They argued that the impact of stigma is grounded in the power held by the dominant group, with Link and Phelan proposing that stigma is attributed over the following steps:

1. Individual differences are assigned and labelled
2. Negative stereotypes are formed based on dominant norms
3. Categorisation/stereotyping creates an in/out group distinction
4. Outgroup status is diminished, leading to poor outcomes (e.g. reduced access to resources).

Steps 1-3 highlight how stigma is reliant upon the homogenising and dehumanising of people in lower status groups, whereby any between group differences are amplified to justify the belief that stigmatised people/groups are fundamentally different in some way to the 'normals'. Dehumanisation relies on the ingroup tendency to attribute their own group members with more agency, emotionality, and distinctly 'human' features compared to outgroup members (Kteily & Landry, 2022).

The structural impact of stigma demonstrates that without power, negative perceptions of outgroup members and their attributes has little effect beyond individual offence. Link and Phelan (p. 376) gave the specific example of how people who have been institutionalised may refer to the staff as 'pill pushers' and associate this description with stereotypes about people who work in this role (e.g. that they are paternalistic), creating an in/outgroup distinction as per steps 1-3 of their model. However as the staff in institutions hold the power they do not lose status or experience poor outcomes as a result- the prejudice does not manifest in discriminatory consequences. Recent discussions around discord between the autistic, and autism research communities mirror this distinction. Some autism researchers have expressed discomfort with the way in which autistic people question or criticise their work, and have suggested that it makes them feel worried about dissemination due to how people may respond. Whilst journalists have highlighted the online reach that some autistic people may have as a source of 'power', autism researchers are in fact the more dominant group with respect to power. Their research shapes public perception (we will return to this point later in this chapter), and has a tangible impact in the lives of autistic people (e.g. how support is designed and offered). Schneidre, (1988) argued that non-disabled 'experts' (i.e.

scientists) prioritise scientific methodology and theory over lived experience, leading to the perpetuation of flawed assumptions about the groups that they study. In this regard, epistemic injustice sustains stigmatising attitudes through shaping the common narratives about a particular group, and providing scientists the means to distance themselves from the consequences through the assertion that their approach is objective. This is not the hallmark of all fields; psychology has had a particular focus on 'objectivity' at the expense of ignoring how our values shape our interpretations (or indeed the questions we ask), however other fields (e.g. sociology) embed reflexivity in the research process (further highlighting the importance of interdisciplinary work). In summary, though autistic people may cause researchers to feel uncomfortable and hurt by their criticisms, they lack the power to cause discriminatory consequences. That is, demanding more stringent ethical requirements, and consideration of dehumanising language does not denigrate non-autistic people and erect systemic barriers to prevent their societal participation, but instead aims simply to improve the lives of autistic people.

The acknowledgement of the role that power has in regards to the impact of stigma is crucial. The power held by the dominant group provides the means to a) shape society so that it is most accessible to those who are in the majority, and b) reinforce the status quo so that those who transgress (e.g. either actively by refusing to conform to normative expectations, or indirectly, by failing to meet them) are punished. Both Corrigan, (2004) and Link & Phelan, (2001) highlight how the consequences of stigma can have both a direct impact on the stigmatised, but that it may also take an indirect route. Direct consequences of stigma are enacted by way of majority discrimination against stigmatised people and groups (termed 'public stigma'), such as preventing people from accessing resources and services (though again this can be explicit, such as refusing to cater to a particular group, or implicit, like lack of funding allocation to particular areas) and fully participating in society. This action enforces lower status for stigmatised people, and is self-perpetuating in that lowered social status prevents a person from changing the system, reinforcing their position and legitimising social dominance to those in power (SDT, Pratto et al., 2006). However this lowered status can also be enforced in an indirect manner (termed 'self-stigma') whereby the stigmatised person *internalises* negative perceptions into their own self-concept which leads to acceptance of lower status, and a belief that it is deserved.

Meyer, (2003) proposed that this lowering of status (both through direct means, and internalisation) increases the risk of excess stress (termed 'minority stress') that results from a mismatch between the world that exists (and the opportunities within it), and the experience of that world that marginalised people have (Major & O'Brien, 2005). He argued that minority stress is enacted through both distal processes (such as discrimination and prejudice), and proximal processes (such as internalisation, and expectations of rejection). Frost, (2011) drew upon Meyer's work to capture the multifaceted nature of stigma and its impact through the development of the process model of social stigma and its consequences (see Figure 7.1)

Frost encapsulated the process that stigma takes, moving from perpetration (e.g. from stereotype, to prejudice and discrimination) of stigma to the experience by the stigmatised (e.g. an increased risk of stressful life events such as employment loss, internalisation of negative stereotypes, and stigma management). He also highlighted the responses that people may have (e.g. seeking out support from similar others, making sense of their experiences) and the associated outcomes. Whilst the negative impacts of stigma are wide ranging (e.g. physical and mental health difficulties, relationship problems), attempts to cope with stigma can also lead to positive outcomes, e.g. resistance and push for social change. Importantly, Frost emphasises how structural inequalities impact at each level of the model, acknowledging the role that power has in shaping each facet. Thus the model presents an integrative account, highlighting the limitations of focussing on one aspect of stigma (e.g. perpetration) without acknowledging how this interacts at other levels (e.g. with the experience of stigma).

Since Goffman's seminal paper, researchers have highlighted how stigma management draws upon SM and IM strategies in an attempt to minimise the risk of harm. One of the unique aspects of SM and IM for stigmatised groups is the impact of the generalised other in driving self-perception. Both Meyer and Frost highlighted that people in stigmatised groups are consistently presented with a generalised other that devalues them and reflects the negative perceptions that society holds about them, thus impacting on their sense of identity and self-concept. Of course, Meyer argued that this impact will be dependent on how central the particular minority identity is to the individual's self-concept. If the minority identity is a prominent aspect of self, negative feedback can cause distress.

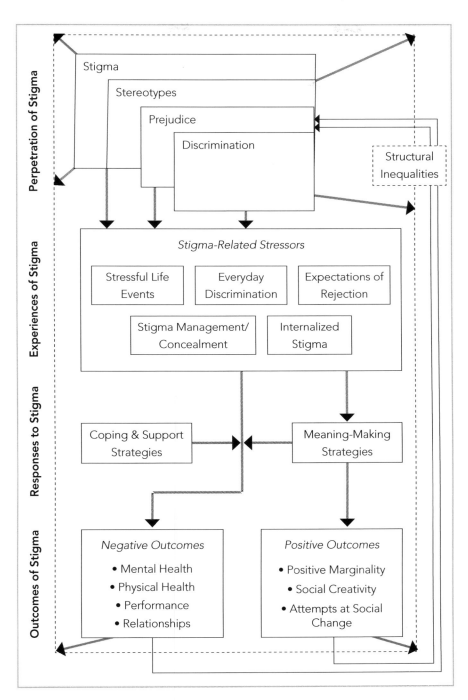

**Figure 7.1:** Process model of social stigma and its consequences (Frost, 2011)

This also leads to a complex relationship between community and minority stress. Close identification with similar others within a minoritised community can provide significant benefits in the face of stigma. Community provides a sense of belonging which fosters positive ingroup associations, and access to material (e.g. mutual aid) and emotional (e.g. support from others) resources that may be more difficult to achieve whilst occupying a stigmatised status. Research has shown that strong community connectedness can lead to ingroup members comparing themselves against each other to achieve a more favourable self-concept, rather than against members of the (dominant) outgroup (Meyer, 2003). However, this positive benefit from strong ingroup identification can also have pitfalls. Those who feel more connected to their community and have a strong sense of coherence with ingroup members are also more likely to be distressed by the stigma enacted on themselves and group members. Identifying more closely with a particular community can buffer against stress caused by being minoritised, but it also means that that particular aspect of identity is more prominent to the individual and thus any negative regard for the group will also take a heavy personal toll (Botha, 2020).

Despite this complex relationship between community connectedness and stigma, community also serves to promote resistance to stigma beyond providing a sense of belonging and social comparison. A strong group identity and connection to others within a stigmatised community can facilitate group members to move beyond passive acceptance of stereotypes and dehumanising rhetoric, and find ways to engage in advocacy and political change. Individual attempts at reframing stigma can often focus on attempts to embed respectability and emphasise similarities with the dominant group (Benoit et al., 2018). Indeed, Coleman-Brown (p.148) argues that stigmatised people have the responsibility to fight for integration into the dominant community. Here the individual is expected to assimilate, rather than shift the focus onto how normative expectations and practices disadvantage and 'other' people who do not fit with these standards as a way of fostering acceptance. Coleman-Brown argues that the stigmatised individual has the choice of "whether to feel inferior or superior", however as outlined by Meyer, a positive self-concept in the face of ongoing stigmatisation is highly distressing for an individual. By contrast, community resistance focuses on challenging systemic barriers and systems (e.g. community organising, influencing policy), and finding allies who can provide support and resources to contribute towards the facilitation of change (Campbell & Deacon, 2006). Thus, instead of placing the onus on the stigmatised individual to affect change, a community approach acknowledges that individuals lack the power to address systemic inequalities and barriers alone.

# Conceptualising stigma management

Autism research has recently started to explore the suggestion that masking is driven by stigma (Pearson & Rose, 2021; Perry et al., 2021). However, there is a rich history of research on the use of identity suppression as a response to stigma across many marginalised people/groups. In this section we will explore some of this research in addition to that on autism, to explore how different approaches to similar concepts might help us to understand how the experience of stigma leads to identity suppression and management.

## Visible Stigmas

In this section we will explore identity management in relation to what Goffman termed 'visible' stigmas, such as race or ('visible') disabilities. Visible stigmas are those that cannot (easily) be concealed, putting the onus on SM and IM strategies to avoid stigma. Here, our emphasis is on the broader theoretical underpinnings, and consideration of how stigma and identity management have been described across various contexts. Whilst the impact of stigma may take a similar shape (e.g. reduction in socio-cultural capital) across various stigmatised groups, there are intersecting factors within the experience of each that lead to unique oppression based upon the interaction with structural and systemic barriers (see Chapter 5 for a full discussion of intersectionality).

As outlined in previous chapters our identities are composed of multiple intersecting aspects, for example our gender, sexuality, race, cultural background, disability etc. For each individual there may be aspects of our identities that are simultaneously protected from negative social judgements and stigma, or that mark us as spoiled (e.g. being white *and* disabled). These intersecting parts of our identity lead to unique experiences and barriers, for example a white disabled person may experience disability related stigma, whereas a Black disabled person may experience racial and disability related stigma. Whilst both of these experiences might lead the stigmatised person to engage in identity management strategies, a white person who experiences disability stigma does not 'know what it is like' to experience racialised stigma or the associated barriers. These experiences also might not prevent a white disabled person from engaging in racially supremacist violence. Thus there is no sense of equivocacy here- stigma manifests in unique perceptions and barriers through its relation to specific aspects of identity. In this chapter we discuss the importance of recognising how the experiences of stigma and IM for Black people (e.g. via DuBois' work) and other marginalised communities may help us to develop a theoretical understanding of IM and SM strategies as a stigma response.

However, it is essential we do not conflate the experiences of stigma across groups. Intersectionality highlights the *unique* experiences that emerge as a result of marginalisation across multiple aspects of identity. It does not seek to make direct comparisons, and neither do we. That is to say, while all of these forms of stigma might result in stigma management strategies such as self-monitoring/masking, how this is internalised and expressed will differ across people and contexts, interacting with other aspects of their identity. Thus though framings around particular kinds of stigma may provide a theoretical understanding of how this impacts people, and there may be shared experiences across these groups, we must be careful not to conflate the two. Not least because many stigmatised people experience stigma across multiple, intersecting aspects of their identity (e.g. being autistic and Black), in ways that cannot be fully understood by people who do not experience this intersection. But additionally, because the experience of stigma across multiple, intersecting aspects of identity is likely to result in loss of power and status across these multiple axes, creating additional tangible barriers to societal participation.

## Example: Racialised Stigma

In 1897 William Edward Burghardt DuBois (Du Bois, 1897) wrote 'Strivings of the Negro people', in which he outlined what he called the 'double consciousness' of living as a Black person in America. DuBois outlined how the experience of being racially othered lead to heightened self-monitoring across multiple contexts, never feeling like one could ever truly live up to their own ideals, or those set by others:

> *"One ever feels his two-ness...He simply wishes to make it possible for a man to be both a Negro and an American without being cursed and spit upon by his fellows, without losing his opportunity for self development".*

Though DuBois was writing in the US, just 30 years after emancipation, the experiences he outlines are neither spatially limited to America, nor temporally limited to that time point in history. DuBois' account highlighted how the experience of being stigmatised can a) lead to the internalisation of negative self-perceptions, and b) lead to engagement in self-monitoring through the eyes of the dominant group. Du Bois' idea of the double consciousness was further expanded by Black women, who argued that their experiences included additional layers of oppression not captured under the binary of living as a Black person in a predominantly white society. Whilst some scholars have used the term 'triple consciousness' to describe this more multifaceted experience (Welang, 2018), King (1988) explained how the multiplicity of oppression experienced by people marginalised across multiple aspects of identity could be difficult to capture with such layered terminology. The avoidance of an additive effect was captured by Crenshaw's work on intersectionality (see chapter 5) which explored the multi-faceted and interactional experiences of Black women. Such work transcends an additive approach (e.g. 'double' or 'triple' stigma, etc) and instead emphasises how different aspects of (stigmatised) identity may lead to unique forms of oppression not experienced by people who do not live at that intersection (e.g. the racism, ableism and sexism that a Black disabled woman may experience).

Franz Fanon's 'Black Skin, White Masks' (Fanon, 1952) also addressed the experiences of Black people living in a predominantly white society, analysing how 'Blackness' is constructed through a colonial and oppressive lens to stigmatise and dehumanise Black people. Fanon focussed on the experiences of Black men, exploring through a psychoanalytical lens how enforced reductions in social capital, and the internalisation of stigma shapes identity. Importantly, he emphasised the importance of first-hand accounts in understanding how racialisation shapes the material reality of Black men.

Whilst first-hand accounts are sometimes dismissed as 'one-off' incidents (in itself an oppressive tool to deny the experiences of marginalised people), Fanon integrates autoethnographic study with exposure of the wider systemic structures that propagate white supremacy, whether explicitly visible to white people or not. He also explicitly addresses the role of the perpetrator in the creation of stigma, stating that 'it is the racist who creates his inferior', that is, perceptions drive stigma, not essentialised differences between individuals or groups. He states that colonisation asserts that 'whiteness' and all that is associated with it is the ideal to strive for, whilst simultaneously devaluing Blackness and creating systemic barriers to flourishing that lead to distress and an attempt to assimilate. Fanon took the view that neither assimilation, nor segregation, were adequate ways to combat racialised stigma.

The structural oppression and racism that Black people (and many other people from an ethnic and/or racialised minority within a predominantly white setting) face is still a prevalent issue. Coleman suggested that context may be an important factor in the impact stigma of (e.g. the experience of being a Black student at a predominantly white university, versus being a Black student at a predominantly Black university may lead to different approaches to assimilation vs. resistance). However, this example fails to acknowledge the transcendent nature of stigma (e.g. internalised stigma) that goes beyond the initial situation. Here the societal power dynamics that construct stigma play a crucial role. Whilst there may be community environments that provide safety and a sense of belonging, the wider societal view of the stigmatised can infect their self-concept (see our discussion of the normative generalised other in chapter 4). Fanon's discussion of assimilation instead can be explored through the lens of 'code switching' (Casimir, 2020) and DuBois concept of the double consciousness, whereby an individual must navigate competing cultural demands in order to try and 'walk in two worlds'. Casimir (2020) outlines how (like autistic masking) there are disagreements within the literature as to how all-encompassing code switching is, with debates as to whether it is linguistic, or includes other aspects of self and identity suppression. Singletary (2020) explored code switching among Black teachers working in predominantly white schools. His findings suggested that despite a strong sense of pride in Black identity, the teachers felt like they were prevented from developing a full sense of belonging in their workplace because they couldn't be their 'true self', monitoring a variety of things including the way they spoke, how they dressed and wore their hair, and which cultural references they could use. Though code switching could allow people to 'blend in more' to the environments they moved through (which one participant likened to learning to communicate with dissimilar others), it was also stressed that code-switching occurred as a way to survive as a minority within a majority culture that devalues Black people. This pressure to suppress aspects of racial identity as a response to external stigmas can have a negative impact on identity, and wellbeing outcomes (Johnson et al., 2022), akin to evidence which is beginning to emerge around the impact of autistic masking (which we will discuss in chapter 10).

A more recent focus broadening discussions around racial stigma in modern society (see the #blacklivesmatter movement, or #blackgirlmagic) have focussed on acceptance, care, and emphasising a positive cultural and community identity that resists the dehumanising tendency to minimise joy and achievement. These radical movements aim not only to dispel stigma, but to push back against the pressure to assimilate and suppress oneself in order to survive in a society which devalues Black people. This model of resistance is consistent with previously discussed suggestions of Campbell & Deacon (2006), whereby stigmatised communities fight for acceptance through challenging systems, and where possible resisting the respectability politics enforced by oppressors.

## Invisible Stigmas

Invisible stigmas are those that can be 'concealed' (e.g. sexuality), resulting in the ability to 'pass for normal' and avoid negative outcomes associated with stigmatisation of the particular characteristic. Concealable stigmas pose their own unique challenges, as those who have a concealable stigma still have to live with the impact of having a devalued characteristic (e.g. internalised stigma), the fear of what will happen if others find out, and the dilemma of whether to disclose one's stigmatised status (Pachankis, 2007). The decision to conceal or disclose may arise across varying circumstances throughout the lifespan, involving regular evaluations of whether to disclose, whom to disclose to, where to disclose and when to disclose. Thus the act of concealing has been conceptualised as the active effort taken to prevent a disclosure, rather than a synonym for non-disclosure itself (Jackson & Mohr, 2016). Pachankis highlights how disclosure decisions can arise on a daily basis, depending on who an individual is interacting with and whether that person may suspect their status. Importantly Pachankis also emphasises the risk associated with the discovery of a concealable stigma, drawing upon literature on mental health and sexuality (Corrigan & Kleinlein, 2005; Herek, 1998) which has demonstrated that job loss, a lack of access to healthcare, social isolation, and victimisation are just some of the negative outcomes that may rise.

Thus, whilst the ability to 'fly under the radar' can provide a protective effect against stigma, it is risky, and it is also more cognitively demanding. Successful concealment relies on the ability to self-monitor one's own appearance and the flow of personal information and modify as needed (a'la Goffman's dramaturgy), and also to keep track of where (and to whom) disclosure has been made. Importantly, a person with a concealable stigma is capable of both concealing aspects of their identity, and engaging in self-monitoring, and the two are not mutually exclusive (e.g. someone may conceal their sexuality, but disclose that they are autistic whilst still masking aspects of their autistic self-presentation). Pachankis captured the complexity of concealment through the development of a process model, capturing the cognitive, behavioural and affective implications of concealment across multiple contexts, and exploring how this impacts on self-concept and self-evaluation (see Figure 7.2).

## Example: Sex and gender minority stigma

Much of the core research around concealment and disclosure has emanated from work done on sexual identity with participants from the Lesbian, Gay, Bisexual, Transgender, and Queer+ (LGBTQ+) communities, exploring the nuance around non-disclosure, concealment, and the concept of 'passing' (or not being visibly identifiable as a member of a sexual or gender minority). The concept of disclosure in particular has become the particular focus of public discourse around LGBTQ+ identity, with 'the closet' or 'coming out of the closet' used as a ubiquitous metaphor to describe the act of disclosing one's sexuality to others, and billed as a 'rite of passage' for LGBTQ+ individuals (Corrigan & Matthews, 2009).

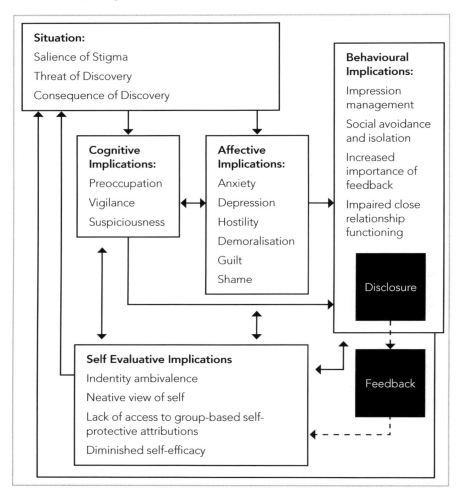

**Figure 7.2:** Process model of the implications of concealing stigma (Pachankis, 2007)

This differentiation between concealment and disclosure echoes current discussions around aspects of masking and concealment, in that someone can be 'out' and still engage in identity management, e.g. a person may both conceal their autistic status, and engage in masking, or engage in masking while being open about being autistic. Disclosure does not necessarily negate masking/concealment, though it might reduce some of the pressure to mask certain aspects of self in particular contexts/situations. Jackson &

Mohr (2016) also specify that concealment and disclosure can be motivated by different psychological functions, i.e. concealment may be driven by stigma avoidance, whereas disclosure may also be driven by a desire to foster trust and authenticity within interpersonal relationships. They argue that concealment can be driven by both stigma perpetuation, and internalised stigma as it is often maintained even in environments where stigmatising attitudes are relatively low. Importantly, they conceptualise IM through concealment in relation to stigma as occurring through a set of distinct, but interrelated processes taking into account concealment motivation and behaviour, internalisation, concerns around acceptance, and social identity. Such a multifaceted understanding of concealment in relation to stigmatised identity may provide a solid theoretical basis for understanding masking.

# Autism and Stigma

The investigation of how stigma impacts autistic people had gone relatively underexplored until very recently (Turnock et al., 2022). Whilst there have been numerous studies examining the experiences of caregivers in regards to the stigma they have experienced through proximity to an autistic person (or 'courtesy stigma'), there has been somewhat less of a focus on the experiences of autistic people themselves. Some researchers have referred to masking as 'attempting to pass as neurotypical' (Libsack et al., 2021), however as can be seen from the discussion on stigma not all masking has the express goal of avoiding being 'found out' or with 'fitting in'. Masking can be unconscious, safety driven, or related to further avoidance of stigma.

Autism poses an interesting challenge to the concept of 'visible vs hidden' disabilities. Whilst some scholars would argue that autism is an invisible disability (Han et al., 2022), in the chapter 6 we explored Radulski's (Radulski, 2022) suggestion that autistic people are often rendered visible due to failing to 'blend into the background' as neurotypical people can due to their majority status. Thus autistic people may be thought of as both 'discreditable' and 'discredited' depending on how visibly autistic they appear. Additionally, research on first impressions of autistic people suggests that autism is not 'invisible'. Multiple studies from Sasson and colleagues (DeBrabander et al., 2019; Morrison et al., 2019; Sasson et al., 2017) have shown that autistic people are judged more negatively by their peers in thin slice interactions when neurotypical observers are presented with visual or audio information, but not transcriptions from these videos. These findings suggest that there is something qualitatively different about how autistic people appear that distinguishes them from non-autistic people (we explored this briefly in relation to action kinematics in chapter 4).

Many autistic people have outlined how visibility can impact the stigmatising perceptions of outsiders, whereby those who appear 'less autistic' through masking are invalidated as 'not autistic enough', and those who are more 'visibly autistic' are assumed to lack competence and capacity (Botha et al., 2022a). This can place autistic people in what Botha has described as a 'double bind', where disclosure results in being discredited, but not disclosing still renders them discreditable through failing to meet normative standards and expectations. Thus, the stigma that autistic people experience occurs at multiple levels, being both a result of how autism itself is perceived (as a deficit or impairment at the group level), and how autistic people as individuals are perceived (e.g. as weird, or lacking in empathy). Milton referred to this as the 'psycho-emotional disablement' of autistic identity (Milton & Sims, 2016), whereby autistic people have to attempt to resolve the mismatch between their own sense of self, and how others expect them to appear. Autism stigma itself appears to be linked to several distinct areas, which Turnock et al., (2022) outlined, arguing that the complexity of stigma among autistic people arises as a results of the interaction between public and professional understanding of autism, and autistic characteristics that are expressed (i.e. what others can externally observe).This relates to Botha's point about autistic people being stigmatised at the group level (due to public and professional perceptions), and at the individual level (due to individual perceptions of otherness). They stressed that a variety of factors moderate the relationship between group/individual perceptions and enacted and felt stigma, such as disclosure, sex/gender, and amount and quality of contact with autistic people.

Fine & Asch, (1988) proposed that disability stigma in particular is inherently linked to the medicalisation of disability. Medicalisation leads to an essentialist approach to disability, which assumes that disability must have a biological cause. This is followed by the assumption that the problems a disabled person faces can all be attributed to the disability, and that they are a victim of it. Disability is seen as the core aspect of the person's identity, and renders a person incapable of living without support. Inherent in this medicalised view is the individualist and capitalist assumption that devalues interdependence, in favour of a view of thriving which is fundamentally linked to one's independence and contributions to the labour market (Chapman & Carel, 2022).

As seen in chapter 2, the medical model has framed the features of autism as inherently negative, and as something that should be diagnosed and remediated. Despite ongoing debates over the biological basis of autism (no singular genetic explanation, no neurological difference can explain the differences seen across autistic people), diagnosis is framed around the experience of 'significant impairment'. This means that autism is framed as both 'inherent to the person' (i.e. the biological difference is the 'cause' of autism and all related traits) and simultaneously based on current societal normative standards of functioning, which are culturally and temporally bound. Thus, under a medical model autistic people are pathologised as both biologically and societally abnormal, and importantly under this framing are theoretically unable to flourish or thrive (Chapman & Carel, 2022). Arguably, if autism is underpinned by a biological difference then we would expect there to be autistic people in society who go unidentified under the current diagnostic criteria (i.e. displaying significant impairment) due to the goodness of fit between themselves and their surroundings (Beardon, 2008). Indeed, some researchers have suggested that autistic people who are living a good life should not require a (formal) diagnosis (Baron-Cohen, in Moorhead, 2021). This simultaneous focus on the 'causes' of autism as an essentialised difference, whilst emphasising that autistic people who are living well should not 'count' formally as autistic is one of the ways in which stigma is enacted against autistic people. As discussed in chapter 5, whilst formal diagnosis should not be (and indeed is not) necessary for someone to recognise that they are autistic, gatekeeping of both identity and access to support hinges on the formal diagnostic label.

## Dehumanisation

The way that autistic people are presented within autism research, and across the wider public consciousness is dehumanising (Botha, 2021; Huws & Jones, 2011; Rose & Michael, 2022), with autistic people labelled as more 'childlike' (Cage et al., 2019), lacking in agency, domestication or culture, and compared to non-human animals (Botha, 2021) and robots (Gernsbacher, 2007). Print media representations of autistic people evoke stereotypes of maleness and deficit based descriptions (Karaminis et al., 2023) and canon and coded representations of autism on screen and in literature are often polarised between stereotypical, negative representations and supercrip narratives or highlighting the 'quirky' and 'loveable' nature of autistic people (Jones, 2022; Jones et al., 2023). The latter may relate to Butler's theorising on proximity (Butler, 1988) whereby representations of marginalised individuals in the media can evoke feelings of compassion and empathy, whereas in person they may evoke fear, disgust and repulsion, furthering the dehumanisation of autistic people.

In chapter 2 we explored how the construction of autism is at its core based on characteristics which differentiate autistic people from the normative majority in society and that these differences are devalued and seen as deficits or impairments that prevent the achievement of normative standards or goals. Yergeau (2013) discusses how autistic embodied experiences are pathologised and othered, often reduced to medicalised descriptions of traits and characteristics, rather than situated within the human they are describing. There are ongoing debates as to whether using more humanising language to describe autistic people as opposed to focussing on deficits removes scientific freedom and limits the 'semantic toolbox' of researchers (Singer et al., 2023). Singer et al. suggest that these 'scientific terms' may "provoke feelings of social stigmatisation in some people", reducing the impact of stigma to individual offence. However, this argument ignores the role of power plays in stigma perpetuation, and the systemic impact of stigma. Power shapes the way that language about autistic people is used (Botha et al., 2020), and consequently, this language shapes outsider understandings of autism (Bottema-Beutel et al., 2020) and the material realities of autistic people. Additionally, as members of a stigmatised group, autistic people lack the power to change this themselves, still making up a minority within the research community. Botha (2021) highlights how autistic people within autism research are frequently presented with dehumanising and stigmatising conceptualisations of their own identities (Lonbay et al., 2021) creating an inhospitable field and preventing long term progression.

The impact of stigma and dehumanisation can be seen across a variety of different domains in Psychology (e.g. autistic play, autistic empathy) where autistic ways of being and doing are interpreted through a deficit focussed lens in comparison to non-autistic people, even if the general difference is positive. For example, research has shown that autistic people are more likely to make fairer judgements in economic decision making tasks (Tei et al., 2019) which has been framed as 'abnormal', and autistic interests and passions are frequently described as 'circumscribed' (Klin et al., 2007) or labelled as 'restricted'. Where autistic participants are found to perform similarly to non-autistic people on cognitive tasks, their performance is labelled as 'intact' or compensatory (Belmonte & Yurgelun-Todd, 2003), resituating this lack of difference within a pathological framework and reminding autistic people of their status. These findings are consistent with theoretical exploration of the social oppression of autistic people (Milton, 2016). Milton drew upon Young's (1990) 'faces of oppression' to explore how economic exploitation, marginalisation, lack of power, and the perpetration of cultural imperialism and violence characterise autistic experience. In particular the imposition of dominant norms here functions as an imperialist suppression of autistic native social skills and behaviours, framing these as impaired in comparison with an assumed normative standard.

As outlined by Link and Phelan, dehumanisation is also perpetuated through stereotyping. The stereotypes most commonly associated with autistic people are negative, and these stereotypes are present both within academia (e.g. in autism researchers), and in the wider community. Botha & Cage (2022) asked autism researchers about their perceptions of autism and autistic people. They found that 55% endorsed a medical-model approach, with autism frequently referred to as a 'disorder' or 'disease', and autistic people referred to as socially withdrawn and unresponsive (aligning with Bleuler's original use), lacking empathy, emotionally flat, and rigid. Researchers also made clear demarcation between autistic people without intellectual disabilities (who were seen as 'capable' of leading a more normative life), and those with (who were seen as lacking value and the capacity to contribute to society). In addition to medicalised language, 60% of participants expressed dehumanising, objectifying and stigmatising views of autistic people.

Wood & Freeth (2016) had 298 students complete a survey asking them to list all of the characteristics that they associated with autism in a free response paradigm. The 10 most common characteristics were: poor social skills (56%), introverted/withdrawn (31%), poor communication (29%), difficult personality/behaviour (28%), poor emotional intelligence (23%), 'special abilities' (18%), high intelligence (16%), awkwardness (12%), obsessiveness (12%) and low intelligence (12%). In a follow-up study they asked 42 students to rate these characteristics on their valence, and found that 8 of the 10 characteristics (all except high intelligence and 'special abilities') were rated negatively.

These studies support the notion that stigma is grounded in the association between perceived negative attributes and stereotyping, as suggested by Link and Phelan. Crucially here the power structures at play can also impact autistic people at both an individual and group level. Negative perceptions of autistic people throughout the general public drive in/outgroup differences, whereby autistic people do not meet normative standards and as a result are likely to be impacted by structural and systemic discrimination (e.g. through reduced socio-cultural capital). However, wider perceptions about autistic people as a group are *shaped* through autism research. Thus negative public perceptions may be influenced by both individual encounters (e.g. meeting an autistic person and thinking that they are 'weird' because they do not conform to societal norms), and through dominant narratives that surround and construct autism (i.e. that autistic is a medical disorder, characterised by deficits and impairments in comparison to the assumed normative population). Here autism researchers have the power to decide what autism *is*, and as outlined by Schneidre (1988), to ensure the perpetuation of negative stereotypes and the power imbalance between autistic and non-autistic people (through asserting what is 'normal' and what is 'impaired').

Though academics may not see the impact of this outside of their field, our work influences professional and public training (Rose & Vivian, 2020) and policy. Though norms are argued to be transient, framings of autism have endured for a significant period of time, having a tangible impact on how autistic people are treated, manifesting in negative outcomes such as underemployment (Finch et al., 2022), heightened risk of bullying (Libster et al., 2022) and victimisation (Weiss & Fardella, 2018), and higher suicide rates (Cassidy et al., 2018).

Negative perceptions of autism and autistic people are cross-cultural in nature. Whilst the participants in Wood and Freeth's study were from the UK, Botha and Cage had an international sample (though most people were still from the UK, US, or Europe). However, research on autism stigma conducted across multiple countries has revealed similar findings. (Kim & Gillespie-Lynch, 2022) found that knowledge about autism in South Korea was more limited than in the US, and attitudes tended to be more stigmatising. In addition, higher expectations of cultural assimilation in South Korea appears to be an important factor in maintaining stigma (Kim et al., 2022). Similar findings have been replicated in Japan (Someki et al., 2018), whereby Japanese participants displayed higher stigma and a desire for social distance compared to participants in the US; Lebanon. (though this appeared to be unrelated to collectivism, Gillespie-Lynch et al., 2019; Obeid et al., 2015) and China (Yu et al., 2020).

## Autistic experiences of stigma

Recent research has started to explore the first-hand experiences of stigmatisation in autistic people, which has provided an important extension to findings from studies on courtesy stigma in the families of autistic people. Research on the experience of stigma in family members gave proximal indication of autistic people as a stigmatised group, however the neglect of autistic perspectives led to the overlooking of what now appears to be a key driving factor in the outcomes of autistic people. To date, there are a small number of studies that have explicitly explored the experience of stigma in autistic people (for a full review see Han et al., 2022).

In alignment with the work of Link and Phelan, Treweek et al., (2019) found that autistic experiences of stigma were related to perceived negative stereotypes, particularly that autistic people felt that they were perceived as homogenous (linking to the dehumanisation of autistic people), and 'weird'. Interestingly, these negative judgments also appear pervasive in the absence of a label of autism (Pearson et al., 2023), whereby autistic people are labelled as 'weird' regardless of whether or not they are explicitly identified as such. This is consistent with the assertion that autistic people can be stigmatised at the group level due to the negative stereotypes associated specifically with the label 'autism' (Farahar, 2021) or at the individual level due to individual violations in normative expectations.

The experience of being stigmatised is frequently internalised into the self-concept of the recipient (Hume & Burgess, 2021; Vogel et al., 2013). There are a small numbers of studies which have explored internalised stigma in autistic people. Bachmann et al., (2019) found that a small number of autistic people displayed severe stigma on the internalised mental illness scale, lower than reported among other groups. However it is worth noting that, as autism is not a mental illness, this may have impacted findings. Botha and Frost (2020) drew upon Meyer's minority stress model to explore the impact of autistic marginalisation on general wellbeing and psychological distress. They found that negative experiences associated with stigma (minority stressors such as victimisation, concealment, internalised stigma, and expectations of rejection) were associated with lower levels of wellbeing and heightened psychological distress. Relatedly, Botha (2020) also found that autistic people who rated themselves as being more connected to the autistic community (higher autistic community connectedness) appeared to have a buffer against stress in that community connectedness moderated the relationship between psychological distress, masking and disclosure. They also found that political community connectedness (e.g. awareness of, and engagement in, advocacy) specifically moderated the impact of internalised stigma on distress. Qualitative exploration of the relationship between community connectedness and wellbeing (Botha et al., 2022b) also highlighted that community fostered a sense of belonging and positive shared identity, whereas disconnection tended to be associated with internalised stigma and a lack of connection to one's own personal autistic identity. Similarly, Huang et al., (2023) explored the internalisation of stigma in late diagnosed autistic adults, finding that internalised stigma was lowered by increased self-understanding. However, the participants in this study acknowledged the complexity of stigma and the different ways that stigma can impact autistic people. In chapter 4 we mentioned the work of Bertilsdotter Rosqvist & Jackson-Perry (2021) who explored the concept of epistemic infection with regards to autistic people. This internalisation of outsider attitudes about what it means to be autistic can create differential ways to cope among autistic people. These are often aligned with the various narratives that have pervaded public consciousness over the years. Whilst some autistic people internalise the belief that being autistic is a 'bad' thing, internalised ableism can manifest in more explicit or subtle ways.

One example of this variation is the concept of 'Aspie supremacy' (De Hooge, 2019), which hearkens back to those early distinctions Asperger made between autistic children who were 'educable' and those who were not. The later association of Aspergers syndrome with 'normal to above average' intelligence served to stratify autistic people with developmental delays or learning disabilities from those who demonstrated a pattern of development which was more consistent with typical expectation (e.g. no language delay in infancy), aligning with the 'high' and 'low' functioning designation that we discussed in chapter 2 (though as de Hooge points out, 'high functioning autism' also referred to those diagnosed with Kanner's autism, but who did not have cognitive developmental delays). Those with a diagnosis of Aspergers were deemed 'high functioning', and as such more capable of being 'productive' and contributing their worth under a capitalist model of value. The ensuing stereotypes associated were those discussed earlier in this book: white, cisgender male and intelligent (the latter also highlighted as an 'autistic strength' in Freeth and Wood's 2016 study on stereotypes), the type of person that typifies the extreme male brain theory of autism. Unsurprisingly given the historical context of autism, this stereotype is aligned with 'ideals' laid out under white supremacy, the idea of a superior, intelligent, white male who is above all else 'rational' (i.e. cold, calculating and uncaring).

Many autistic people have aligned themselves with this narrative, viewing themselves as 'superior' not only to those autistics deemed as 'lower functioning', but also to neurotypicals whom they view as being below themselves, asserting themselves to be the next point in human evolution. This serves as an attempt to both distance oneself from negative perceptions of other ingroup members and assert oneself as aligning with (or above) the dominant societal group. Interestingly, this form of internalised stigma has recently been argued to put individuals at risk of radicalisation from alt-right groups seeking to recruit technical 'geniuses' (referred to as 'weaponised autists') to wage terror online through their superior coding skills (Welch et al., 2022). This stereotype of autistic people (but particularly autistic men) as a potential tool of white supremacy is disturbingly analogous to Aspergers initial assertions that autistic people might be supreme codebreakers (de Hooge, 2019).

Relatedly, there has been a focus on labelling autism as a 'superpower', a direct response to ableism that panders to capitalist conceptualisations of worth. This representation of disability has been referred to in the disability studies literature as the 'supercrip' (Schalk, 2016), and can take different forms, e.g. autism has been constructed as an oppressive force to be pushed against through its description from outsiders (Schalk, page 78), or as the source of extraordinary abilities that others lack. For example a disabled person may be positioned as inspirational, 'special' and overcoming the 'shortcomings' meted out by their disability through the use of language (e.g. 'special'), archetypes, such as exceptional mundanity (where what are usually viewed as everyday achievements are emphasised as spectacular due to being situated within the narrative of disablement) versus being extraordinary, and how much they stand out within their current context. Conversely, their disability may be framed as the superpower itself (e.g. autistic 'attention to detail' being framed as a superpower, or a focus on autistic savantism). Within a supercrip narrative the disability and the person are somewhat disconnected- despite disability being essentialised, there is often a sense that it can be fought, and won, or that it gives someone an innate benefit.

Whilst emphasising positive aspects of identity is not inherently ableist, supercrip narratives about autism are underpinned by, and perpetuate ableism through the underlying suggestion that there is something that needs to be compensated for. This narrative arises as a direct response to narratives which frame autistic (and disabled existence more broadly) as a tragedy, and a source of grief (Piepmeier, 2012). As we outlined in chapter 2, we personally view autism to be value neutral. Autistic people are inherently valuable and valid by virtue of existing, and not because of the 'special skills' they may or may not possess. We should not need to emphasise autistic capacity for greatness in order to be treated with basic dignity and respect. As autistic poet Joanne Limburg (Limburg, 2021, p. 15) remarks "I don't want to have to argue that I'm special in order to justify my existence. That is not autism acceptance. Acceptance isn't about being celebrated; it's about being unremarked and unremarkable, the opposite of uncanny".

Another aspect of internalised stigma manifests in depersonalisation (as discussed in chapter 3) interacting with epistemic infection, leading to the internalisation of stereotypes about what it means to be autistic to one's own self-concept, beyond the notion of 'autism as negative'. What we mean here is that some people will minimise their own uniqueness in favour of accepting stereotypical or prototypical descriptions of autism and autistic characteristics, in order to align themselves with the perceived broader autistic community, or autistic people as a 'social group'. For example, this might include describing one's own social skills as 'poor' or ascribing oneself a lack of theory of mind regardless of how true it is about that person as an individual. Whilst this may appear to be an uncritical acceptance of outsider narratives, we think it is worth emphasising the context that feeds into this form of internalised ableism. Many autistic people engage with reading research in an attempt to understand themselves in more depth, however the prevailing narrative around autism has emphasised a medicalised, deficit focussed conceptualisation. This attempt to gain self-understanding interacts with hermeneutical injustice - the language of the oppressor is accepted and internalised in order to validate one's proximity and deservingness of their own label. This is a direct result of both the medical shaping of the autism narrative, and the gatekeeping of access to self-actualisation that comes with it.

This response is not surprising given the questioning and invalidation that surrounds autistic identity, particularly for those who do not fit with the stereotypical profile of autism. This may lead people to 'lean in' to autistic stereotypes (though not necessarily consciously) in an attempt to seek validation for their autistic identity. We will discuss this phenomena with specific relation to masking in chapter 11, when we outline the projection of acceptability.

Lilley et al., (2023) found that late diagnosed people question their autistic validity due to not meeting narrow stereotypes, which often interacts with a lifetime of masking. Some participants in Lilley's study expressed feeling like they were not 'autistic enough', however others questioned the validity of others' autistic status (stating that other autistic people 'appeared normal' to them). This suggests the internalisation of norms and stereotypes linked to autism interacts with stigma, which can result in lateral ableism against those who are perceived to not be struggling as much as the observer.

Discussions of this nature have become more prescient in recent years as diagnostic gaps have started to close, prompting the questioning from autistic people themselves as to whether late identified (women in particular) people are *really* autistic. These discussions are often centred on perceptions that many late identified people have met 'normal' milestones such as developing romantic relationships, or having a career, which others may not have achieved themselves. Here, the internalisation of norms (e.g. the milestones that a person should achieve in life) occurs alongside the internalisation of negative narratives around autism (e.g. that it prevents the achievement of these norms), which can lead to several resultant narratives, including the narrative that 'truly' autistic people are defined through their struggles, or that these achievements were only possible through engaging in masking. Where some people may feel like the latter has been personally true for them as an individual, this sort of lateral ableism facilitates a dangerous rendering of autistic existence, and attempts to re-homogenise autistic people as opposed to emphasising the different trajectories that people may follow. Again, this is impacted by the subtle ways in which stigma may impact an individual. What we mean here is that the experiences of autistic people diagnosed both earlier, and later in life are shaped by the perceptions and expectations that other people have. For people identified early, people may have lower expectations due to negative perceptions of the autism label (as outlined by the young people in Mesa and Hamilton's school study) and thus provide lower support and guidance around things like employment. Thus it is difficult to disentangle the impact of stigma upon both how we view ourselves as autistic people, and how we view autistic others. However, unsurprisingly, research has shown that people who are self-identified as autistic (who may have struggled to achieve a formal diagnosis) have experienced similar levels of stigma and internalised stigma to those with a formal diagnosis (McDonald, 2020).

## Autism and intersectional stigma

As highlighted in chapter 5, many autistic people experience marginalisation across multiple aspects of identity. In addition to the intersection of autism and race, gender and sexuality, autistic people are also more likely to be disabled in other ways, and of a lower socio-economic status. Understanding how stigma manifests for autistic people marginalised across multiple aspects of identity is crucial for improving conditions and fostering autistic flourishing, in addition to understanding the complexities of autistic self-monitoring and impression management.

### Autism and Racialised stigma

Autistic people of the global majority experience the intersection of racism and ableism (and potentially other forms of marginalisation) in a way that manifests in unique barriers not experienced by white autistic people (Jones et al., 2020). Ventour-Williams (2022) has written about the intersection of being autistic and Black, and the difficulty navigating both spaces whilst dealing with systemic and pervasive ableism and racism that create a hostile world.

Likewise, some autistic scholars have referenced the idea of the 'triple consciousness' (Simmonds, 2021) in explaining the multi-layered IM processes that they engage in in navigating different identity relevant spaces. Simmonds (2021) has spoken about masking in Black spaces to avoid autism-related stigma, and masking in (white) autistic spaces to avoid racialised stigma. DuBois' work on the double consciousness outlines the pressure of attempting to 'walk in multiple worlds', highlighting how attempting to please both can result in failing to please either. This is consistent with an intersectional perspective on stigma and 'punishment' for failing to perform not only neurotypicality, but other aspects of identity that make up the expected self (e.g. gender, culture, race etc). This can be especially alienating for those who experience marginalisation across several aspects of identity like autistic Black women, who are subject to ableism, sexism and gender stereotypes, and racism which may intersect in unique ways. For example, the expectations attached to identity signifiers such as race and gender mean that engaging in IM in an interaction with a non-autistic white woman, a Black autistic woman may have to consider racist stereotypes, white gendered stereotypes around femininity, and how the risk of ableism intersects with each of these (Burkett, 2020).

The experience of intersectional stigma for autistic people who are racially minoritised can result in specific dangers and negative outcomes compared to white counterparts. As outlined in chapter 5, autistic Black people are at a significantly higher risk of being incarcerated or killed during interactions with law enforcement (Dababnah et al., 2022), and are also less likely to be employed compared to white peers, experience significant healthcare disparities including lack of access to diagnosis and mental health supports (Malone et al. 2022), educational disparities (Diemer et al., 2022), in addition to being more likely to experience negative life events associated with minority stress. Davis et al., (2022) explored understanding discrimination, everyday discrimination, perceived stress, autistic characteristics and black identity regard, alongside self-determination and psychological empowerment in a sample of autistic and non-autistic African American/Black (AAB) participants. Interestingly, the authors did not find that AAB autistic young adults experience more discrimination than non-autistic AAB young adults. However, around a third of the AAB autistic participants reported intersectional discrimination (being Black and autistic) as a main factor in their experiences of discrimination, compared to single issue discrimination (being Black).

In chapter 5 we briefly explored the concept of 'code switching' among Black people as a response to racialised stigma and systemic white supremacy, which can manifest in overt (e.g. explicit supremacist actions such as segregation) or covert (e.g. white people not engaging in cross-cultural competence, instead claiming not to 'see' colour) actions. Whilst masking and code-switching are not equivalent (that is, a white autistic person will not inherently understand code-switching because they experience stigma-driven masking), they can both be seen to arise as a response to differing forms of marginalisation and stigma perpetuated by imperialist and supremacist systems. Thus examining stigma through an intersectional lens can help us to understand the unique forms of oppression that Black autistic people, and autistic people from other racialised minorities, experience.

## Autism and Gender-related Stigma

The intersection of gender and autism related stigma impacts on autistic people of all genders, through both intergroup and intragroup norms.

Intergroup stigma interacts with expectations of gender performativity for all autistic people regardless of gender. Milton, (2018b) has described growing up feeling like he did not meet stereotypical expectations of what a 'boy' should be, likewise participants in Kourti and MacLeod's (Kourti & MacLeod, 2019) study on gender in autistic people raised as girls described not identifying with typical expected gender norms. Many autistic people 'fail' to perform gender (or as can be seen from the previous section on race, any normative aspect of identity) in a way that is consistent with normative expectations. Whilst this can be a source of neuroqueering or emancipatory action for some autistic people, it can also deepen the relationship between gender and masking, whereby autistic people feel the need to 'perform' gender in a way that aligns with external societal expectations to avoid further punishment. Moore et al., (2022) have outlined how autism discourse (e.g. EMB theory) has shaped and limited perceptions of gender among some autistic people.

As with our previous discussion of autism and Blackness, or autism and womanhood (of which the experience of autistic trans women has been notably absent from the literature thus far), autistic TNB + people experience marginalisation across multiple aspects of their identity. As outlined in chapter 5 society is particularly hostile to people who are TNB + , with many places revoking rights and actively attempting to suppress authentic expression within this population. Autistic people who are TNB + experience not only ableism, but cis-heterosexism, through which norms about gender (and frequently sexuality, as many autistic people are part of the wider LGBTQIA + community) shape their access to societal participation and the unique barriers that they might face (such as issues in gender affirming healthcare). Strang, Powers, et al., (2018) described how autistic TNB + young people worried about a lack of acceptance, and the harassment that they might experience because of their identity. Their identity has been questioned by professionals who suggested that their gender was an 'autistic obsession', using pathologising language to invalidate self-insight and authenticity. Likewise, McAuliffe et al., (2022) found that autistic LGBTQIA + adults (some of whom were also TNB + ) reported intersectional oppression from within the LGBTQIA + community, where they experienced ableism and gatekeeping around aspects of their identity, as well as the identities of others (e.g. invalidating asexual people). Participants in McAuliffe's study highlighted how intracommunity stigma could arise as a result of new expected norms (here termed 'homonormative' in comparison to heteronormative) to replace dominant wider societal norms, and engagement in identity policing and other forms of respectability politics.

Additional gender related stigma is perpetuated across all groups (i.e. women, TNB + people, cis men who do not fit narrow stereotypes) through academic (e.g. Frith, 2021) and public (e.g. see Clements, 2019) debates about the 'broadening' of the diagnostic criteria. These debates have led to gatekeeping discussions about who should and shouldn't be defined as autistic in relation to how they fit with the medicalised criteria specifying 'significant impairment'. This can lead to a double bind for autistic people of all genders, who simultaneously may not see themselves in pervading stereotypes about autism, but feel like they need to justify why they meet the criteria. The idea that autistic people should look or appear a particular way continues to feed stigma about autistic people, as it creates confirmation bias around what autism is (i.e. a tragedy, a deficit, 'significant impairment') and what autistic people's lives should look like (i.e. miserable, traumatic).

In summary, understanding how different forms of stigma surrounding gender, sexuality and autism can provide insight into the unique and overlapping forms of identity suppression that arise as a result of marginalisation and minority stress.

## Stigma experienced by Autistic people with Learning Disabilities

As outlined in both chapter 2 and chapter 5, the entire history surrounding our understanding of how autistic people with learning disabilities have been constructed has been through a pathologising and neuronormative lens. Han et al., (2023) highlighted how non-speaking autistic people and those with learning disabilities are frequently ignored, patronised and assumptions made about their capacity to understand that they are being stigmatised. Accordingly there is very little empirical research into their experiences of stigma, with research focussing on their families (Mitter et al., 2019).

Notions of 'functioning', severity and capacity have led to the conceptualisation of autistic people with learning disabilities (*and* those who are non-speaking) as less than human and disposable, referred to in demeaning terms that reduce autistic embodiment to external perceptions of undesirability such as "head-bangers," "biters," "runners," and "shit-smearers" (Broderick & Roscigno, 2021). Autistic people with learning disabilities are more likely to experience institutionalisation (Care Quality Comission, 2020a, 2020b), and be forced to undergo traumatic interventions and restrictive practice (Anderson, 2023; Hayward et al., 2023), which we will discuss in further detail in chapter 9). Broderick & Roscigno, (2021) highlights how neoliberal perceptions of productivity have facilitated the development of the autism industrial complex, centred on the idea that the worst thing a person could be is autistic, and dependent on others. Activist Cal Montogomery highlights how perceptions of dependence are construed negatively (Montgomery, 2001), and are used to obscure the nature of how support of disabled people is often used as a means for control (Montgomery, 2021).

The concept of 'normalisation' (Wolfensberger & Tullman, 1982) emerged as an approach to ensure that disabled people had access to the 'normal rhythms of life' (Cocks, 2001). Here the emphasis was on the ability to display agency over one's own daily routines, including getting out of bed, the option to go to work, and to socialise, eat, sleep etc in the same way that non-disabled people do. The term normalisation was later shifted to 'social role valorisation', to emphasise that all lives and social roles have value, and the theoretical framework aimed to reduce the attribution of social stigma by "enhancing the social image of disabled people and enhancing their competencies". Despite the focus here on improving the lives of disabled people rather than attempting to force the appearance of normativity, the approach resulted in the policing and controlling of disabled people in an attempt to foster respectability (Montgomery, 2021). This is consistent with discussions earlier in this chapter, which emphasised how attempts to reduce stigma by emphasising similarities between the stigmatised and dominant groups often result in attempts at assimilation (Benoit et al., 2018) rather than meaningful community change.

Historically, many people with learning disabilities (including those who are autistic) have been institutionalised. Though community living can provide an important opportunity for agency and interdependence to co-exist, the enduring assumption that normative is the ideal, coupled with a poor understanding of the needs of people with learning disabilities has led to restrictive practices within these places of living. Frameworks such as 'positive behavioural support' have been developed to reduce 'challenging behaviour', in other words to control and reduce the externalised distress responses of people who often have very little agency, and live in highly unsuitable environments (Hayward et al., 2023; Jorgensen et al., 2023). Such frameworks reinforce the need for normative behaviour, often relying upon coercive and controlling tactics to try and 'reduce behaviour', rather than modifying the environment to reduce the distress.

Overall, autistic people who are non-speaking and/or have a learning disability experience the same types of stigma as other autistic people, this however is amplified by outsider perceptions of what it means to be intellectually disabled. These perceptions manifest in additional barriers such as a lack of access to communication, institutional oppression, and a heightened risk of experiencing particular forms of trauma which are justified under the notion that people with learning disabilities are 'less human'. We will explore these in more depth in chapter 9.

## The Concept of Disclosure

Recent research has focussed on the concept of disclosure among autistic people. As highlighted in the section on concealable stigmas, the need to disclose or conceal is driven by the avoidance of shifting from the category of 'discreditable' into 'discredited'. Botha et al., (2022a) highlighted how disclosure placed autistic people in a 'double bind', whereby disclosure could lead to negative responses from others due to negative perceptions of autism, but nondisclosure could also lead to negative individual judgements of 'weirdness'.

Motivations for disclosure include seeking support and understanding (Farsinejad et al., 2022; Love et al., 2023) however disclosure does not come with the guarantee of a helpful response making decisions around disclosure difficult. Love and colleagues collected real-time data on the disclosure opportunities of autistic adults, finding that disclosure led to a range of responses, both positive (such as being validated), neutral, and negative (such as being patronised or othered by the recipient of the disclosure information). This led to a sense that it was only worth disclosing if the individual felt that there was something positive to gain from doing so, as disclosure could be resource heavy (e.g. draining in terms of time and energy). Context also played a major role, with the safety of the immediate environment (e.g. place of work, familiarity) dictating whether people felt able to share that they were autistic. Their findings are consistent with previous research into disclosure and concealment (Jackson & Mohr, 2016), that disclosure decisions are frequent; participants in Love's study experienced a disclosure decision an average of 6.42 times over the course of 2 months with the majority occurring in a workplace or community setting. This suggests that autistic people face a constant and ongoing stressor in the form of making decisions about their identity and how much of themselves that they can authentically let show.

## Attempts to reduce autism-related stigma

There have been multiple attempts so far to reduce autism-related stigma, which have had varying levels of success. The development of education and training, particularly that which is developed by/with and delivered by/with autistic people is ongoing. Findings so far have been inconsistent, with some studies showing a decrease in explicit negative bias towards autistic people (Gillespie-Lynch et al., 2015), but no reduction in implicit bias (Jones et al., 2021). Likewise, there has been uptake of the neurodiversity paradigm within the recruitment sector, which has focused on how certain 'autistic strengths' can contribute positively to the workplace in an attempt to reduce stigma and increase positive outcomes for autistic people. Grinker, (2020) highlights how this view relates to the concept of the ideal 'modern worker' emphasising autonomy and self-reliance, however Crocker & Lutsky (1986) have argued that emphasising cooperative interdependence between dominant and marginalised groups may change how marginalised people are viewed through encouraging both groups to view each other as mutually useful. However, this approach may reinforce capitalist and eugenecist ideals about worth (e.g. people shouldn't be stigmatised if they can be useful), and arguably this approach would not reduce stigma towards those who did not meet a specific desired profile (e.g. 'the detail focussed autistic'). Link and Phelan (2001) also argue that approaches that focus on a specific intervention (e.g. through employment or education) are limited in their scope as they neglect the broader context, and their success is open to erosion over time. Thus they argue that reducing stigma must take into account the multifaceted and multilevel nature of its impact, so that the mechanisms underpinning systemic barriers are removed, and individual and structural discrimination is limited.

Link and Phelan highlight how groups are constructed based on perceived binary variables (e.g. Black and white, male and female) which oversimplify variability within those categories (a hallmark of dehumanisation). This could be argued to be evidence in favour of shifting away from binary labels such as 'autistic' and neurotypical', or put emphasis on the idea that the 'autistic spectrum' ranges from autistic at one end, all the way to neurotypical at the other. Indeed the phrase "we're all a little bit autistic" is often used to discredit Autistic experience, or conversely emphasise that autistic and non-autistic people have shared experiences. However, with the latter, this attempt to humanise autistic people places emphasis on similarity to perceived normality, as opposed to reducing stigma and fostering acceptance of difference. Thus, this is less likely to lead to changes at the structural level.

Han et al. (2023) explored the views of autistic adults, and caregivers/parents of autistic people on what stigma-related support might be needed for autistic people and what this might look like in practice. Their participants highlighted the need for society to be more understanding and educated about the reality of being autistic, and the need for community support to mitigate the difficulty of dealing with stigma alone. This is consistent with our previous discussion of how community can buffer the impact of stigma, with intra-group support providing positive identity role models, and inter-group support providing understanding via allyship, and practical help (e.g. how to identify and deal with stigma). There was a sense that a shift away from a pathological model of autism would be helpful in fostering a positive sense of identity among all autistic people.

A more emancipatory approach can be seen within the application of the neurodiversity paradigm (which emphasises that humans can exist, think, feel and act in multifarious ways), and neuroqueering. The neurodiversity paradigm, despite criticisms that it excludes 'low functioning' individuals, seeks to provide a space in which to recognise that neurocognitive variation and disability are not inherently positive or negative, but simply part of human diversity. It seeks to reduce stigma by noting the value neutral status of autism and other forms of neurodivergence, and establish the value neutral status of typicality, as opposed to facilitating its occupation as the virtuous norm that all should aim to achieve. Accordingly, from a neuroqueer perspective, Walker (2021) advocates for a move away from essentialist or binary conceptions of autism (and neurodiversity more broadly). She discusses how the rejection of cognitive normativity and assertions that 'normal' objectively exists can facilitate a future where all kinds of people exist alongside each other without a hierarchy assigned to particular ways of being and doing. She described this potential future as one that is 'neurocosmopolitan' (Walker & Raymaker, 2021), a future where: "an individual accepts and welcomes neurocognitive differences in experience, communication, and embodiment in the same sort of enlightened way that a cosmopolitan individual accepts and welcomes cultural differences in dining habits". We will explore this theory more in Chapter 12, thinking about how it may contribute towards fostering authenticity for autistic people.

## Conclusion

In this chapter we explored the concept of stigma, what that means, and how it might impact on marginalised people; including autistic people. It is important that we understand the different ways in which stigma may impact an individual, and interact with intersecting aspects of identity (that may themselves be stigmatised). In the next chapter we explore how trauma impacts autistic people, much of which is underpinned by the experiences of stigma outlined here.

# Chapter 8: Trauma

## What is trauma?

Trauma is difficult to define given the nebulous nature of both its causes, and effects (Levine, 2021). The American Psychiatric Association (2013) define it as "an emotional response to a terrible event like an accident, rape, or natural disaster", and whilst the NHS describe it as "a response to a discreet or prolonged circumstance; which at some point is perceived by the person to be an uncontrollable serious threat to physical or psychological integrity and which overwhelms emotional resources or a capacity to function" (NHS, 2023)." Historically, trauma was both defined by, and associated with a response to the experience of a potentially life-threatening event (or witnessing such an event), limiting the subjective nature of trauma (e.g. what is defined as traumatic to one person may not be to another). However, more recently there has been a shift towards recognising that trauma is incredibly subjective, and is also an intersectional issue that can be driven by prolonged exposure to living within an oppressive system (Nadal et al., 2019). The exclusion of non-life threatening events was driven by the research context of the majority of early trauma research, and the (as with everything) historical context of how we considered responses to negative life events.

There are many issues to consider with regards to the emergence of trauma research. Prior to the recognition that adverse circumstances could cause prolonged psychological distress, distressed people in the western world were often diagnosed with other nebulous psychiatric conditions such as 'hysteria'. Hysteria was associated with a variety of 'symptoms' including anxiety, sexual desire, and vomiting, and was thought originally to be caused by mechanisms in the uterus, though during the 18th century it was re-attributed to the brain. Early work on trauma theory was grounded in the psychoanalytic approach to understanding hysteria, including work from Charcot and Freud (Ringel & Brandell, 2011) who argued that hysteria was a psychological disorder that both men and women could experience (though seen as more common in women), caused by previous trauma. Though hysteria through a historical lens is a highly politicised (as a diagnosis it was instrumental in the oppression of women through a variety of medical practices such as forced hysterectomy), the later work on it did underpin recognition that adverse life experiences could have prolonged psychological effects (though hysteria was more likely to represent ongoing chronic stress in the face of the oppressive historical treatment of women).

In the post-war period trauma research experienced a resurgence, and was centered around the experiences of veterans who had returned from war experiencing psychological distress, which continued beyond the expected timeframe for recovery (Woodlock, 2020). As outlined by Jones & Wessely (2006), prior to the 1970s, displaying prolonged and chronic distress as a result of experiencing a negative event was considered to be a form of neurosis, and a character flaw, rather than a response to the trauma itself. Whilst there was some effort made to establish the impact of war on psychiatric outcomes (e.g. 'shell shock'), it was only in the 1980's that Post Traumatic Stress Disorder (PTSD) was formally recognised within the DSM and our understanding of what causes and constitutes trauma is constantly evolving. PTSD was recently reclassified from an anxiety disorder to a trauma and stressor related disorder, and there has also been a shift towards recognising that defining a post-traumatic stress as the result of a single (life-threatening) event may be limiting.

As trauma research has developed, there has been a shift away from both the limited conceptualisation of prolonged traumatic distress emerging solely as the result of a singular event (e.g. a car accident), and of it being something that is situated solely within an individual (or individuals), despite it's highly subjective nature. Kira (2001) highlights how traumatic events are "more diverse than just survival traumas, and the trauma response is greater than simple PTSD". He provides a detailed taxonomy of trauma, which outlines both subjective and objective features of traumatogenic experiences and events which can be used to understand and assess trauma across the lifespan (Table 8.1).

Recent research has examined how trauma can be facilitated and driven by structures and systems of power. For example, Nadal and colleagues (2019) explored how racism at multiple levels can lead to racial trauma. An individual may experience overt (e.g. racially motivated hate crime), or covert (e.g. more "subtle and automatic" microaggressions) racism, alongside systemic racism. Some of this trauma is enacted through "unjust institutional policies and societal norms" (Nadal et al., 2019), e.g. violence from law enforcement directed at Black people in the US, and some manifests in more covert discrimination. The pervasive and often chronic nature of covert and systemic racism can have a cumulative impact on both an individual and the wider group, through the proliferation of stigma and minority stressors. Nadal and colleagues note the importance of recognising

| Classification 1 | | Classification 2 | |
|---|---|---|---|
| **Item** | **Description** | **Item** | **Description** |
| Attachment trauma | Shared affective bond disruption between dyad (e.g. death of a parent, divorce). | Factitious trauma or trauma like events | Accumulation of stressors over time (e.g. experience of racism). |
| Autonomy/Identity/ Individuation (personal, or collective) trauma | Traumas which disrupt identity formation and sense of agency (e.g. sexual abuse). | Indirect or vicarious trauma | Trauma transmitted between individuals or generations, through one (e.g. person to person) or multiple (generation, or societally) steps, e.g. lasting generational impacts of poverty. |
| Interdependence or Disconnectedness Trauma | Threat to social network and community (e.g. moving schools). | Direct Traumas | Singular unexpected traumas (e.g. a violent physical attack), or complex traumas (e.g. prolonged emotional abuse). |
| Achievement/Self- actualization trauma | Failure to achieve a goal that is viewed as crucial for progression (e.g. job loss) | | |
| Survival Trauma | Witnessing or participating in an event which poses a threat to own life, or lives of others (e.g. vehicle accident). | | |

**Table 8.1:** Kira's (2001) taxonomy of trauma

the impact of chronic stressors upon the development of post-traumatic symptoms. They argue that during the treatment of PTSD practitioners focus on the external event as the stressor, rather than (as was historically the case) an individual neuroses or weakness of character. The exclusion of often systemic and chronic stressors such as racism (and other forms of oppression) from the 'causes' of trauma can lead to the internalisation of blame for psychological distress. Here people may blame themselves for 'lacking resilience' to cope with chronic stressors rather than recognise their distress as a normal response to unescapable trauma (Nadal, 2018).

The notion that psychological distress is a form of individual weakness is compounded by how subjective the experience of trauma can be, that is, people do not respond to aversive experiences in the same way. Historically, research into trauma took an individualistic approach, by which the distress response was considered to be caused by the individual experience of a particular event. The psychological impact, associated distress and temporal features of trauma experienced by a person will be impacted by myriad factors (Levine, 2021) such as their age, upbringing and culture, and as Nadal (2018) highlights, how chronic the exposure to the stressor may be. Thus it is important that we do not minimise the distress that one individual experiences because another appears to be unaffected by the same stimulus. This can be explored across two levels; the first is the acknowledgement of oppressive systems that act as a chronic stressor. For those who do not live within these systems (i.e. do not experience racism, or ableism), a one-off discriminatory event may not provoke the same distress response as someone who is perpetually exposed to a stressor over time. The second is how oppressive systems can shape responses to stressors. Let us take the example of getting removed from an internet forum. Whilst one individual might not find this particularly traumatic (e.g. they may have a good social support system offline), another might find this highly distressing, particularly if they have previously experienced social exclusion. This is important to keep in mind as we move on to discuss trauma among the autistic population.

There has been an attempt more recently to capture the multidimensional nature of trauma as described here, under the label of 'complex trauma' and complex PTSD (c-PTSD). The UK Trauma Council defines complex trauma as "traumatic experiences involving multiple events with interpersonal threats during childhood or adolescence. That is, the accumulation of traumas across the lifespan that can vary in perceived severity. Such events may include abuse, neglect, interpersonal violence, community violence, racism, discrimination, and war". Here the developmental and prolonged nature of trauma is acknowledged, in addition to more systemic stressors such as racism and other forms of discrimination. c-PTSD may result from complex trauma, though may also develop in adulthood through the experience of recurring or long term adverse circumstances such as abuse or neglect. Though there is overlap in the symptomology between PTSD and c-PTSD, c-PTSD is additionally defined through the presence of emotional and interpersonal difficulties (e.g. internalised shame, worthlessness and guilt, and difficulties connecting to and maintaining relationships with others). It is important to note here that the chronic experience of stigma and discrimination has also been found to relate to post-traumatic stress symptoms such as intrusive thoughts and heightened arousal (Kennedy et al., 2014), which is unsurprising given that internalised shame and relationship difficulties are common outcomes of social stigma (Frost, 2011).

# Trauma and Autism

There is a growing interest into the impact of trauma on autistic people (Kildahl et al., 2019). Whilst it has been debated as to whether increased incidence of trauma in the autistic population may arise as a result poorer ability to cope with stress in everyday life (Haruvi-Lamdan et al., 2020), evidence suggests that autistic people experience stressors at a much higher rate than the general population. Autistic people experience negative life events such as abuse (see Weiss & Fardella, 2018) and sexual violence (Gibbs et al., 2022) at an alarmingly high rate (Griffiths et al., 2019). As outlined in chapter 8, the heightened risk of these negative life events is often attributable to stigma and a common outcome of minority stress. Whilst there is an emerging body of evidence on the impact of these adverse circumstances, we do know that these negative experiences manifest in higher rates of mental health difficulties in the autistic population (Reuben et al., 2021), in particular higher likelihood of PTSD or cPTSD (Rumball et al., 2020). However, autistic trauma is more multifaceted than a risk of 'adverse events' (Kerns et al., 2022). Autistic people, by nature of our disability experience the world in a way that differs to the majority; this can include our experience of what it means to be 'human' (whereby autistic people are dehumanised and pathologised), our ability to access societal participation (whereby our needs are not considered or actively discouraged), and our sensory affordances (whereby the interaction between our sensory processing, and the environment we exist in can be at odds, Fulton et al., 2020). The multidimensional nature of autistic trauma was captured by participant 'Luna' in Pearson et al., (2023):

> *"The idea that trauma is just one event you can recover from and one day feel safe again is not really relevant when the world is not built for you, and in many cases, is actively built to harm you"*

(Watermeyer & Swartz, 2016) describe the existential, psychological trauma that can arise as a result of this mismatch, of existing as a disabled person in a world not designed to facilitate your belonging: *"In this sense, then, a traumatic experience of disability may centre on the subjective meaning one makes of being starved of the means to take on the basic challenges and pleasures of life while surrounded by fellow citizens granted full access"*

In addition to the construction of autism as deficit, and the person-environment mismatch, aspects of autistic cognition may also contribute towards heightened risk of PTSD developing, and the perpetuation of symptoms (Rumball et al., 2021). Consistent with our earlier discussions of Milton's conceptualisation of autistic memory as rhizomatic (Milton, 2018a), a lack of linear narrative may make it more difficult for autistic people to contextualise their traumatic experiences and integrate them with sensory and emotional elements. This may also be impacted by the presence of alexithymia in the autistic population making it more difficult for an individual to access, connect with, and identify emotional experiences in order to integrate these different aspects of trauma. It is worth keeping in mind that certain emotional and behavioural responses often associated with autism (e.g. meltdowns and shutdowns, fawning) can also be understood through the lens of a trauma response (e.g. meltdowns as a 'fight' response, shutdowns as a 'freeze' response, etc).

Kildahl et al., (2020) highlighted the importance of research into understanding the experience of trauma among autistic people, arguing that autistic people were at risk of diagnostic overshadowing in this area (e.g. clinicians attributing symptoms of PTSD to autism or 'challenging behaviour', which we will discuss later in this chapter). They interviewed professionals working with autistic people in mental health services, who reported that trauma appeared to manifest differently in autistic people, leading to an increase in characteristics associated with autism such as insistence on routine, or a loss of functional language. This is consistent with Hume & Burgess (2021), who highlighted the overlap between some of the characteristics we associate with both autism and trauma and how these may lead to conflation of the two. Such evidence has led to community discussions on whether some of the characteristics that we typically associate with autism could occur as a result of trauma, prompting some to ask what a non-traumatised autistic person would actually look like (Gray-Hammond & Adkin, 2021). Participants in Kildahl's study also highlighted how interpretations of behaviour could make it harder to recognise distress, as this could be coded as 'challenging' rather than trauma-driven, and that trauma expression could vary largely from day-to-day. Importantly professionals highlighted how trauma has previously been overlooked in autistic people and the need for sensitive and multidimensional assessments that take into account how things that non-autistic people do not consider traumatic (e.g. sensory experiences) may impact on autistic people in the long term.

Multiple studies have suggested that autistic people are more likely to experience PTSD as a result of events that are not included in the (arguably limited) description in the DSM (Haruvi-Lamdan, 2020; Rumball et al. 2020; Kildahl et al. 2019; Kerns et al. 2022). Rumball et al (2020) emphasised how the recognition that non-DSM events could cause PTSD in autistic people is crucial to ensure that a diagnosis and any associated treatment and support is not withheld. Researchers have started to assess and validate tools for the measurement of trauma in autistic people (McKinnon et al., 2021; Wigham et al., 2021). However additionally our understanding of autistic trauma may be better informed through the use of a holistic framing such as Kira's taxonomy (2001), whereby we can consider how multiple dimensions of experience may manifest in differential sources and expressions of trauma between autistic (and other neurodivergent) and non-autistic people. For example, Kerns and colleagues (2022) found that autistic people reported frequent loss of autonomy and feelings of entrapment, which led to diminished self-determination, which is consistent with Kira's classification of identity trauma. Understanding this form of trauma may be particularly relevant for understanding the masking-trauma relationship. However as we will explore throughout this chapter, there is an interaction between different aspects and classifications within Kira's model in relation to autistic people that can lead to masking as a consequence regardless of how identity related the initial trauma appears to be (e.g. the relationship between sensory trauma and masking being facilitated through external invalidation).

Whilst the majority of research thus far on masking has focussed on masking as a social strategy, more recent conceptualisations from autistic scholars (Lawson, 2020; Pearson & Rose, 2021) has suggested that masking develops as a response to trauma (of which stigma and the associated outcomes plays an important role) and as a survival mechanism to cope with a world that is hostile towards autistic people. However, masking as a social affiliation technique and masking as a trauma response are not necessarily distinct. In previous chapters we have discussed masking as a form of social self-monitoring that can facilitate our attempts to manage our reputation and what others think of us. We have also discussed the role that stigma plays in the development of masking in marginalised populations, drawing upon Frost's Social Process model and minority stress to explore why marginalised people may need to try and control different forms of information about themselves compared to non-marginalised people. In the following sections, we will explore some different types of trauma that autistic people may experience across the lifespan (though by no means exhaustive), and the relationship that these may have to the development and maintenance of masking. It is worth noting here that we focus on 'broad strokes' exploration of trauma, but as with our earlier discussions there will be intersectional considerations here that impact autistic people in important ways (e.g. our discussion of the use of severely restrictive and dangerous practices being overwhelmingly levelled at Black autistic youth).

# A taxonomy of autistic trauma

## Generational trauma

Generational trauma is defined as the "transmission of traumatic practices and their effects" (Kira, 2001) through multiple generations of a family (e.g. cycles of abuse, and the associated normalisation). Dekel & Goldblatt (2008), argue that this transmission may include both biological (e.g. genetic transmission of attenuated hormonal stress responses between parent and child) and environmental (e.g. parenting style) inputs. Epigenetic research suggests that genetic transmission may occur through stress impacting on long term DNA expression whereby the structure of DNA is unchanged, but the expression is altered. This can result in heightened vulnerability to chronic physiological stress and ill health (Ramo-Fernández et al., 2015). Environmental inputs on the other hand, are transmitted generationally through the transmission of norms and learned behaviours, and how this may interact with factors such as attachment and parenting style, and the environments and interactions we find ourselves in regularly during our developmental years.

There is very little exploration of genetic contributions to intergenerational trauma in autistic people. Warrier & Baron-Cohen (2021) explored the relationship between polygenic risk (i.e. likelihood based on genetic material) of autism, and experiences of childhood trauma, suicidal ideation, and self-harm in the UK Biobank database. The authors examined both whether autistic people were more likely to report childhood trauma, suicidal ideation, and self-harm, in addition to whether polygenic risk score for autism was associated with these in non-autistic (or not identified as autistic) people. They found that autistic people were more likely to report experiencing all three, as were people who displayed higher polygenic risk scores for autism (that is, whose genetic data shared more in common with the expected profile related to autism). The authors argue that heightened risk of childhood abuse among those with heightened polygenic risk of autism may be driven by three distinct factors:

1. the presence of autistic characteristics (e.g. differences in social communication) causing neglect or abuse from caregivers and peers,

2. autistic people being socially naive which may make them 'more vulnerable' and put them at risk of adverse life situations, and

3. how autistic people perceive an event (e.g. the subjective nature of trauma).

In addition, they note that stigma, and a lack of societal supports for autistic people may contribute towards heightened suicidal ideation and self-harm. The authors conclude that the three factors are associated with a predisposition to autism but caution against making causal claims due to the underpowered dataset. However, it is also important to recognise the potential interaction here between non-genetic transmission of generational trauma. The authors do acknowledge the potential for a lack of supports due to late diagnosis and identification linking to suicidal ideation and self-harm, however they do not consider the role that this may have played in the transmission of intergenerational difficulties between the potentially undiagnosed parents of these individuals (possibly because they do not want to speculate beyond their current data).

Indeed, community accounts have highlighted how being late identified has led people to recognise autism within their family members, including parents (Lilley et al., 2023). These accounts have included retrospective reports of parents reinforcing the need for normative behaviour, having internalised themselves the need to avoid stigma and discrimination from others. Here caregivers simultaneously invalidate the needs of their child and themselves, in an effort to avoid external traumas. This transmission of the normative gaze through generations within a family can contribute towards the development of masking, reinforcing the need to suppress natural ways of being, and adopt external norms in order to survive. Though we will address explicit social skills training later in this chapter, the experience of invalidation within a family system can lead to a sense of otherness and drive the development of masking in young people. In our study on interpersonal violence (Pearson et al., 2023), we found that many autistic people reported being singled out and pressured by their own families for their difference which led to a sense of otherness and identity shame.

Similarly, heightened risk of negative life events due to minority stress within these families may also have a negative impact across generations. We recently explored the experience of intimate violence and abuse among autistic people (the manuscript is currently in preparation), finding that for some their experiences were normalised from witnessing similar abuse across generations of their family, making it difficult to recognise that their experiences were harmful. Distinct from family pressure to conform, these issues may be underpinned by similar cyclical issues leading to the proliferation of violence, difficulty ascertaining whether this is 'normal' compared to others, and identity suppression as a safety mechanism. There is currently very little research into how certain coping strategies (e.g. self-medication) are transmitted within autistic families, and may contribute towards a higher likelihood of adverse childhood experiences, or ACES. However similar research has been conducted with ADHD (of which there is considerable co-occurrence among autistic people) young people (Brown et al., 2017), and has demonstrated that parental relationship difficulties and higher likelihood of substance misuse are two of the most frequently occurring sources of familial trauma.

Relatedly, another potential source of generational trauma among autistic people may be caused by attachment difficulties (Teague et al., 2017). It is worth considering here that, given the double empathy problem, traditional models of attachment may not be sufficient to explain what a healthy attachment bond looks like in autistic children and caregivers. Teague and colleagues found that around 50% of autistic children display secure parental attachment, and that attachment was impacted by perceived functional skill of the child. Whilst the authors suggest that autistic lack of interpersonal relatedness may impact on the attachment bond, we think it is worth considering these issues through the lens of the double empathy problem. Regardless of whether a parent of autistic children is autistic themselves, a secure attachment between autistic children and their caregivers may not look the same as in neurotypical bonds. However, this may interact with distinct external issues. Firstly, parents may find it difficult to relate to their children if the two have disparities in their social communication, and this may foster a sense of shame in parents further impacting the quality of the attachment bond. Secondly, research suggests that the pathologisation of autism and the lack of support to parents in raising an autistic child can be a significant source of difficulty, alongside the trauma experiences of parents.

Grey et al., (2021) outline how perceptions of autistic children can impact on families via courtesy stigma, leading mothers in particular to feel judged and morally inept for outsider judgements of their children's difference. They argue that whilst a diagnosis can help families to make sense of their experiences, the stigma and shame is passed on from parent to child, with the child embodying disappointment (Oprea & Stan, 2012). They interviewed parents of autistic children, finding that all reported emotional neglect and feelings of rejection from their own families in childhood. Some of the parents attempted to create different parenting scripts, which unintentionally led to the othering of their own children from the sense that the children were not 'responding correctly' to the parents' attempt to share emotions. The authors outline how this creates a cycle whereby the attempts to eschew an implicit trauma script leads to a ruptured caregiver child bond, followed by defensive caregiving, which feeds into further distress for the child. Some of the parents in this study explicitly reflected on seeing similarities between themselves and their children, which led to a sense of warmth and understanding. However, it is unclear how many of the parents in this study were (unknowingly) autistic. Grey and colleagues emphasise the importance of supporting parents to see themselves in their children, and helping them to recognise their effectiveness as parenting in order to encourage the sense that they are on a shared journey, with their children as opposed to feeling trapped by previous trauma scripts and external expectations of parenting.

As can be seen from the evidence here, and previous discussion of stigma in chapter 7, the marginalisation and social stigma levelled at autistic people can impact on their caregivers perception of their child, themselves, and as a result feed into the maintenance of generational trauma. Whilst there has been very little exploration of the direct impact of attachment and early caregiver relationships on masking in autistic people thus far, Grey's note about children embodying the shame of the parent support the notion that the autistic young person will develop strategies to cope with familial othering and stigma.

## Sensory processing

Autistic people experience differences in sensory processing compared to the non-autistic population (MacLennan et al., 2022).These differences include hypersensitivity (e.g. being more sensitive to certain frequencies of sound), and hyposensitivity (e.g. being less sensitive to temperature changes). Many autistic people experience fluctuations in both directions that are influenced by contextual factors (e.g. being more sensitive to sound when in a busy environment, but listening to loud music as sensory seeking behaviour when alone). Fulton and colleagues have described the relationship between autistic sensory processing and the outside world through the concept of 'affordances'(Fulton et al., 2020).

They highlight how individual differences to affordances within the same environment can vary, leading to people responding in varying ways (e.g. one person needing to wear earplugs at a busy event, and another feeling the noise level is just right). In the non-autistic population these varying sensory affordances might offer a particular level of stimulation depending on the context (e.g. how they are feeling at the time) but are unlikely to show a large amount of variation, providing a linear relationship between stimulation and chosen response. For the autistic person, the authors argue that this relationship is not so straightforward. The felt response to the sensory stimulus for them might also vary based on contextual information such as how they are feelings, yes (e.g. stressed or calm), but also the degree to which the stimulus is registered within the body through the sensitivity of the sensory system (e.g. sound registering as pain). Rather than frame this as pathological or disordered, Fulton and colleagues suggest that we instead view these experiences as simply an interaction between an autistic person and their environment, acknowledging their different ways of experiencing the world, and validating them.

These differences in sensory processing are often alien to people who do not experience them (e.g. 'What sound? I can't hear anything), which can lead to incredulity and disbelief when faced with someone who is becoming (increasingly) dysregulated by something they themselves are not experiencing. Here the double empathy problem manifests in the autistic person (often a child) being told to 'stop overreacting' or 'being fussy', and attempts to minimise the behaviour associated with dysregulation, rather than the source of the dysregulation itself. These responses invalidate the response of the autistic person, and can lead to a) questioning whether their response is reasonable, and b) learning to ignore internal signals of stress. It is worth noting here that this invalidation is not intentional; many people simply do not consider the variations in how others process the world until this is explicitly pointed out to them. The proliferation of social media has, in recent years, led to an increased interest among the general public in how different people experience sensory and perceptual stimuli. 'The Dress' (in 2015) was a viral example of how two people could look at the same image and see completely different things. However, gaining knowledge that sensory experience may vary across interlocutors, and applying this knowledge consistently takes conscious and ongoing effort. As a result this invalidation can lead autistic people to engage in masking their response to sensory stimuli. This can function as a protective measure to avoid further invalidation, and to avoid being the 'odd one out' (Miller et al., 2021). Sensory invalidation can be particularly risky for autistic people, with the possibility of sensory processing differences being interpreted as features of a mental health condition such as psychosis, and being (needlessly) prescribed the associated antipsychotics used to treat it (Fulton et al., 2020). However it can also lead to the internalisation of invalidation, with the autistic person doubting their own responses, and disconnecting from their own interoceptive awareness.

Autistic people experience the sensory world in a way that differs to the majority. This can result in both sensory bombardment and overwhelm due to an inability to escape a chronic stressor, but also the experience of invalidation due to experiencing sensory stimuli that others do not (e.g. sounds, smells, etc). Recent research and community accounts suggest that sensory trauma may be one facet of trauma more unique (but not limited) to autistic people. The impact of chronic sensory bombardment on autistic people can contribute towards mental health difficulties, and risk of burnout (which we will discuss in further detail in chapter 10).

Sensory trauma, alongside other areas, may be particularly useful towards an understanding of masking in a school or workplace setting, where autistic people experience a high level of sensory input (Jones et al., 2020). These environments may place pressure on suppressing a response to sensory bombardment in order to avoid standing out or being invalidated. This can lead to heightened dysregulation (Fulton et al., 2020) alongside an inability to escape this due to situational demands (Beardon, 2008). Chapman and colleagues (Chapman et al., 2022) highlight how the interaction between masking and sensory distress can be particularly draining, whereby the suppression of sensory distress within social interactions that require other aspects of masking (e.g. forcing eye contact) places increasing demand on cognitive and sensory resources, leading to extreme exhaustion. We will discuss this particular issue with reference to autistic burnout in chapter 10.

In summary, the experience of sensory trauma can act as both a cause of masking (suppressing distress) and interact with masking (competing for cognitive resources) among autistic people.

## Interpersonal victimisation

Whilst it is difficult to stratify the impact of individual traumatic occurrences in the development of mental health difficulties, research has suggested that one particular type of trauma appears to be a) more prevalent in autistic people and b) directly related to both mental health outcomes (Reuben et al., 2021) and masking (Pearson et al., 2023): Interpersonal victimisation, or IPV.

Interpersonal victimisation is defined as violence and abuse that occurs within a close personal relationship (Pearson et al., 2022). Whilst the definition of a 'close personal relationship' is broad, and highly subjective, typically here we are referring to people like friends, family members and partners, though some people may include other relationships, such as with teachers, colleagues and carers. Violence and abuse from people known to the victim (e.g. a neighbour) but not well enough to be classified as a close interpersonal relationship have been captured within the definition of 'hate relationships' provided by Macdonald et al., (2021), which is frequently driven by stigma (e.g. ableism, racism). Though we will not discuss them in detail here, it is worth noting that institutional abuse scandals that have been revealed in recent years (e.g. see Pearson et al., 2020, 2023) meet criteria for both IPV and hate relationships, and have caused immense trauma to many people who are autistic and/or have learning disabilities.

IPV is also distinguished from bullying on the basis that bullying, though similar to IPV in that there is an intent to harm which tends to be perpetrated via repeated actions (Olweus, 1997) is usually perpetrated by someone who is not defined as being in a close personal relationship with the victim. Shakespeare (2012) has also noted that labelling abuse as bullying suggests that it is 'low level' in nature (though the impact of both can lead to long term trauma). Autistic people also experience higher incidence of bullying experiences compared to non-autistic people (Morton, 2021) however as outlined by participants in a study by Forster & Pearson, (2020) bullies tend to be more obvious in their dislike of a victim, whereas IPV can include more complex and manipulative actions from people who are supposedly trustworthy. The scope of IPV is also notoriously broad, and may include hateful, but not criminal acts such as manipulation and 'cruelty', alongside criminal acts such as physical, sexual and emotional violence, and financial or sexual exploitation (Pearson et al., 2022). Though prevalence is hard to estimate, studies suggest that between 50-89% of the autistic population have experienced IPV (Griffiths et al., 2019; Papadopoulos, 2016).

Whilst IPV occurs as a result of a set of complex and interactional factors (see Bronfenbrenner, 1977), crucial factors in its occurrence appear to be stigma and dehumanisation (Gibbs & Pellicano, 2023; Pearson et al., 2023). The presence of difference or 'weirdness' can act as a cue for dehumanisation, by which a victim is considered to be 'less than human'. This can lead to a complex relationship with others, including a sense of thwarted belonging despite a need to depend on those doing the thwarting (Watermeyer & Swartz, 2016), example teachers and family, or being perceived as 'lesser' by others and therefore more deserving of violence or easier to perpetrate against. It is worth stressing here that these actions are not always conscious, that is, we are not suggesting that all people seek out autistic people as victims, or that the perpetrators are always non-autistic (our own work suggests that this is not the case). What we are saying here is that societal perceptions and devaluations of difference create systemic violence against those who fail to meet normative standards, which can manifest in increased risk of violence even from those classified as more vulnerable themselves (Quarmby, 2011). The avoidance of stigma (and victimisation) can lead to the implementation of stigma avoidance (e.g. concealment), and IM to minimise the appearance of vulnerability or appear in a way that is more attractive or amenable to a perpetrator (Frost, 2011).

In a study on the impact of interpersonal victimisation on autistic adults, we (Pearson, Rose and Rees, 2023) found that the experience of IPV had often started in childhood, whereby our participants had experienced abuse from people they thought they should be able to trust (e.g. family members, teachers). This abuse often centred on perceptions of the participants as 'other', being 'too weird', and deserving of any negative attention that they received from others. Importantly, these perceptions occurred regardless of diagnostic status (i.e. the perpetrator, and often the victim, did not know that the victim was autistic) and led to the internalisation of the belief that there was something bad or wrong about the participant that made them deserving of this abuse. Indeed, earlier discussions in chapter 7 about thin slice judgements support the notion that people are able to sense difference, and more importantly, respond negatively to this difference, without knowing about diagnostic label. The longitudinal nature of victimisation had a striking impact on identity and self-monitoring, whereby masking was described as a key survival strategy. Here masking was not simply a tool used to 'fit in' in social situations, but was an essential method of avoiding further harm from others.

In this context, masking was viewed by participants as a trauma response. Whilst minimising certain aspects of our identity as we move through different contexts may allow us to align ourselves more effectively with the social demands of the situation, suppressing aspects of self for fear of physical or emotional harm is a very different beast. Whilst the methods (e.g. mimicking the social styles of others) and the impact (feelings of loss, burnout) were the same, the way that participants described masking (e.g. as a 'trauma response' or a 'hard won battle scar') reinforced the perception of masking as something unavoidable.

These findings were reinforced by (Gibbs & Pellicano, 2023) who also found that the experience of lifelong invalidation and abuse led autistic people to feel like they were broken in comparison to their peers, and to fawn and comply with the demands of others. Participants in both Pearson (2023) and Gibbs' (2023) research described fawning as a form of people pleasing that they engaged in in order to try and stay safe and avoid further abuse. We posit that fawning is an aspect of masking, whereby an individual suppresses their own needs/identity, instead presenting a compliant and pliable demeanour.

Overall, research into the experience of interpersonal victimisation so far suggests that its relationship to masking may be both causal (though not a singular cause) and perpetuating. Autistic people respond to early stigmatisation and abuse by suppressing aspects of themselves in order to try and maintain safety, which feeds into a cycle through which aspects of masking (such as increased compliance and fawning) lead to increased risk of polyvictimisation, and the continuation of masking as both a survival strategy and risk factor.

## Invalidation/Pathologisation

The experience of invalidation is commonplace for autistic people, due to growing up in a world where the majority of people do not think or experience the world in the same way. Although some invalidation (such as that by way of stigma as discussed in the previous chapter) is intentional, much of it is *not* intentional, but rather a result of non-autistic people lacking insight into, and empathy with, autistic experiences due to the double empathy problem resulting in micro-aggressive actions that can have a cumulative impact on autistic people.

Despite this invalidation occurring unintentionally at an individual level, it is worth pointing out that this devaluing and invalidation of autistic ways of being also occurs at a societal level, by pathologising people who do not meet normative expectations. The framing of autistic cognition and behaviour as impaired, and the narratives that have developed around this (e.g. 'challenging behaviour') implicitly infer that autistic people are broken versions of 'normal' people, and that it is not just kind but *imperative* to ensure that they act as normally as possible in order to meet societal standards of functionality. This pathologisation leads to the justification of practices which are harmful to autistic people (which often disproportionately impact on non-speaking autistic people and those with learning disabilities, who are viewed as less 'human'), and that actively encourage masking as a strategy to appear more normative (that is, more acceptable) to external observers.

In previous chapters we have outlined how the conceptualisation of autism as a diagnosis developed (and was maintained) through pathological interpretations of autistic ways of being, e.g. emotion expression, movement, sensory processing, etc. Here we will explore some of the ways in which autistic modes of being have been pathologised and how this has led to masking and self-suppression, before moving on to specifically discuss how interventions designed to increase normative behaviours have specifically contributed to the development and maintenance of masking.

## Social and Emotional Modes of Being

As outlined in previous chapters, until recently autistic communication was primarily viewed through a pathological lens which stated that communication was disordered and deficient in comparison to neurotypical peers. Whilst this is still the prevailing narrative within a clinical and academic understanding of autism, small pockets of autistic-affirming work has started to emerge. Within the remit of communication as a whole, the pathologisation of autistic communication was all encompassing, focussed on both verbal communication (i.e. speech development), non-verbal communication (e.g. 'appropriate' use of gestures), and style (e.g. 'monologuing', preferring parallel or solo play to interactive play with others). The ways that autistic people tried to communicate with non-autistic others were wrong, disordered and required intervention in order to facilitate the development of relationships with others, who found autistic communication confusing and unusual.

As described in chapter 4, this approach led to assumptions about the meaning of autistic communication and behaviour. A focus was placed on the development of 'functional' language skills, often leading to the withholding of alternative forms of communication such as AAC (Zimmerman, 2022). Autistic use of gestures and body language were assumed to lack intentionality (Tomasello & Camaioni, 1997) and autistic social overtures were assumed to lack relationality (e.g. talking about a favourite topic was viewed as 'monologuing' as opposed to sharing). Gernsbacher et al., (2008) invited non-autistic people to try and understand the communication styles of autistic people, however this approach remained relatively unexplored until Milton's work on the double empathy problem in 2012 (Milton, 2012).

Alongside similar theories such as Beardon's cross-neurological theory of mind (Beardon, 2008), or Bolis's Dialectical Misattunement Hypothesis (Bolis et al., 2017), Milton's double empathy problem was ground-breaking in its resituating of the social into social communication. Whereas previous research had seen any difficulties between autistic and non-autistic people as resulting from inherent deficits within the autistic person, Milton's work emphasised the bi-directional nature of social communication, resituating communication difficulties as existing in the space *between* interlocutors as opposed to inherent in one party. His work emphasised how research into social communication skills in autistic people took any aspect of difference between autistic and non-autistic people as evidence that autistic people were impaired at understanding the non-autistic mind (and, as we discussed earlier, their own minds), but the inverse had gone unexplored and assumed to be intact. As empirical work on the double empathy problem has emerged, research has shown that non-autistic people are worse at recognising autistic emotional expressions (Alkhaldi et al., 2019), and that information transfer between autistic and non-autistic people is less effective compared to within group (autistic-autistic and non-autistic to non-autistic) transfer (Crompton et al., 2020).

The pathologisation of autistic social communication is a direct path to masking. The understanding of, and engagement with non-native social communication may be useful as a cross-neurotype tool for developing shared understanding. However, due to the normative standards dictated by society (i.e. that autistic social skills are impaired and need to be remediated) autistic people experience pressure to draw upon these non-native social skills whereas non-autistic people experience no such expectation. The internalisation of normative standards is not always a conscious decision. Many autistic people report growing up being bullied or singled out for the way that they communicate, and being blamed for any misinterpretations or miscommunications that occur (Spaeth & Pearson, 2021). These experiences constitute social trauma, which occurs frequently due to existing as a minority within a majority non-autistic society. Autistic people have reported the experience of constant misinterpretation from others, e.g. directness being taken as rudeness, or a lack of empathy, attempts to share passion (i.e. infodumping) being labelled as annoying or leading to accusations of 'showing off', tone of voice being interpreted as aggressive or boring…the list is near endless. For non-autistic people, a communicative misunderstanding may be a minor inconvenience, but for an autistic person who is frequently on the receiving end of the blame for such misunderstandings the thought of 'getting it wrong' can be harrowing.

## Emotional Experiences

Emotional processing differences have long been posited as one of the cognitive contributions towards autistic socio-communicative and interactional style (Nuske et al., 2013). Autistic people have been described as 'cold' and 'lacking empathy', unable to understand the thoughts and feelings of other people. In this section we will unpack how these perceptions may relate to masking.

Early research into autistic socio-cognitive ability posited that we lack the ability to understand the beliefs, desires and intentions of other (non-autistic) people (Baron-Cohen, 1997; Baron-Cohen et al., 1985; Frith, 2001), displaying a general 'failure of empathy' (see Hume & Burgess, 2021). Despite later work asserting that autistic people lacked cognitive empathy (that is, mentalising skills), whilst arguing that affective empathy (e.g. feeling moved by the emotions of others) was intact, perceptions of autistic people as self-centred and lacking care for others has become a pervasive myth impacting on how autistic people are viewed and constructed (Bergenmar et al., 2015). As outlined in the previous chapter, the notion that autistic people lack features posited to be 'uniquely human' places autistic people outside of the sphere of humanity (Baron-Cohen, 1997). Of course, the double empathy problem outlines how non-autistic interpretations of autistic sociality and emotionality have situated difficulties in cross-group understanding as flaws inherent in the autistic person. In addition to research showing that non-autistic people are impaired at recognising autistic facial expressions (Alkhaldi et al., 2019), there have also been debates around the way empathy is constructed and operationalised (Nicolaidis et al., 2019) and how this may implicitly overlook the double empathy problem. For example, in Nicolaidis et al., (2019) Yergeau points out that the relational nature of empathy and attempts to externally measure it are interpreted through a normative lens, with little consideration of how empathy can be used to marginalise through assumptions about 'correct' ways to empathise, or assumptions that one can truly put themselves in another shoes to understand their experiences. Yergeau (2013) and Hume and Burgess (2021) argue that assumptions about autistic empathy are used to reinforce dominant norms, and to actively advocate for the forced normalisation and disposability of autistic people. As Yergeau elucidates, historical narratives around autistic people as unreliable narrators of their own experiences negate the need to build inroads to mutual understanding: autistic people are empathically impaired, lacking the (meta) understanding to understand their own deficits.

Yergeau's assertions explain how autistic trauma via violence against autistic people is justifiable under the narrative that autistic people lack a theory of mind. If we lack the capacity to understand the mental states and feelings of others, as well as our own, we are effectively 'un-people'. This trope is echoed in Hume and Burgess (2021), where after discussing the recognition of their own capacity for affective empathy, HB opines at the closing of the article "I guess I'm human after all". It is further discussed by Rose & Vivian (2020) in an article titled 'Regarding the use of dehumanising rhetoric', which discusses Vivian's experience of this narrative as an autistic person studying neuroscience at a UK University, and having witnessed debates over the definition of humanity that actively excluded autistic people on the basis of lacking theory of mind, to which the university's response to a complaint was: 'evidence the harm'.

There are multiple issues arising from the notion that autistic emotional processing and understanding is impaired. Firstly, there has been a lack of recognition of how autistic modes of processing may lead to differential experiences of emotionality, and what this means for cross-neurotype empathy. Secondly, as outlined in Hume and Burgess, there has been little exploration of how *trauma* may shape these differences. Here we unpack both of these in a little more detail before considering how they may lead to masking.

Autistic people have described a range of empathic experiences that go beyond a 'lack of empathy', including the experience of hyper-empathic states (i.e. intensely feeling the emotional states of others), and difficulties with understanding and identifying their own emotional states, known as Alexithymia (Milosavljevic et al., 2016). Milton (in Nicolaidis et al., 2019) highlights how salience of meaning, and context alongside autistic disposition and perception (e.g. monotropism) can help us to start to explore autistic empathy from a more neutral standpoint, taking into account how differences are shaped and what they mean for developing an understanding of autistic social relationality. This is consistent with suggestions in chapter 4 that empathy is a nebulous and difficult to define term (Fletcher-Watson & Bird, 2020), likely impacted by the factors that influence our own 'mindspace', e.g. the contextual information we draw upon to make inferences about our own minds, and the minds of others (Conway et al., 2019).

There is currently very little research into hyper-empathy among autistic people, however (Jordan, 1999) described an autistic person as akin to "a phenomenologist, trying to learn from what is seen, heard, felt, smelt, rather than from what can be implied or inferred from these sensations'; Some Autistic people may also be described as 'emotional sponges', experiencing strong affective components of the emotions of others. This means that the interpretation of other people's emotions may be different, and therefore empathy with that person may be expressed differently. Often Autistic people relate to each other empathetically by sharing concrete examples of similar experiences, this done as a logical evidenced way of saying "I understand how you feel". This is not how non-autistic people tend to express empathy for another person's situation, so it is not uncommon for autistic people who express empathy in this way to be dismissed as selfish or self-involved.

Alexythymia has garnered more attention, and is posited to have a prevalence of around 50-60% in the autistic population (Kinnaird et al., 2019; Milosavljevic et al., 2016). The relationship between trauma and alexithymia is argued to be somewhat bi-directional, whereby trauma can trigger a disconnection between an emotional response an emotional labelling (i.e. difficulty recognising emotions), but can also be caused through the invalidation and stigma attached to difficulty interpreting and intimating one's own emotional states. There can be a sense of shame in the experience of alexithymia, via the notion that a person is not 'responding correctly' within an emotionally charged situation (e.g. a bereavement). This may be due to difficulty identifying an emotion, or taking longer to process an emotional response that can result in a delayed emotional expression. This can result in a direct pressure to mask, to avoid being viewed as cold, inappropriate or unfeeling, or being seen to 'over-react' while a stress response has been building, unknown to the experiencer. In our 2021 paper on masking, we theorise that there may be a relationship between masking, alexithymia and instances of burnout, whereby difficulty recognising internal states, and further disconnection from internal states via masking, results in a build of stress that is only noticeable once it is too late to prevent severe outcomes (i.e. burnout).

Alexithymia may also be important for understanding the impact of sensory trauma. While monotropism is usually described only in terms of attentional differences, it is important to understand what monotropism may mean for sensory and emotional processing. It has been suggested that sensory processing differences are directly related to autistic sensory processing; that in order to maintain monotropic flow and attentional states, an increased flow of sensory information is needed to drive it. Neurological function can be described as the body taking in sensory information, processing it, and responding to it. If the autistic brain is processing that sensory information differently to the non-autistic brain, then the bodily response to that sensory information is also going to be different. Sensory processing and emotional states are intrinsically interconnected for autistic people, with sensory dysregulation and emotional dysregulation often co-occurring. If someone is sensorially overwhelmed, then that in turn can trigger emotional dysregulation (Fulton et al., 2020). The sometimes extreme differences of sensory perception can therefore trigger extreme differences in emotional responses and emotional processing. These responses can appear strange and sometimes even alarming to non-autistic people, leading to a higher likelihood of dismissal as a response to autistic expression. It may also lead to the assumption that an autistic person is over-reacting, or lead the observer to pathologise an emotional response through the lens of challenging behaviour.

Thus far, we have discussed how deficit narratives of emotionality have impacted on assumptions about autistic empathy, and autistic communication. However, as Yergeau points out, autism itself is imbued with a sense of agency when describing the actions of autistic people, and autistic people are simultaneously stripped of agency through the way that their interpretations of the world are described. The narrative around 'challenging behaviour' and 'meltdowns' is one such example. The experience of significant distress or overwhelm among autistic people can manifest in an involuntary response characterised by an outpouring of anxiety and externally directed energy (Phung et al., 2021). However meltdowns are frequently framed as 'tantrums', 'manipulation' and 'challenging behaviour' as opposed to an involuntary distress response. This framing of autistic emotional expression and overwhelm as 'behaviour' hearkens back to early narratives around autistic communication lacking 'function' (i.e. an involuntary distress response is certainly communicating that a person is overwhelmed, in pain, needs to leave a situation, etc, but is often interpreted as a symptom of autism rather than a person/environment issue).

Quinn (2018) has written about how the pathologisation of autistic responses to distress can lead to further trauma from attempts to 'treat' it. Autistic people are more likely to experience institutionalisation and punitive treatment for displaying 'unusual' responses to distress such as a need to stim, or frequent meltdowns within a therapeutic or educational setting. Neuronormative interpretations of autistic distress responses imbue them with intentionality (e.g. a person is being 'challenging' by avoiding a group therapy session, or wanting to sit on the floor), not considering how autistic needs (e.g. minimal sensory arousal) may not be being met within these environments. The drive to enforce neurotypical norms, and to interpret a lack of their presence as a lack of engagement leads to further trauma for autistic people by way of invalidation and coercion to mask, or through attempts to minimise 'behaviour' (e.g. solitary confinement).

So far we have outlined how the interpretation of autistic ways of being may be misinterpreted and pathologised, leading to invalidation and a risk of traumatic punitive treatment. In the following section we focus specifically upon the impact of behavioural interventions upon autistic people, and how these may lead to both trauma, and masking.

## Behavioural Interventions

In chapter 2, we discussed the history of autism knowledge creation, and the use of behavioural therapies as a 'treatment' to encourage autistic people to develop normative social skills. Behavioural interventions and frameworks (e.g. Applied Behaviour Analysis, or Positive Behaviour Support) frame 'autistic behaviour' (i.e. that is, what is externally visible to others) as impaired, lacking functionality, and/or challenging. As outlined in the previous section, there is a tendency to view autistic communication through a behavioural lens, by which intentionality is ascribed to the visible manifestation of a particular internal state. However due to misalignments in empathy and social communication (i.e. the DEP), non-autistic people may be unlikely to accurately interpret autistic communication (e.g. mistaking distress for intentional aggression).

Abaable.co.uk describe the main aims of ABA as: "ABA aims to increase socially important behaviours such as **communication, play skills, social skills, academic skills and daily living skills.**" In chapter 2 we outlined the development of ABA by Lovaas, who believed that autistic people were empty vessels that had the appearance of a human, in need of behavioural shaping in order to ensure that their development aligned with that of their typical peers. Lovaas recommended that children were enrolled children in 40 hour per week ABA training, where behaviourists used both positive (e.g. offering chocolates each time a given behaviour is expressed, giving them a favourite toy to play with) and negative (the use of aversives, such as removing a favourite item, or in extreme cases physical violence such as electric shock) reinforcement in order to train children to act accordingly. ABA has been compared to conversion therapy (Pyne, 2020), which is unsurprising given Lovaas' input into the development of both.

Autistic community discussions have long featured disclosure of trauma from being entered into early interventions aimed at reducing 'autistic behaviour' in an attempt to make the receiver appear neurotypical (Bascombe, 2011). Autistic adults have discussed how 'positive' reinforcement using food has led to an unhealthy or disordered relationship with food (Kraemer, 2021). There are ongoing discussions about the inhumane use of negative reinforcement. Whereas many modern ABA proponents denounce the use of physical aversives, they have been maintained in a variety of settings, including institutional facilities such as the Judge Rotenberg Centre, or JRC (Neumeier & Brown, 2020). Up until US congress passed an amendment in December 2022 following the tireless work of advocates (ASAN, 2023), the JRC had been using gradual electronic decelerators (electric shock devices) on disabled children. The devices were used as a punishment for behaviour such as physical (e.g. hand flapping) and vocal stimming, causing acute pain to the recipient. Additionally, these practices have been shown to disproportionately be used on Black autistic people, highlighting the intersectional impact of stigma upon risk of trauma (Neumeier & Brown, 2020). Autistic people have spoken at length about the trauma of experiencing such shocks, and how it has led to secondary mental health difficulties as a result of the fear that they experienced within these institutions (Neumeier & Brown, 2020).

Recent research into the impact of ABA has shown similar findings. McGill & Robinson (2021) interviewed autistic adults who had been enrolled in ABA programmes as children. They highlighted feeling harmed by the intervention, recalling physical restraint and feeling dehumanised and treated 'like an animal'. The process led them to shut off from their 'true selves', likening this to being 'taught to fool people' that they were neurotypical. Participants explicitly spoke about how ABA led to masking, and difficulty forming relationships with others due to the effort spent pretending to 'be someone else'. This led to long term mental health difficulties, and difficulties expressing agency due to the coercion and focus on compliance that they experienced. These findings are particularly important when we consider the impact of victimisation on autistic people, and the role that compliance plays in facilitating manipulation, and in perpetuating abuse. Autistic people have highlighted how compliance has put them at risk, and interventions that focus on training compliance may contribute towards compliance and fawning within interpersonal relationships. Additionally, teaching autistic people that they need to suppress their own needs and comfort, and to prioritise that of others puts autistic people at risk from nefarious others who may take advantage of this (Sandoval-Norton et al., 2019).

As previously discussed in Chapter 2, divergence from neurotypical standards have been framed as 'deficits' in these areas (Walker, 2021). However though autistic people may differ in how certain skills are expressed, for example those who do not use spoken language to communicate are still able to communicate using different methods such as AAC (Heyworth et al., 2022; Zimmerman, 2022), or engage in play through sensory engagement (Conn, 2015), they are still present. The inference that only forms of communication, play etc. that are aligned with the skills of the majority are valid form a kind of imperialism (e.g. oralism), and importantly, prevent the recognition that these skills already exist in autistic people, allowing us to develop cross-neurotype communication strategies. Instead, autistic people are encouraged (or forced) through the use of positive or negative reinforcement to suppress their native skills, and use those of non-autistic people instead. This is particularly true of non-speaking autistic people, and autistic people with LDs, who are more likely to be enrolled into intensive programmes based around coercive principles and stringent expectations (Sandoval-Norton et al., 2019).

It is worth noting that we are not suggesting that it is not useful for autistic people to learn about non-native strategies, cross-neurotype communication indeed goes both ways. However there is an aspect of the 'illusion of choice' present in the suggestion that learning neuronormative forms of communication will automatically help autistic people to 'fit in' (as can be seen of the impact of masking in chapter 10). When autistic people are taught to suppress their native skills and only use those of the dominant group, what we are reinforcing is the need to mask, even if this may seem at the time like a viable way for the autistic person themselves to navigate society. It may feel like a choice to develop these skills, but when stigma is a strong reinforcer, very little choice actually exists.

Leadbitter et al., (2021) have written on the potential for neurodiversity informed and affirming interventions. They argue that such interventions should avoid 'curative' approaches that encourage masking, and focus instead on helping autistic people to thrive within their given environment. Many autistic people (particularly children) may have little choice over the environments that they have to navigate (e.g. school), and many interventions serve to force a square peg into a round hole, so to speak, as opposed to finding ways to make the environment more suitable to facilitate a better person-environment match. Leadbitter and colleagues propose that one of key factors in supportive interventions is acknowledgement that interventions often focus on externally perceivable behaviour (stimming, echolalia), as opposed to internal experiences (e.g. dysregulation). Understanding the latter helps to foster autonomy and functional skills by helping people to recognise their own internal states and develop coping strategies, rather than simply focussing on making an autistic person 'appear' less autistic to interlocutors. Indeed, autistic people have highlighted how important stimming in particular can be for our own regulation (Kapp et al., 2019). This approach can help autistic people to develop desired skills at their own pace, and does not rely upon forcing normative goals but in recognising what people need to navigate the environment they inhabit.

Overall, compliance based, normativity focussed interventions are both traumatic and highly implicated in the development of masking among autistic people who have experienced them (Pukki et al., 2022). These interventions teach autistic people that expressing themselves in native ways are impaired and undesirable, and that they should ignore their own needs in favour of the needs of others.

# Education and well-being

In addition to the normative practices instilled during social and behavioural interventions, the education system can be a significant source of trauma for many autistic people, and a crucial factor that is implicated in the development of masking (Chapman et al., 2022; Smitten, 2022). Schools are full of intense sensory information, social expectations, and normative/authoritarian practices which harm neurodivergent children. In this section we will discuss how some of these issues contribute towards trauma, and masking in autistic young people (though much of the research here is also relevant to autistic adults in higher education, see Spaeth & Pearson, 2021) We will begin by outlining some of the key aspects of school trauma, followed by a discussion of normative practices and unmet needs.

## Sensory environment

There is an emerging knowledge base on the sensory impact of the school environment on autistic young people. McDougal et al., (2020) highlighted the impact that sensory processing could have on autistic young people, creating a barrier to learning. Autistic students have to deal with classroom shifts, crowds, noise, classroom displays etc, all of which can be an overwhelming source of sensory information (Goodall, 2018). As highlighted in our earlier subsection on sensory trauma, the dysregulation that overwhelming sensory input can cause has a negative impact on autistic people and can lead to anxiety and distress (Jones et al., 2020). Autistic pupils in particular may struggle due to the lack of agency and autonomy they have to remove themselves from overwhelming environments, effectively forced to endure sensory distress until they can leave (i.e. go home at the end of the day). This can impact on both the learning experience, and their social and emotional wellbeing (Howe & Stagg, 2016), and lead to immediate (e.g. meltdown, or the 'coke bottle effect') and long term consequences (e.g. burnout).

Autistic young people have highlighted how the school environment is not designed for them, having been formulated with a neurotypical student in mind (Birkett et al., 2022). This issue links all the way back to our earlier discussions in chapter 2, about the development of compulsory schooling and the expectation of homogenous pupil needs. Birkett and colleagues found that autistic students may attempt to cope by finding muted spaces (such as the school (library). They highlight how the attempt to develop coping mechanisms (e.g. seeking out quieter environments) are only partial solutions to coping with an environment not designed for them, and may lead to social exclusion and prevent opportunity for interpersonal connection.

## Normative practices and unmet needs

The experience of unmet needs within an educational setting is common among autistic young people (and adults in higher education), which can be seen to directly relate to the way that autistic (and neurodivergent needs in general) are framed: as special, or additional. The majority of autistic young people are educated in mainstream school settings as opposed to specialist schools (Birkett et al., 2022), leading to calls for a focus on 'inclusion'. However, the framing of the majority groups' (i.e. neurotypical students) needs as the norm, and everything else as exceptional can lead to a) a sense that encouraging normativity is the most utilitarian practice, and b) that the needs or neurodivergent people are an optional extra rather than a necessary implementation to make learning spaces more accessible (Hummerstone & Parsons, 2023). Indeed, in a meta-synthesis of the literature on how autistic pupils make sense of themselves in a mainstream school setting (Williams et al., 2019), overwhelmingly highlights the impact of the accessibility of the school environment in influencing autistic young people internalising stigma linked to 'being different in a negative way'.

Time, lack of resources and training, and performance pressures (e.g. an emphasis on academic attainment) can impact on the ability of schools and educators to meet the needs of the children that they teach (Hummerstone & Parsons, 2023; Moyse, 2021). Additionally, a focus on a techno-rationalist approach (emphasising productivity, adapting to external demands, etc) places the burden for outcomes on the learner (Conn, 2019; Fataar et al., 2022). Rather than meeting the needs of the students, students are expected to meet the needs of the school. Some autistic students may internalise these expectations and attempt to meet them in order to cope (e.g. attempting to be a 'good student' and developing perfectionist and fawning behaviours), giving educators the perception that they are not experiencing difficulties. Those pupils who struggle to meet expectations are labelled as 'challenging' and 'difficult' for failing to appear to thrive in a system that fails to meet their needs. As a result, there can be a focus on trying to instil normative behaviour among these children, or alternatively, 'off-rolling' them (i.e. removing pupils from the school roll without officially excluding them, (McShane, 2020).

The instilling of normative values can be seen in some of the basic assumptions about what it means to be engaged within a school setting. The concept of 'whole body listening' emphasises 'eyes to the front' when in class, drawing upon the notion that looking = learning. Research has shown that this is often not the case for autistic young people (Doherty-Sneddon et al., 2012), who may display focussed attention in unexpected ways.

This may include avoiding eye contact to avoid being overwhelmed, and using stimming/movement as a regulatory tool to aid learning. Additionally, co-occurring issues such the prevalence of joint hypermobility that goes unrecognised which might make things like sitting crossed legged on a carpet or a hard chair in a restricted space difficult for neurodivergent children. This places students in a bind as to whether to appear to 'pay attention' through engagement in normative practices (leading to an inability to pay attention due to cognitive resource being spent on masking), or whether to actually pay attention, and risk being perceived as disengaged (Spaeth & Pearson, 2021). Thus, the learning needs and styles of autistic pupils may go unrecognised at best, and actively discouraged at worst.

Attempts to 'correct' the behaviour of autistic young people reinforces neuronormative supremacy, and encourages masking through the implicit suggestion that autistic ways of engaging are wrong. Wood & Lawson, (2019) highlight how this approach emphasises sanction over understanding, widening the double empathy gap between educators and students, and disenfranchises autistic young people within the education system. In addition to  emphasising the importance of normativity, the focus on behaviourism in educational settings has led to the proliferation of a focus on external behaviour (as opposed to the underlying causes), and the use of dangerous and restrictive practices such as restraint and seclusion (ICARS, 2023). The ICARS report revealed that such practices were being used frequently as a way to address dysregulation, which arose out of a lack of accessible learning environments. Far from a last resort, restraint and seclusion were highlighted as a common approach taken to 'reduce challenging behaviour' as opposed to making environmental changes to support student learning. Almost half of all respondents to the report identified that the experience of restraint and seclusion had led to a lasting physical or psychological impact.

As highlighted in the section on behavioural interventions, these restrictive and dangerous practices disproportionately affect autistic people from racialised minorities. Sassu & Volkmar, (2023) have highlighted how unrecognised intersectional issues can compound the impact of educational trauma, in addition to the unmet needs that arise as a result of poor insight into how to support neurodivergent students. They highlight a need for enhanced knowledge of how intersectionality (e.g. race, socio-economic status) may impact on autistic students, to develop "thoughtful, well-informed, evidence-based practices that benefit diverse learners".

## The impact on identity

Research into the impact of school on the development of identity in the general population has shown that professionals may unintentionally limit the identity development of young people through biased inferences about their ingroup (Verhoeven et al., 2019). In chapters 3 and 4 we explored the perceptions of young people with regards to their own identity, with many highlighting how teachers stigmatised them, drawing upon stereotypes of autistic people in their interactions with autistic pupils. The young people in Verhoeven's study felt stifled by the expectations of others, and lacking in the support needed to achieve their own goals with educators often focussing on normalisation, or lowered expectations.

Moyse (2021) explored the experiences of autistic adolescent girls who had experienced school refusal. She found that they were less likely to have received a referral for autism compared to male peers, and more likely to experience persistent absenteeism due to environmental pressures and bullying from peers. The young people highlighted not being included in discussions about their own needs, which reduced feelings of agency and disenfranchised them, leading to disengagement and poor mental health outcomes. They felt pressure to mask both their needs with regards to their work, but also within social interactions to avoid bullying and victimisation.

The experience of masking within a school setting as a response to school-based trauma can result in further invalidation from educators, who do not see the distress that school causes, believing that pupils are 'fine' at school, and that the expression of distress at home is related to home life and parenting. Cunningham (2022) found that autistic pupils would suppress their distress in front of teachers, sometimes going to the bathroom to cry. Likewise, a study from Carrington & Graham (2001) explicitly highlighted autistic pupils' engagement in masking, followed by expressing significant dysregulation upon returning home. This has been referred to as the 'coke bottle' effect by some professionals (Fisher, 2021), likening the experience of the young person to a bottle of fizzy drink that has been shaken up all day leading to a build-up of pressure, only to explode upon opening (or leaving school).

## Developing better practice

Creating a less traumatising and more supportive educational experience means recognising the differences that autistic (and other neurodivergent children) display as necessitating an approach that meets their needs, as opposed to forcing them to assimilate. This may mean recognising the double empathy problem in education and encouraging educators and other school staff to look beyond 'behaviour' to address the causes of unmet needs.

More recently, there has been a shift within education towards neurodivergent affirmative strategies for support. Programmes such as the 'Triple A' intervention led by Hanley and colleagues (https://tripleadurham. co.uk) are aimed at educators rather than students, and aim to provide educators with the understanding and tools to provide a more inclusive environment for autistic students as opposed to expecting the student to learn how to 'fit in' (i.e. mask). Research has shown that the creation of an inclusive school environment is underpinned by developing a sense of trust between educators and pupils, and creating a place where all students feel like valued members. Here teaching educators how to recognise distress, instead of putting the onus on the student to 'unmask' (as we will discuss further in chapter 12) shifts the responsibility back to the person who holds the power in the relationship- the educator.

Neurodiversity-affirming (that is, recognising the needs of both neurotypical and neurodivergent students alike) approaches also open up the opportunity to develop collaborative and reflective practice, whereby educators are able to work with students to foster a positive learning experience that minimises the need to mask, and prevents a need for masking in the first place. We certainly acknowledge that educational professionals have a lot on their plates, and are often working with limited time, resources and support. However, ensuring accessibility and developing a relationship with students that is built upon trust is invaluable for fostering positive outcomes for autistic children.

# Conclusion

Overall, our aim for this chapter was to highlight just some of the many ways that autistic people may a) be at higher risk of trauma, and b) how many of these experiences have both a direct (through explicitly encouraging masking) and indirect (through fostering internalised stigma and the notion that authenticity is unsafe) impact on the development of masking. Autistic people experience commonly established sources of trauma (e.g. interpersonal victimisation and abuse) frequently, however they also experience some forms of trauma that are more closely intertwined with being autistic (e.g. sensory trauma, autism stigma and invalidation).

# Chapter 9: Research to date

The aim of this chapter is to provide a (non-exhaustive) overview of the present state of the masking literature, exploring what we know about masking across the lifespan, and discussing how it relates to the theory we discussed in the previous chapter. For a recent and in-depth systematic review of masking research, we recommend Cook et al., 2021). We will also address the literature around masking and gender in more detail, before addressing other aspects of intersectionality. It is worth noting that we may touch on marginalisation here, but we will specifically discuss masking in relation to autism, stigma and intersectionality in the following chapter. We begin this chapter by outlining the different approaches (i.e. discrepancy vs. reflective approaches) before moving on to explore masking across the lifespan.

## Approaches to masking

In chapter 6, we introduced the concept of discrepancy approaches and reflective approaches to masking, albeit with specific reference to compensation. However, much of the research into masking so far has been explored using these two distinct approaches. Hull et al presented a detailed outline of the two in their 2020 review of the literature. Here we outline the key differences in these approaches before moving on to discuss research to date.

### Discrepancy approaches

Discrepancy approaches seek to examine masking from what is argued to be a more 'objective' position. Here a clinical measure of autistic behaviour (such as the ADOS) is compared to self-reported autistic characteristics, in order to identify whether there is a 'discrepancy' between how autistic a person identifies themselves to be on a questionnaire, or performs in a task designed to assess core features of autism (e.g. theory of mind), and how autistic they outwardly appear to be when interacting with a clinical professional. Whilst this approach may seem more 'objective' it has a number of issues. One issue is that assessments of 'autistic behaviour' have been developed from a normative perspective (Timimi et al., 2019) and as discussed, may have a bias towards recognising particular presentations in autistic people (that is, in white young boys who have a stereotyped profile that clinicians are familiar with). An autistic person's presentation may not be consistent with their self-report (or caregiver report) scores on an (arguably rigid and decontextualised) questionnaire measure, but this does not necessarily suggest that they are masking. This relates to Milton's concept of autism from the inside out. Behavioural measures of autism assess the externally visible characteristics, whilst self-report or cognitive measures assess internal states. A discrepancy between these two factors does not necessarily indicate masking but may relate to their interpretation of situational norms or demands (e.g. a person may not talk about a strong interest with the researcher because it seems irrelevant to the situation, but report themselves to have strong interests in the measure). Here the assumption within the clinical context is that autistic people's 'repetitive interests' will be obvious, and result in an interruption to the flow of the assessment, and if they do not then they must be suppressed.

Another issue is the context in which these measures are gathered, whereby autistic people perform artificial social situations within a clinical setting. This environment does not particularly facilitate 'acting naturally', and the ADOS itself may appear confusing and nonsensical to the person being assessed (e.g. having to make up a story to match a picture book without words). Timimi et al. outline how within the context of the assessment, a practitioner is trained to view all autistic behaviour through the lens of pathology, providing an objectifying standard against which to measure all aspects of the interaction. Interestingly, this approach is similar to the historical evidence gathering used by the Maudsley Children's Hospital (Evans, 2014), by which all behaviour was coded within the expectation of abnormality, and measured against an artificial standard of 'normal behaviour'. In addition, Timimi and colleagues highlight how the behaviour of the researcher (or clinician) may influence the behaviour of the person being assessed, despite assumptions that the relationality between the observer and observed play no part in the assessment. They draw upon the double empathy problem, asserting that measures like the ADOS ignore the inter-subjective nature of relationships, setting up an artificially one-sided interaction and then penalising the autistic person for failing to meet the 'objective' standards set.

The subjective-objective, socially artificial nature of measures such as the ADOS lead to a difficulty knowing what a discrepancy approach is actually measuring. Though they might obtain a difference between performance on a behavioural, and an internal measure of autistic characteristics, Timimi et al. point out that several assumptions underlie the utility of behavioural measures, i.e. that autism is discrete and essentialised, and that it can be assessed and quantified through behavioural means because autistic characteristics are visible and easy to identify. As we have outlined previously, autistic people present in a variety of ways that do not meet with clinical stereotypes (rendering them less 'visible' to external observers) AND may mask. Whilst the foundation of a discrepancy approach acknowledges that autistic people might appear 'less autistic', there is less consideration of whether this may be due to a) individual differences in presentation, b) flawed assumptions underlying behavioural measures of autism, and c) the context of the assessment itself (which does lend itself to the notion of impression management).

A strength of a discrepancy approach is that it does not necessarily rely upon the conscious awareness of masking (in comparison to the reflective approach). A person may mask during the ADOS, but does not have to explicitly reflect upon this, or be aware that they are doing it. The implicit assumption is that if there is a difference between external presentation (i.e. they appear 'less autistic' by way of the assessment) and internal presentation (e.g. they score higher in a measure of self-report autistic characteristics) then masking may be the explanation. However as outlined above, discrepancies between internal and external presentation may vary for reasons aside from masking. This makes the approach useful for exploring discrepancies between behavioural and internal 'autistic characteristics', but not necessarily for operationalising masking.

## Observational/Reflective Approaches

Observational and reflective approaches examine how autistic people describe the act of masking, looking at the strategies or behaviours that they might (consciously) engage with in order to present themselves differently depending on the situation or who they are interacting with. Observational approaches rely upon observing the autistic person within a more naturalistic social interaction and tracking behaviour previously associated with masking (e.g. weaving in and out of social activities, (Dean et al., 2017). Whilst these approaches may be useful for assessing differences in behaviour between socialising and solo activity, they have a similar issue to a discrepancy approach in that they rely upon external ratings of behaviour and may be impacted by the double empathy problem (e.g. a neurotypical coder lacking insight into nuanced aspects of autistic social interaction). The experience and insight of the coder will affect how they interpret autistic external behaviour, with the potential for every action to be coded with reference to a pathological lens (e.g. interpreting an autistic child lining up toys as repetitive behaviour, and a non-autistic child lining up toys as demonstrating a 'meaningful' action such a queuing). Timimi et al. (2019) highlight how coders will often make erroneous inferences about autistic social communication (e.g. labelling a smile as a smirk), rendering judgements of autistic social behaviour through a non-autistic lens to have questionable authority.

Reflective approaches place value on the experience of the informant, drawing upon autistic insight into their own experiences in order to understand the different ways in which masking may develop and manifest. Hull and colleagues (Hull et al., 2020b) outline how reflective approaches (unlike a discrepancy approach) do not rely upon the 'success' of masking in order to assess it (i.e. a person can reflect on their attempts to mask and the impact it has on them regardless of whether their autistic characteristics are externally visible other people). However, this also results in the key limitation with this method. Within the use of a reflective approach, researchers are reliant on explicit and conscious knowledge of masking. Among autistic people who are aware of aspects of their own masking, some have described how masking is multifaceted and not always under conscious control (Pearson et al., 2023; Pearson & Rose, 2021; Wharmby, 2022, p. 31). This means that participants may be limited in the descriptions of their own strategies, behaviour and the underlying drivers of masking.

# Masking in children and young people

There is a small but growing body of literature on masking in children and young people (CYP). Whilst the majority of early research into masking in young people used discrepancy approaches more recent work has used a reflective approach, drawing upon both quantitative and qualitative methods. This research is important as it provides insight into how masking may develop across the lifespan, and the underlying factors which contribute towards its development and maintenance.

Several studies have used a discrepancy approach to explore masking in CYP. The majority of these studies have used the ADOS as an objective clinical measure of external behaviour, alongside parent report measures like the social communication questionnaire, or SCQ (Rynkiewicz et al., 2016), theory of mind tasks (Corbett et al., 2021) and the social responsiveness scale or, SRS, a parent-report measure of autistic characteristics and clinical interview (Ratto et al., 2018). Both Rynkiewcz and Ratto found gender differences in their samples, with autistic girls showing evidence of masking between the ADOS and questionnaire/interview measures compared to autistic boys, whereas Corbett found that girls had lower repetitive behaviour scores but that masking (here compensation) was not impacted by gender.

Wood-Downie et al., (2020) used the Interactive Drawing Test as an alternative to the ADOS, attempting to create a more naturalistic social interaction between participant and researcher. They also took a parent-report of autistic characteristics using the Social and Communication Disorders Checklist, or SCDC (Skuse et al., 2005), a measure of IQ, and the reading the mind in the eyes test for children (RMET-C, Baron-Cohen et al., 2001) They operationalised masking in two different ways- comparing behaviour in the task compared to non-autistic peers to parent report (behavioural masking), and comparing behaviour in the task compared to non-autistic peers to performance in the theory of mind task (compensatory masking). They found that autistic girls performed similarly to non-autistic girls on the IDT task, and had higher scores than autistic boys, but had similar levels of parent-report autistic characteristics as the autistic boys, and similar theory of mind scores. The authors suggest that these differences provide evidence of more frequent masking among autistic girls compared to autistic boys. However, Mattern et al., (2023) found that sex differences between autistic girls and boys with regards to social insight were comparable to sex differences between non-autistic children, which they suggest is evidence of a general sex difference (e.g. due to socialisation) rather than masking.

Ross et al., (2023) used the ADOS, SRS and the child behaviour checklist (CBCL: Achenbach, 2011) to explore the relationship between masking and mental health  in young people aged 4-17 years. They found that parents rated girls as having more communication difficulties than boys, though both showed similar scores on the ADOS and masking was not found to be significantly different across the groups. Masking did predict internalising symptoms of mental health difficulties, consistent with the suggestion that masking results in poor mental health outcomes for autistic people (which we will discuss in chapter 10) and providing evidence that this begins early in life.

Hannon et al., (2023) conducted a systematic review of the different quantitative methods used to examine masking across autistic young people and adults, revealing 13 different observational/reflective measures had been developed (though two were variations on the CAT-Q). Hull et al., (2019) developed the CAT-Q to provide a quantitative assessment of masking in autistic adults, though the measure has since been validated for use online, in adolescents and parent-report (Hannon et al., 2023). Of all measures reported, the CAT-Q was the only measure to demonstrate test-re-test reliability, though Williams has noted that CAT-Q scores may be confounded by social anxiety (Williams, 2022) and should be assessed further for psychometric utility. Multiple studies of masking in CYP have used the CAT-Q in order to assess the relationship between masking, autistic characteristics, and underlying mechanisms (e.g. cognition) and outcomes (e.g. mental health).

Jorgenson et al., (2020) found that age appeared to impact on masking in autistic young people (measured using the CAT-Q), which supports the notion of a developmental component to masking and aligns with broader research on impression management in young people. However Hull et al., (2020a) examined the relationship between self-reported masking via the CAT-Q and social cognition, IQ, autistic characteristics and executive function (EF) among autistic young people and interestingly, they found no relationship between age and masking (their sample ranged from 13-18). This is unexpected given the impact of adolescence on identity management (see chapter 3). They also found no relationship with IQ, supporting the idea that autistic people with learning disabilities do mask (contrary to previous discourse that masking is a feature of 'high functioning' autistics), and no relationship with social cognition. The latter is unsurprising given previous evidence that performance on socio-cognitive tasks may not relate to everyday social interaction skills (Sasson et al., 2020). They did find a relationship between EF and masking, which supports the notion that masking and IM requires the ability to track and manage multiple cues within the social context in relation to self-presentation.

Hannon et al., (2023) explored the utility of the CAT-Q for use with young people and their parents, by adapting the CAT-Q to include a parent report measure and comparing this to self-reported masking in their young person. Results showed a strong positive correlation between the two, suggesting that parents had good insight into their young person's masking (although some discrepancies were found). The authors also found that CAT-Q scores were weakly correlated with discrepancy measures of masking, and that neither were associated with social difficulties, which they suggest may support the notion that masking and appearing socially competent by neurotypical standards are not interchangeable (as we have previously discussed).

Reflective insights into masking among autistic young people have also been gathered using interviews. Chapman et al., (2022) interviewed autistic adolescents about their experiences of masking and how it impacted on their identity. They found 7 key themes, including balancing suppression and hiding aspects of self with being one's true self, the impact of environment and context (e.g. schools), and internal experiences (e.g. anxiety) on masking, and the sense of a self-fulfilling prophecy. The data suggested that masking was a response to the way that others treated them, with the young people describing how they had been stigmatised and bullied (echoing reports from retrospective adult accounts of how early victimisation led to the development of masking). This led to low self-image and a sense among the young people that autism was perceived negatively by non-autistic people who were viewed as having 'superior' social skills (emphasising the internalisation of stigma and dominant narratives). The young people highlighted how masking intersected with other aspects of their identity (such as gender) and overall had a negative impact on their mental health. These findings are directly comparable to those emerging in adults, and support the idea that masking in autistic people is primarily driven by stigma. Overall, they support the notion of masking as a multifaceted and complex response to living in a world that does not respond kindly to difference.

Similarly Smitten, (2022) used a participatory approach to explore masking among autistic CYP, interviewing four young people from a phenomenological perspective. She found 9 key themes, which focussed on masking as both suppression of external authentic self-representation and internal states, masking as an exaggerated or 'made up' version of self, masking occurring as a response to stigma and a sense that masking was not intentional or agentic. The young people placed particular emphasis on the school context as a source of masking, and specified how they desired educators to empathise with them (bridging the double empathy gap). The study highlighted some important aspects of masking that have received less attention within the literature so far, such as emotional suppression and the need for adults to work hard to bridge the double empathy gap and foster safer and more inclusive environments for CYP.

Together these studies use a reflective first person perspective to highlight the complexity of masking among young people in a way that goes beyond a social IM strategy and emphasises how both societal narratives about autistic people, and individual responses to difference lead autistic young people to recognise that it is not safe to be themselves, and find a way to cope with the tools that they have.

Overall, research into masking among young people suggests that it develops early in life as an attempt to navigate an often hostile social world. It also appears to be distinct from the appearance of (neuronormative) social competence, supporting the suggestion that autistic people vary in terms of their external social presentation and that a normatively more acceptable outer appearance is not necessarily an indication that someone is masking (calling into question the discrepancy method). In the next section we will discuss research conducted with adults, and what this adds to our understanding.

# Masking in adulthood

Much of the initial research into masking in adulthood emerged as a result of discussions around the gender disparity in autism diagnosis. Arguments around the masking hypothesis of 'female autism' started to surface around 2016 when a study from Bargeila and colleagues (Bargiela et al., 2016) exploring the experiences of late diagnosed autistic women revealed how their experiences of masking had led to difficulties in external recognition of their autistic characteristics. Whilst masking had been discussed previously in the autistic community (Holliday-Willey, 2014)and in sociological literature (Milton & Sims, 2016), this study was one of the first to explore masking through a Psychological lens, and bring it to the forefront of autism researchers' minds. Suddenly, the existence of autistic women was of interest, as well as the key question of why they were only identified at a ratio 7:1 (Loomes et al., 2017) compared to autistic men (at the time of writing this gap is argued to be closer to 4:1, (Lord et al., 2020) or 2:1 (Zeidan et al., 2022).

Judith Gould (Gould, 2017) proposed that masking was likely a crucial explanation. Autistic women were more capable of 'appearing normal' than their male peers, making more frequent eye contact, and displaying more 'normative' interests (though still very passionate in nature). Gould referred to these women as 'the lost girls'. A generation of autistic women, hiding in plain sight, able to pass as non-autistic due to their social skills, or as we sometimes jokingly refer to it, 'sneaky autism'. This increased interest in masking led to a growth in empirical research, much of which initially focussed on gender. We will begin by discussing this literature, before moving on to a more general discussion of masking in adulthood.

Discrepancy studies on autistic adults have demonstrated inconsistent results with regards to gender differences. Lai (Lai et al., 2017, 2019) used the ADOS alongside the RMET and AQ to explore gender differences in masking in autistic adults. In both studies they found that autistic women showed a higher discrepancy between ADOS performance and RMET/AQ scores, indicating a higher level of masking compared to autistic men. Schuck et al., (2019) used the same measures in an attempted replication, alongside several other measures of social communication, and anxiety. Their findings did replicate those of Lai and colleagues, suggesting that women had similar self-reported levels of autistic characteristics, but lower ADOS scores. As previously discussed, there have been discussions as to whether the ADOS is sensitive to characterising autism outside of a stereotypical sample. This makes it difficult to ascertain whether gender differences on these tasks reflects an actual difference in masking between autistic men and women, or whether it may reflect more general sex and gender differences in social interaction.

Milner et al., (2023) examined both discrepancy and reflective accounts of masking among autistic adults and adults with high autistic traits but no diagnosis, using a similar method to Hanlon (2021). They found that autistic males showed a stronger correlation between discrepancy scores, and that participants with high traits scored higher than diagnosed participants on discrepancy measures but not on reflective measures. Their findings suggest that masking may be a barrier to diagnosis for both men and women, supporting the notion that it is the lack of a stereotypical profile, rather than a gendered phenotype, that drives under-diagnosis. Relatedly, a follow up study from Milner et al., (2023) which explored the relationship between masking and outcomes. They found that formally diagnosed autistic women reported masking more than diagnosed autistic men, but no gender differences in masking in the high traits group, again suggesting that masking may form a barrier to diagnosis regardless of gender. Finally, masking predicted poor psychological outcomes for the diagnosed participants and the high trait groups, however upon closer inspection this relationship was only significant for male participants. The authors suggest that this may be related to socialised expectations of women leading to the normalisation of masking and thus better coping mechanisms, or that the measures used may not have captured aspects of masking that relate to poor outcomes for autistic women. Indeed, as mentioned in chapter 6, the CAT-Q is limited in scope with regards to capturing particular aspects of masking (e.g. unconscious and internalised strategies), and may have limited cross-cultural utility (Lundin Remnélius & Bölte, 2023).

Cage & Troxell-Whitman (2019) used the CAT-Q alongside a measure of reasons/contexts for masking across autistic men and women, finding no difference in CAT-Q scores across gender (though as mentioned in Chapter 6, they did find gender differences in motivations). Similar findings have emerged in qualitative reflective studies which have compared whether gender impacts on self-reported masking (in men, women, and non-binary participants). These studies have generally shown that gender does not manifest in differences in masking. Here autistic people of all genders have spoken about their need to mask to 'fit in' socially, as well as to avoid harm and abuse from others (see chapter 8). Participants in Hull et al.s 2017 study highlighted that both autistic and non-autistic people engage in IM, but that they were motivated by threat reduction, and a desire to survive in hostile environments. Masking was used across participants of all genders as both a defence mechanism, and a way to foster social acceptance. Similar themes were highlighted by Atherton et al., (2022) by late diagnosed adults, with participants emphasising the impact of growing up feeling like an outsider.

More recently, researchers have attempted to measure masking within situations that are closer to everyday social interactions. Cook et al., (2021, 2022) had participants take part in a brief social interaction task and then watched a video of the interaction with the researcher, describing examples of their own masking during the interaction. In Cook et al. 2021 participants' motivations for masking were developed using thematic analysis of their masking descriptions. They highlighted a desire for connection with others, and the use of general IM as a value expressive function to show themselves as a desirable and responsible social partner. However, they also used masking to avoid being perceived as autistic, with some responses highlighting internalised ableism (e.g. not wanting to appear like a stereotypically autistic person) in their motivations. In Cook et al. 2022 the behaviour used to mask were analysed and split into 4 clusters, focussed on suppressing autistic aspects of self and identity, using superficial social behaviours, modelling neurotypical forms of social communication, and using active self-monitoring to establish themselves as a competent (by non-autistic standards) social partner.

Overall, the research into masking in adulthood highlights similar motivations and mechanisms to those seen in young people (e.g. stigma, intersecting aspects of socialisation). In the following section, we unpack the relationship between masking and gender, and masking and stigma in more depth, with consideration of issues highlighted in previous chapters.

# The relationship between gender and masking

Research discussed in the previous sections has highlighted a complex relationship between masking and gender (with very little consideration of non-binary participants). So what is the impact of gender on masking and the expression of autistic characteristics? In order to answer this question, we need to take a step back and think about the broader aspects of our identities. Whilst debates rage about a social versus medical approach to understanding neurodivergent people, the enactivist model (Jurgens, 2020) has gained somewhat less attention. However an enactivist approach is crucial in understanding how our identities are shaped. From birth, our biology (e.g. genetics), cognition (i.e. how we think), and behaviour (i.e. how we act or appear to others) interact with our environment (e.g. our culture, our caregivers) in order to shape who we are. Socio-cultural factors such as culture-bound gender roles (Butler, 1988) impact on our sense of self, and how we want others to perceive us.

In order to understand an enactivist approach to the perception of autistic characteristics, we highlight findings from Mandy et al., (2018). Mandy and colleagues examined the developmental trajectory of autistic traits in young people, finding that girls are often rated as displaying lower levels of autistic traits earlier in childhood, with an increase in adolescence. The authors argue that this may be when autistic traits in girls start to develop, however, it is possible that what we are seeing here is a change in the perception of certain traits over time. Earlier in childhood, young girls bond over shared interests, with a passionate investment in a band, or tv show viewed as 'normal' childhood behaviour. As girls transition into secondary education, social interactions begin to become more complex and are often centred more on sharing emotions and discussing social information (Sedgewick et al., 2018). Here, an autistic young girl who is able to engage with others over passionate shared interests is likely to feel more at ease socially, and may only appear to be 'struggling' when social demands change. Here we can see that it is the external expectations (e.g. how to interact at different developmental stages, and how certain behaviours are perceived at different developmental stages) that dictate what is considered to be 'impaired social skills' relative to peers. Cook et al., (2018) highlight how gender stereotypes may impact on autistic girls in social settings, with the heightened expectation of intimacy within social relationships harder to navigate due to the double empathy problem.

Thus as we highlighted in chapter 5, the relationship between gender and masking is unlikely to be driven by a 'female phenotype', but related to the experience of being on the intersection of autistic and female (or the intersection of autism and upbringing, culture etc. which impact on individual presentations). Consideration of individual or group differences in masking through an intersectional lens provides a more nuanced understanding of disparities in identification, without unintentionally blaming women (and other people who may go un/misdiagnosed) for their under-recognition. An intersectional approach also highlights the need for consideration of other aspects of identity in ameliorating issues around recognition of the diverse way in which autism may present in interaction with other aspects of identity. The majority of research on masking and gender has been in white women, and as we highlight in chapter 5, racism also impacts on access to diagnosis and recognition of autism in BAWG and autistic people of all genders from racialised minorities. By focussing on masking as part of 'a female autism phenotype' we risk creating another white-centric narrative which further excludes and marginalises other racialised groups.

# Masking and stigma

Moving away from a narrative which conceptualises masking as a core aspect of a 'female autism phenotype' and towards an intersectional perspective allows for a more fine grained consideration of the interaction between stigma and masking. Cage and Troxell-Whitman's (2019) work on reasons, contexts and costs of masking among autistic adults highlighted the role of stigma in the use of masking as impression management, feeling a need to avoid victimisation from others. Similarly, Schneid & Raz (2020) explored masking as a form of impression management, interviewing 24 autistic adults on their experiences. They found that impression management was seen as a social asset with masking highlighted as only one aspect of IM, though masking itself was primarily stigma driven in nature as opposed to functioning as a general. Their participants also referred to taking the role of the generalised other, and using IM and SM to express their values (e.g. behaving in a way that they saw as consistent with who they wanted to be, and how they wanted others to see them). Masking as a form of IM was seen as limited as though it could provide a way to 'pass' in social situations it could not always breach the double empathy divide to help them understand the social requirements of the situation, and was exhausting. Participants highlighted the importance of authentic expression, and how developing relationships with autistic people had helped them to develop a sense of belonging, though this was not always enough to combat internalised stigma.

Further qualitative support for the relationship between masking and stigma comes from Miller and colleagues (Miller et al., 2021) who explored masking among autistic and non-autistic people. They found that  all participants highlighted masking as a form of IM/SM. Autistic people emphasised some autism-specific aspects (e.g. suppressing stimming for fear of negative social judgements) of masking, however the sense that masking was a response to a marginalising social world was found across both autistic and non-autistic participants, highlighting the general role that stigma plays in IM. Participants also highlighted the role of trauma in the development of masking, reflecting on experiences of victimisation that led them to engage in IM as a survival strategy in addition to using IM to indicate a social alignment with others. Quantitative support for the relationship between masking and stigma comes from Perry et al., (2021), who examined the relationship between masking, stigma and social identity strategies among autistic adults, and how this impacted on mental wellbeing. They found that stigma significantly predicted masking (measured using the CAT-Q), and interestingly, that both individualistic social identity strategies (e.g. distancing oneself as an individual from autistic identity), and collective social identity strategies (e.g. engaging in autism advocacy) were associated with higher masking. These findings are consistent with Botha's work on ACC, showing that a sense of belonging could actually predict higher perceptions of stigma (and thus a need for masking).

## Conclusion

In summary, the research discussed in this chapter has provided insight into the emerging field of autistic masking across the lifespan. Both discrepancy and observational approaches have strengths and weaknesses in helping us to understand how masking may impact on how autistic people may present within social interactions, how it develops and what motivates it. In the next chapter we will outline the impact of masking on autistic people, taking into consideration masking as a form of social IM, and masking as a response to stigma.

# Chapter 10: Impact of masking

To date, literature exploring the impact of masking upon autistic people suggests that the impact is overwhelmingly negative. Whilst general impression management strategies may allow for more positive outcomes (e.g. making a positive impression, being able to express different aspects of self in relevant contexts), IM through masking may be more related to what Ai and colleagues refer to as being "below the baseline of social favourability'. That is, when a stigmatised person engages in IM, there may always be a bias towards maintaining safety due to prior negative experiences and a stigmatised social status, with more ground to 'make up' to gain a favourable social judgement. Thus, stigmatised people may not 'benefit' from impression management in the same way as non-stigmatised people, as disentangling voluntary IM from pressured IM may be difficult to achieve (though is certainly a worthwhile endeavour for future research).

As such, this chapter aims to examine how masking relates to poor outcomes (such as mental health difficulties, burnout and suicidality) among autistic people. We will discuss how masking may relate to more positive aspects of impression management in Chapter 12, where we address whether and how it is possible to safely foster authenticity.

## Difficulties in recognising autism

We will begin the chapter by discussing how masking might impact on diagnosis and identification, given that it has been proposed as a core reason that autistic people may go unidentified until later in life (Gould, 2017; Leedham et al., 2020).

Throughout this book we have discussed the tension between the suggestion that masking impacts on diagnosis and identification, and a more recent recognition that autistic people present in a range of ways that do not necessarily meet clinical stereotypes. This tension is important to consider in discussions about later, missed and mis-diagnosis, because as we discussed in chapter 9, an autistic person not meeting stereotypical expectations is not necessarily indicative of masking. However, masking *does* impact on access to diagnosis for a variety of different reasons.

The developmental nature of masking can lead to many of the associated strategies and mechanisms operating at a primarily unconscious level (Leedham et al., 2020; Pearson & Rose, 2021). Autistic people have recounted feeling like they are struggling, not knowing why things seem to be so much harder for them than others, and having to work hard to cope in a world that did not feel designed for them (Miller et al., 2021). As we discussed in chapters 4 and 7, the internalisation of stereotypes about autistic people can also lead to difficulty recognising autism in oneself (Cage et al., 2022). Here internalised stigma may interact with self-blame to create a sense that an individual just needs to 'try harder' (i.e. mask more) in order to cope.

Many autistic people are diagnosed with mental health difficulties or other psychiatric conditions prior to receiving an autism diagnosis (de Broize et al., 2022; Fusar-Poli et al., 2022; Leedham et al., 2020). This can lead to diagnostic overshadowing ( e.g. struggling to form relationships being attributed to social anxiety, as opposed to recognising that a person may be autistic). Autistic women in particular are likely to receive an inaccurate diagnosis prior to being identified as autistic, with borderline personality disorder (BPD) being one of the most prevalent (Belcher et al., 2022), which is thought to be due to some overlap in an expected profile (McQuaid et al., 2022). The experience of misdiagnoses can be traumatising, and lead to inappropriate forms of medication and therapy which can worsen any secondary mental and even physical health difficulties (McQuaid et al., 2022).

Recently, there has been a push for clinicians to consider that a person may be masking during the diagnostic process (Beck et al., 2020), with tools like the CAT-Q available for them to use alongside diagnostic measures. However the autism assessment pathway itself is often fraught with barriers and gatekeepers (e.g. general practitioners, or GPs) who may not be as knowledgeable about recent advances in autism research or practice. Some practitioners may not be aware of what autism can look like outside of a stereotype, and may also be faced with autistic people who are masking and/ or fawning and/or projecting whilst engaging with healthcare professionals.

The diagnostic process itself can be traumatic for those who have spent a lifetime masking. Autistic people have recounted having to re-process their entire life through a new lens, and experiencing a crisis of identity when they become aware of masking, which can be utterly exhausting (Lilley et al., 2022). Throughout this book we have discussed the impact of masking on both personal and social identity among autistic people, however, much of this research has been explored in an indirect manner due to the difficulty in measuring masking, and the lack of coherent consensus on what personal and social identity look like more broadly among autistic people *outside* of masking.

Autistic people have reported that masking has led to difficulties in developing a sense of identity (Pearson et al., 2023), and a loss of identity (Hull et al., 2017; Miller et al., 2021). The identity crisis that emerges with regards to masking is sometimes centred on feelings of deceit in relation to others (e.g. 'no-one knows who I really am') and what would happen if people found out (e.g. 'they would reject me'), alongside a sense that the person themselves do not know who they truly are. The latter can be incredibly distressing, with people reporting high levels of anxiety about what exists 'underneath the mask' and whether they even have an identity (Hull et al., 2017). There have been suggestions that better support is needed around a positive autistic identity at all levels of the diagnostic process, due to variable waiting times (in the UK these can be anywhere from 2-5 years), to help people during this time of moratorium while they make sense of their experiences and adapt to a new identity.

In summary, masking and internalised stigma may make it more difficult for someone to identify themselves as autistic and seek diagnosis. However, masking may also impact on the likelihood of being correctly identified as autistic, and also impact on one's sense of self and identity as they begin to explore the possibility that they are.

# Masking and wellbeing

Recent research has started to explore the relationship between masking and wellbeing outcomes for autistic people (Cremone et al., 2023). Autistic people are more likely to be diagnosed with depression and anxiety (Linden et al., 2023) compared to non-autistic peers, and are at a higher risk of suicidality and suicidal ideation (Cassidy et al., 2018). Researchers have suggested that masking may contribute towards these poor outcomes, drawing upon literature surrounding minority stress to support (Botha & Frost, 2020; Miller et al., 2021).

A small number of studies have explicitly examined the relationship between masking and mental health outcomes using both quantitative and qualitative methods. Quantitative data has been gathered using validated questionnaire measures. Ross et al., (2023) found a relationship between masking and internalising mental health difficulties (anxiety) in autistic young people, suggesting that the masking begins to have a negative impact on mental health early in the lives of autistic people. Similar results have been found among autistic adults (Hull et al., 2021; Lai et al., 2017), with masking related to both anxiety (both generalised and social) and depression. Similar research into the impact of masking on mental health in adulthood has been conducted on people with and without a formal autism diagnosis. Beck et al., (2020) explored the relationship between mental health, masking and autistic characteristics in women without an autism diagnosis, finding high levels of distress, suicidal ideation and difficulties in everyday functioning. Their findings provide evidence that clinicians should consider the potential for autism in women in particular who display social and mental health difficulties across the lifespan, taking masking into account. Such work has recently been integrated into advice for psychiatric management among autistic adults (Royal College of Psychiatrists, 2020).

Cage et al., (2018) explored the link between autism acceptance and mental health outcomes using questionnaire measures, alongside open text responses. The quantitative data suggested that anxiety and depression were impacted by both personal and external autism acceptance, while qualitative data highlighted the impact of masking on personal wellbeing. They completed further analysis on whether mental health outcomes differed in those who reported masking compared to those who didn't, finding that those who reported masking had higher self-reported depression scores.

With regards to qualitative research to support the relationship between masking and mental health outcomes, several studies on masking more generally (Hull et al., 2017; Miller et al., 2021) have found that participants perceived masking to impact negatively on mental health. Direct qualitative study on the impact of masking on wellbeing comes from Bradley et al., (2021) who asked autistic adults about how masking impacts on their mental health. Their participants highlighted how masking could lead to heightened anxiety, risk of breakdowns in mental health, and suicidal ideation. Importantly, they also found that participants related masking to increased exhaustion (similarly to Hull et al., 2017) and risk of autistic burnout.

Autistic burnout is currently characterised by a loss of functional skill previously held by an individual, that occurs in conjunction with extreme physical and mental exhaustion and the increased manifestation of autistic traits (Higgins et al., 2021; Raymaker et al., 2020). Burnout can be both long term and acute in nature (Higgins et al. 2021), and often includes the need for social withdrawal and a lowering of social demands (Arnold et al., 2023a) alongside a range of other indicators (see Figure 10.1). There is currently a limited (but emerging) body of academic literature on autistic burnout, with much of the discussion taking place in a community context (Dwyer, 2019; Rose, 2018a). To date, seven studies have explicitly explored the phenomena of autistic burnout, with an attempt to define it and explore the impact that it has. Five of these have explored the relationship that burnout has with masking.

---

## Indicators of Autistic Burnout

- Lethargy
- Increased irritability
- Increased anxiety
- Increased sensory dysregulation
- Heightened auditory processing problems
- Decreased communication
- Narrowed vision
- Increased Shutdowns and heightened withdrawn state Increased frequency and severity of Meltdowns Diminished ability for self-regulation of emotional state
- Mood swings
- Slowed down cognitive processes (Brain fog)
- Memory loss/forgetfulness
- Decreased motivation
- Migraines
- Inability to be Monotroplc (Poor hyperfocus, inertia, lock of flow}
- Extreme overwhelm more regularly

- Decreased mental flexibility/narrowing of thinking Increased guilt/self blame
- Increased Executive Dysfunction
- Increased Demond Avoidance
- Increased digestive issues
- Increased Slimming (more frantic)
- Decreased immune function (auto-immune issues} Increased dissociative episodes
- Increased suicidal ideation
- Increased self-harm
- Increased restriction of diet
- Reduced self core
- Significant changes in sleep patterns

### What it can appear like:

- Skills loss/regression
- An inability to sustain a Mask
- School 'refusal' /Workplace anxiety
- Depression

---

**Figure 10.1:** Indicators of autistic burnout (with permission from www.theautisticadvocate.com)

Raymaker et al. (2020) were the first to explore autistic burnout among autistic people, using a combination of interviews and public community internet resources (e.g. blog posts). Their findings highlighted the sheer exhaustion and loss of skill that burnout brought, alongside secondary mental health difficulties such as depression. Masking was also highlighted in relation to burnout, being both a prominent stressor that contributed towards its occurrence, and the need to 'un-mask' viewed as crucial to the recovery process. This work was followed by Mantzalas et al., (2022) who also completed a thematic analysis of online community posts about burnout, finding that masking was viewed as instrumental in the development of burnout, and as such people felt that they were in a bind whereby they were damned if they did mask (to experience burnout and mental health difficulties) and damned if they didn't (to experience stigma and risk of victimisation). Arnold et al., (2023a, 2023b) have examined the nature and measurement of autistic burnout among autistic adults. In their paper confirming the nature of autistic burnout they found masking to be a crucial factor in the experience of burnout. In their paper exploring the measurement of burnout they found that masking (measured using the CAT-Q) and depression were associated with more severe burnout.

Additional research has highlighted the bi-directional relationship between masking and burnout. In our (Pearson et al., 2023) study on interpersonal victimisation participants highlighted how masking to avoid stigma and abuse led to burnout that had been difficult to recover from, but also that burnout had then made it difficult for them to engage in masking. Whilst Raymaker et al's (2020) participants emphasised the importance of unmasking in recovery from burnout, our participants' reflections on not being able to mask also aligned with participants in Mantzalas et al's (2022) work, who said they felt damned if they did, and damned if they didn't. Masking was viewed as a survival strategy (we will discuss this in further detail at the end of this chapter), and not being able to mask left our participants feeling at risk of further stigma and victimisation.

Mantzalas et al., (2022) have used evidence on the relationship between masking and burnout to propose a conceptual model of autistic burnout (CMAB). They integrate theory from the social-relational model of disability and neurodiversity paradigm with two theories of stress and burnout: the Job Demands-Resources model (Bakker et al., 2004) and Conservation of Resources theory (Hobfoll, 1989). Their CMAB hypothesises a relationship between personal demands and resources, mental strain, wellbeing and additional variables. Masking is defined here as a personal demand which may play both a drain and gain role for autistic people, demanding and exhausting both cognitive and physical energy, but providing a way to stay safe in a hostile society.

In summary burnout appears to be one consequence of masking, however the relationship between masking and burnout is not unidirectional and requires further study in order to assess to how a) safely prevent burnout whilst not needlessly denigrating the need for a coping strategy such as masking, and b) how to ameliorate the impact of both burnout and masking.

As highlighted in several of the aforementioned studies, there also appears to be a link between masking, and risk of suicidality and/or suicidal ideation among autistic people. Cassidy et al. (2018) found that masking was a significant predictor of suicidality among autistic adults after controlling for additional factors (including anxiety and depression, employment status, etc). Their findings suggested that masking could explain suicidality independent of mental health, highlighting the unique risk that masking may pose to autistic suicidality.

Cassidy et al., (2019) followed up this work with an examination of the relationship between masking, autistic characteristics, and suicidal thoughts and behaviours among undergraduate students. Their findings showed that masking was associated with feelings of thwarted belonging amongst people with more autistic characteristics, and that this was in turn related to an increase in suicidal thoughts and behaviours. Importantly their findings highlight how the relationship between masking and suicidality may be seen more generally among marginalised populations who experience thwarted belonging due to stigmatised social status, supporting the notion that masking is a stigma driven impression management strategy.

The relationship between masking and suicidality has also been highlighted in qualitative studies, among autistic adults (Bradley et al., 2021; Miller et al., 2021) and autistic young people (Chapman et al., 2022). It has also been overwhelmingly highlighted in community accounts, for example Forbes, (2020) wrote:

> "The elimination of autistic behaviour encourages us to mask all our lives, it doesn't make us non autistic. The discouraging of autistic expression robs our non-speaking autistic kin of communication completely. It creates a narrative of shame, fear and panic that is passed down through bloodlines over generations, resulting in intergenerational trauma. It results in unidentified autistic people seeking respite and reprieve in the first thing that eases the pain, grief, trauma and isolation of the unspoken knowledge that we are unacceptable.

*Alcoholism, drug addiction, sex addiction, eating disorders, hoarding, anything that we are able to centre our focus on, anything that we can exercise the illusion of control over, all whilst slowly killing ourselves...*

*...It is a direct contribution to the higher rates of poor mental health outcomes, chronic long term illness and co-occurring conditions and the suicide rates amongst our community."*

Additionally, Rose, (2018)  published community responses from the 2018 #TakeTheMaskOff campaign organised by Rose and Molesworth, highlighting the impact of masking on suicidality:

*"I've been suicidal many times in my life and most times it's because I simply cannot cope with the way the world works (the layers of 'truths' and the sensory overload). This campaign has really made me question who I am without the 'good girl/ nice girl' mask, and I realise I don't know"*

These accounts and more also often highlight the complex relationship between suicidality and masking. Rose, (2018a, 2018b, 2018c) emphasises the relationship between masking, burnout and suicidality, stating that autistic suicidality may necessarily be a direct response to stigma, but also an indirect way to escape the crushing weight of burnout. Mantzalas et al., (2022) exploration of community accounts of burnout highlighted this link more broadly, with multiple examples of given of suicide being seen as a way to escape burnout, and not necessarily reflecting a wish to die.

These experiences truly underscore the importance of further research into the impact of masking on mental health, and the need to account for complex relationships between masking and potential negative outcomes.

# Self-Medication

There is currently very little academic exploration into the use of self-medication as a way to cope with masking. Livingston (2021) highlights the importance of more explicit research in this area given the link between masking and poor mental health outcomes, particularly in autistic people identified later in life. Weir et al., (2021) found that autistic people highlighted self-medication as a way to 'manage behaviours' (e.g. making them feel like they could socialise more easily). Relatedly, Levy (2022) found a relationship between substance use, autistic characteristics and social anxiety among college students. Taken together these findings suggest that masking via self-medication may be an indirect side effect, or unconsciously motivated by the apparent ease in socialising that arises during substance use.

Autistic participants in our 2021 study on masking (Miller et al., 2021) highlighted the use of alcohol as both a social lubricant, and a way to cope with masking. Additionally, Bowri et al., (2021) explored the relationship between masking, mental health and alcohol consumption. Though they found higher mean masking scores (measured via the CAT-Q) in people classed as 'hazardous' drinkers, they found no direct significant relationship between the two, which may have been related to the generally high masking scores across all groups.

Community accounts of self-medication offer an explicit link between masking and self-medication. Sykes, (2023) states:

> *"My drinking was, at that time, a confidence booster, a way to brave the world and calm my ragged nerves, and my tolerance for alcohol was high… Having a few drinks relaxed me, then adopting a devil-may-care attitude would descend, and more drinks would follow."*

Gray-Hammond (2023) has written extensively on substance use as a way to explore and 'try on' different aspects of identity, with an aim to assimilate into neurotypical culture. This 'normalising' motivation to engage in substance use is also highlighted by Flood (2023) and Rebarbar (2021) who have written about the use of substances to ease social anxiety among autistic people. The limited and mostly anecdotal evidence presented here suggests that much more research is needed to explore the relationship between self-medication and masking among autistic people.

# Masking and Safety

Though the impact of masking has been highlighted as overwhelmingly negative so far, it is important that we acknowledge masking as a way to try and stay safe, and avoid (further) trauma. Participants in Pearson et al., (2023) emphasised that masking was a survival strategy that arose as a result of experiencing trauma, and that it helped to keep them safe despite the debilitating impact that it had on their mental health. Likewise, autistic adults in a study by Bradley et al., (2021) outlined that masking provided them access to the social world, and allowed them to develop a way to cope and feel safe in a world that did not feel built for them. However, they also highlighted that this was 'surviving' rather than 'thriving', because it was driven by maintenance of safety and avoidance of negative outcomes (e.g. bullying and victimisation) rather than a contextual expression of self.

Though we will highlight the importance of recognising masking as a (necessary) tool for survival further in chapter 11, it should be noted that there are intersectional considerations that should be taken into account when examining masking as a way to stay safe. Black autistic scholars and activists have highlighted that unmasking is a privilege not afforded to members of the Black autistic community (Gulley & Hammond, 2022), due to the existing dangers around perceptions of the behaviour of Black people, and risk of brutality and death (Dababnah et al., 2022; Epstein et al., 2017; Hutson et al., 2022; Spence, 2020). Some Black parents of autistic children have discussed the use of behavioural interventions as a way to keep their children safe (Jeffrey-Wilensky, 2020). Though we do not endorse interventions such as ABA, we also acknowledge that our position here comes from a place of privilege, and that the argument surrounding behavioural intervention for safety is far more nuanced (Gulley & Hammond, 2022). Black autistic adults have emphasised the double bind of masking (Thornton, 2021; Ventour-Williams, 2022) and the importance of instead fostering a more understanding society, and dismantling racism (Gulley & Hammond, 2022) Black scholars (Lovelace et al., 2022) have also suggested that there are ways to keep young Black people safe whilst taking a neurodiversity-paradigm aligned, disability studies informed approach. Thus fostering as much safety as possible for Black autistic people whilst avoiding the additional trauma that can arise from social and behavioural intervention. It is essential that discussions around masking/unmasking recognise this nuance moving forward, and that we work to dismantle oppressive systems more broadly as opposed to simply working to encourage (white) autistic people to 'be themselves.

# Conclusion

In summary, this chapter has explored the impact of masking, with the current available literature suggesting that the impact of autistic masking is negative. In addition to contributing towards missed and misdiagnosis, masking can lead to poor mental health outcomes and higher risk of suicidality. Masking may also be related to substance use, however the research in this area is incredibly limited. Thus, though masking may serve to keep autistic people safe in a society which devalues difference, this can come at a significant cost.

# Chapter 11: Reframing and expanding the concept of masking

Throughout this book we have discussed the many overlapping yet disparate approaches to understanding masking, from the terminology used (e.g. masking, camouflaging, concealment, passing, adaptive morphing, self-monitoring, etc) to the underlying motivations (fitting in, stigma, the experience of trauma). Our aim for this chapter is to discuss the different components involved in masking, before moving on to introduce the concept of 'projecting acceptability' in order to expand prevailing narratives on who masking impacts.

## Understanding the Current Narrative

Masking research has generally been predicated on the assumption that masking involves a suppression of self and identity, in order to navigate and 'fit in' in a predominantly non-autistic society. However, much of the narrative so far has focussed on the idea that autistic people want to be *liked* by neurotypical people, rather than be *accepted by* neurotypical people for who they are. This likely relates to an enduring emphasis on the importance of neurotypical expectations, and the assumption that being neurotypical is both desirable and the 'correct' way to exist. Autistic people, given the choice, would rather not have to fundamentally change who they are (Chapman et al, 2022) in order to be accepted.

Whilst early masking research led to a narrative predominantly framed around gender differences in autistic presentation, more recent contributions have recognised how masking aligns with previously theorised social impression management and self-monitoring strategies used across the general population (i.e. these are not neurodivergent specific strategies, though aspects *may* be specific to particular groups). These contributions situate masking as arising out of a dynamic interaction between person and context, aligning with an enactivist approach to development. Some research has prioritised understanding the strategies involved in masking, and operationalising them to gain further insight into their underlying cognitive components, and impact (Hull et al., 2017; Livingston et al., 2020), whilst other research has focussed on integrating what we know about masking within existing conceptual and theoretical frameworks to develop a clearer picture of the foundations, motivations, involved factors, and consequences (Ai et al., 2022; Lawson, 2020; Pearson & Rose, 2021). Taken together, this research positions masking as a complex phenomenon composed of many aspects (see Figure 11.1), that develops as a response to misaligned external social demands, and the experience of stigma and the associated marginalisation and trauma that it perpetuates.

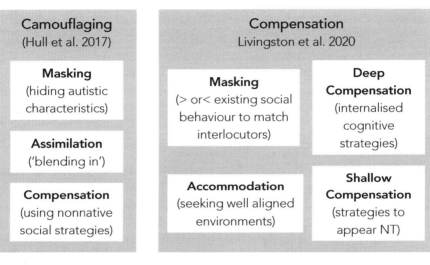

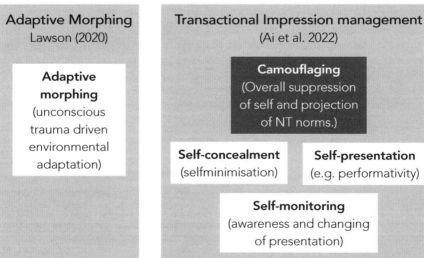

**Figure 11.1:** Current conceptualisations of masking described in the literature to date

Both Radulski's (2022) work on understanding autistic masking as a response to being positioned as a neurominority and Ai's work on transactional impression management explore the concept of social prediction. Radulski's work focuses more upon the societal level, drawing upon Butler's work on performativity to explore how masking involves the performance of a constructed self, based on perceptions of societal norms and accepted modes of being (i.e. neurotypicality). Ai's work focuses in on the individual level, examining the concept of self-presentation and how this may relate to the attempt to gauge what our interlocutor is expecting, and present ourselves accordingly. Here the broader concept of masking transgresses the notion that autistic people are socially unmotivated and 'mindblind' (Baron-Cohen, 1997; Chevallier et al., 2012) and instead explores the suggestion that autistic people actively engage in attempting to figure out what is socially acceptable to (non-autistic) others, and expressing that in order to increase positive social judgements, and reduce negative ones. Ai's work in particular posits that impression management among autistic people may be impacted by the DEP/DMH. Here, masking/IM can be understood via the need to figure out the expectations of a dissimilar other (here a non-autistic person). Ai et al. outline how neurotypical people appear to be able to compute IM in a fairly effortless and automatic way, responding reflexively to the needs of the context. Autistic people may find this slower, due to a higher degree of uncertainty about the expectations of their social partner. Given our discussions in chapter 4 surrounding autistic differences in movement and expression it is unsurprising that misalignment occurs between autistic and non-autistic people. However, autistic people also have the disadvantage of being in the minority. Small misalignments between non-autistic people may be swiftly traversed due to an overall increase in similarity in communicative style (e.g. higher resonance between communicative partners). However this is not the case for autistic people, for whom resonance is reduced. This leaves autistic people in the position of not just suppressing aspects of self, or managing what people can see, but attempting to work out what both society, and individuals within that society expect of them in order to stay safe.

## Projecting acceptability

In this section, we are going to outline the concept of the 'projection of acceptability', developed by Rose (2023). The projection of acceptability is a self-presentation tool grounded in attempting to understand the expectations of others, and how autistic people, in order to avoid being further stigmatised, may unconsciously and consciously play into those expectations. We avoid use of the word strategy here to emphasise that this is not always a conscious choice. Projecting acceptability can be understood as both the integration of impression management, *and* as a response to stigma and trauma, which result in the development of a projection of self that is designed to meet the expectations of external observers and foster acceptance. For some autistic people the projection of acceptability may include an attempt to appear 'more neurotypical' or to 'pass' as non-autistic, however projecting acceptability may also include attempts to appear 'more Autistic', or presenting an infinite mix of characteristics to the world around us that seek to sooth the confirmation bias of others and give them what they expect to see. Broadening the concept of masking to explore the projection of acceptability takes us beyond the limited and somewhat superficial suggestion that masking is **only** about concealment and 'fitting in' and allows us to incorporate the intersectional experiences of being autistic with other aspects of identity across a far greater spectrum of experience.

As has been established in earlier chapters, much of the emerging masking narrative to date has been framed around the concept that not only is masking about an autistic person's desire to 'fit in' or pass as neurotypical, but that those 'desires' are enacted through conscious choices on multiple levels, for instance mimicking the facial expressions of others, or forcing oneself to make eye contact. There are certainly conscious decisions involved within some aspects of masking (e.g. see Ai's model of transactional impression management), however the underlying motivation to mask can be driven by (as Snyder outlined in 1987) conscious attempts to engagement in voluntary strategic or value expressive IM, *and* the avoidance of harm which may develop via explicit (i.e. conscious) and implicit (i.e. unconscious) means. The latter may involve the internalising of outside social judgements, which then shapes behaviour without the individual being explicitly aware. This is what we referred to in our conceptual paper as the 'illusion of choice' - masking may feel like a choice, but when it also feels like the only way to survive, or stay safe, there isn't much of a choice at all.

The projection of acceptability draws upon these factors to help us understand how the perceptions of others shape everyone's behaviour, and that this does not always mean hiding or suppression, but may also involve actively attempting to meet the expectations of others, or *performing* an identity. Radulski's discussion of 'visible invisibility' is relevant to understanding this concept. Though autistic people are often considered to have an invisible disability, Radulski argues that our differences render us visible, whether it is named (i.e. recognised as autism) or not. As has been described throughout earlier chapters, much of the masking narrative is framed around the misperceptions of others, the lenses they view autistic people through, and the assumptions they make as a result of those perceptions. This has led to the development of a sense of confirmation bias about what autism 'looks like', with the limited stereotypes we have about autistic people (i.e. white, and male) and the diagnostic disparities that arise as a result of these stereotypes creating a feedback loop where we expect autistic people to look a certain way, and when they do indeed look like that we congratulate ourselves on recognising it.

The concept of projecting acceptability is also centered on confirmation bias, however in this case it is about meeting the biases and expectations of others, e.g. monitoring self-presentation and presenting oneself accordingly. Whereas this may sometimes be conceptualised through wanting to manage and curate a positive impression of ourselves in interactions with others, wider community accounts of masking suggest that positive self-presentation is not always necessarily the aim.

For some autistic people masking may mean a combination of matching or mirroring other people's behaviours, fawning, and suppressing certain aspects of their sensory, physical, or emotional being. For others it may mean filling social niches, and developing social personalities (e.g. being the 'class clown', Rowland, 2020). However, one lesser considered aspect of masking is the exaggeration of aspects of identity, which may include attempting to appear 'more Autistic', or develop 'challenging behaviours' in order to give others what is expected of them. Due to this 'the projection of acceptability' incorporates a much larger range of behaviours that might not previously have been considered under the masking narrative, and recognises that masking is primarily about protecting oneself, by giving others what they want and expect to see, which will differ for each person depending on how aspects of their identity intersect.

## Safety in predictability

Prediction is important for all humans (Bervoets et al., 2021). It allows us to incorporate past experiences, understand what might happen to us in given contexts, allows us to think critically about situations, and can help us to reduce anxiety (Stark et al., 2021a).

As autistic people, we (unconsciously and consciously) learn that in order to try and avoid being excluded, marginalised, invalidated and ill-treated, we have to be 'acceptable' to external others. Whilst all people may draw upon the lens of the generalised other in order to engage in self-monitoring, the risk of being misinterpreted, and the consequences that come along with that, will vary based on identity features (such as race, gender, etc). Thus for marginalised people the risk in 'getting it wrong' is higher, which can lead to heightened anxiety (Spaeth & Pearson, 2021). The attempt to 'get it right' can be complicated by the complexity of social context, which may show incredible variation. For people who inhabit the majority, they may navigate these contexts with the (implicit) knowledge that for the most part, they will be able to draw upon their own embodied experiences to satisfy the social expectations of others. However, for autistic people (and other marginalised individuals) this variation might be driven by the need to minimise harm and a need to stay safe. This might include looking for what people expect of us, anticipating how we might be treated, or attempting to make sure the other person feels safe and comfortable in their experience of us. Often comfort for the observer comes in the form of autistic people being more predictable for them in whatever form this may take (e.g. based on prior interactions with other autistic people, having read about autistic people, etc). This in turn can also help make other people's behaviour predictable to us.

The greater need for predictability among autistic people has long been framed as an intolerance of uncertainty (Jenkinson et al., 2020). However, more recent work has begun to explore the response to uncertainty through the lens of predictive coding (similar to Ai's work on impression management). Stark et al. (2021) highlight how cognitive style among autistic people may impact on making social predictions about the non-autistic social world (attenuated priors), leading to increased anxiety over unpredictable outcomes. They propose that attenuated priors interact with environmental factors (e.g. stigma and associated negative outcomes) to lead to heightened anxiety among autistic people. Whilst this model presents a less neuronormative approach to understanding autistic drive to establish predictability, concerns have been expressed over maintenance of the term 'intolerance of uncertainty' due to the implied irrationality of the distress response (Bervoets et al. 2021). Indeed, Stark and colleagues acknowledge that the term is not ideal and may require re-naming or re-framing in order to proceed with a more constructive approach, suggesting the term 'uncertainty attunement' may be more appropriate (Stark et al., 2021b).

We suggest that this reframing from intolerance of uncertainty to uncertainty attunement may be more easily conceptualised for a broader audience through the notion of 'safety in predictability'. Stark and colleagues highlight how attenuated uncertainty among autistic people can currently be explained via multiple pathways, e.g. difficulty predicting the world based upon prior experience and a reliance on bottom up sensory information (Pellicano & Burr, 2012), or through difficulty in estimating the precision of predictions (Friston et al., 2013) which may align with a double empathy perspective, in that autistic-non-autistic interactions are inherently more ambiguous due to mutual misalignments).

With relation to projecting acceptability, the concept of safety in predictability can help us to understand why it is sometimes safer to expect to be perceived negatively (and treated accordingly), than it is to be unsure as to how we will be treated, and risk a potentially worse outcome. Here the emphasis is not on 'acceptability' by way of normative standards, but acceptability with regards to the individual bias of the observer. As autistic people experience a higher degree of uncertainty within social interactions due to the DEP, impression management may be impacted by uncertainty attunement, leading some autistic people to look for the quickest (and thus most energy efficient) route. Importantly, Stark et al. (2021) highlight that uncertainty attunement (and associated ways of responding) may include an unconscious element ("mental processes that operate below the level of subjective awareness").

Evidence for the projection of acceptability can currently be seen in community discussions of masking, even when those participating do not recognise that this is what they are discussing, because the framework of masking they associate with is limited to masking being about 'fitting in' and 'appearing more neurotypical', or other limited conceptualisations. Rose (2020) describes an interaction with a client who denied engaging in masking, but described their social approach as polishing "my 'not normal' till it shone; and showed it off." Their discussion of disclosure highlighted a need to manage the expectations and responses of others, making it seem safer to exaggerate being autistic. Their comments aligned with the double bind outlined by Botha et al., (2022) whereby disclosing and exaggerating their behaviour would lead others to believe that they were 'different', but not disclosing would lead to the same response, with additional feelings of exclusion. These comments have been echoed by participants in our research on autistic identity (currently unpublished), where participants have described assessing who external others expect them to be, and then presenting this to them.

Our current understanding of masking as purely suppressive may risk excluding autistic people who cannot see themselves in that description, and thus also lead to the misconception that only certain autistic people can mask. These misconceptions have already started to emerge in community discussions, with the use of the term 'high masking' entering vocabulary and creating implicit arbitrary distinctions between people who are aware that they mask and people who are not aware. Whilst recognition of one's own masking behaviour can be important for reducing distress and fostering more positive individual outcomes, masking is, as we have highlighted, not always a conscious decision. The focus on masking as a conscious (and also somewhat binary) behaviour may unintentionally exclude people who do not fit with popular notions of what masking might look like. Part of this connects with the notion of functioning - assumptions that 'high masking' is a skill of those who are 'high functioning'. The use of functioning labels, and binary demarcations to explain the facets of being autistic provide no meaningful insight into the multifaceted and complex lives of autistic people. The use of 'high masking' to describe the perceived ability to 'fit in' with neuronormative expectations aligns itself with a societal assertion that someone who appears to 'function' is a 'better' contributor to society. Those labelled as low functioning, or low in 'masking' are deemed as low value, drains on society rather than contributors, being seen as a burden emotionally and financially on families and society at large (Baggs, 2020). Importantly, with specific regards to masking and IM, assumptions about who can mask mean that the development of supportive strategies and attempts at ameliorating poor outcomes are limited to one particular group of people. Thus they will not be suitable for those who do not meet stereotypical expectations of 'masking', and as such, replicate oppressive structures that exist with regards to autistic presentation.

Overall, both the diagnostic criteria for autism and the societal understanding of autism is limited, and our current understanding of what autism 'looks like' relies both upon stereotype and emerging knowledge about IM. Researchers have attempted to address these issues by proposing the introduction of phenotypes/subtypes, keeping the core construct of autism intact. However, these divides are based on the assumption that the core construct is actually correct in the first place, and worth preserving. Rather than subtyping autistic people based on arbitrary notions of societal functionality, broadening the concept of masking makes it a more inclusive paradigm that recognises that even though a group is subject to similar ill-treatment and even though responses within that group can be very similar, there are enough differences among members of that group to mean that while responding in very similar ways, not all members will respond identically.

## Expanding our notions of masking

As discussed in previous chapters, perceptions of masking as a barrier to recognition of autistic people among professionals has led to somewhat of a misconception that people who are more 'obviously' autistic (i.e. autistic people who are non-speaking or have a learning disability) do not have the capacity to mask. This is reinforced by the lack of research to date in this area (Petrolini et al., 2023). This is a dangerous narrative to develop, as it a) can lead to further dehumanisation via the demarcation of autistic people, and b) the exclusion of non-speaking autistic people and those with learning disabilities in future research that aims to prevent the negative impact of masking.

To address the first point, impression management is viewed as a universal human response to navigating the social world (Goffman, 1959; Snyder, 1987). Exploring autistic masking through a developmental lens that integrates knowledge of trauma allows us to broaden our understanding of who engages in masking and how, then it logically follows that all autistic people will mask to some degree. If we assume that autistic masking is a response to forms of autistic invalidation, uncertainty, pathologisation and stigma alongside the broader notion of general transactional impression management. Here different aspects of IM can be teased out, to examine those which impact all humans in the form of context switching, self-monitoring and self-presentation; and which are more specific to marginalised groups as a response to stigma and trauma. The notion that only particular types of autistic people engage in IM reinforces stigma towards non-speaking autistic people and autistic people with learning disabilities, implicitly suggesting that they are lacking another aspect of 'human' behaviour. It is also inconsistent with the knowledge that non-speaking autistic people and autistic people with learning disabilities are more likely to be enrolled in compliance based social interventions, which actively focus on developing neurotypical modes of communication. If we reduce masking to successful (or partially successful) 'passing' as neurotypical we risk creating a narrow definition of what masking is, and suggest that those who may be more 'visibly' autistic are incapable of masking, which is not the case. With regards to the second point, there is a growing body of research (as discussed in the previous chapter) to suggest that masking can lead to negative outcomes for autistic people. Emancipation from pressures to appear 'normal', and amelioration of poor outcomes needs to include *all* autistic people, not just those who have been most vocal about masking so far. Much more research is needed to explore IM, and related experiences among non-speaking autistic people, and autistic people with learning disabilities.

## Disentangling masking from impression management (IM)

The research reviewed throughout this book (both autism specific, such as that of Ai et al. 2022, and the broader literature on identity management) suggests that impression management is much broader than masking (or camouflaging, if one considers masking to be one component of this model). Here the role of context might be an important factor in understanding where autistic masking sits within a broader model of impression management. For non-autistic (and other non-stigmatised people) the managing of identity and impression appears to be based around the expression of different aspects of self, in a way that is most relevant to that context, e.g. wanting to make a good impression at work through being your best 'professional self'. However with stigma-driven IM, inauthenticity seems to be a core issue (See Figure 11.2), whereby there is a suppression of authentic self, or projection of inauthentic self, rather than a highlighting or softening of contextually less relevant aspects of identity. The latter may allow someone to feel like they are still expressing themselves more authentically as different aspects of self eb and flow, whereas the former creates disjunction.

The possibility that general IM works by highlighting or softening different aspects of self supports the notion that what is considered 'the self' is actually composed of multiple selves, each holding different relevances for specific contexts and interlocutors, but each reflecting some authentic aspect of the holder. Though autistic people are also likely to have multiple selves, there is currently very little understanding of how non-stigma driven context switching looks and works among autistic people. It is possible that some autistic people may describe context switching in a way that differs from the concept of 'masking', however it is also possible that growing up as a stigmatised person 'infects' general impression management, and makes it difficult to see where general context-switching ends, and inauthenticity begins. Much more research is needed on autistic identity and impression management in future in order to explore this issue.

## Operationalising 'masking'

So far in this chapter we have discussed the expansion of the notion of masking to include projecting an 'acceptable' self-presentation, and the recognition that masking may occur among all autistic people, not just those who are explicitly aware, or can report their experiences fluently. In this section we will outline some of the various ways in which masking may present, in order to develop a more complex picture of areas that have been explored (and have significant empirical evidence), and areas we may want to explore in future. Instead of breaking these down into areas traditionally defined in research (e.g. masking, assimilation, as already outlined in Ai at al. 2022), we discuss the specific (conscious and unconscious) strategies acknowledging that some aspects might span various proposed conceptual variables. We have split some of these into domains (e.g. linguistic) but it is worth noting that there is significant overlap in motivation and purpose, making it difficult to truly separate any of these out.

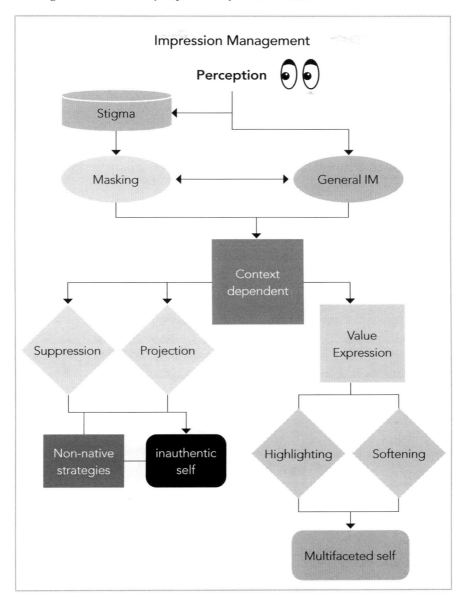

**Figure 11.2:** Model displaying the differential pathways that traditional impression management and masking may follow

As we discussed earlier in this chapter, some aspects of masking relate specifically to a drive to project an acceptable persona to others to avoid negative social judgements, or physical and emotional harm. Some autistic people may suppress, exaggerate or construct situational personalities in order to meet the expectations of those they are interacting with. One aspect of projecting acceptability that is beginning to emerge in the empirical literature is the concept of 'fawning', whereby autistic people may engage in people-pleasing in order to try and stay safe. This may include saying yes when you want to say no (e.g. to sex, to doing someone a favour), telling people what you think they want to hear, or taking on more than you can cope with. Fawning may also lead to taking the blame for something you didn't do (Chandler et al., 2019) which puts autistic people who encounter the criminal justice system particularly at risk of false confession and coercion.

Masking may also include engaging in gender performativity (alongside other aspects of identity performativity), such as embodying expected gender roles (e.g. binary expectations of feminine or masculine) through physical expression (e.g. clothing, makeup) and interests (e.g. football, pop music). As discussed throughout this book, having traditionally 'normative' interests is not necessarily an indicator of masking, as autistic people have interests that vary as much as other people, but autistic people have expressed trying to align their interests with those of their peers in order to 'fit in'. This may also provide autistic people with the means to enter a social group, particularly subcultures which occupy a particular social niche (e.g. fandoms, football).

Relatedly, some autistic people may engage in forms of behavioural mirroring, including mirroring the movements and behaviour of others, which may include attempts to change one's own natural body posture, use of gesture, and mirroring those of interlocutors. This may also extend into emotional mirroring, whereby some autistic people describe the feeling of being an 'emotional sponge', and reflecting back the emotional experiences of others.

## Linguistic

Linguistic aspects of masking and IM may involve traditional forms of scripting typically used by autistic (and other neurodivergent people) in order to minimise uncertain outcomes and negative social judgements in conversations with others (Hull et al., 2017). Autistic people have reported scripting topics of conversation (e.g. music) and rehearsing potential interactions in order to minimise perceptions of awkwardness or social misalignment. Autistic people display differential markers of rapport when interacting with other autistic people (e.g. lower eye gaze frequency, reduced verbal back-channelling) compared to when they are interacting with non-autistic people (Rifai et al., 2022), suggesting that autistic people are aware of the norms used in non-autistic communication and attempt to align with these in cross-neurotype interactions. This can also be seen in the syntactic alignment that autistic people display in both scripted and naturalistic conversations with others (Hopkins et al., 2016). These findings align with those of Williams et al., (2021) who found that conversational dyads between autistic strangers showed increased rapport, flow, and intersubjective attunement compared to autistic and non-autistic stranger interlocutor dyads, and autistic-familar non-autistic interlocutor dyads.

Boorse et al., (2019) suggest that autistic girls may engage in linguistic masking relative to autistic boys from an early age, demonstrating a unique linguistic style that is fully aligned with neither autistic boys or non-autistic girls, through the utilisation of both cognitive process words (e.g. 'think') and nouns. However, more research is needed to explore explicit linguistic masking in adulthood, and whether these differences may be primarily related to sex/gender differences.

In addition to the content of speech, autistic people may also attempt to change the pitch and tone of their voice (e.g. to appear less monotone), or may mimic the accents of others (Hull et al., 2017). Community accounts of masking have also highlighted several aspects of linguistic masking yet to be formally explored in the literature, including playing for time through vocal strategies (e.g. repeating the question back to the interlocutor while thinking, or using filler words to give yourself time to process the question and form a response), and directed hyperlexia, or the use of advanced language skills (Solazzo et al., 2021) in order to project a neurotypical conceptualisation of social competence. Alternatively, some autistic people may avoid speaking, and stay quiet, being labelled as 'shy'.

## Suppression

The act of suppressing aspects of self has been reported as one of the core aspects of masking across a range of different domains. This can include the suppression of emotional responses (e.g. not crying when upset, not showing joy) and sensory (e.g. overwhelm and dysregulation) for fear of being mocked or invalidated, as we outline in chapter 8. However suppression of emotions and sensory responses may also be internalised, leading to a disconnection from recognising these as a source of anxiety and distress (Fulton et al., 2020; Pearson & Rose, 2021). Suppression may also involve the preventing or redirecting of physical responses such as stimming, suppressing the stim entirely (Miller et al., 2021), or stimming in a more subtle manner that may be less noticeable to others.

As outlined throughout the book, suppression may also directly relate to the expression of personal identity and values, such as hiding passionate interests and avoiding sharing personal information about oneself with others. This may interact with identity projection, by which core identity is suppressed and a more acceptable sense of self projected to outsiders. This suppression may also function as a form of self-regulation, through which autistic people minimise their engagement in a promotion mindset (e.g. seeking their own ideals and desires) and instead engage in a prevention mindset (trying to appease the desires, expectations and needs of others to minimise harm).

## Cognitive

Though we find the term compensation somewhat unhelpful with regards to reinforcing neuronormative modes of being, more research is needed into the use of non-native cognitive strategies among autistic people. Whilst research on compensation does suggest that some people utilise strategies that lead to similar outcomes to non-autistic people, it is currently unclear as to whether this is due to general heterogeneity within the autistic population, or the internalisation of different strategies from prolonged and practised use. The shift towards conceptualising autistic cognition in and of itself, as opposed to comparatively, before examining differences between autistic people, and across autistic and non-autistic people would provide insight into this issue.

Developing a knowledgeable approach to understanding masking/IM among autistic people would benefit professionals across a range of areas, in addition to academics who seek to understand masking as a phenomenon. Indeed, the overall aim of such research is to understand how to better support autistic people across the lifespan, and foster the potential for autistic people to thrive, however that looks for them personally (Chapman & Carel, 2022). By understanding that masking may be motivated by various external pressures, manifest in a range of different ways, and is context-driven, professionals can be mindful of factors that might contribute to masking, the way it may look, and what can be done to support people. In the next chapter we explore how to safely support authenticity, whilst acknowledging that this is not always possible due to societal harms.

# Conclusion

In this chapter we have explored different aspects of masking and impression management that autistic people may engage in in order to avoid harm and make more positive social impressions. We outlined the concept of 'projecting acceptability', to highlight that masking is not always suppressive, but may involve the projection of a range of characteristics and behaviours in order to meet the expectations of others. Finally, we explored some of the different ways in which autistic people may engage in masking.

# Chapter 12: How to safely foster authenticity

Throughout this book we have discussed how masking can arise out of a need for self-protection, and to avoid stigma and the harm that comes with it. However, as outlined in chapter 10, the impact of masking (as opposed to general impression management) appears to be overwhelmingly negative. Whilst the solution to this may appear straightforward ('taking off the mask'), the relationship between masking and safety makes it anything but. In this chapter we will discuss whether and how it is possible to (safely) foster authenticity for autistic people, taking an intersectional approach that acknowledges that what may be safe for one group of people, may not be safe for another.

## Recognising masking

The understanding of masking as a series of conscious behaviours and choices, centred around notions of autistic people striving to be less autistic and to 'fit in' has in turn led to the idea that if the mask can simply be 'put on', it can also be removed relatively simply. The phrases 'dropping the mask', 'taking off the mask', and 'unmasking' have become common across autistic spaces on social media, and recently we have even seen the emergence of 'autism coaches' who state that they are able to instruct and teach autistic people how to stop masking. Much of this focus has been grounded in the findings from research, which has taken a component approach to masking (Hull et al., 2017) and revealed some of the factors involved (e.g. mimicry of others' facial expressions, or suppression of stims). Here some strategies for masking appeared to be under more conscious control and well-rehearsed, with people aware, or becoming aware, that they were engaging in these behaviours, suggesting that they can also be 'stopped'. Additionally, recent research has suggested that autistic people may be able to retrospectively identify aspects of their own masking when watching clips of their own interactions (see Cook et al., 2021, 2022). This suggests that there may be some additional facets of masking that, even if they are less consciously driven in the moment, may be possible to identify (and therefore moderate) afterwards.

Throughout this book we have discussed some of the underlying factors that can contribute towards masking among autistic people. From childhood, autistic people experience explicit (e.g. bullying) and implicit (e.g. microaggressions) stigmatisation that reflects a generalised attitude that their embodied identity is spoiled and in some way 'other'. Masking is shaped by this experience, with even the more conscious aspects of masking that is used to avoid this stigma or to build social relationships with others, underpinned by the notion that the way that the person exists in the world is wrong or will lead to rejection. Autistic people often experience a traumatic developmental trajectory, with some experiences of invalidation (across a range of domains), so normalised that it is difficult to recognise it as trauma. Masking may become the default response in order to try and gain/maintain some semblance of safety (in whatever form that takes, as we discuss in chapter 11). However as we outline earlier in this book (and in Pearson & Rose, 2021) it would be a misnomer to say that this is a choice. Some aspects of masking may begin under more conscious control (e.g. making eye contact after being repeatedly accused of not listening, or being told that it is rude) but become automatic over time, however others may simply emerge as an attempt to stay safe (e.g. reducing more visible stims) with little active reflection on their development or use.

Though masking is arguably complex, the primary reasons given for masking so far in both the literature (e.g. Chapman et al., 2022; Hull et al., 2017; Miller et al., 2021; Pearson et al., 2023) and across community discussions have centred on safety, avoiding negative social judgements, and building connections with others (with the latter two overlapping with general impression management). Masking can be protective, or provide access to otherwise inaccessible spaces. It keeps people safe from harm, intersects with multiple aspects of identity and allows people to navigate different social situations, responding to contextual cues. Discussions of masking and unmasking can lose nuance when we conflate the impact of masking with masking itself, deciding that masking is 'bad' when it is the *need* for masking that is the problem (Gulley & Hammond, 2022). It is somewhat hubristic to encourage autistic people to unmask when society does not make it safe to do so and can lead to (unintentionally) victim-blaming autistic people for the negative impact that masking has on them, making them responsible for the way society treats them and the impact this has. The encouragement to unmask can also lead to pressure for autistic people to act in a more 'visibly autistic' manner, which again may not necessarily represent authenticity but a projection of acceptability (Adkin, 2023).

A related problem with the onus on autistic people to unmask is that the notion of unmasking is embedded in privilege. The intersectional nature of being autistic means that it *may* be safer for certain autistic people (e.g. a white autistic woman) to identify and change these behaviours than it is for others (e.g. a black autistic woman). As we discussed in chapters 5 and 7, many autistic people experience stigma across multiple intersecting aspects of their identities, with masking (and associated stigma avoidance strategies such as code switching) functioning as a way to keep them safe. Thus, for many autistic people it is not safe to simply 'unmask' for a variety of reasons. Making it safe for autistic people to unmask means dismantling other oppressive structures that harm autistic people, such as white supremacy and racism (Gulley & Hammond, 2022), transphobia, homophobia. Though masking might be considered an individualistic approach to stigma – in that it involves an individual modifying how they appear – a focus on the individual as a means to reduce stigma (and the need for masking) itself often relies upon assimilation into the dominant group (which may be more viable for cis-hetero, white autistic people), as opposed to emancipation and justice (which would benefit all autistic people).

Thus, given that autistic people (as the stigmatised group) do not generally hold the power to shape the narrative, it is important when discussing how to foster authenticity that we take into account a) how safe this may be, and b) the agency that an individual has within the different levels of power. In the following sections we will discuss factors that *may* be within the power of an individual, factors which are unlikely to be within the power of an individual, including systemic factors.

# Fostering Authenticity

In order to provide space for autistic people to live authentically, we need to consider what can be done beyond the responsibility of the individual. As we have acknowledged, autistic people (and marginalised people more broadly) have limited power to shape the narrative, and thus to lead to social and cultural changes needed to safely foster authenticity. Here the hunt for authenticity may be best understood through an ecological systems approach (Bronfenbrenner, 1977), which importantly takes into account wider systemic and intersectional issues that may impact on an individual in addition to more interpersonal and local factors (see Figure 12.1). Relatedly, an ecological approach can help us to shift away from a narrative of independent responsibility to a broader understanding of the importance of interdependence. Though neoliberal framings of worth often focus on self-reliance and independence, nobody is solely reliant on themselves and our identities and self-understanding are shaped by systems much broader than the individual. Thus, consideration of factors across multiple levels can help us to understand how the responsibility for authenticity (and safety to express it) cannot be attributed to the individual alone.

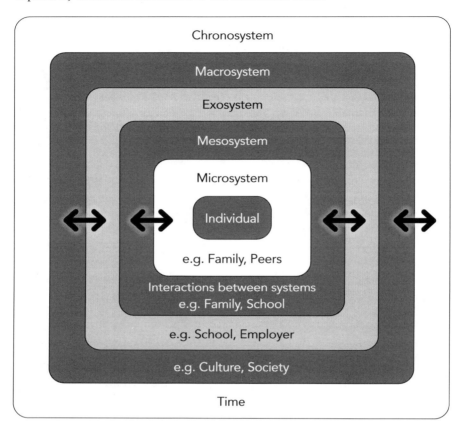

**Figure 12.1:** An ecological systems representation of masking

## Things somewhat within an individual's power to control (privilege dependent)

The idea of unmasking suggests that the mask, and the ability to take it off, exist as a tangible thing. We do not of course mean literally, but that the idea of taking off the mask situates 'the mask' as a singular and somewhat integrated entity that can be 'removed', rather than a collection of conscious and unconscious features across a variety of domains and aspects of identity. We suggest here that developing a sense of authenticity is instead reliant upon further development of self-insight and self-understanding.

That is not to suggest that masking is always predicated upon a lack of self-understanding, but community reflections, particularly from late-identified people, have emphasised the importance of self-understanding in becoming aware of masking, and attempts to mitigate its impact through developing agency and insight into one's own needs.

As we discussed in chapter 4, research into the impact of late diagnosis has highlighted the reprocessing and revision of autobiographical narrative in light of new information about the self (Lilley et al., 2022). Becoming personally aware of masking can have a similar impact (Hull et al., 2017; Miller et al., 2021), with people experiencing distress about the nature of their own identity and who they really are. Unpacking and processing the how, why and where of masking can itself be incredibly traumatic for people who were not aware that what they were doing differed to the general impression-management strategies used by other people, and for late identified people this often occurs in parallel to reprocessing their autobiographical narrative. Additionally, it may also include the need to process the experience of trauma itself; autistic people have spoken about making sense of their own experiences, gaining the appropriate language to describe and glean meaning from what has happened to them throughout their lives (hermeneutical justice, Fricker, 2007).This can be an arduous process, and again may be incredibly distressing as people recognise that the harm and invalidation that they have experienced is not universal, and has led to an injured sense of self. It takes time for people to work through their experiences, learning about themselves and thinking about how to apply this knowledge in future.

The process of developing one's authentic self also requires recognition of autistic ways of being, including gaining insight into sensory and social needs. Building up this understanding can help autistic people to understand when a particular stimulus or situation is stressful, and how to develop coping strategies that do not rely on response suppression. Recognition of one's own needs can also help autistic people to start to ameliorate the impact of internalised ableism and the self-blame that can arise as a result (e.g. 'everyone else seems to be able to do this, so I'll just force myself'). Whilst these factors can help to foster a sense of comfort in expressing (or at least recognising) one's authentic self, it can also reduce the impact of related variables that interact with masking and contribute towards poor mental health (e.g. increased sensory overload and the stress that can accumulate from a perceived inability to escape it).

The latter is particularly important for autistic people who are experiencing/ attempting to recover from (both short and long-term) autistic burnout.

Participants in Raymaker et al., (2020) highlighted the importance of being able to reduce the demand of masking in order to recover physically and mentally. Masking may place a particularly high demand on cognitive resources (Hull et al., 2020), which appears to be significantly depleted during burnout, manifesting in a loss of functional skill that can be difficult to recover (Higgins et al., 2021; Raymaker et al., 2020). Thus, the ability to be authentic can aid recovery, though it is important to note that – alongside other aspects of individual action – this may be more or less viable based on a variety of factors. For example, young people may lack the opportunity to learn about themselves (Riccio et al., 2021), or have less avoidable external pressures such as school (Chapman et al., 2022) which may make it difficult to express authenticity whilst staying safe.

Here it may be important to ensure that people know that masking can be used as a tool, much like general impression management. Becoming aware of one's own inauthenticity and ability to express this when 'necessary' can provide a sense of agency and control to the person masking. This in turn can help them to learn to acknowledge their own identity and where masking is situated in relation to that, giving a more empowering approach. It may not always be safe or viable for someone to be their true selves, but having an awareness to recognise that and not dissociate from it can, in itself, allow an individual to feel more in control, despite not being able to change society (we will address this in more detail in the following sections). Here we are not providing an excuse for professionals and systems to disengage with the changes *they* need to make for it to be safer for autistic people (which we discuss later in this chapter). The use of masking as a tool to navigate different contexts safely, does not negate the need for these contexts to become more generally accessible to autistic people.

Finally it can be important for autistic people to learn where their boundaries lie, and how to assert them when developing the ability to safely express authenticity. Many autistic people experience heightened compliance and fawning as a response to having grown up in environments where their boundaries were either not respected, or it was not safe to assert them (Montgomery, 2021; Zimmerman, 2022). As such, the development of self-insight and the expression of a more authentic self may also include learning about boundaries (e.g. when to say no), and how to use these in order to ensure that needs are met (e.g. telling others about the impact of particular environments on your social energy and your need to leave, as opposed to suppressing the distress they cause, resulting in extreme exhaustion).

The assertion of boundaries may also relate to recognising your 'safety bubble', that is, knowing your needs within a particular context and what adjustments might be needed in order to cope. For example, you may be able to spend more time out with friends in a bar if you take noise-reducing earplugs or are able to choose a venue that is smaller and quieter. The ability to apply this knowledge is based on self-insight, and the amount of privilege you have to control particular aspects of your environment. For example, an autistic person who is able to work at home may be able to retain more energy than someone who goes to work in an office, but the person working in the office may be able to increase their bubble at work through personal (e.g. noise-cancelling headphones) and environmental (e.g. a single office) adjustments.

## Validating spaces

Many of the issues that we have discussed here relate to the key objectives, defined as 'the Four A's, outlined in Rose's Advoc8 framework (see Table 12.1): acceptance, agency, autonomy and authenticity. Though these objectives do not relate *specifically* to masking (that is, they are broadly applicable as a means to encourage flourishing among autistic people), masking is one of the key areas that they are applied to in order to explore how to support a positive sense of autistic identity. These objectives are also inherently intertwined and the relationship between them can be multi-directional in nature (e.g. recognising aspects of your authentic self may increase agency through opening up new coping strategies and knowledge about your own needs).

| Key objectives (The Four A's) | Descriptions |
|---|---|
| Acceptance | To accept oneself internally by understanding one's own needs; and to be accepted externally, by others. |
| Agency | Understanding oneself and being understood by others offers the opportunity for choice and the ability to make meaningful decisions around ones wants and needs |
| Autonomy | Making choices requires the ability to act on them. Autonomy means to be enabled and supported to act on those choices, either independently, or interdependently with support. |
| Authenticity | The enablement of agency and autonomy leads to feeling in more control of oneself and one's environment, creating a feeling of greater safety which offers the opportunity for authenticity to develop.  ➔ |

| The eight pillars | Descriptions |
|---|---|
| Understanding the societal & historical narrative | Using constructive & positive sources of knowledge to understand the context within which autistic people are framed. This provides the opportunity for greater understanding and the validation of the experiences of autistic people beyond a pathological lens. It also helps understand and remedy the lack of intersectional recognition. It provides an opportunity for decolonisation. |
| The Neurodiversity Paradigm | Provides a humanising and intersectional framework that focuses on individual needs and provides context for shared experiences, rather than focusing on a deficit model which suggests there is a 'perfect person'. This offers the opportunity for services and systems to be flexible and responsive to need rather than a 'one size fits all' approach. |
| Utilising Double Empathy | A Double Empathy approach forces us to reflect on the inequality in how people are treated and the barriers faced by some that are not experienced by others.  It requires us to reflect on our thinking and practice and develop thinking that focuses on equitable intersectionality. |
| Cultural diversity in social intelligence | Evolving from double empathy to focus on communication differences instead of deficits, and on diverging social motivations rather than an inability to socialise. A cultural or even neuro-cultural framework creates an environment that focuses on translation rather than a colonialist imposition of social requirements. |
| Understanding Monotropism | The key factor in difference between autistic and non-autistic attentional, sensorial, emotional and behavioural divergences. Understanding monotropism is a step toward understanding autistic experiences |
| Diversity in movement, sensory, neurobiology & trauma response | Recognising the impact of trauma on Autistic people & how trauma is received and experienced differently by them is key to the validation of autistic experience. Understanding this diversity in experience offers us the opportunity to validate communication, sensory, behavioural & experiential differences; allowing us to meet & be led by those needs. ➜ |

| The Environment | Along with an understanding of the impact of sensory input, focusing on the environment allows us to reflect on the impact of carer/peer/practitioner behaviour on autistic people. It provides a reframing of the notions around challenging behaviour and other pathologising and reductive ideologies that ignore the impact of other people and their behaviour. This also allows us to focus on removing confirmation bias & societal conformity/norms/expectations |
|---|---|
| Identity and it's relationships with stigma, masking, burnout and mental health outcomes | Focusing on positive and constructive self-identity, promoting that via family, services & peers, and societally. Preventing neuronormative ideologies and reducing stigma allows us to understand and mitigate the impact on autistic mental health and wellbeing. |

**Table 12.1:** Rose 2020 Advoc8 framework. (© Kieran Rose, 2023)

We have briefly discussed the role that autonomy and agency can play in fostering authenticity, through providing an individual more power and control to make decisions about their own needs based on an increased understanding of self. The ability to display autonomy and agency will vary across the lifespan, as young people (and people assumed to 'lack capacity') may be infrequently afforded the capacity to make decisions about their own lives. However, supporting people to develop autonomy and agency, particularly around safe self-expression or authenticity, can empower them and may act as a protective factor against the negative impact of stigma and the stress associated with stigma management strategies. Here authenticity goes beyond masking/unmasking, whereby an autistic person uses that self-knowledge to create or shape an environment which meets their needs more effectively, within the sphere of power that they have. This will lessen the overall burden of stress upon the individual and can give them the opportunity to thrive.

The relationship between authenticity and acceptance can be complicated, as acceptance can be both under the control of the individual (i.e. self-acceptance), or less under individual control (external acceptance). Self-acceptance can include embracing one's own identity and recognising one's own needs. Aspects of Brach's notion of 'radical self-acceptance' in particular may be useful, and can be compatible with a neurodiversity approach (Brach, 2000). Here the focus is on eschewing notions of 'productivity' and perfection and instead focusing on developing an embodied awareness of yourself and your needs outside of shame and stigma (both external, and internalised).

External acceptance can also be a powerful tool for fostering authenticity. In our 2023 paper on victimisation (Pearson et al., 2023), our participants highlighted the need for community spaces where neurodivergent people can express themselves authentically, and feel validated by others. As discussed in chapter 4, having the opportunity to interact with other autistic people from a young age can have a positive impact on autistic identity and self-expression. However, it is important that the opportunity for these interactions occurs outside of prescribed facilitation (e.g. as part of a social skills group).

The need for autistic spaces is consistent with Botha's work on community connectedness, and highlights the importance of belonging and connection with others in both healing from trauma, and feeling able to be one's authentic self (Botha, 2020). Farahar and Foster (who created soyoureautistic.com) have developed a programme that provides an exploration of an autistic identity, focussing on developing self-insight and self-esteem, and helping autistic people to express their authentic selves.

Though there has been a focus in the literature so far on autistic-only (or more broadly, neurodivergent-only) spaces, this sense of validation may also be found from non-neurodivergent allies who value and validate differences in other people. The double empathy divide may be hard to bridge, but the capacity for genuine relationships founded on mutual respect, trust, and understanding can provide a space for the expression of authenticity (we will discuss this with specific reference to the relationship between autistic people and professionals such as therapists later in this chapter).

# Things outside of an individual's power to control

Some factors may be more difficult to account for in the attempt to express authenticity, for example the response and support of other people, and wider societal systems. Towards the end of the last section, we discussed the importance of community and peer relationships, and how these can engender a sense of belonging and validation for an individual. However, as we have discussed throughout the book, the dehumanisation and stigmatisation of autistic people is entrenched and can be difficult to resist, both individually and as a wider community. It infects both how autistic people view themselves, and how others view us (whether they know we are autistic or not).

Societal normativity can pervade both individual responses to, as well as general attitudes towards, autistic people (and difference more broadly), emphasising the importance of an ecological approach to masking and authenticity. In particular, understanding the interaction between the different levels of the ecological system and how this may influence a person's experiences. As discussed in earlier chapters, the pathological construction of autism influences how autistic people are viewed at the societal and individual level, and shapes responses at each of these in return. The ability of an autistic person to express themselves authentically will not only be shaped by their interactions with others, but the search for authentic self and attempts to engage in authentic self-expression may also be thwarted (or encouraged) by others (e.g. family members, or professionals). Beardon (2022), has described how societal norms and their influence on the environment of autistic people (both people and place) have a destructive impact on autistic lives, and lead to what Milton and Sims have referred to as 'psycho-emotional disablement' (Milton & Sims, 2016).

## Microsystem and mesosystem

As we discussed in chapter 8, autistic people often experience invalidation from others within their microsystem based on other's difficulty understanding the autistic experience. This invalidation can be traumatic for autistic people and can contribute towards masking through a) encouraging the autistic person not to trust their own interpretation of experiences, and b) a desire to avoid further invalidation. When this invalidation comes from within close personal relationships (e.g. friends, family) it can thwart belonging and make it difficult for the autistic person to feel safe within the relationship. When this invalidation comes from professionals (e.g. educators), it cements the person's perception that their experience of the world is somehow flawed and that nowhere is safe for them to express themselves authentically. Importantly, we may also see mesosystem influences play a part here, such as in the example of the 'coke bottle' effect outlined in chapter 8, whereby interactions between parents and school shape how the behaviour of the autistic child is conceptualised and responded to. The framings within these systems will also be influenced by the wider macrosystem, feeding down into narratives around how autistic behaviour and communication should be interpreted, and the language used to describe this (as we will discuss shortly).

## Macrosystem

Throughout this book we have discussed how wider socio-cultural perceptions of autism and autistic people, shape both societal knowledge in addition to autistic access to self-knowledge (Fricker, 2007) and self-understanding, which impact on the ability to express authenticity. The stigmatising construction of autistic people as deficient, impaired and less than human impacts upon perceptions of autistic people as a group, and as individuals who fail to meet normative expectations. Society makes it unsafe for autistic people to be their authentic selves and devalues autistic people in comparison to the presumed norm.

At the macrosystem level, other forms of stigma and systemic oppression shape the experience of the individual and dictate how safe it might be to express different aspects of self. For example, Simmonds (2021) outlined the difficulty in finding spaces where it was safe to unmask, due to experiences of ableism in Black spaces, and racism in autistic spaces. Here autistic people who experience intersectional forms of oppression may be pressured to suppress their authenticity in different ways, across different environments. Thus, we cannot consider autistic authenticity as something that exists in a vacuum and that can be achieved through seemingly simple actions such as stimming in public. Firstly, intersectional societal perceptions can impact on how safe this is from person to person (e.g. it may be incredibly unsafe for a Black autistic man to stim publicly), but crucially, autistic people are never *just* autistic. We are multifaceted, and as such, until it is safe to be our *whole* selves, autistic authenticity is not achievable as it cannot be isolated from other intersections of self-expression.

## Shifting responsibility

As can be seen from the discussion of the ecological systems that impact on authenticity, autistic people may have *some* control over *some* aspects of authentic self-expression, but these are heavily impacted by the broader systems surrounding us. For autistic people to develop and express authentically, wider cultural and societal change is needed. The neurodiversity paradigm and a shift towards a value neutral conceptualisation of autism (and neurodivergence) plays an important part here, as it emphasises the need to eschew normative expectations of flourishing and a shift away from label-based support to a needs-based approach. Likewise, a neuroqueer approach facilitates the emancipation of autistic people by encouraging the exploration of difference and the transgression of norms as a way to achieve joy. A future where autistic (and other neurodivergent) people can (safely) be themselves is a neurocosmopolitan future (Walker & Raymaker, 2021), where a) 'normative' standards are not enforced and b) we remove broader and intersectional forms of oppression (e.g. racism, sexism, transphobia) to ensure that *all* neurodivergent people have access to emancipation.

Of course, reshaping society is no easy feat, nor one that can be achieved in the same way cross-culturally as definitions of flourishing and individual and collective goals may differ widely. It is important, however, that we strive for and attempt to embed change across systems (e.g. among friends and family, in schools and healthcare, in policy) in order to create a society where autistic people do not *need* to mask.

Both Beardon (2022) and Rose (see Table 12.1) have provided guidance on how to create a more autistic-friendly society that integrates an understanding of up-to-date knowledge about autistic people, such as the double empathy problem and monotropism, with a shift towards neurodiversity-affirmative principles. The idea of making 'reasonable adjustments' for neurodivergent people (and disabled people more broadly) is grounded in the conceptualisation of need as homogenous among the dominant group, with changes to be implemented ad-hoc and 'as necessary' to support those who diverge. However, recognising diversity and embedding a proactive – rather than a responsive – approach (such as the use of Universal Design for Learning (or UDL) in education, see Waisman, 2020) can foster autistic authenticity and flourishing by treating needs as equivalent, and not 'special'. Here we are advocating for an approach which centres equity and justice, as opposed to 'equality' (which can obscure need).

In the following section, we discuss how systems external to the individual (and individuals within these systems) might work to foster authenticity, within the scope of power that they have.

## The power of language

There are ongoing debates about the language used to describe autistic people and their experiences (Botha et al., 2020; Bottema-Beutel et al., 2020; Natri et al., 2023; Singer et al., 2023), and how important this is for reducing stigma towards autistic people and making society a safer place for us to be ourselves. We have provided previous discussion in this book as to how terminology and rhetoric may shape perceptions of, and thus responses towards, autistic people, for example the use of the terms 'challenging behaviour' to describe what is most commonly the expression of distress among autistic people. However, there are similar issues in the way we discuss and construct masking and authenticity. In discussions of the 'coke bottle' effect, children are described as 'unmasking' once they leave the school environment. This framing unintentionally situates the child's behavioural response (e.g. a meltdown, or a shutdown) to suddenly leaving an 'unsafe' environment and entering a safe one as a choice, rather than an automatic response to suddenly exiting a stressful environment and feeling safe enough to externalise their dysregulation. Importantly, shifting away from language of choice moves the onus for 'intervention' away from the autistic person, and resituates it as an external need that must be addressed (e.g. creating a safer school environment). The same principles apply regardless of point in the lifespan and the environment that the person is in (e.g. the workplace); creating safer environments for autistic people will reduce the need for masking, and by association lessen its impact on the individual.

## Building genuine professional relationships

Earlier in the chapter we wrote about the importance of validating peer relationships and community spaces in fostering authenticity among autistic people. However, autistic people also benefit from validation and understanding within their relationships with professionals (e.g. therapists, educators, healthcare professionals, etc). The double empathy problem can lead to difficulty in empathy and mutual understanding between autistic people and non-autistic professionals (Jellett & Flower, 2023). However, Pavlopoulou (2020) developed a useful framework for helping professionals to take an experience-sensitive approach when working with autistic people. Within her lifeworld framework, developed from work by Todres (2005), she outlines eight dimensions (see Table 12.2) which can be used to develop a meaningful relationship with an autistic person, taking into account factors such as promoting agency (consistent with Rose's Advoc8 framework), autistic embodiment, and togetherness. Pavlopoulou's work acknowledges that it is the professional who has the power to shape their relationship with the autistic person, and as such it is their responsibility to develop what Jellett has referred to as 'cultural competency' with regards to understanding autistic people.

Part of this competency requires the acknowledgement of the weight of developmental and socio-cultural trauma experienced by autistic people, that impacts on their ability to self-actualise. This acknowledgement can help to reframe the relationship between professionals and autistic people and shift the focus away from trying to instil normativity towards validating experiences and providing safety for autistic people to flourish in their own way. This also necessitates understanding what safety, objectives and a good quality of life look like to autistic people, as these are often framed through non-autistic understandings (Lam et al., 2021), which may not capture autistic needs.

| Dimensions | Descriptions |
| --- | --- |
| Objectification to Insiderness | Valuing the subjective experiences of the person. Seeing past diagnostic expectations to unique perspectives, strengths, and challenges. |
| Passivity to Agency | Promoting autistic decision making in collaboration with caregivers and practioners. Supporting personal dignity. |
| Homogenisation to Uniqueness | Recognising the unique aspects that make up an autistic person's identity (e.g. friend, male, son, pupil). No one size fits all approach. |
| Loss of Meaning to Sense Making | Listening to autistic interpretations of their own experiences. Enabling autistic people to make sense of their experiences and the contexts of the situations they are in, is an important aspect of humanising practice. |
| The importance of Personal Journey | Recognising and faciliating individual pathways and aspirations. Humanising practice recognises the importance of maintaining a sense of continuity. It seeks to keep people connected to their histories and plans for their future. |
| Dislocation to a Sense of Place | Ensuring autistic people feel included and welcome across different environments. Imagine having everything you know stripped away from you, with no access to the familiar, with nothing to remind you of love or comfort. Where the things or activities you hold dear are seen as representing a risk to yourself or to others. Contrast this with a humanising approach or place that feels more like 'home'. |
| Reductionism to Embodiment | Exploring the experience of autistic being without defaulting to a deficit narrative and enabling them in their personal development. |
| Isolation to Belonging | Creating a safe place for autistic people to share their worries and joys. Build a sense of community and belonging. |

**Table 12.2:** Lifeworld Framework (Pavlopoulou, 2020)

It is also important that professionals are aware of masking beyond the basic narrative that 'it's something that autistic girls do that make them harder to spot and diagnose', and thinking about how to reduce the need for masking to mitigate its impact even if it remains hard to recognise. Fostering authenticity means creating a safe environment for autistic people to be themselves, and responding to them with an approach that recognises their humanity.

For educators this may mean taking into account how they might misinterpret communication differences, and attentional and sensory needs, and working to move past educator's own biases. As outlined in chapter 8, some young people may respond to stressful environments by attempting to please educators and developing perfectionist tendencies as a form of masking. Some young people may respond by externalising their distress, consistent with what has been conceptualised as challenging behaviour. Recognising that masking (whether through suppression or projection) is a response to both the environment, and the behaviour and responses of educators, empowers educators to make changes which can foster authenticity within a safer educational environment. For therapists it might mean recognising that an autistic client may not communicate or reflect on their emotions in an expected way, and that you might have to work to meet them where they are rather than where you expect them to be.

Importantly, supporting autistic authenticity requires cross-disciplinary knowledge and interactions between specialists in these areas who have moved beyond theoretical knowledge and incorporate cultural competence, and know how to work together to foster autistic flourishing. For example, occupational therapists who are aware of how to minimise sensory distress and create sensory joy beyond meeting normative targets (e.g. pencil grasp), and speech and language therapists who can facilitate the development of meaningful communication in whatever form that takes, work with educators and families to support autistic people to thrive.

## Conclusion

Fostering authenticity among autistic people must be approached with sensitivity and nuance, that recognises the impact of intersectional factors and acknowledges that masking is situated within an ecological framework. It is not solely the responsibility of the autistic person to 'unmask', but an interaction between individuals and systems at multiple levels that can allow for the development of a) the self-knowledge needed to develop a more authentic sense of self, and b) a society in which it is safe to express this.

Here much of the onus is on exosystem and macrosystem inhabitants (e.g. schools, employers, society) to do the work to make the world a safer place for *all* autistic people to be their authentic selves (i.e. not just white, cis-het autistic people).

# Chapter 13: Conclusions: Towards a better future

In the introduction to this book, we outlined our aim to expand upon our conceptual paper (Pearson & Rose, 2021), drawing together research from across different areas and attempting to take a somewhat interdisciplinary approach to masking. The order of the chapters aimed to tell a story, starting with the conceptualisation of autism and how this has evolved over time in chapter 2. With this chapter, we hoped that the reader would understand how pathological views about autism and autistic people have enacted violence upon the identities of autistic people in both overt and subtle ways. Following this, chapters 3 and 4 explored identity development across the lifespan among both non-autistic and autistic people. Due to the limited research into autistic identity thus far, we theorised about how general social theory might apply to our understanding of autistic identity. Chapter 5 introduced the (crucial) concept of intersectionality and explored other factors which shape and interact with autistic identity. Here we discussed a small range of intersecting factors such as race, gender and additional disabilities, noting that our identities often intersect in complex and multifarious ways that mean we can never be reduced to *just* being autistic. With this understanding under our proverbial belts, we then presented the reader with current theories about what masking is, deconstructing our current understandings before moving on to *reconstruct* our understandings in the following chapters within the broader context of autistic social experience. Chapters 7 and 8 explored the impact of both stigma and trauma upon autistic people, contextualising masking within the broader concept of stigma management and acknowledging how a stigmatised identity can lead to an increase in stressors (as seen in the trauma chapter) that underpin the sense that expressing authenticity is unsafe. In chapter 9 we discussed research to date, taking into account how the factors we had discussed (e.g. intersectionality, stigma) had been addressed in the literature, before moving on to talk about the impact of masking in chapter 10. Finally, in chapters 11 and 12, we explored the mechanisms involved in masking, drawing in the factors we had introduced throughout the book and discussing how these relate to current theory, before discussing the possibility of a more authentic life for autistic people.

It has been difficult to finish this book because it is such a complex topic. There is a sense from us both that we could probably keep writing for a very long time and never quite achieve the level of nuance that we think this topic needs. Part of the issue we have faced is that autism research and masking research are both fast-evolving fields, and we are faced with a nagging concern that the shelf life of what we have written is short-lived as we understand more and conceptualise better. We'd love to think that the blood and tears that have been poured into this book will stand the test of time, and that the language we use and the way that we've described things are, at their heart, humanistic and won't be looked at in the future as evidence of further dehumanisation and harm.

As we outlined in the introduction though, no discussion of such a complex topic will ever be perfect. We hope that anyone who reads this and notes what they would view to be a glaring omission (particularly those people in fields outside of psychology), consider diving into this research area and contributing their ideas towards the broader understanding of masking. We hope this book functions somewhat as a wider call to arms, for more people to engage with developing a nuanced and critical understanding of masking, that acknowledges the complexity of the factors that shape autistic identity, and thus its management. We see this book as a stepping stone to ensuring a more interdisciplinary approach to understanding masking; one that integrates knowledge from across areas including cognitive science and psychology, sociology, philosophy to shape an understanding that goes beyond individual strategies used to fit in. There is a much broader body of intersectional work out there, and we feel that we are only scratching the surface with the issues that we have discussed, particularly with regards to racialised autistic experiences. Most importantly we hope that this body of work is both developed and led by autistic people, the people with the most at stake and whose lives are impacted so powerfully and negatively.

## Changing the narrative - changing the future

Given that we aimed this book primarily at an academic audience, we want to spend a little bit of time in this conclusion addressing what we, as academics, (though a lot of what we say will be relevant to professionals of any field, and to non-autistic people in general) can do given the information we have presented about the broader narratives that shape autistic experience.

As we have outlined in previous chapters, the work we do as academics does not exist in a vacuum. The way that we construct knowledge about autistic people, speak about autistic people, and the way that our work about (or with) autistic people is implemented outside of academia has a tangible impact on the lives of autistic people. Whilst debating heterogeneity or sex differences may feel to many of us like just ensuring that the science is 'right', there are wider considerations to be made about how these debates filter down into societal discourse, services offered, and access to identification and support.

Masking is an incredibly young and emerging research area within autism research (though as we have discussed, not so new with regards to other marginalised populations), and as such it is crucial that we avoid the proliferation of, and contribution to, limited or under-developed narratives about who masks, how, and the impact that it might have. Those of us who interact regularly with professionals and families outside of academia will already have seen the emerging discourse around masking being a 'girl' thing, and about it amounting to 'hiding autism'. Whilst it is essential to recognise how masking does indeed contribute towards under-recognition (and find ways to implement this knowledge into clinical practice) we must be careful about ensuring that we do not further marginalise autistic people in our attempts to make quick improvements based on limited knowledge. If we are to achieve meaningful and sustainable change in the lives of autistic people, and within the services that support us, we need to ensure that the frameworks we develop are considerate of the wider social context that shapes autistic lives, and not just an isolated snapshot of our behaviour in the moment. There is an important place for all of the approaches we have discussed towards understanding masking, but these need to be integrated, not least through a wider intersectional lens, in order to advance both the field and improve autistic lives. Given the statistics on autistic life outcomes – such as suicide and self-injury, eating disorders, poor mental health, higher rates of physical poor health and early death – we do not think it is hyperbolic to say that these improvements can and will be a matter of life or death for autistic people.

As such, we have a responsibility within academia not only to ensure a nuanced narrative around masking, but to lead the charge in shaping a more nuanced narrative around autism and autistic people. Change is underway in pockets of autism research, with more researchers engaging with the neurodiversity paradigm, and engaging in co-production and collaboration as a means to strengthen the work we do, meet autistic priorities, and create a better future for autistic people (Pearson et al., 2022). Part of this change has been driven by the recognition that autism research should focus on the needs and priorities of autistic people (Pellicano et al., 2014), rather than neuronormative and curative research agendas. However, as can be seen in the work of Botha & Cage (2022) that we discussed in chapter 7 (and that are visible across the wider research sphere if those of us who work predominantly within the neurodiversity paradigm dare to look outside of our immediate areas), autism research is still built upon the dehumanisation of autistic people. It can be hard as a researcher to acknowledge your own bias, particularly those of us who are convinced that what we are doing *helps* autistic people. But this is not about us, or our feelings. It is about ensuring that autistic people in future get to live in a society where stigma is less of a problem, and the need to mask dwindles. It is our responsibility to ensure that this change happens, and that if we want to see it happen, we lead from the front and put our own egos and feelings aside. Our research is accessible to the wider community and the people we are meant to serve – off of whose lives we earn our living – are going to hold us to account, so we may as well start to do that with ourselves. This is about recognising our privilege and being responsible, humanising the people we study, working *with* them, not *on* them (Michael, 2021) and considering the potential negative impacts on them of our language, behaviour, theorising and publishing. None of us are perfect, but being *better* is a start.

We can also foster change by increasing the impact of our work, shifting from 'what are we seeing?' (information gathering), to 'what are we going to do about it?' (ensuring impact). Of course, both of these approaches are important, particularly when developing an evidence base in an emerging area (for which masking provides a key example, we do not need to rush into 'intervention' without first establishing a solid theoretical understanding). However, thinking with impact in mind when approaching research is one way to ensure that what we are doing will benefit autistic people now, or in future.

We also need to consider how our research is applied at the service level for autistic people. Academic conceptualisations of autism underpin how autistic people are understood and treated within a variety of other fields, including education. The narrative of 'special needs', and the focus on normative behaviour and communication does immense harm to autistic people (by way of encouraging masking, and the psycho-emotional disablement and trauma that arises as a result of the dire person-environment fit). Work like that of Alcorn et al. (2023) and Brownlow et al. (2021), highlight the importance of embedding a humanising approach that is informed by, designed with, or led by autistic (young) people within the educational setting. Shifting away from changing the young person, and instead focusing on changing the environment to make it more accessible will reduce the need for masking and have a long-term positive impact on the lives of autistic people. This change comes from not only ensuring that research filters into schools, but also in the way that professionals train other professionals (Rose & Vivian, 2020). Pathologising narratives can proliferate when people and organisations do not engage with contemporary knowledge surrounding autistic people and rely upon a 'business as usual' understanding. Radical changes are needed to improve knowledge and practice, and the outcomes that result from an inadequate understanding.

Change is also very much needed across society more broadly (this might be the understatement of the century). As we outlined in chapter 7, media representations of autistic people are often heavily stereotyped, and propagate dehumanising and tragedy-focused narratives about autistic people. These narratives feed into wider societal conceptualisations of normality, and are drawn upon in campaigns which rely on the notion of autism as a tragedy in order to generate income (ASAN, 2009). Autistic people are currently at the forefront of driving change and have been the ones doing the 'heavy lifting' with regards to societal change (Botha, 2021), advocating for acceptance (self-understanding), autonomy, agency and authenticity. However, we cannot do this work alone. Strong allies are needed both within and outside of academia who can co-advocate alongside autistic people and use the power that they have to push for the change that will lead to a reduction in stigma and flawed narratives.

# Future directions for masking research

Given that autistic masking is an emerging area, there is a broad scope for development in both theoretical and empirical work. In chapter 12 we outlined how an ecological framework might be applied to understanding how masking is shaped by the broader societal context. This model can be used to consider how factors across multiple levels (e.g. individual, societal) shape masking and the associated outcomes (see Table 13.1).

| Level | Example Factors |
| --- | --- |
| Individual | Uncertainty attunement, social interaction style |
| Microsystem | Peer relationships, family environment |
| Mesosystem | Family-school interactions |
| Exosystem | School, the workplace |
| Macrosystem | Societal stigma, cultural notions of autism |
| Chronosystem | Lifespan development |

**Table 13.1:** An ecological framework for understanding autistic masking

The use of an ecological framework of autistic masking also provides space for various theories and approaches to masking to co-exist, acknowledging that they may provide knowledge at different levels of the framework (e.g. Ai et al.s, (2022) work on transactional impression management may be primarily concerned with individual and microsystem factors, but also takes into account the impact of macrosystem factors and time, whereas Livingston & Happé's (2017) work on compensation is mostly concerned with individual factors such as cognitive and social style). Here knowledge from multiple theories may provide insight into different aspects of masking, and importantly this provides scope for interdisciplinary understandings to emerge which can be integrated into future models (e.g sociological and psychological approaches co-existing to produce more meaningful knowledge).

Additionally, significant gaps in literature have been identified, which are not surprising given how new the area is. Researchers have highlighted (Lai et al., 2020; Petrolini et al., 2023) that masking research so far has mostly focused on conscious knowledge of masking, contexts in which it occurs and intentionality to mask. However there has been less focus on the 'success' of masking (Belcher et al., 2022) and the unconscious aspects (the latter for fairly obvious reasons). There is also a need to explore the notion that masking can be encouraged and even enforced (e.g. through both social skill and behavioural interventions, frameworks and ideologies). It is also important that we explore the experiences of autistic people who state that they cannot create the appearance of conforming to social rules (e.g. who state that they cannot mask). In chapter 11 we explored whether the notion of projection acceptability might be more helpful for understanding certain aspects of masking/stigma related impression management that do not rely on the concept of suppression.

Milton's double empathy problem (2012) positions difficulties in social interaction and communication between autistic and non-autistic people as bi-directional, emphasising how it may be difficult for one group to empathise with another, when their experiences are so disparate. One of the reasons for the increase in popularity of co-production and participatory research is that that research done in this way not only centres the voices and more adequately meets the needs of the people the research is studying, but it also means that there is greater opportunity to communicate more clearly and interpret responses in a more insightful way. Participatory research and co-production should be embedded in research on masking where possible in order to minimise misinterpretations of autistic experiential accounts, and to avoid problematic framings (e.g. the language used to describe masking unintentionally framing it as a conscious and deliberate attempt to 'fit in' as opposed to a response shaped by stigma and societal trauma). While there may be a level of intent for some aspects of masking and for some Autistic people, as both autistic people and academics, this interpretation is only a partial picture of what is being experienced. If we are to understand masking as both a social strategy and a human behavioural response to being marginalised, then we have to factor in that in many ways there is very little aspect of choice to it and how masking may manifest in a variety of different ways. Throughout this book we have laid out a narrative outlining what we know about autistic people and how they are constructed, the issues we may face in navigating the social world as (intersectionally) marginalised people, and how these framings directly feed into the heightened risk of, and experiences of, trauma.

Finally, we need more research into the impact of masking on autistic people, including the relationship between masking and burnout, mental health difficulties and suicidality. From a critical realist perspective, exploring the impact of masking allows us to access the 'unseen' – we cannot necessarily 'see' masking, or get at the unconscious mechanisms involved, but we *can* measure the impact and see the tangible effect it has on people.

We also need to consider this impact in thinking about how to intervene. As outlined in chapter 12, focusing on 'unmasking' in autistic people as individuals does little to reduce the societal pressure to mask, and may not reduce poor outcomes for autistic people in the face of continuing stigma and dehumanisation. As we discussed at the start of this chapter, society is in need of intervention. Though we may look for ways to support autistic people to safely display authenticity, we must work more broadly to develop a society that is more inclusive of all forms of difference (not just neurodivergence).

## Concluding thought

Whilst we have spent much of this book advocating for stigma reduction and understanding, applying these aims in an autism-specific manner is only part of a wider picture. People do not need to simply 'understand autism', they need to be open to the possibility of difference in all manner of ways – we need to expect and support different communication styles, different cognitive styles, different behaviours, different cultures and be better at encouraging critical thought and reflecting on our own behaviours, heuristics and biases. We need to question the push for normativity, acknowledge the limitations of averages, means and bell curves and develop meaningful and sustainable practice for supporting all kinds of people. We need to acknowledge our own fears and desire for control and learn to sit uncomfortably with our practice.

We want a future where there is facilitation of meaningful communication for non-speaking autistics. Where there is a better recognition and understanding of the variety of and impact of co-occurring conditions.

We want to see platforms for autistic people who are marginalised in multiple ways, and opportunities for autistic people in positions of influence.

We want policies that actively work to improve autistic lives, fuelled by the priorities of autistics.

We want to see an end to the practice of dividing autistic people up into subgroups, which are then used to decide who is 'useful' but never get the right support, and those who are deemed 'burdens' and who are tossed aside with assumed incompetence.

We want autistic people not to have to 'take the mask off', because they never experience the stigma, trauma and lack of safety that causes it to develop in the first place.

We want to see a world in which "We don't have to fall into the same category to be of equal value." (Chambers, 2021).

We hope that this book functions as a call to action for researchers, professionals, autistic people, family members: anyone who wants to see a better future for autistic people. We invite anyone who shares this aim to use your knowledge and whatever control and power you have, big or small, to advocate for cultural and social change and embed your values into your practice to be the change you want to see.

# References

## Chapter 1

Ai, W., Cunningham, W. A., & Lai, M.-C. (2022). Reconsidering autistic 'camouflaging' as transactional impression management. *Trends in Cognitive Sciences*.

Astle, D. E., Holmes, J., Kievit, R., & Gathercole, S. E. (2022). Annual Research Review: The transdiagnostic revolution in neurodevelopmental disorders. *Journal of Child Psychology and Psychiatry*, **63**(4), 397–417.

Bertilsdotter Rosqvist, H., Stenning, A., & Chown, N. (2020). Neurodiversity studies: Proposing a new field of inquiry. In H. Bertilsdotter Rosqvist, A. Stenning, & N. Chown (Eds.), *Neurodiversity Studies. A New Critical Paradigm*. Routledge.

Botha, M., Hanlon, J., & Williams, G. (2020). *Does language matter? Identity-first versus person-first language use in autism research: A response to Vivanti*.

Bottema-Beutel, K., Kapp, S. K., Lester, J. N., Sasson, N. J., & Hand, B. N. (2020). Avoiding ableist language: Suggestions for autism researchers. *Autism in Adulthood*.

Cascio, M. A., Weiss, J. A., & Racine, E. (2021). Making autism research inclusive by attending to intersectionality: A review of the research ethics literature. *Review Journal of Autism and Developmental Disorders*, **8**, 22–36.

Forster, S., & Pearson, A. (2020). "Bullies tend to be obvious": Autistic adults perceptions of friendship and the concept of 'mate crime'. *Disability and Society*. https://doi.org/10.1080/0968759 9.2019.1680347

Giwa Onaiwu, M. (2020). "They Don't Know, Don't Show, or Don't Care": Autism's White Privilege Problem. *Autism in Adulthood*, 2(4), 270–272. https://doi.org/10.1089/aut.2020.0077

Hull, L., Petrides, K. V., Allison, C., Smith, P., Baron-Cohen, S., Lai, M. C., & Mandy, W. (2017). "Putting on My Best Normal": Social Camouflaging in Adults with Autism Spectrum Conditions. *Journal of Autism and Developmental Disorders*. https://doi.org/10.1007/s10803-017-3166-5

Kapp, S. (2019). How social deficit models exacerbate the medical model: Autism as case in point. *Autism Policy & Practice*, 2(1), 3–28.

Lawson, W. B. (2020). Adaptive Morphing and Coping with Social Threat in Autism: An Autistic Perspective. *Journal of Intellectual Disability-Diagnosis and Treatment*, **8**, 519–526.

Livingston, L. A., & Happé, F. (2017). Conceptualising compensation in neurodevelopmental disorders: Reflections from autism spectrum disorder. *Neuroscience and Biobehavioral Reviews*. https://doi.org/10.1016/j.neubiorev.2017.06.005

Lockwood Estrin, G., Milner, V., Spain, D., Happé, F., & Colvert, E. (2021). Barriers to autism spectrum disorder diagnosis for young women and girls: A systematic review. *Review Journal of Autism and Developmental Disorders*, **8**(4), 454–470.

Milton, D. E. (2014). Autistic expertise: A critical reflection on the production of knowledge in autism studies. *Autism*, **18**(7), 794–802.

Milton, D., & Sims, T. (2016). How is a sense of well-being and belonging constructed in the accounts of autistic adults? *Disability & Society*, **31**(4), 520–534.

Rosqvist, H. B., Botha, M., Hens, K., O'Donoghue, S., Pearson, A., & Stenning, A. (2023). Being, Knowing, and Doing: Importing Theoretical Toolboxes for Autism Studies. *Autism in Adulthood*, **5**(1), 15–23.

Stenning, A. (2020). Understanding empathy through a study of autistic life writing: On the importance of neurodiverse morality. *Neurodiversity Studies*.

Waltz, M. (2008). Autism = death: The social and medical impact of a catastrophic medical model of autistic spectrum disorders. Popular *Narrative Media*, **1**(1), 13–23. https://doi.org/10.3828/pnm.1.1.4

Willey, L. H. (2014). *Pretending to be normal: Living with asperger's syndrome (autism spectrum disorder) expanded edition*. Jessica Kingsley Publishers.

Woods, R., & Waldock, K. E. (2021). Critical autism studies. *Encyclopedia of Autism Spectrum Disorders*, 1240–1248.

Yergeau, M. (2013). Clinically significant disturbance: On theorists who theorize theory of mind. *Disability Studies Quarterly*, **33**(4).

# Chapter 2

American Psychiatric Association. (2013). *Diagnostic and statistical manual of mental disorders (DSM-5®)*. American Psychiatric Pub.

Armstrong, T. (2015). The Myth of the Normal Brain: Embracing Neurodiversity. *AMA Journal of Ethics*, **17**(4), 348–352. https://doi.org/10.1001/journalofethics.2015.17.4.msoc1-1504

Astle, D. E., Holmes, J., Kievit, R., & Gathercole, S. E. (2022). Annual Research Review: The transdiagnostic revolution in neurodevelopmental disorders. *Journal of Child Psychology and Psychiatry*, **63**(4), 397–417.

Ballou, E. (2018, February 6). WHAT THE NEURODIVERSITY MOVEMENT DOES—AND DOESN'T—OFFER. *Thinking Person's Guide to Autism*. https://thinkingautismguide.com/2018/02/what-neurodiversity-movement-doesand.html

Baron-Cohen, S. (1997). *Mindblindness: An essay on autism and theory of mind*. MIT press.

Baron-Cohen, S., Leslie, A. M., & Frith, U. (1985). Does the autistic child have a "theory of mind"? *Cognition*, **21**(1), 37–46. https://doi.org/10.1016/0010-0277(85)90022-8

Beardon, L. (2008). Is Autism really a disorder part 2: Theory of Mind? Rethink how we think. The *Journal of Inclusive Practice in Further and Higher Education*, **1**(1), 19–21.

Bettelheim, B. (1967). *The empty fortress: Infantile autism and the birth of the self*. Free Press of Glencoe.

Bleuler, E. (1924). *Textbook of psychiatry*. (p. Pp. 635). Macmillan.

Bolis, D., Balsters, J., Wenderoth, N., Becchio, C., & Schilbach, L. (2017). Beyond Autism: Introducing the Dialectical Misattunement Hypothesis and a Bayesian Account of Intersubjectivity. *Psychopathology*, **50**(6), 355–372. https://doi.org/10.1159/000484353

Boogert, N. J., Madden, J. R., Morand-Ferron, J., & Thornton, A. (2018). Measuring and understanding individual differences in cognition. *Philosophical Transactions of the Royal Society B: Biological Sciences*, **373**(1756), 20170280. https://doi.org/10.1098/rstb.2017.0280

Botha, M. (2021). Academic, Activist, or Advocate? Angry, Entangled, and Emerging: A Critical Reflection on Autism Knowledge Production. In *Frontiers in Psychology* (Vol. 12). https://www.frontiersin.org/article/10.3389/fpsyg.2021.727542

Brignell, A., Chenausky, K. V., Song, H., Zhu, J., Suo, C., & Morgan, A. T. (2018). Communication interventions for autism spectrum disorder in minimally verbal children. *Cochrane Database of Systematic Reviews*, **2018**(11). https://doi.org/10.1002/14651858.CD012324.pub2

Caçola, P., Miller, H. L., & Williamson, P. O. (2017). Behavioral comparisons in Autism Spectrum Disorder and Developmental Coordination Disorder: A systematic literature review. *Research in Autism Spectrum Disorders*, **38**, 6–18. https://doi.org/10.1016/j.rasd.2017.03.004

Chance, P. (1974, January). 'After you hit a child you can't just get up and leave him; you are hooked to that kid'. Conversation with Ivar Lovaas about self-mutilating children and how their parents make it worse. *Psychology Today*, **76**.

Chapman, R. (2020). The reality of autism: On the metaphysics of disorder and diversity. *Philosophical Psychology*, **33**(6), 799–819. https://doi.org/10.1080/09515089.2020.1751103

Chapman, R. (2021). Neurodiversity and the Social Ecology of Mental Functions. *Perspectives on Psychological Science*, **16**(6), 1360–1372. https://doi.org/10.1177/1745691620959833

Chevallier, C., Kohls, G., Troiani, V., Brodkin, E. S., & Schultz, R. T. (2012). The social motivation theory of autism. *Trends in Cognitive Sciences*, **16**(4), 231–239.

Collis, R. (2023). A response to Singer, Lutz, Escher, and Halladay's "a full semantic toolbox is essential for autism research and practice to thrive" in Autism Research (published online 12 Dec 2022). *Autism Research*, **16**(4), 679–680. https://doi.org/10.1002/aur.2902

Crompton, C. J., Ropar, D., Evans-Williams, C. V. M., Flynn, E. G., & Fletcher-Watson, S. (2020). Autistic peer-to-peer information transfer is highly effective. *Autism*. https://doi.org/10.1177/1362361320919286

Csikszentmihalyi, M., Abuhamdeh, S., & Nakamura, J. (2005). *Flow. In Handbook of competence and motivation*. (pp. 598–608). Guilford Publications.

Czech, H. (2018). Hans Asperger, National Socialism, and "race hygiene" in Nazi-era Vienna. *Molecular Autism*, **9**(1), 29. https://doi.org/10.1186/s13229-018-0208-6

den Houting, J. (2019). Neurodiversity: An insider's perspective. *Autism*. https://doi.org/10.1177/1362361318820762

Dwyer, P. (2022). The Neurodiversity Approach(es): What Are They and What Do They Mean for Researchers? *Human Development*, **66**(2), 73–92. https://doi.org/10.1159/000523723

Evans, B. (2013). How autism became autism: The radical transformation of a central concept of child development in Britain. *History of the Human Sciences*, **26**(3), 3–31. https://doi.org/10.1177/0952695113484320

Evans, B. (2014). The Foundations of Autism: The Law Concerning Psychotic, Schizophrenic, and Autistic Children in 1950s and 1960s Britain. *Bulletin of the History of Medicine*, **88**(2), 253–285. https://doi.org/10.1353/bhm.2014.0033

Folstein, S., & Rutter, M. (1977). Genetic influences and infantile autism. *Nature*, **265**(5596), 726–728. https://doi.org/10.1038/265726a0

Fombonne, E. (2023). Editorial: Is autism overdiagnosed? *Journal of Child Psychology and Psychiatry*, **64**(5), 711–714. https://doi.org/10.1111/jcpp.13806

Foucault, M. (1977). *Discipline and Punish: The Birth of the Prison*. Random House.

Fricker, M. (2007). *Epistemic injustice: Power and the ethics of knowing*. https://books.google.co.uk/books?hl = en&lr = &id = lncSDAAAQBAJ&oi = fnd&pg = PR9&dq = Fricker, + M. + Epistemic + injustice + : + power + and + the + ethics + of + knowing. + Oxford: + Oxford + University + Press % 3B + 2007. + &ots = 3fJeUPHdO-&sig = YfmkI6737W45ABxUXAy-3tVYRuc

Frith, U. (2001). Mind Blindness and the Brain in Autism. *Neuron*, **32**(6), 969–979. https://doi.org/10.1016/S0896-6273(01)00552-9

Frith, U., & Happe, F. (1999). Theory of Mind and Self-Consciousness: What Is It Like to Be Autistic? *Mind and Language*, **14**(1), 82–89. https://doi.org/10.1111/1468-0017.00100

Frith, U., & Mira, M. (1992). Autism and Asperger Syndrome. *Focus on Autistic Behavior*, **7**(3), 13–15. https://doi.org/10.1177/108835769200700302

Hens, K. (2019). The many meanings of autism: Conceptual and ethical reflections. *Developmental Medicine & Child Neurology*, **61**(9), 1025–1029. https://doi.org/10.1111/dmcn.14278

Heyworth, M., Chan, T., & Lawson, W. (2022). Perspective: Presuming Autistic Communication Competence and Reframing Facilitated Communication. *Frontiers in Psychology*, **13**. https://www.frontiersin.org/articles/10.3389/fpsyg.2022.864991

Hippler, K., & Klicpera, C. (2003). A retrospective analysis of the clinical case records of 'autistic psychopaths' diagnosed by Hans Asperger and his team at the University Children's Hospital, Vienna. Philosophical Transactions of the Royal Society of London. *Series B: Biological Sciences*, **358**(1430), 291–301. https://doi.org/10.1098/rstb.2002.1197

Jellett, R., & Muggleton, J. (2022). Implications of Applying "Clinically Significant Impairment" to Autism Assessment: Commentary on Six Problems Encountered in Clinical Practice. *Journal of Autism and Developmental Disorders*, **52**(3), 1412–1421. https://doi.org/10.1007/s10803-021-04988-9

Jurgens, A. (2020). *Neurodiversity in a neurotypical world. In Neurodiversity Studies: A new critical paradigm* (pp. 73–88). Routledge.

Kanner, L. (1949). Problems of nosology and psychodynamics of early infantile autism. *American Journal of Orthopsychiatry*, **19**, 416–426. https://doi.org/10.1111/j.1939-0025.1949.tb05441.x

Kapp, S. K. (Ed.). (2020). *Autistic Community and the Neurodiversity Movement: Stories from the Frontline*. Springer Singapore. https://doi.org/10.1007/978-981-13-8437-0

Kirkham, P. (2017). 'The line between intervention and abuse' – autism and applied behaviour analysis. *History of the Human Sciences*, **30**(2), 107–126. https://doi.org/10.1177/0952695117702571

Lai, M.-C., & Baron-Cohen, S. (2015). Identifying the lost generation of adults with autism spectrum conditions. *The Lancet Psychiatry*, **2**(11), 1013–1027. https://doi.org/10.1016/S2215-0366(15)00277-1

Lai, M.-C., Kassee, C., Besney, R., Bonato, S., Hull, L., Mandy, W., Szatmari, P., & Ameis, S. H. (2019). Prevalence of co-occurring mental health diagnoses in the autism population: A systematic review and meta-analysis. *The Lancet Psychiatry*, **6**(10), 819–829. https://doi.org/10.1016/S2215-0366(19)30289-5

Lawson, W. (2011). *The passionate mind: How people with autism learn* (1. publ). Jessica Kingsley Publ.

Lovaas, O. I., Berberich, J. P., Perloff, B. F., & Schaeffer, B. (1966). Acquisition of Imitative Speech by Schizophrenic Children. *Science*, **151**(3711), 705–707. https://doi.org/10.1126/science.151.3711.705

Milton, D. (2017). *A mismatch of salience: Explorations of the nature of autism from theory to practice*. Pavilion Press. https://www.pavpub.com/a-mismatch-of-salience/

Milton, D. E. M. (2012). On the ontological status of autism: The 'double empathy problem'. *Disability & Society*, **27**(6), 883–887.

Murray, D., Lesser, M., & Lawson, W. (2005). Attention, monotropism and the diagnostic criteria for autism. *Autism*, **9**(2), 139–156.

Natri, H. M., Abubakare, O., Asasumasu, K., Basargekar, A., Beaud, F., Botha, M., Bottema-Beutel, K., Brea, M. R., Brown, L. X. Z., Burr, D. A., Cobbaert, L., Dabbs, C., Denome, D., Rosa, S. D. R., Doherty, M., Edwards, B., Edwards, C., Liszk, S. E., Elise, F., … Zisk, A. H. (2023). Anti-ableist language is fully compatible with high-quality autism research: Response to S inger et al. (2023). *Autism Research*, **16**(4), 673–676. https://doi.org/10.1002/aur.2928

Oliver, M. (1983). *Social Work with Disabled People*. Macmillan.

O'Nions, E., Petersen, I., Buckman, J. E., Charlton, R. A., Cooper, C., Corbett, A., Happé, F., Manthorpe, J., Richards, M., & Saunders, R. (2023). Autism in England: Investigating underdiagnosis in a population-based cohort. *The Lancet Regional Health Europe*.

Pearson, A., & Rose, K. (2021). A Conceptual Analysis of Autistic Masking: Understanding the Narrative of Stigma and the Illusion of Choice. *Autism in Adulthood*. https://doi.org/10.1089/aut.2020.0043

Peña, E. V. (Ed.). (2019). *Communication alternatives in autism: Perspectives on typing and spelling approaches for the nonspeaking*. Toplight.

Pollak, R. (1998). *The creation of doctor B: A biography of Bruno Bettelheim*. Simon and Schuster.

Quarmby, K. (2011). *Scapegoat: How we are failing disabled people*. Portobello.

Reichow, B., Hume, K., Barton, E. E., & Boyd, B. A. (2018). Early intensive behavioral intervention (EIBI) for young children with autism spectrum disorders (ASD). *Cochrane Database of Systematic Reviews*, **2018**(10). https://doi.org/10.1002/14651858.CD009260.pub3

Sher, D. A., & Gibson, J. L. (2023). Pioneering, prodigious and perspicacious: Grunya Efimovna Sukhareva's life and contribution to conceptualising autism and schizophrenia. *European Child & Adolescent Psychiatry*, **32**(3), 475–490. https://doi.org/10.1007/s00787-021-01875-7

Silberman, S. (2015). *Neurotribes: The legacy of autism and the future of neurodiversity*. Penguin.

Sinclair, J. (1993). *Don't Mourn for Us*. International Conference on Autism, Toronto. https://www.autreat.com/dont_mourn.html

Singer, A., Lutz, A., Escher, J., & Halladay, A. (2023). A full semantic toolbox is essential for autism research and practice to thrive. *Autism Research*, **16**(3), 497–501. https://doi.org/10.1002/aur.2876

Singer, J. (1999). Why can't you be normal for once in your life? From a 'Problem with no Name'to a new category of disability. *Disability Discourse*, 59–67.

Sukhareva, G. (1925). Shizoidnyye psixopatii v detskom vozraste [Schizoid personality disorders of childhood]. In *Gurevich MO* (ed) Voprosy pedologii i detskoĭ psikhonevrologii (2nd ed., pp. 157–187). Zhizn' i Znanie.

Thomas, C. (2004). Rescuing a social relational understanding of disability. *Scandinavian Journal of Disability Research*, **6**(1), 22–36. https://doi.org/10.1080/15017410409512637

Walker, N. (2021). *Neuroqueer Heresies*. Autonomous Press.

Waltz, M. (2015). Mothers and Autism: The Evolution of a Discourse of Blame. *AMA Journal of Ethics*, **17**(4), 353–358. https://doi.org/10.1001/journalofethics.2015.17.4.mhst1-1504

Waltz, M. (2020). The production of the 'normal'child: Neurodiversity and the commodification of parenting. In *Neurodiversity Studies: A New Critical Paradigm* (pp. 15–26). https://www.taylorfrancis.com/chapters/edit/10.4324/9780429322297-3/production-normal-child-mitzi-waltz

WHO. (2022). *International Classification of Diseases 11th Revision*. World Health Organisation. https://icd.who.int/en

Williams, G. L., Wharton, T., & Jagoe, C. (2021). Mutual (Mis)understanding: Reframing Autistic Pragmatic "Impairments" Using Relevance Theory. *Frontiers in Psychology*, **12**. https://www.frontiersin.org/articles/10.3389/fpsyg.2021.616664

Wing, L. (2000). Past and future of research on Asperger syndrome. In F. R. Volkmar & S. S. Sparrow (Eds.), *Asperger syndrome* (pp. 418–432). Guilford Press.

Wing, L., & Gould, J. (1979). Severe impairments of social interaction and associated abnormalities in children: Epidemiology and classification. *Journal of Autism and Developmental Disorders*, **9**(1), 11–29. https://doi.org/10.1007/BF01531288

# Chapter 3

Arnett, J. J. (2000). Emerging adulthood: A theory of development from the late teens through the twenties. *American Psychologist*, **55**(5), 469–480. https://doi.org/10.1037/0003-066X.55.5.469

Bem, D. J. (1972). Self-perception theory. *Advances in Experimental Social Psychology*, **6**(1), 1–62.

Blumer, H. (1986). *Symbolic interactionism: Perspective and method*. Univ of California Press.

Brewer, M. B., & Gardner, W. (1996). Who is this 'We'? Levels of collective identity and self representations. *Journal of Personality and Social Psychology*, **71**, 83–93. https://doi.org/10.1037/0022-3514.71.1.83

Butterworth, G. (1995). *An ecological perspective on the origins of self*.

Caracciolo, M. (2012). Narrative, meaning, interpretation: An enactivist approach. *Phenomenology and the Cognitive Sciences*, **11**(3), 367–384. https://doi.org/10.1007/s11097-011-9216-0

Carver, C. S., & Scheier, M. F. (1981). Self-consciousness and reactance. *Journal of Research in Personality*, **15**(1), 16–29. https://doi.org/10.1016/0092-6566(81)90003-9

Cook, J. (2016). From movement kinematics to social cognition: The case of autism. *Philosophical Transactions of the Royal Society B: Biological Sciences*, **371**(1693), 20150372.

Duval, S., & Wicklund, R. A. (1972). *A theory of objective self awareness*. (pp. x, 238). Academic Press.

Erikson, E. H. (1993). *Childhood and society*. WW Norton & Company.

Festinger, L., & Carlsmith, J. M. (1959). Cognitive consequences of forced compliance. *The Journal of Abnormal and Social Psychology*, **58**, 203–210. https://doi.org/10.1037/h0041593

Gergen, K. J. (1971). *The concept of self*. (pp. x, 106). Holt, Rinehart & Winston.

Goffman, E. (1959). *The presentation of self in everyday life*. (Vol. 259). Garden City.

Haslam, S. A., Jetten, J., Postmes, T., & Haslam, C. (2009). Social identity, health and well-being: An emerging agenda for applied psychology. *Applied Psychology: An International Review*, **58**, 1–23. https://doi.org/10.1111/j.1464-0597.2008.00379.x

Higgins, E. T. (1987). Self-discrepancy: A theory relating self and affect. *Psychological Review*, 94(3), **319**.

James, W. (1890). *Principles of psychology*. Henry Holt.

Jones, E., & Pittman, T. (1982). Toward a general theory of strategic self-presentation. *Psychological Perspectives on the Self*, **1**(1), 231–262.

Jurgens, A. (2020). *Neurodiversity in a neurotypical world. In Neurodiversity Studies: A new critical paradigm* (pp. 73–88). Routledge.

Lodi-Smith, J., & Roberts, B. W. (2010). Getting to Know Me: Social Role Experiences and Age Differences in Self-Concept Clarity During Adulthood: SCC in Adulthood. *Journal of Personality*, **78**(5), 1383–1410. https://doi.org/10.1111/j.1467-6494.2010.00655.x

Lodi-Smith, J., Spain, S. M., Cologgi, K., & Roberts, B. W. (2017). Development of identity clarity and content in adulthood. *Journal of Personality and Social Psychology*, **112**, 755–768. https://doi.org/10.1037/pspp0000091

Marcia, J. (1980). Identity in adolescence. In *Handbook of adolescent psychology* (Vol. 9).

Mead, G. H. (1934). Taking the role of the other. In *Mind, self, and society*.

Mentzou, A., & Ross, J. (2023). A developmental understanding of the self may provide valuable insight into the experience of selfhood in dementia. *Infant and Child Development*, **32**(1). https://doi.org/10.1002/icd.2388

Morin, A. (2011). Self-Awareness Part 1: Definition, Measures, Effects, Functions, and Antecedents: Self-Awareness. *Social and Personality Psychology Compass*, **5**(10), 807–823. https://doi.org/10.1111/j.1751-9004.2011.00387.x

Neisser, U. (1991). Two perceptually given aspects of the self and their development. *Developmental Review*, **11**(3), 197–209. https://doi.org/10.1016/0273-2297(91)90009-D

Pfeifer, J. H., & Berkman, E. T. (2018). The Development of Self and Identity in Adolescence: Neural Evidence and Implications for a Value-Based Choice Perspective on Motivated Behavior. *Child Development Perspectives*, **12**(3), 158–164. https://doi.org/10.1111/cdep.12279

Rochat, P. (1998). Self-perception and action in infancy. *Experimental Brain Research*, **123**(1–2), 102–109. https://doi.org/10.1007/s002210050550

Rochat, P., & Striano, T. (2000). Perceived self in infancy. *Infant Behavior and Development*, **23**(3), 513–530. https://doi.org/10.1016/S0163-6383(01)00055-8

Saxe, R., Moran, J. M., Scholz, J., & Gabrieli, J. (2006). Overlapping and non-overlapping brain regions for theory of mind and self reflection in individual subjects. *Social Cognitive and Affective Neuroscience*, **1**(3), 229–234. https://doi.org/10.1093/scan/nsl034

Sebastian, C., Burnett, S., & Blakemore, S.-J. (2008). Development of the self-concept during adolescence. *Trends in Cognitive Sciences*, **12**(11), 441–446. https://doi.org/10.1016/j.tics.2008.07.008

Snyder, M. (1987). *Public appearances, Private realities: The psychology of self-monitoring*. WH Freeman/Times Books/Henry Holt & Co.

Tajfel, H., & Turner, J. C. (1986). The social identity theory of intergroup behavior. In S. Worchel & W. G. Austin (Eds.), *Psychology of intergroup relations* (pp. 7–24). Nelson Hall.

Tajfel, H., Turner, J. C., Austin, W. G., & Worchel, S. (1979). *An integrative theory of intergroup conflict. Organizational Identity: A Reader*, 56, 65.

Tanti, C., Stukas, A. A., Halloran, M. J., & Foddy, M. (2011). Social identity change: Shifts in social identity during adolescence. *Journal of Adolescence*, **34**(3), 555–567. https://doi.org/10.1016/j.adolescence.2010.05.012

# Chapter 4

Afsharnejad, B., Falkmer, M., Picen, T., Black, M. H., Alach, T., Fridell, A., Coco, C., Milne, K., Perry, J., Bölte, S., & Girdler, S. (2022). "I Met Someone Like Me!": Autistic Adolescents and Their Parents' Experience of the KONTAKT® Social Skills Group Training. *Journal of Autism and Developmental Disorders*, **52**(4), 1458–1477. https://doi.org/10.1007/s10803-021-05045-1

Ai, W., Cunningham, W. A., & Lai, M.-C. (2022). Reconsidering autistic 'camouflaging' as transactional impression management. *Trends in Cognitive Sciences*.

Alkhaldi, R. S., Sheppard, E., & Mitchell, P. (2019). Is There a Link Between Autistic People Being Perceived Unfavorably and Having a Mind That Is Difficult to Read? *Journal of Autism and Developmental Disorders*, **49**(10), 3973–3982. https://doi.org/10.1007/s10803-019-04101-1

Baron-Cohen, S. (1997). *Mindblindness: An essay on autism and theory of mind*. MIT press.

Belcher, H. L., Morein-Zamir, S., Mandy, W., & Ford, R. M. (2022). Camouflaging Intent, First Impressions, and Age of ASC Diagnosis in Autistic Men and Women. *Journal of Autism and Developmental Disorders*, **52**(8), 3413–3426. https://doi.org/10.1007/s10803-021-05221-3

Bertilsdotter Rosqvist, H., & Jackson-Perry, D. (2021). Not Doing it Properly? (Re)producing and Resisting Knowledge Through Narratives of Autistic Sexualities. *Sexuality and Disability*, **39**(2), 327–344. https://doi.org/10.1007/s11195-020-09624-5

Botha, M. (2020). *Autistic community connectedness as a buffer against the effects of minority stress*. University of Surrey.

Botha, M., Dibb, B., & Frost, D. M. (2022). 'It's being a part of a grand tradition, a grand counter-culture which involves communities': A qualitative investigation of autistic community connectedness. *Autism*, **26**(8), 2151–2164. https://doi.org/10.1177/13623613221080248

Brewer, R., Biotti, F., Catmur, C., Press, C., Happé, F., Cook, R., & Bird, G. (2016). Can Neurotypical Individuals Read Autistic Facial Expressions? Atypical Production of Emotional Facial Expressions in Autism Spectrum Disorders: Expression production in autism. *Autism Research*, **9**(2), 262–271. https://doi.org/10.1002/aur.1508

Bury, S. M., Jellett, R., Spoor, J. R., & Hedley, D. (2023). "It Defines Who I Am" or "It's Something I Have": What Language Do [Autistic] Australian Adults [on the Autism Spectrum] Prefer? *Journal of Autism and Developmental Disorders*, **53**(2), 677–687. https://doi.org/10.1007/s10803-020-04425-3

Cage, E., Bird, G., & Pellicano, L. (2016). 'I am who I am': Reputation concerns in adolescents on the autism spectrum. *Research in Autism Spectrum Disorders*, **25**, 12–23. https://doi.org/10.1016/j.rasd.2016.01.010

Cage, E., Botha, M., McDevitt, L., King, K. N., Biscoe, L., Tucker, K., & Pearson, A. (2022). *Diagnosis as a new beginning not an end: A participatory photovoice study on navigating an autism diagnosis in adulthood* [Preprint]. PsyArXiv. https://doi.org/10.31234/osf.io/qg9bt

Cage, E., & Troxell-Whitman, Z. (2019). Understanding the Reasons, Contexts and Costs of Camouflaging for Autistic Adults. *Journal of Autism and Developmental Disorders*. https://doi.org/10.1007/s10803-018-03878-x

Chapman, R. (2020). The reality of autism: On the metaphysics of disorder and diversity. *Philosophical Psychology*, **33**(6), 799–819. https://doi.org/10.1080/09515089.2020.1751103

Chapman, R., & Carel, H. (2022). Neurodiversity, epistemic injustice, and the good human life. *Journal of Social Philosophy*, **53**(4), 614–631. https://doi.org/10.1111/josp.12456

Chevallier, C., Kohls, G., Troiani, V., Brodkin, E. S., & Schultz, R. T. (2012). The social motivation theory of autism. *Trends in Cognitive Sciences*, **16**(4), 231–239.

Conway, J. R., Catmur, C., & Bird, G. (2019). Understanding individual differences in theory of mind via representation of minds, not mental states. *Psychonomic Bulletin & Review*, **26**(3), 798–812. https://doi.org/10.3758/s13423-018-1559-x

Cook, J. (2016). From movement kinematics to social cognition: The case of autism. *Philosophical Transactions of the Royal Society B: Biological Sciences*, **371**(1693), 20150372.

Cooper, K., Russell, A. J., Lei, J., & Smith, L. G. (2023). The impact of a positive autism identity and autistic community solidarity on social anxiety and mental health in autistic young people. *Autism*, **27**(3), 848–857. https://doi.org/10.1177/13623613221118351

Cooper, K., Smith, L. G. E., & Russell, A. (2017). Social identity, self-esteem, and mental health in autism: Social identity, self-esteem, and mental health in autism. *European Journal of Social Psychology*, **47**(7), 844–854. https://doi.org/10.1002/ejsp.2297

Cooper, R., Cooper, K., Russell, A. J., & Smith, L. G. E. (2021). "I'm Proud to be a Little Bit Different": The Effects of Autistic Individuals' Perceptions of Autism and Autism Social Identity on Their Collective Self-esteem. *Journal of Autism and Developmental Disorders*, **51**(2), 704–714. https://doi.org/10.1007/s10803-020-04575-4

Corden, K., Brewer, R., & Cage, E. (2021). Personal Identity After an Autism Diagnosis: Relationships With Self-Esteem, Mental Wellbeing, and Diagnostic Timing. *Frontiers in Psychology*, **12**, 699335. https://doi.org/10.3389/fpsyg.2021.699335

Crane, L., Jones, L., Prosser, R., Taghrizi, M., & Pellicano, E. (2019). Parents' views and experiences of talking about autism with their children. *Autism*, **23**(8), 1969–1981. https://doi.org/10.1177/1362361319836257

Crane, L., Lui, L. M., Davies, J., & Pellicano, E. (2021). Autistic parents' views and experiences of talking about autism with their autistic children. *Autism*, **25**(4), 1161–1167. https://doi.org/10.1177/1362361320981317

Crawshaw, D. (2023). *Should We Continue to Tell Autistic People that Their Brains are Different?* *Psychological Reports*, 003329412311743. https://doi.org/10.1177/00332941231174391

Cresswell, L., & Cage, E. (2019). 'Who Am I?': An Exploratory Study of the Relationships Between Identity, Acculturation and Mental Health in Autistic Adolescents. *Journal of Autism and Developmental Disorders*, **49**(7), 2901–2912. https://doi.org/10.1007/s10803-019-04016-x

Cresswell, L., Hinch, R., & Cage, E. (2019). The experiences of peer relationships amongst autistic adolescents: A systematic review of the qualitative evidence. *Research in Autism Spectrum Disorders*, **61**, 45–60. https://doi.org/10.1016/j.rasd.2019.01.003

DeBrabander, K. M., Morrison, K. E., Jones, D. R., Faso, D. J., Chmielewski, M., & Sasson, N. J. (2019). Do First Impressions of Autistic Adults Differ Between Autistic and Nonautistic Observers? *Autism in Adulthood*, **1**(4), 250–257. https://doi.org/10.1089/aut.2019.0018

Ellis, J. (Manidoomakwakwe). (2023). Imagining Neurodivergent Futures from the Belly of the Identity Machine: Neurodiversity, Biosociality, and Strategic Essentialism. *Autism in Adulthood*, aut.2021.0075. https://doi.org/10.1089/aut.2021.0075

Evans, B. (2014). The Foundations of Autism: The Law Concerning Psychotic, Schizophrenic, and Autistic Children in 1950s and 1960s Britain. *Bulletin of the History of Medicine*, **88**(2), 253–285. https://doi.org/10.1353/bhm.2014.0033

Forster, S., & Pearson, A. (2020). "Bullies tend to be obvious": Autistic adults perceptions of friendship and the concept of 'mate crime'. *Disability and Society*. https://doi.org/10.1080/09687599.2019.1680347

Frith, U., & De Vignemont, F. (2005). Egocentrism, allocentrism, and Asperger syndrome. *Consciousness and Cognition*, **14**(4), 719–738. https://doi.org/10.1016/j.concog.2005.04.006

Frith, U., & Happe, F. (1999). Theory of Mind and Self-Consciousness: What Is It Like to Be Autistic? *Mind and Language*, **14**(1), 82–89. https://doi.org/10.1111/1468-0017.00100

Gaigg, S. B., & Bowler, D. M. (2008). Free recall and forgetting of emotionally arousing words in autism spectrum disorder. *Neuropsychologia*, **46**(9), 2336–2343. https://doi.org/10.1016/j.neuropsychologia.2008.03.008

Gallup, G. G. (1979). Self-Awareness in Primates: The sense of identity distinguishes man from most but perhaps not all other forms of life. *American Scientist*, **67**(4), 417–421. JSTOR.

Gernsbacher, M. A., Stevenson, J. L., Khandakar, S., & Goldsmith, H. H. (2008). Why Does Joint Attention Look Atypical in Autism? *Child Development Perspectives*, **2**(1), 38–45. https://doi.org/10.1111/j.1750-8606.2008.00039.x

Grisdale, E. (2014). *Dimensions of the Self-Concept in Autism Spectrum Disorder* [Durham University]. http://etheses.dur.ac.uk/10750/

Harmens, M., Sedgewick, F., & Hobson, H. (2022). Autistic women's diagnostic experiences: Interactions with identity and impacts on well-being. *Women's Health*, **18**, 174550572211374. https://doi.org/10.1177/17455057221137477

Higgins, E. T. (1998). Promotion and Prevention: Regulatory Focus as A Motivational Principle. In *Advances in Experimental Social Psychology* (Vol. 30, pp. 1–46). Elsevier. https://doi.org/10.1016/S0065-2601(08)60381-0

Huang, Y., Arnold, S. R., Foley, K.-R., & Trollor, J. N. (2020). Diagnosis of autism in adulthood: A scoping review. *Autism*, **24**(6), 1311–1327. https://doi.org/10.1177/1362361320903128

Huang, Y., Trollor, J. N., Foley, K.-R., & Arnold, S. R. C. (2023). "I've Spent My Whole Life Striving to Be Normal": Internalized Stigma and Perceived Impact of Diagnosis in Autistic Adults. *Autism in Adulthood*, aut.2022.0066. https://doi.org/10.1089/aut.2022.0066

Humphrey, N., & Lewis, S. (2008). `Make me normal': The views and experiences of pupils on the autistic spectrum in mainstream secondary schools. *Autism*, **12**(1), 23–46. https://doi.org/10.1177/1362361307085267

Keates, N. (2022). A Letter to the Editor Regarding Bambara et al. (2021), "Using Peer Supports to Encourage Adolescents With Autism Spectrum Disorder to Show Interest in Their Conversation Partners". *Journal of Speech, Language, and Hearing Research*, **65**(4), 1600–1603. https://doi.org/10.1044/2022_JSLHR-22-00028

Keating, C. T., Sowden, S., & Cook, J. L. (2022). Comparing internal representations of facial expression kinematics between autistic and non-autistic adults. *Autism Research*, **15**(3), 493–506. https://doi.org/10.1002/aur.2642

Kelly, C., Sharma, S., Jieman, A.-T., & Ramon, S. (2022). Sense-making narratives of autistic women diagnosed in adulthood: A systematic review of the qualitative research. *Disability & Society*, 1–33. https://doi.org/10.1080/09687599.2022.2076582

Kelly, G. (1955). *Personal construct psychology*. Nueva York: Norton.

Kinnaird, E., Stewart, C., & Tchanturia, K. (2019). Investigating alexithymia in autism: A systematic review and meta-analysis. *European Psychiatry*, **55**, 80–89.

Kteily, N. S., & Landry, A. P. (2022). Dehumanization: Trends, insights, and challenges. *Trends in Cognitive Sciences*, **26**(3), 222–240. https://doi.org/10.1016/j.tics.2021.12.003

Lee, A., Hobson, R. P., & Chiat, S. (1994). I, you, me, and autism: An experimental study. *Journal of Autism and Developmental Disorders*, **24**(2), 155–176. https://doi.org/10.1007/BF02172094

Leedham, A., Thompson, A. R., Smith, R., & Freeth, M. (2020). 'I was exhausted trying to figure it out': The experiences of females receiving an autism diagnosis in middle to late adulthood. *Autism*, **24**(1), 135–146.

Lewis, L. F. (2016). Exploring the Experience of Self-Diagnosis of Autism Spectrum Disorder in Adults. Archives of Psychiatric Nursing, 30(5), 575–580. https://doi.org/10.1016/j.apnu.2016.03.009

Lilley, R., Lawson, W., Hall, G., Mahony, J., Clapham, H., Heyworth, M., Arnold, S. R., Trollor, J. N., Yudell, M., & Pellicano, E. (2022). 'A way to be me': Autobiographical reflections of autistic adults diagnosed in mid-to-late adulthood. *Autism*, **26**(6), 1395–1408. https://doi.org/10.1177/13623613211050694

Lilley, R., Lawson, W., Hall, G., Mahony, J., Clapham, H., Heyworth, M., Arnold, S., Trollor, J., Yudell, M., & Pellicano, E. (2023). "Peas in a pod": Oral History Reflections on Autistic Identity in Family and Community by Late-Diagnosed Adults. *Journal of Autism and Developmental Disorders*, **53**(3), 1146–1161. https://doi.org/10.1007/s10803-022-05667-z

Lind, S. E., & Bowler, D. M. (2009). Delayed Self-recognition in Children with Autism Spectrum Disorder. *Journal of Autism and Developmental Disorders*, **39**(4), 643–650. https://doi.org/10.1007/s10803-008-0670-7

Linden, A., Best, L., Elise, F., Roberts, D., Branagan, A., Tay, Y. B. E., Crane, L., Cusack, J., Davidson, B., Davidson, I., Hearst, C., Mandy, W., Rai, D., Smith, E., & Gurusamy, K. (2023). Benefits and harms of interventions to improve anxiety, depression, and other mental health outcomes for autistic people: A systematic review and network meta-analysis of randomised controlled trials. *Autism*, **27**(1), 7–30. https://doi.org/10.1177/13623613221117931

Livingston, L. A., & Happé, F. (2017). Conceptualising compensation in neurodevelopmental disorders: Reflections from autism spectrum disorder. *Neuroscience and Biobehavioral Reviews*. https://doi.org/10.1016/j.neubiorev.2017.06.005

Lombardo, M. V., & Baron-Cohen, S. (2010). Unraveling the paradox of the autistic self. WIREs *Cognitive Science*, 2(3), 393–403. https://doi.org/10.1002/wcs.45

Maitland, C. A., Rhodes, S., O'Hare, A., & Stewart, M. E. (2021). Social identities and mental well-being in autistic adults. *Autism*, 25(6), 1771–1783. https://doi.org/10.1177/13623613211004328

Mandy, W. (2019). Social camouflaging in autism: Is it time to lose the mask? *Autism*, 23(8), 1879–1881. https://doi.org/10.1177/1362361319878559

McDonald, T. A. M. (2020). Autism Identity and the "Lost Generation": Structural Validation of the Autism Spectrum Identity Scale and Comparison of Diagnosed and Self-Diagnosed Adults on the Autism Spectrum. *Autism in Adulthood*, 2(1), 13–23. https://doi.org/10.1089/aut.2019.0069

McLeod, J. D., Meanwell, E., & Hawbaker, A. (2019). The Experiences of College Students on the Autism Spectrum: A Comparison to Their Neurotypical Peers. *Journal of Autism and Developmental Disorders*, 49(6), 2320–2336. https://doi.org/10.1007/s10803-019-03910-8

Mesa, S., & Hamilton, L. G. (2022). "We are different, that's a fact, but they treat us like we're different-er": Understandings of autism and adolescent identity development. *Advances in Autism*, 8(3), 217–231. https://doi.org/10.1108/AIA-12-2020-0071

Milton, D. (2018). Autistic Development, Trauma and Personhood: Beyond the Frame of the Neoliberal Individual. In K. Runswick-Cole, T. Curran, & K. Liddiard (Eds.), *The Palgrave Handbook of Disabled Children's Childhood Studies* (pp. 461–476). Palgrave Macmillan UK. https://doi.org/10.1057/978-1-137-54446-9_29

Milton, D., & Sims, T. (2016). How is a sense of well-being and belonging constructed in the accounts of autistic adults? *Disability & Society*, 31(4), 520–534.

Morgan, R. (2023). How do adolescent autistic girls construct self-concept and social identity? A discourse analysis. *Educational Psychology in Practice*, 1–23. https://doi.org/10.1080/02667363.2023.2181316

Morin, A. (2011). Self-Awareness Part 1: Definition, Measures, Effects, Functions, and Antecedents: Self-Awareness. *Social and Personality Psychology Compass*, 5(10), 807–823. https://doi.org/10.1111/j.1751-9004.2011.00387.x

Murray, D., Lesser, M., & Lawson, W. (2005). Attention, monotropism and the diagnostic criteria for autism. *Autism*, 9(2), 139–156.

Nation, K., & Penny, S. (2008). Sensitivity to eye gaze in autism: Is it normal? Is it automatic? Is it social? *Development and Psychopathology*, 20(1), 79–97. https://doi.org/10.1017/S0954579408000047

Nijhof, A. D., & Bird, G. (2019). Self-processing in individuals with autism spectrum disorder. **Autism Research**, 12(11), 1580–1584. https://doi.org/10.1002/aur.2200

Oyserman, D., Uskul, A. K., Yoder, N., Nesse, R. M., & Williams, D. R. (2007). Unfair treatment and self-regulatory focus. *Journal of Experimental Social Psychology*, 43(3), 505–512. https://doi.org/10.1016/j.jesp.2006.05.014

Paton, B., Hohwy, J., & Enticott, P. G. (2012). The Rubber Hand Illusion Reveals Proprioceptive and Sensorimotor Differences in Autism Spectrum Disorders. *Journal of Autism and Developmental Disorders*, 42(9), 1870–1883. https://doi.org/10.1007/s10803-011-1430-7

Paul, R., Augustyn, A., Klin, A., & Volkmar, F. R. (2005). Perception and Production of Prosody by Speakers with Autism Spectrum Disorders. *Journal of Autism and Developmental Disorders*, 35(2), 205–220. https://doi.org/10.1007/s10803-004-1999-1

Pearson, A., Ropar, D., & De C. Hamilton, A. F. (2013). A review of visual perspective taking in autism spectrum disorder. *Frontiers in Human Neuroscience*, 7. https://doi.org/10.3389/fnhum.2013.00652

Pearson, A., Rose, K., & Rees, J. (2023). 'I felt like I deserved it because I was autistic': Understanding the impact of interpersonal victimisation in the lives of autistic people. *Autism*, 27(2), 500–511. https://doi.org/10.1177/13623613221104546

Pyne, J. (2021). Autistic Disruptions, Trans Temporalities. *South Atlantic Quarterly*, **120**(2), 343–361. https://doi.org/10.1215/00382876-8916088

Riby, D. M., Hancock, P. J., Jones, N., & Hanley, M. (2013). Spontaneous and cued gaze-following in autism and Williams syndrome. *Journal of Neurodevelopmental Disorders*, **5**(1), 13. https://doi.org/10.1186/1866-1955-5-13

Riccio, A., Kapp, S. K., Jordan, A., Dorelien, A. M., & Gillespie-Lynch, K. (2021). How is autistic identity in adolescence influenced by parental disclosure decisions and perceptions of autism? *Autism*, **25**(2), 374–388. https://doi.org/10.1177/1362361320958214

Sasson, N. J., Faso, D. J., Nugent, J., Lovell, S., Kennedy, D. P., & Grossman, R. B. (2017). Neurotypical Peers are Less Willing to Interact with Those with Autism based on Thin Slice Judgments. *Scientific Reports*, **7**. https://doi.org/10.1038/srep40700

Schneid, I., & Raz, A. E. (2020). The mask of autism: Social camouflaging and impression management as coping/normalization from the perspectives of autistic adults. *Social Science & Medicine*, **248**, 112826.

Schröer, L., Çetin, D., Vacaru, S. V., Addabbo, M., Van Schaik, J. E., & Hunnius, S. (2022). Infants' sensitivity to emotional expressions in actions: The contributions of parental expressivity and motor experience. *Infant Behavior and Development*, **68**, 101751. https://doi.org/10.1016/j.infbeh.2022.101751

Sedgewick, F., Crane, L., Hill, V., & Pellicano, E. (2019). Friends and lovers: The relationships of autistic and neurotypical women. *Autism in Adulthood*, **1**(2), 112–123.

Sedgewick, F., Hill, V., Yates, R., Pickering, L., & Pellicano, E. (2016). Gender Differences in the Social Motivation and Friendship Experiences of Autistic and Non-autistic Adolescents. *Journal of Autism and Developmental Disorders*, **46**(4), 1297–1306. https://doi.org/10.1007/s10803-015-2669-1

Senju, A., & Johnson, M. H. (2009). Atypical eye contact in autism: Models, mechanisms and development. *Neuroscience & Biobehavioral Reviews*, **33**(8), 1204–1214. https://doi.org/10.1016/j.neubiorev.2009.06.001

Shrauger, J. S., & Schoeneman, T. J. (1999). *Symbolic interactionist view of self-concept: Through the looking glass darkly.* (p. 42). Psychology Press.

Spiker, D., & Ricks, M. (1984). Visual Self-Recognition in Autistic Children: Developmental Relationships. *Child Development*, **55**(1), 214. https://doi.org/10.2307/1129846

Stenning, A. (2020). Understanding empathy through a study of autistic life writing: On the importance of neurodiverse morality. *Neurodiversity Studies*.

Tajfel, H., & Turner, J. C. (1986). The social identity theory of intergroup behavior. In S. Worchel & W. G. Austin (Eds.), *Psychology of intergroup relations* (pp. 7–24). Nelson Hall.

Thapar, A., & Rutter, M. (2021). Genetic Advances in Autism. *Journal of Autism and Developmental Disorders*, **51**(12), 4321–4332. https://doi.org/10.1007/s10803-020-04685-z

Tice, D. M. (1992). Self-concept change and self-presentation: The looking glass self is also a magnifying glass. *Journal of Personality and Social Psychology*, **63**(3), 435–451. https://doi.org/10.1037/0022-3514.63.3.435

Watermeyer, B., & Swartz, L. (2016). Disablism, Identity and Self: Discrimination as a Traumatic Assault on Subjectivity: Disablism as a traumatic assault. *Journal of Community & Applied Social Psychology*, **26**(3), 268–276. https://doi.org/10.1002/casp.2266

Zahavi, D. (2010). Complexities of self. *Autism*, **14**(5), 547–551. https://doi.org/10.1177/1362361310370040

# Chapter 5

Almeida, R. A., Dickinson, J. E., Maybery, M. T., Badcock, J. C., & Badcock, D. R. (2010). A new step towards understanding Embedded Figures Test performance in the autism spectrum: The radial frequency search task. *Neuropsychologia*, **48**(2), 374–381. https://doi.org/10.1016/j.neuropsychologia.2009.09.024

Baron-Cohen, S. (2002). The extreme male brain theory of autism. *Trends in Cognitive Sciences*, **6**(6), 248–254.

Baron-Cohen, S. (2015). Leo Kanner, Hans Asperger, and the discovery of autism. *The Lancet*, **386**(10001), 1329–1330. https://doi.org/10.1016/S0140-6736(15)00337-2

Baron-Cohen, S. (2017). Editorial Perspective: Neurodiversity – a revolutionary concept for autism and psychiatry. *Journal of Child Psychology and Psychiatry and Allied Disciplines*. https://doi.org/10.1111/jcpp.12703

Baron-Cohen, S., Tsompanidis, A., Auyeung, B., Nørgaard-Pedersen, B., Hougaard, D. M., Abdallah, M., Cohen, A., & Pohl, A. (2020). Foetal oestrogens and autism. *Molecular Psychiatry*, **25**(11), 2970–2978. https://doi.org/10.1038/s41380-019-0454-9

Belcher, H. L., Morein-Zamir, S., Mandy, W., & Ford, R. M. (2022). Camouflaging Intent, First Impressions, and Age of ASC Diagnosis in Autistic Men and Women. *Journal of Autism and Developmental Disorders*, **52**(8), 3413–3426. https://doi.org/10.1007/s10803-021-05221-3

Belcher, H. L., Morein-Zamir, S., Stagg, S. D., & Ford, R. M. (2022). Shining a Light on a Hidden Population: Social Functioning and Mental Health in Women Reporting Autistic Traits But Lacking Diagnosis. *Journal of Autism and Developmental Disorders*. https://doi.org/10.1007/s10803-022-05583-2

Bertilsdotter Rosqvist, H., Botha, M., Hens, K., O'Donoghue, S., Pearson, A., & Stenning, A. (2022). Cutting our own keys: New possibilities of neurodivergent storying in research. *Autism*, 13623613221132108.

Betts, K., Creechan, L., Cawkwell, R., Finn-Kelcey, I., Griffin, C. J., Hagopian, A., Hartley, D., Manalili, M. A. R., Murkumbi, I., O'Donoghue, S., Shanahan, C., Stenning, A., & Zisk, A. H. (2022). Neurodiversity, Networks, and Narratives: Exploring Intimacy and Expressive Freedom in the Time of Covid-19. *Social Inclusion*, **11**(1). https://doi.org/10.17645/si.v11i1.5737

Bobb, V. (2019). Black girls and autism. In B. Carpenter, F. Happé, & J. Egerton (Eds.), *Girls and autism: Educational, family and personal perspectives*. Routledge.

Botha, M., & Gillespie-Lynch, K. (2022). Come as You Are: Examining Autistic Identity Development and the Neurodiversity Movement through an Intersectional Lens. *Human Development*, **66**(2), 93–112. https://doi.org/10.1159/000524123

Brown, L. X. Z., Ashkenazy, E., & Onaiwu, M. G. (Eds.). (2017). *All the weight of our dreams: On living racialized autism*. DragonBee Press, an imprint of the Autism Women's Network.

Butler, J. (1988). Performative Acts and Gender Constitution: An Essay in Phenomenology and Feminist Theory. *Theatre Journal*, **40**(4), 519. https://doi.org/10.2307/3207893

Cage, E., Botha, M., McDevitt, L., King, K. N., Biscoe, L., Tucker, K., & Pearson, A. (2022). *Diagnosis as a new beginning not an end: A participatory photovoice study on navigating an autism diagnosis in adulthood* [Preprint]. PsyArXiv. https://doi.org/10.31234/osf.io/qg9bt

Cascio, M. A., Weiss, J. A., & Racine, E. (2021). Making autism research inclusive by attending to intersectionality: A review of the research ethics literature. *Review Journal of Autism and Developmental Disorders*, **8**, 22–36.

Cheng, Y., Tekola, B., Balasubramanian, A., Crane, L., & Leadbitter, K. (2023). Neurodiversity and community-led rights-based movements: Barriers and opportunities for global research partnerships. *Autism*, **27**(3), 573–577. https://doi.org/10.1177/13623613231159165

Cheon, B. K., Melani, I., & Hong, Y. (2020). How USA-Centric Is Psychology? An Archival Study of Implicit Assumptions of Generalizability of Findings to Human Nature Based on Origins of Study Samples. *Social Psychological and Personality Science*, **11**(7), 928–937. https://doi.org/10.1177/1948550620927269

Collis, R. (2023). A response to Singer, Lutz, Escher, and Halladay's "a full semantic toolbox is essential for autism research and practice to thrive" in Autism Research (published online 12 Dec 2022). *Autism Research*, **16**(4), 679–680. https://doi.org/10.1002/aur.2902

Cooper, K., Mandy, W., Butler, C., & Russell, A. (2022). The lived experience of gender dysphoria in autistic adults: An interpretative phenomenological analysis. *Autism*, **26**(4), 963–974. https://doi.org/10.1177/13623613211039113

Cooper, K., Smith, L. G. E., & Russell, A. J. (2018). Gender identity in autism: Sex differences in social affiliation with gender groups. *Journal of Autism and Developmental Disorders*, **48**(12), 3995–4006.

Crenshaw, K. (1990). Mapping the margins: Intersectionality, identity politics, and violence against women of color. *Stan. L. Rev.*, **43**, 1241.

Crenshaw, K. W. (2017). *On intersectionality: Essential writings*. The New Press.

Dababnah, S., Kim, I., & Shaia, W. E. (2022). 'I am so fearful for him': A mixed-methods exploration of stress among caregivers of Black children with autism. *International Journal of Developmental Disabilities*, **68**(5), 658–670. https://doi.org/10.1080/20473869.2020.1870418

Davis, A. Y., & Martínez, E. (1993). *Coalition Building Among People of Color: A discussion with Angela Y. Davis and Elizabeth Martínez* [Interview]. https://culturalstudies.ucsc.edu/inscriptions/volume-7/angela-y-davis-elizabeth-martinez/

Dewinter, J., De Graaf, H., & Begeer, S. (2017). Sexual orientation, gender identity, and romantic relationships in adolescents and adults with autism spectrum disorder. *Journal of Autism and Developmental Disorders*, **47**(9), 2927–2934.

Diemer, M. C., Gerstein, E. D., & Regester, A. (2022). Autism presentation in female and Black populations: Examining the roles of identity, theory, and systemic inequalities. *Autism*, **26**(8), 1931–1946. https://doi.org/10.1177/13623613221113501

Dupree, C. H., & Kraus, M. W. (2022). Psychological Science Is Not Race Neutral. *Perspectives on Psychological Science*, **17**(1), 270–275. https://doi.org/10.1177/1745691620979820

Epstein, R., Blake, J. J., & González, T. (2017). *Girlhood Interrupted: The Erasure of Black Girls' Childhood*. Georgetown Law Center on Poverty and Inequality. https://genderjusticeandopportunity.georgetown.edu/wp-content/uploads/2020/06/girlhood-interrupted.pdf

Fombonne, E. (1999). The epidemiology of autism: A review. *Psychological Medicine*, **29**(4), 769–786. https://doi.org/10.1017/S0033291799008508

Fombonne, E. (2020). Camouflage and autism. *Journal of Child Psychology and Psychiatry*, **61**(7), 735–738. https://doi.org/10.1111/jcpp.13296

Fombonne, E., & Zuckerman, K. E. (2022). Clinical Profiles of Black and White Children Referred for Autism Diagnosis. *Journal of Autism and Developmental Disorders*, **52**(3), 1120–1130. https://doi.org/10.1007/s10803-021-05019-3

Forbes, S. H., Aneja, P., & Guest, O. (2022). *The myth of normative development. Infant and Child Development*. https://doi.org/10.1002/icd.2393

Frith, U. (2001). Mind Blindness and the Brain in Autism. *Neuron*, **32**(6), 969–979. https://doi.org/10.1016/S0896-6273(01)00552-9

Frith, U. (2021). When diagnosis hampers research. *Autism Research*, **14**(10), 2235–2236. https://doi.org/10.1002/aur.2578

Gesi, C., Migliarese, G., Torriero, S., Capellazzi, M., Omboni, A. C., Cerveri, G., & Mencacci, C. (2021). Gender Differences in Misdiagnosis and Delayed Diagnosis among Adults with Autism Spectrum Disorder with No Language or Intellectual Disability. *Brain Sciences*, **11**(7), Article 7. https://doi.org/10.3390/brainsci11070912

Giwa Onaiwu, M. (2020). "They Don't Know, Don't Show, or Don't Care": Autism's White Privilege Problem. *Autism in Adulthood*, **2**(4), 270–272. https://doi.org/10.1089/aut.2020.0077

Giwa Onaiwu, M., Montgomery, C., Latimer, O., Brown, L. X. Z., & Gardiner, F. (2021). *Hear Our Cry: Call for Solidarity with Autistic BIPoC and Autistic People with Intellectual Disabilities: Demands presented to the Autistic Self-Advocacy Network (ASAN) for their June 20th Board Meeting*. https://morenikego.com/memo-to-asan-2021/

Henrich, J., Heine, S. J., & Norenzayan, A. (2010). Most people are not WEIRD. *Nature*, **466**(7302), 29–29. https://doi.org/10.1038/466029a

Hens, K., & Van Goidsenhoven, L. (2023). Developmental diversity: Putting the development back into research about developmental conditions. *Frontiers in Psychiatry*, **13**, 986732. https://doi.org/10.3389/fpsyt.2022.986732

Hodgetts, S., & Hausmann, M. (2022). Sex/Gender Differences in Brain Lateralisation and Connectivity. In C. Gibson & L. A. M. Galea (Eds.), *Sex Differences in Brain Function and Dysfunction* (Vol. 62, pp. 71–99). Springer International Publishing. https://doi. org/10.1007/7854_2022_303

Hoekstra, R. A. (2022). Serving the underserved: How can we reach autism families who systemically miss out on support? *Autism*, **26**(6), 1315–1319. https://doi. org/10.1177/13623613221105389

Hongo, M., Oshima, F., Guan, S., Takahashi, T., Nitta, Y., Seto, M., Hull, L., Mandy, W., Ohtani, T., Tamura, M., & Shimizu, E. (2022). *Reliability and Validity of the Japanese Version of the Camouflaging Autistic Traits Questionnaire* [Preprint]. PsyArXiv. https://doi.org/10.31234/osf.io/ zdc6g

Hughes, J. A. (2021). Does the heterogeneity of autism undermine the neurodiversity paradigm? *Bioethics*, **35**(1), 47–60. https://doi.org/10.1111/bioe.12780

Hull, L., Petrides, K. V., Allison, C., Smith, P., Baron-Cohen, S., Lai, M. C., & Mandy, W. (2017). "Putting on My Best Normal": Social Camouflaging in Adults with Autism Spectrum Conditions. *Journal of Autism and Developmental Disorders*. https://doi.org/10.1007/s10803-017-3166-5

Hull, L., Petrides, K. V., & Mandy, W. (2020). The Female Autism Phenotype and Camouflaging: A Narrative Review. *Review Journal of Autism and Developmental Disorders*. https://doi.org/10.1007/ s40489-020-00197-9

Hutson, T. M., McGhee Hassrick, E., Fernandes, S., Walton, J., Bouvier-Weinberg, K., Radcliffe, A., & Allen-Handy, A. (2022). "I'm just different–that's all–I'm so sorry … ": Black men, ASD and the urgent need for DisCrit Theory in police encounters. *Policing: An International Journal*, **45**(3), 524–537. https://doi.org/10.1108/PIJPSM-10-2021-0149

Jadav, N., & Bal, V. H. (2022). Associations between co-occurring conditions and age of autism diagnosis: Implications for mental health training and adult autism research. *Autism Research*, **15**(11), 2112–2125. https://doi.org/10.1002/aur.2808

Jellett, R., & Muggleton, J. (2022). Implications of Applying "Clinically Significant Impairment" to Autism Assessment: Commentary on Six Problems Encountered in Clinical Practice. *Journal of Autism and Developmental Disorders*, **52**(3), 1412–1421. https://doi.org/10.1007/s10803-021-04988-9

Jones, D. R., & Mandell, D. S. (2020). To address racial disparities in autism research, we must think globally, act locally. *Autism*, **24**(7), 1587–1589. https://doi.org/10.1177/1362361320948313

Jones, D. R., Nicolaidis, C., Ellwood, L. J., Garcia, A., Johnson, K. R., Lopez, K., & Waisman, T. (2020). An Expert Discussion on Structural Racism in Autism Research and Practice. *Autism in Adulthood*, **2**(4), 273–281. https://doi.org/10.1089/aut.2020.29015.drj

Kanner, L. (1944). Early infantile autism. *The Journal of Pediatrics*, **25**, 211–217. https://doi. org/10.1016/S0022-3476(44)80156-1

Kassous, I. Z. (2023). Researching autism in the Global South (MENA region): To what extent is Western autism research inclusive towards the Global South? *Women's Health*, **19**, 174550572311563. https://doi.org/10.1177/17455057231156315

Keating, C. T., Hickman, L., Geelhand, P., Takahashi, T., Leung, J., Schuster, B., Rybicki, A., Girolamo, T. M., Clin, E., Papastamou, F., Belenger, M., Eigsti, I.-M., Cook, J. L., Kosaka, H., Osu, R., Okamoto, Y., & Sowden, S. (2021). Global perspectives on autism acceptance, camouflaging behaviours and mental health in autism spectrum disorder: A registered report protocol. *PLOS ONE*, **16**(12), e0261774. https://doi.org/10.1371/journal.pone.0261774

King, D. K. (1988). Multiple Jeopardy, Multiple Consciousness: The Context of a Black Feminist Ideology. *Signs: Journal of Women in Culture and Society*, **14**(1), 42–72. https://doi. org/10.1086/494491

Koffer Miller, K. H., Cooper, D. S., Song, W., & Shea, L. L. (2022). Self-reported service needs and barriers reported by autistic adults: Differences by gender identity. *Research in Autism Spectrum Disorders*, **92**, 101916. https://doi.org/10.1016/j.rasd.2022.101916

Kung, K. T. F., Thankamony, A., Ong, K. K. L., Acerini, C. L., Dunger, D. B., Hughes, I. A., & Hines, M. (2021). No relationship between prenatal or early postnatal androgen exposure and autistic traits: Evidence using anogenital distance and penile length measurements at birth and 3 months of age. *Journal of Child Psychology and Psychiatry*, **62**(7), 876–883. https://doi.org/10.1111/jcpp.13335

Kyselicová, K., Belica, I., Vidošovičová, M., Janšáková, K., Neščáková, E., Špajdel, M., Navarová, S., & Ostatníková, D. (2021). Autism spectrum disorder and new perspectives on the reliability of second to fourth digit ratio. *Developmental Psychobiology*, **63**(6). https://doi.org/10.1002/dev.22122

Lai, M.-C., Kassee, C., Besney, R., Bonato, S., Hull, L., Mandy, W., Szatmari, P., & Ameis, S. H. (2019). Prevalence of co-occurring mental health diagnoses in the autism population: A systematic review and meta-analysis. *The Lancet Psychiatry*, **6**(10), 819–829. https://doi.org/10.1016/S2215-0366(19)30289-5

Lewis, L. F. (2016). Exploring the Experience of Self-Diagnosis of Autism Spectrum Disorder in Adults. *Archives of Psychiatric Nursing*, **30**(5), 575–580. https://doi.org/10.1016/j.apnu.2016.03.009

Loomes, R., Hull, L., & Mandy, W. P. L. (2017). What Is the Male-to-Female Ratio in Autism Spectrum Disorder? A Systematic Review and Meta-Analysis. *Journal of the American Academy of Child & Adolescent Psychiatry*, **56**(6), 466–474. https://doi.org/10.1016/j.jaac.2017.03.013

Lord, C., Brugha, T. S., Charman, T., Cusack, J., Dumas, G., Frazier, T., Jones, E. J. H., Jones, R. M., Pickles, A., & State, M. W. (2020). Autism spectrum disorder. *Nature Reviews Disease Primers*, **6**(1), 1–23.

Lord, C., Charman, T., Havdahl, A., Carbone, P., Anagnostou, E., Boyd, B., Carr, T., De Vries, P. J., Dissanayake, C., Divan, G., Freitag, C. M., Gotelli, M. M., Kasari, C., Knapp, M., Mundy, P., Plank, A., Scahill, L., Servili, C., Shattuck, P., … McCauley, J. B. (2022). The Lancet Commission on the future of care and clinical research in autism. *The Lancet*, **399**(10321), 271–334. https://doi.org/10.1016/S0140-6736(21)01541-5

Lovelace, T. S., Comis, M. P., Tabb, J. M., & Oshokoya, O. E. (2022). Missing from the Narrative: A Seven-Decade Scoping Review of the Inclusion of Black Autistic Women and Girls in Autism Research. *Behavior Analysis in Practice*, **15**(4), 1093–1105. https://doi.org/10.1007/s40617-021-00654-9

Mallipeddi, N. V., & VanDaalen, R. A. (2022). Intersectionality within critical autism studies: A narrative review. *Autism in Adulthood*, **4**(4), 281–289.

Malone, K. M., Pearson, J. N., Palazzo, K. N., Manns, L. D., Rivera, A. Q., & Mason Martin, D. L. (2022). The Scholarly Neglect of Black Autistic Adults in Autism Research. *Autism in Adulthood*, **4**(4), 271–280. https://doi.org/10.1089/aut.2021.0086

Manalili, M. A. R., Pearson, A., Sulik, J., Creechan, L., Elsherif, M., Murkumbi, I., Azevedo, F., Bonnen, K. L., Kim, J. S., Kording, K., Lee, J. J., Obscura, M., Kapp, S. K., Röer, J. P., & Morstead, T. (2023). From Puzzle to Progress: How Engaging With Neurodiversity Can Improve Cognitive Science. *Cognitive Science*, **47**(2), e13255. https://doi.org/10.1111/cogs.13255

Mandy, W., Pellicano, L., St Pourcain, B., Skuse, D., & Heron, J. (2018). The development of autistic social traits across childhood and adolescence in males and females. *Journal of Child Psychology and Psychiatry*, **59**(11), 1143–1151.

Manning, J. T., Baron-Cohen, S., Wheelwright, S., & Sanders, G. (2001). The 2nd to 4th digit ratio and autism. *Developmental Medicine and Child Neurology*, **43**(03), 160. https://doi.org/10.1017/S0012162201000317

Maye, M., Boyd, B. A., Martínez-Pedraza, F., Halladay, A., Thurm, A., & Mandell, D. S. (2022). Biases, Barriers, and Possible Solutions: Steps Towards Addressing Autism Researchers Under-Engagement with Racially, Ethnically, and Socioeconomically Diverse Communities. *Journal of Autism and Developmental Disorders*, **52**(9), 4206–4211. https://doi.org/10.1007/s10803-021-05250-y

Milton, D. (2016). *Re-thinking autism: Diagnosis, identity and equality: Re-thinking autism: diagnosis, identity and equality*, edited by Katherine Runswick-Cole, Rebecca Mallet and Sami Timimi, London, Jessica Kingsley Publishers, 2016, 336 pp.,\pounds 18.99 (paperback), ISBN 978-1-78-450027-6. Taylor & Francis.

Morgan, E. H., Rodgers, R., & Tschida, J. (2022). Addressing the Intersectionality of Race and Disability to Improve Autism Care. *Pediatrics*, **149**(Supplement 4), e2020049437M. https://doi.org/10.1542/peds.2020-049437M

Natri, H. M., Abubakare, O., Asasumasu, K., Basargekar, A., Beaud, F., Botha, M., Bottema-Beutel, K., Brea, M. R., Brown, L. X. Z., Burr, D. A., Cobbaert, L., Dabbs, C., Denome, D., Rosa, S. D. R., Doherty, M., Edwards, B., Edwards, C., Liszk, S. E., Elise, F., … Zisk, A. H. (2023). Anti-ableist language is fully compatible with high-quality autism research: Response to S inger et al. (2023). *Autism Research*, **16**(4), 673–676. https://doi.org/10.1002/aur.2928

NHS. (2016). *Adult Psychiatric Morbidity Survey: Survey of Mental Health and Wellbeing, England*, 2014.

NHS. (2018, April 9). *Learning disabilities*. Nhs.Uk. https://www.nhs.uk/conditions/learning-disabilities/

Obeid, R., Bisson, J. B., Cosenza, A., Harrison, A. J., James, F., Saade, S., & Gillespie-Lynch, K. (2021). Do Implicit and Explicit Racial Biases Influence Autism Identification and Stigma? An Implicit Association Test Study. *Journal of Autism and Developmental Disorders*, **51**(1), 106–128. https://doi.org/10.1007/s10803-020-04507-2

O'Brien, G., & Pearson, J. (2004). Autism and Learning Disability. *Autism*, **8**(2), 125–140. https://doi.org/10.1177/1362361304042718

Offord, J. (n.d.). A conversation with Simon Baron-Cohen (No. 34). https://podcasters.spotify.com/pod/show/differentminds/episodes/A-conversation-with-Simon-Baron-Cohen-emudeb

Oshima, F., Tamura, M., Cage, E., Perry, E., Hongo, M., Seto, M., Takahashi, T., & Shimizu, E. (2023). *Understanding camouflaging, stigma, and mental health for autistic people in Japan* [Preprint]. In Review. https://doi.org/10.21203/rs.3.rs-2614748/v1

Paul, S., Maria, C., & Chiedza, K. (2020). Supporting people with learning disabilities and mental health issues: Service users' experiences. *Learning Disability Practice*, **23**(4), 16–26. https://doi.org/10.7748/ldp.2020.e2037

Pavlopoulou, G. (2020). A Good Night's Sleep: Learning About Sleep From Autistic Adolescents' Personal Accounts. *Frontiers in Psychology*, **11**, 583868. https://doi.org/10.3389/fpsyg.2020.583868

Pearson, A., & Rose, K. (2021). A Conceptual Analysis of Autistic Masking: Understanding the Narrative of Stigma and the Illusion of Choice. *Autism in Adulthood*. https://doi.org/10.1089/aut.2020.0043

Pearson, A., Woods, R., Morgan, H., & Botha, M. (2021). Creating truly radical change in autism research: A response to FRITH and MOTTRON. *Autism Research*, **14**(10), 2243–2244. https://doi.org/10.1002/aur.2605

Pellicano, E., Dinsmore, A., & Charman, T. (2014). What should autism research focus upon? Community views and priorities from the United Kingdom. *Autism*, **18**(7), 756–770. https://doi.org/10.1177/1362361314529627

Radulski, E. M. (2022). Conceptualising Autistic Masking, Camouflaging, and Neurotypical Privilege: Towards a Minority Group Model of Neurodiversity. *Human Development*, **66**(2), 113–127. https://doi.org/10.1159/000524122

Roman-Urrestarazu, A., van Kessel, R., Allison, C., Matthews, F. E., Brayne, C., & Baron-Cohen, S. (2021). Association of Race/Ethnicity and Social Disadvantage With Autism Prevalence in 7 Million School Children in England. *JAMA Pediatrics*, **175**(6), e210054–e210054. https://doi.org/10.1001/jamapediatrics.2021.0054

Rose, K. (2018a). *Masking: I am not OK*. https://theautisticadvocate.com/2018/07/masking-i-am-not-ok/

Rose, K. (2018b). We are not ok. *The Autistic Advocate*. https://theautisticadvocate.com/2018/08/we-are-not-ok/

Russell, G., Mandy, W., Elliott, D., White, R., Pittwood, T., & Ford, T. (2019). Selection bias on intellectual ability in autism research: A cross-sectional review and meta-analysis. *Molecular Autism*, **10**(1), 9. https://doi.org/10.1186/s13229-019-0260-x

Schulz, J., Bahrami-Rad, D., Beauchamp, J., & Henrich, J. (2018). The Origins of WEIRD Psychology. *SSRN Electronic Journal*. https://doi.org/10.2139/ssrn.3201031

Sedgewick, F., Hill, V., & Pellicano, E. (2018). 'It's different for girls': Gender differences in the friendships and conflict of autistic and neurotypical adolescents. *Autism*, **23**(5), 1119–1132. https://doi.org/10.1177/1362361318794930

Silberman, S. (2015). *Neurotribes: The legacy of autism and the future of neurodiversity*. Penguin.

Singer, A., Lutz, A., Escher, J., & Halladay, A. (2023). A full semantic toolbox is essential for autism research and practice to thrive. *Autism Research*, **16**(3), 497–501. https://doi.org/10.1002/aur.2876

Singh, L., Cristia, A., Karasik, L. B., Rajendra, S. J., & Oakes, L. (2021). *Diversity and Representation in Infant Research: Barriers and bridges towards a globalized science of infant development* [Preprint]. PsyArXiv. https://doi.org/10.31234/osf.io/hgukc

Smilges, J. L. (2022). Neurotrans. *TSQ: Transgender Studies Quarterly*, **9**(4), 634–652. https://doi.org/10.1215/23289252-10133831

Smith, K. (2020). *AUTISM INTERVIEW #140: KAYLA SMITH ON THE INTERSECTIONALITY OF RACE AND AUTISM* [Written]. https://learnfromautistics.com/autism-interview-140-kayla-smith-on-the-intersectionality-of-race-and-autism/

Spence, O. (2020). "Zero Tolerance" of Black Autistic Boys: Are schools failing to recognise the needs of African Caribbean Boys with a diagnosis of autism? In *The Neurodiversity Reader: Exploring Concepts, Lived Experience and Implications for Practice* (pp. 41–47). Pavilion.

Strand, L. R. (2017). Charting Relations between Intersectionality Theory and the Neurodiversity Paradigm. *Disability Studies Quarterly*, **37**(2). https://doi.org/10.18061/dsq.v37i2.5374

Strang, J. F., Klomp, S. E., Caplan, R., Griffin, A. D., Anthony, L. G., Harris, M. C., Graham, E. K., Knauss, M., & van der Miesen, A. I. R. (2019). Community-based participatory design for research that impacts the lives of transgender and/or gender-diverse autistic and/or neurodiverse people. *Clinical Practice in Pediatric Psychology*, **7**, 396–404. https://doi.org/10.1037/cpp0000310

Strang, J. F., Meagher, H., Kenworthy, L., De Vries, A. L. C., Menvielle, E., Leibowitz, S., Janssen, A., Cohen-Kettenis, P., Shumer, D. E., Edwards-Leeper, L., Pleak, R. R., Spack, N., Karasic, D. H., Schreier, H., Balleur, A., Tishelman, A., Ehrensaft, D., Rodnan, L., Kuschner, E. S., … Anthony, L. G. (2018). Initial Clinical Guidelines for Co-Occurring Autism Spectrum Disorder and Gender Dysphoria or Incongruence in Adolescents. *Journal of Clinical Child & Adolescent Psychology*, **47**(1), 105–115. https://doi.org/10.1080/15374416.2016.1228462

Strang, J. F., van der Miesen, A. I. R., Caplan, R., Hughes, C., daVanport, S., & Lai, M.-C. (2020). Both sex- and gender-related factors should be considered in autism research and clinical practice. *Autism*, **24**(3), 539–543. https://doi.org/10.1177/1362361320913192

Teatero, M. L., & Netley, C. (2013). A Critical Review of the Research on the Extreme Male Brain Theory and Digit Ratio (2D:4D). *Journal of Autism and Developmental Disorders*, **43**(11), 2664–2676. https://doi.org/10.1007/s10803-013-1819-6

Timimi, S., Milton, D., Bovell, V., Kapp, S., & Russell, G. (2019). Deconstructing Diagnosis: Four Commentaries on a Diagnostic Tool to Assess Individuals for Autism Spectrum Disorders. *Autonomy* (Birmingham, England), **1**(6), AR26.

Waldock, K. E. (2019). Commentary on "Thinking differently? Autism and quality of life". *Tizard Learning Disability Review*, **24**(2), 77–81. https://doi.org/10.1108/TLDR-02-2019-0006

Walker, N. (2021). *Neuroqueer Heresies*. Autonomous Press.

Wing, L., & Gould, J. (1979). Severe impairments of social interaction and associated abnormalities in children: Epidemiology and classification. *Journal of Autism and Developmental Disorders*, **9**(1), 11–29. https://doi.org/10.1007/BF01531288

Wood, C., & Freeth, M. (2016). Students' Stereotypes of Autism. *Journal of Educational Issues*, **2**(2), 131–140.

Woods, R., Waldock, K. E., Keates, N., & Morgan, H. (2023). Empathy and a Personalised Approach in Autism. *Journal of Autism and Developmental Disorders*, **53**(2), 850–852. https://doi.org/10.1007/s10803-019-04287-4

Zeidan, J., Fombonne, E., Scorah, J., Ibrahim, A., Durkin, M. S., Saxena, S., Yusuf, A., Shih, A., & Elsabbagh, M. (2022). Global prevalence of autism: A systematic review update. *Autism Research*, **15**(5), 778–790. https://doi.org/10.1002/aur.2696

Zimmerman, J. (2022). Jordyn Zimmerman's Remarks to the Interagency Autism Coordinating Committee. *Communication FIRST*. https://communicationfirst.org/jordyn-zimmermans-remarks-to-the-interagency-autism-coordinating-committee/

# Chapter 6

Ai, W., Cunningham, W. A., & Lai, M.-C. (2022). Reconsidering autistic 'camouflaging' as transactional impression management. *Trends in Cognitive Sciences*.

Bargiela, S., Steward, R., & Mandy, W. (2016). The Experiences of Late-diagnosed Women with Autism Spectrum Conditions: An Investigation of the Female Autism Phenotype. *Journal of Autism and Developmental Disorders*. https://doi.org/10.1007/s10803-016-2872-8

Botha, M., & Frost, D. M. (2020). Extending the Minority Stress Model to Understand Mental Health Problems Experienced by the Autistic Population. *Society and Mental Health*, **10**(1), 20–34. https://doi.org/10.1177/2156869318804297

Cage, E., & Burton, H. (2019). Gender Differences in the First Impressions of Autistic Adults. *Autism Research*, **12**(10), 1495–1504. https://doi.org/10.1002/aur.2191

Cage, E., & Troxell-Whitman, Z. (2019). Understanding the Reasons, Contexts and Costs of Camouflaging for Autistic Adults. *Journal of Autism and Developmental Disorders*. https://doi.org/10.1007/s10803-018-03878-x

Conway, J. R., Catmur, C., & Bird, G. (2019). Understanding individual differences in theory of mind via representation of minds, not mental states. *Psychonomic Bulletin & Review*, **26**(3), 798–812. https://doi.org/10.3758/s13423-018-1559-x

Corbett, B. A., Schwartzman, J. M., Libsack, E. J., Muscatello, R. A., Lerner, M. D., Simmons, G. L., & White, S. W. (2021). Camouflaging in Autism: Examining Sex-Based and Compensatory Models in Social Cognition and Communication. *Autism Research*, **14**(1), 127–142. https://doi.org/10.1002/aur.2440

Fombonne, E. (2020). Camouflage and autism. *Journal of Child Psychology and Psychiatry*, **61**(7), 735–738. https://doi.org/10.1111/jcpp.13296

Gibbs, V., & Pellicano, E. (2023). 'Maybe we just seem like easy targets': A qualitative analysis of autistic adults' experiences of interpersonal violence. *Autism*, 136236132211503. https://doi.org/10.1177/13623613221150375

Hannon, B., Mandy, W., & Hull, L. (2023). A comparison of methods for measuring camouflaging in autism. *Autism Research*, **16**(1), 12–29. https://doi.org/10.1002/aur.2850

Hull, L., Mandy, W., Lai, M. C., Baron-Cohen, S., Allison, C., Smith, P., & Petrides, K. V. (2019). Development and Validation of the Camouflaging Autistic Traits Questionnaire (CAT-Q). *Journal of Autism and Developmental Disorders*. https://doi.org/10.1007/s10803-018-3792-6

Hull, L., Petrides, K. V., Allison, C., Smith, P., Baron-Cohen, S., Lai, M. C., & Mandy, W. (2017). "Putting on My Best Normal": Social Camouflaging in Adults with Autism Spectrum Conditions. *Journal of Autism and Developmental Disorders*. https://doi.org/10.1007/s10803-017-3166-5

Lawson, W. B. (2020). Adaptive Morphing and Coping with Social Threat in Autism: An Autistic Perspective. *Journal of Intellectual Disability-Diagnosis and Treatment*, **8**, 519–526.

Livingston, L. A., Colvert, E., the Social Relationships Study Team, Bolton, P., & Happé, F. (2019). Good social skills despite poor theory of mind: Exploring compensation in autism spectrum disorder. *Journal of Child Psychology and Psychiatry*, **60**(1), 102–110. https://doi.org/10.1111/jcpp.12886

Livingston, L. A., Shah, P., Milner, V., & Happé, F. (2020). Quantifying compensatory strategies in adults with and without diagnosed autism. *Molecular Autism*. https://doi.org/10.1186/s13229-019-0308-y

Livingston, L. A., Shah, P., White, S. J., & Happé, F. (2021). Further developing the Frith–Happé animations: A quicker, more objective, and web-based test of theory of mind for autistic and neurotypical adults. *Autism Research*, **14**(9), 1905–1912. https://doi.org/10.1002/aur.2575

Morrison, K. E., DeBrabander, K. M., Jones, D. R., Ackerman, R. A., & Sasson, N. J. (2020). Social Cognition, Social Skill, and Social Motivation Minimally Predict Social Interaction Outcomes for

Autistic and Non-Autistic Adults. *Frontiers in Psychology*, **11**, 591100. https://doi.org/10.3389/fpsyg.2020.591100

Pearson, A., Rose, K., & Rees, J. (2023). 'I felt like I deserved it because I was autistic': Understanding the impact of interpersonal victimisation in the lives of autistic people. *Autism*, **27**(2), 500–511. https://doi.org/10.1177/13623613221104546

Radulski, E. M. (2022). Conceptualising Autistic Masking, Camouflaging, and Neurotypical Privilege: Towards a Minority Group Model of Neurodiversity. *Human Development*, **66**(2), 113–127. https://doi.org/10.1159/000524122

Rose, K. (2018). *Masking: I am not OK*. https://theautisticadvocate.com/2018/07/masking-i-am-not-ok/

Sasson, N. J., Faso, D. J., Nugent, J., Lovell, S., Kennedy, D. P., & Grossman, R. B. (2017). Neurotypical Peers are Less Willing to Interact with Those with Autism based on Thin Slice Judgments. *Scientific Reports*, **7**. https://doi.org/10.1038/srep40700

Sasson, N. J., Morrison, K. E., Kelsven, S., & Pinkham, A. E. (2020). Social cognition as a predictor of functional and social skills in autistic adults without intellectual disability. *Autism Research*, **13**(2), 259–270.

Walker, N. (2021). *Neuroqueer Heresies*. Autonomous Press.

# Chapter 7

Anderson, L. K. (2023). Autistic experiences of applied behavior analysis. *Autism*, **27**(3), 737–750. https://doi.org/10.1177/13623613221118216

Bachmann, C. J., Höfer, J., Kamp-Becker, I., Küpper, C., Poustka, L., Roepke, S., Roessner, V., Stroth, S., Wolff, N., & Hoffmann, F. (2019). Internalised stigma in adults with autism: A German multi-center survey. *Psychiatry Research*, **276**, 94–99. https://doi.org/10.1016/j.psychres.2019.04.023

Beardon, L. (2008). Is Autism really a disorder part 2: Theory of Mind? Rethink how we think. *The Journal of Inclusive Practice in Further and Higher Education*, 2(1), 19–21.

Belmonte, M. K., & Yurgelun-Todd, D. A. (2003). Functional anatomy of impaired selective attention and compensatory processing in autism. *Cognitive Brain Research*, **17**(3), 651–664. https://doi.org/10.1016/S0926-6410(03)00189-7

Benoit, C., Jansson, S. M., Smith, M., & Flagg, J. (2018). Prostitution Stigma and Its Effect on the Working Conditions, Personal Lives, and Health of Sex Workers. *The Journal of Sex Research*, **55**(4–5), 457–471. https://doi.org/10.1080/00224499.2017.1393652

Bertilsdotter Rosqvist, H., & Jackson-Perry, D. (2021). Not Doing it Properly? (Re)producing and Resisting Knowledge Through Narratives of Autistic Sexualities. *Sexuality and Disability*, **39**(2), 327–344. https://doi.org/10.1007/s11195-020-09624-5

Botha, M. (2020). *Autistic community connectedness as a buffer against the effects of minority stress*. University of Surrey.

Botha, M. (2021). Academic, Activist, or Advocate? Angry, Entangled, and Emerging: A Critical Reflection on Autism Knowledge Production. In *Frontiers in Psychology* (Vol. 12). https://www.frontiersin.org/article/10.3389/fpsyg.2021.727542

Botha, M., & Cage, E. (2022). "Autism research is in crisis": A mixed method study of researcher's constructions of autistic people and autism research. *Frontiers in Psychology*, **13**, 1050897. https://doi.org/10.3389/fpsyg.2022.1050897

Botha, M., Dibb, B., & Frost, D. M. (2022a). 'Autism is me': An investigation of how autistic individuals make sense of autism and stigma. *Disability & Society*, **37**(3), 427–453. https://doi.org/10.1080/09687599.2020.1822782

Botha, M., Dibb, B., & Frost, D. M. (2022b). 'It's being a part of a grand tradition, a grand counter-culture which involves communities': A qualitative investigation of autistic community connectedness. *Autism*, **26**(8), 2151–2164. https://doi.org/10.1177/13623613221080248

Botha, M., Hanlon, J., & Williams, G. (2020). *Does language matter? Identity-first versus person-first language use in autism research: A response to Vivanti*.

Bottema-Beutel, K., Kapp, S. K., Lester, J. N., Sasson, N. J., & Hand, B. N. (2020). Avoiding ableist language: Suggestions for autism researchers. *Autism in Adulthood*.

Broderick, A. A., & Roscigno, R. (2021). Autism, Inc.: The Autism Industrial Complex. *Journal of Disability Studies in Education*, 2(1), 77–101. https://doi.org/10.1163/25888803-bja10008

Burkett, C. (2020). 'Autistic while black': How autism amplifies stereotypes. *Spectrum News*. https://www.spectrumnews.org/opinion/viewpoint/autistic-while-black-how-autism-amplifies-stereotypes/

Butler, J. (1988). Performative Acts and Gender Constitution: An Essay in Phenomenology and Feminist Theory. *Theatre Journal*, **40**(4), 519. https://doi.org/10.2307/3207893

Cage, E., Di Monaco, J., & Newell, V. (2019). Understanding, attitudes and dehumanisation towards autistic people. Autism, 23(6), 1373–1383.

Campbell, C., & Deacon, H. (2006). Unravelling the Contexts of Stigma: From Internalisation to Resistance to Change. *Journal of Community & Applied Social Psychology*, **16**, 411–417. https://doi.org/10.1002/casp.901

Care Quality Comission. (2020a). *Out of sight – who cares?: Restraint, segregation and seclusion review*. Care Quality Comission. https://www.cqc.org.uk/publications/themed-work/rssreview

Care Quality Comission. (2020b). *CQC demands national system change to prevent future generations of autistic people and/or people with a learning disability from 'falling through the gaps'*. https://www.cqc.org.uk/news/releases/cqc-demands-national-system-change-prevent-future-generations-autistic-people-andor

Casimir, J. (2020). The Cost of Fitting In: *An Investigative Analysis of Race-Based Code-Switching and Social Exclusion*. https://doi.org/10.17615/WMK4-MF65

Cassidy, S., Bradley, L., Shaw, R., & Baron-Cohen, S. (2018). Risk markers for suicidality in autistic adults. *Molecular Autism*. https://doi.org/10.1186/s13229-018-0226-4

Chapman, R., & Carel, H. (2022). Neurodiversity, epistemic injustice, and the good human life. *Journal of Social Philosophy*, **53**(4), 614–631. https://doi.org/10.1111/josp.12456

Clements, T. (2019). What is autism? How the term became too broad to have meaning any more. *The Guardian*. https://www.theguardian.com/commentisfree/2019/aug/26/autism-neurodiversity-severe

Cocks, E. (2001). Normalisation and social role valorisation: Guidance for human service development. *Hong Kong Journal of Psychiatry*, **11**(1), 12 + . Gale Academic OneFile.

Coleman-Brown, L. (2013). Stigma: An Enigma Demystified. In L. J. Davis (Ed.), *The Disability Studies Reader* (pp. 147–160). Taylor & Francis.

Corrigan, P. (2004). How stigma interferes with mental health care. *American Psychologist*, **59**, 614–625. https://doi.org/10.1037/0003-066X.59.7.614

Corrigan, P., & Matthews, A. (2009). Stigma and disclosure: Implications for coming out of the closet. *Journal of Mental Health*. https://doi.org/10.1080/0963823031000118221

Corrigan, P. W., & Kleinlein, P. (2005). The Impact of Mental Illness Stigma. In On the stigma of mental illness: Practical strategies for research and social change. (pp. 11–44). *American Psychological Association*. https://doi.org/10.1037/10887-001

Crocker, J., & Lutsky, N. (1986). Stigma and the Dynamics of Social Cognition. In S. C. Ainlay, G. Becker, & L. M. Coleman (Eds.), *The Dilemma of Difference* (pp. 95–121). Springer US. https://doi.org/10.1007/978-1-4684-7568-5_6

Dababnah, S., Kim, I., & Shaia, W. E. (2022). 'I am so fearful for him': A mixed-methods exploration of stress among caregivers of Black children with autism. *International Journal of Developmental Disabilities*, **68**(5), 658–670. https://doi.org/10.1080/20473869.2020.1870418

Davis, A., Solomon, M., & Belcher, H. (2022). Examination of Race and Autism Intersectionality Among African American/Black Young Adults. *Autism in Adulthood*, **4**(4), 306–314. https://doi.org/10.1089/aut.2021.0091

De Hooge, A. N. (2019). Binary Boys: Autism, Aspie Supremacy and Post/Humanist *Normativity*. *Disability Studies Quarterly*, **39**(1). https://doi.org/10.18061/dsq.v39i1.6461

DeBrabander, K. M., Morrison, K. E., Jones, D. R., Faso, D. J., Chmielewski, M., & Sasson, N. J. (2019). Do First Impressions of Autistic Adults Differ Between Autistic and Nonautistic Observers? *Autism in Adulthood*, **1**(4), 250–257. https://doi.org/10.1089/aut.2019.0018

Diemer, M. C., Gerstein, E. D., & Regester, A. (2022). Autism presentation in female and Black populations: Examining the roles of identity, theory, and systemic inequalities. *Autism*, **26**(8), 1931–1946. https://doi.org/10.1177/13623613221113501

Du Bois, W. E. B. (1897). *Strivings of the Negro People*. The Atlantic. https://www.theatlantic.com/magazine/archive/1897/08/strivings-of-the-negro-people/305446/

Fanon, F. (1952). *Black skin, white masks* (1st Evergreen ed). Grove Press.

Farahar, C. (2021). A rose by any other name would smell…of stigma (or, the psychologically important difference between being a "person with autism" or an Autistic person). *Unit for Stigma Research*. https://blogs.ucl.ac.uk/stigma-research/2021/06/25/a-rose-by-any-other-name-would-smellof-stigma-or-the-psychologically-important-difference-between-being-a-person-with-autism-or-an-autistic-person-by-dr-chloe-farahar/

Farsinejad, A., Russell, A., & Butler, C. (2022). Autism disclosure – The decisions autistic adults make. *Research in Autism Spectrum Disorders*, **93**, 101936. https://doi.org/10.1016/j.rasd.2022.101936

Finch, T. L., Mackintosh, J., Petrou, A., McConachie, H., Le Couteur, A., Garland, D., & Parr, J. R. (2022). "We couldn't think in the box if we tried. We can't even find the damn box": A qualitative study of the lived experiences of autistic adults and relatives of autistic adults. *PLOS ONE*, **17**(3), e0264932. https://doi.org/10.1371/journal.pone.0264932

Fine, M., & Asch, A. (1988). Disability Beyond Stigma: Social Interaction, Discrimination, and Activism. *Journal of Social Issues*, **44**(1), 3–21. https://doi.org/10.1111/j.1540-4560.1988.tb02045.x

Frost, D. M. (2011). Social stigma and its consequences for the socially stigmatized. *Social and Personality Psychology Compass*, **5**(11), 824–839.

Gernsbacher, M. A. (2007). On not being human. *APS Observer*, **20**(2), 5.

Gillespie-Lynch, K., Brooks, P. J., Someki, F., Obeid, R., Shane-Simpson, C., Kapp, S. K., Daou, N., & Smith, D. S. (2015). Changing College Students' Conceptions of Autism: An Online Training to Increase Knowledge and Decrease Stigma. *Journal of Autism and Developmental Disorders*, **45**(8), 2553–2566. https://doi.org/10.1007/s10803-015-2422-9

Gillespie-Lynch, K., Daou, N., Sanchez-Ruiz, M.-J., Kapp, S. K., Obeid, R., Brooks, P. J., Someki, F., Silton, N., & Abi-Habib, R. (2019). Factors underlying cross-cultural differences in stigma toward autism among college students in Lebanon and the United States. *Autism*, **23**(8), 1993–2006. https://doi.org/10.1177/1362361318823550

Goffman, E. (1963). *Stigma: Notes on the management of spoiled identity*. Penguin Books.

Grinker, R. R. (2020). Autism, "Stigma," Disability: A Shifting Historical Terrain. *Current Anthropology*, **61**(S21), S55–S67. https://doi.org/10.1086/705748

Han, E., Scior, K., Avramides, K., & Crane, L. (2022). A systematic review on autistic people's experiences of stigma and coping strategies. *Autism Research*, **15**(1), 12–26. https://doi.org/10.1002/aur.2652

Han, E., Scior, K., Heath, E., Umagami, K., & Crane, L. (2023). Development of stigma-related support for autistic adults: Insights from the autism community. *Autism*, 136236132211435. https://doi.org/10.1177/13623613221143590

Hayward, B. A., McKay-Brown, L., & Poed, S. (2023). Restrictive Practices and the 'Need' for Positive Behaviour Support (PBS): A Critical Discourse Examination of Disability Policy Beliefs. *Journal of Intellectual Disabilities*, **27**(1), 170–189. https://doi.org/10.1177/17446295211062383

Herek, G. (2009). Sexual Stigma and Sexual Prejudice in the United States: A Conceptual Framework. In R. Thomas & European Molecular Biology Organization (Eds.), *Kinetic logic: A Boolean approach to the analysis of complex regulatory systems: Proceedings of the EMBO course 'Formal analysis of genetic regulation,' held in Brussels, September 6-16, 1977*. Springer-Verlag.

Herek, G. M. (1998). *Stigma and sexual orientation* (Vol. 4). Sage.

Huang, Y., Trollor, J. N., Foley, K.-R., & Arnold, S. R. C. (2023). "I've Spent My Whole Life Striving to Be Normal": Internalized Stigma and Perceived Impact of Diagnosis in Autistic Adults. *Autism in Adulthood*, aut.2022.0066. https://doi.org/10.1089/aut.2022.0066

Hume, R., & Burgess, H. (2021). "I'm Human After All": Autism, Trauma, and Affective Empathy. *Autism in Adulthood*, **3**(3), 221–229. https://doi.org/10.1089/aut.2020.0013

Huws, J. C., & Jones, R. S. P. (2011). Missing voices: Representations of autism in British newspapers, 1999-2008: Missing voices. *British Journal of Learning Disabilities*, **39**(2), 98–104. https://doi.org/10.1111/j.1468-3156.2010.00624.x

Jackson, S. D., & Mohr, J. J. (2016). Conceptualizing the closet: Differentiating stigma concealment and nondisclosure processes. *Psychology of Sexual Orientation and Gender Diversity*, **2**(1), 80–92. https://doi.org/10.1037/sgd0000147

Johnson, D. G., Mattan, B. D., Flores, N., Lauharatanahirun, N., & Falk, E. B. (2022). Social-Cognitive and Affective Antecedents of Code Switching and the Consequences of Linguistic Racism for Black People and People of Color. *Affective Science*, **2**(1), 5–13. https://doi.org/10.1007/s42761-021-00072-8

Jones, D. R., DeBrabander, K. M., & Sasson, N. J. (2021). Effects of autism acceptance training on explicit and implicit biases toward autism. *Autism*, **25**(5), 1246–1261. https://doi.org/10.1177/1362361320984896

Jones, D. R., Nicolaidis, C., Ellwood, L. J., Garcia, A., Johnson, K. R., Lopez, K., & Waisman, T. (2020). An Expert Discussion on Structural Racism in Autism Research and Practice. *Autism in Adulthood*, **2**(4), 273–281. https://doi.org/10.1089/aut.2020.29015.drj

Jones, S. C. (2022). Hey look, I'm (not) on TV: Autistic people reflect on autism portrayals in entertainment media. *Disability & Society*, 1–18. https://doi.org/10.1080/09687599.2022.2150602

Jones, S. C., Gordon, C. S., & Mizzi, S. (2023). Representation of autism in fictional media: A systematic review of media content and its impact on viewer knowledge and understanding of autism. *Autism*, 136236132311557. https://doi.org/10.1177/13623613231155770

Jorgensen, M., Nankervis, K., & Chan, J. (2023). 'Environments of concern': Reframing challenging behaviour within a human rights approach. *International Journal of Developmental Disabilities*, **69**(1), 95–100. https://doi.org/10.1080/20473869.2022.2118513

Karaminis, T., Gabrielatos, C., Maden-Weinberger, U., & Beattie, G. (2023). Portrayals of autism in the British press: A corpus-based study. *Autism*, **27**(4), 1092–1114. https://doi.org/10.1177/13623613221131752

Kim, S. Y., Cheon, J. E., Gillespie-Lynch, K., & Kim, Y.-H. (2022). Is autism stigma higher in South Korea than the United States? Examining cultural tightness, intergroup bias, and concerns about heredity as contributors to heightened autism stigma. *Autism*, **26**(2), 460–472. https://doi.org/10.1177/13623613211029520

Kim, S. Y., & Gillespie-Lynch, K. (2022). Do Autistic People's Support Needs and Non-Autistic People's Support for the Neurodiversity Movement Contribute to Heightened Autism Stigma in South Korea vs. The US? *Journal of Autism and Developmental Disorders*. https://doi.org/10.1007/s10803-022-05739-0

King, D. K. (1988). Multiple Jeopardy, Multiple Consciousness: The Context of a Black Feminist Ideology. *Signs: Journal of Women in Culture and Society*, **14**(1), 42–72. https://doi.org/10.1086/494491

Klin, A., Danovitch, J. H., Merz, A. B., & Volkmar, F. R. (2007). Circumscribed Interests in Higher Functioning Individuals with Autism Spectrum Disorders: An Exploratory Study. *Research and Practice for Persons with Severe Disabilities*, **32**(2), 89–100. https://doi.org/10.2511/rpsd.32.2.89

Kourti, M., & MacLeod, A. (2019). "I Don't Feel Like a Gender, I Feel Like Myself": Autistic Individuals Raised as Girls Exploring Gender Identity. *Autism in Adulthood*, **1**(1), 52–59. https://doi.org/10.1089/aut.2018.0001

Kteily, N. S., & Landry, A. P. (2022). Dehumanization: Trends, insights, and challenges. *Trends in Cognitive Sciences*, **26**(3), 222–240. https://doi.org/10.1016/j.tics.2021.12.003

Libsack, E. J., Keenan, E. G., Freden, C. E., Mirmina, J., Iskhakov, N., Krishnathasan, D., & Lerner, M. D. (2021). A Systematic Review of Passing as Non-autistic in Autism Spectrum Disorder. *Clinical Child and Family Psychology Review*, **24**(4), 783–812. https://doi.org/10.1007/s10567-021-00365-1

Libster, N., Knox, A., Engin, S., Geschwind, D., Parish-Morris, J., & Kasari, C. (2022). Personal victimization experiences of autistic and non-autistic children. *Molecular Autism*, **13**(1), 51. https://doi.org/10.1186/s13229-022-00531-4

Lilley, R., Lawson, W., Hall, G., Mahony, J., Clapham, H., Heyworth, M., Arnold, S., Trollor, J., Yudell, M., & Pellicano, E. (2023). "Peas in a pod": Oral History Reflections on Autistic Identity in *Family and Community by Late-Diagnosed Adults.* Journal of Autism and Developmental Disorders, **53**(3), 1146–1161. https://doi.org/10.1007/s10803-022-05667-z

Limburg, J. (2021). *Letters to my weird sisters: On autism and feminism*. Atlantic Books.

Link, B. G., & Phelan, J. C. (2001). Conceptualizing Stigma. *Annual Review of Sociology*, **27**(1), 363–385. https://doi.org/10.1146/annurev.soc.27.1.363

Lonbay, S., Pearson, A., Hamilton, E., Higgins, P., Foulkes, E., & Glascott, M. (2021). Trauma informed participatory research: Reflections on co-producing a research proposal. *Gateways: International Journal of Community Research and Engagement*, **14**(1). https://doi.org/10.5130/ijcre.v14i1.7728

Love, A. M. A., Edwards, C., Cai, R. Y., & Gibbs, V. (2023). Using Experience Sampling Methodology to Capture Disclosure Opportunities for Autistic Adults. *Autism in Adulthood*, aut.2022.0090. https://doi.org/10.1089/aut.2022.0090

Major, B., & O'Brien, L. T. (2005). The Social Psychology of Stigma. *Annual Review of Psychology*, **56**(1), 393–421. https://doi.org/10.1146/annurev.psych.56.091103.070137

McAuliffe, C., Walsh, R. J., & Cage, E. (2022). " My whole life has been a process of finding labels that fit ": A Thematic Analysis of Autistic LGBTQIA + Identity and Inclusion in the LGBTQIA + Community. *Autism in Adulthood*, aut.2021.0074. https://doi.org/10.1089/aut.2021.0074

McDonald, T. A. M. (2020). Autism Identity and the "Lost Generation": Structural Validation of the Autism Spectrum Identity Scale and Comparison of Diagnosed and Self-Diagnosed Adults on the Autism Spectrum. *Autism in Adulthood*, **2**(1), 13–23. https://doi.org/10.1089/aut.2019.0069

Meyer, I. H. (2003). Prejudice, social stress, and mental health in lesbian, gay, and bisexual populations: Conceptual issues and research evidence. *Psychological Bulletin*, **129**(5), 674–697. https://doi.org/10.1037/0033-2909.129.5.674

Milton, D. (2018). Milton, Damian (2018) *'Here comes trouble': Autism and gender performance.* Gendering Autism, Strathclyde, UK. https://kar.kent.ac.uk/66024/1/Here%20comes%20trouble.pdf

Milton, D. E. M. (2016). Disposable dispositions: Reflections upon the work of Iris Marion Young in relation to the social oppression of autistic people. *Disability & Society*, **31**(10), 1403–1407.

Milton, D., & Sims, T. (2016). How is a sense of well-being and belonging constructed in the accounts of autistic adults? *Disability & Society*, **31**(4), 520–534.

Mitter, N., Ali, A., & Scior, K. (2019). Stigma experienced by families of individuals with intellectual disabilities and autism: A systematic review. *Research in Developmental Disabilities*, **89**, 10–21. https://doi.org/10.1016/j.ridd.2019.03.001

Montgomery, C. (2001). Critic of the Dawn. *Ragged Edge Online*. http://www.raggededgemagazine.com/0501/0501cov.htm

Montgomery, C. (2021). Wolfensberger at the Door. *Cal's Blog: A Blog about Disability*. https://montgomerycal.wordpress.com

Moore, I., Morgan, G., Welham, A., & Russell, G. (2022). The intersection of autism and gender in the negotiation of identity: A systematic review and metasynthesis. *Feminism & Psychology*, **32**(4), 421–442. https://doi.org/10.1177/09593535221074806

Moorhead, J. (2021). 'A lot fell into place': The adults who discovered they were autistic – after their child was diagnosed. *The Guardian*. https://www.theguardian.com/society/2021/dec/16/adults-discovered-autistic-child-diagnosed-autism

Morrison, K. E., DeBrabander, K. M., Faso, D. J., & Sasson, N. J. (2019). Variability in first impressions of autistic adults made by neurotypical raters is driven more by characteristics of the rater than by characteristics of autistic adults. *Autism*, **23**(7), 1817–1829. https://doi.org/10.1177/1362361318824104

Obeid, R., Daou, N., DeNigris, D., Shane-Simpson, C., Brooks, P. J., & Gillespie-Lynch, K. (2015). A Cross-Cultural Comparison of Knowledge and Stigma Associated with Autism Spectrum Disorder Among College Students in Lebanon and the United States. *Journal of Autism and Developmental Disorders*, **45**(11), 3520–3536. https://doi.org/10.1007/s10803-015-2499-1

Pachankis, J. E. (2007). The psychological implications of concealing a stigma: A cognitive-affective-behavioral model. *Psychological Bulletin*, **133**(2), 328–345. https://doi.org/10.1037/0033-2909.133.2.328

Pearson, A., & Rose, K. (2021). A Conceptual Analysis of Autistic Masking: Understanding the Narrative of Stigma and the Illusion of Choice. *Autism in Adulthood*. https://doi.org/10.1089/aut.2020.0043

Pearson, A., Rose, K., & Rees, J. (2023). 'I felt like I deserved it because I was autistic': Understanding the impact of interpersonal victimisation in the lives of autistic people. *Autism*, **27**(2), 500–511. https://doi.org/10.1177/13623613221104546

Perry, E., Mandy, W., Hull, L., & Cage, E. (2021). Understanding camouflaging as a response to autism-related stigma: A Social Identity Theory approach. *Journal of Autism and Developmental Disorders*, 1–11.

Piepmeier, A. (2012). Saints, Sages, and Victims: Endorsement of and Resistance to Cultural Stereotypes in Memoirs by Parents of Children with Disabilities. *Disability Studies Quarterly*, **32**(1). https://doi.org/10.18061/dsq.v32i1.3031

Pratto, F., Sidanius, J., & Levin, S. (2006). Social dominance theory and the dynamics of intergroup relations: Taking stock and looking forward. *European Review of Social Psychology*, **17**(1), 271–320. https://doi.org/10.1080/10463280601055772

Radulski, E. M. (2022). Conceptualising Autistic Masking, Camouflaging, and Neurotypical Privilege: Towards a Minority Group Model of Neurodiversity. *Human Development*, **66**(2), 113–127. https://doi.org/10.1159/000524122

Rose, K., & Michael, C. (2022). Re: Older Age Autism Research: A Rapidly Growing Field, but Still a Long Way to Go by Mason et al.; DOI: 10.1089/aut.2021.0041 ( Previously titled: The Rising Tide of "Gerontautism"). *Autism in Adulthood*, **4**(2), 173–175. https://doi.org/10.1089/aut.2022.0023

Rose, K., & Vivian, S. (2020). *Regarding the use of Dehumanising Rhetoric*. https://theautisticadvocate.com/2020/02/regarding-the-use-of-dehumanising-rhetoric/

Sasson, N. J., Faso, D. J., Nugent, J., Lovell, S., Kennedy, D. P., & Grossman, R. B. (2017). Neurotypical Peers are Less Willing to Interact with Those with Autism based on Thin Slice Judgments. *Scientific Reports*, 7. https://doi.org/10.1038/srep40700

Schalk, S. (2016). Reevaluating the Supercrip. *Journal of Literary & Cultural Disability Studies*, **10**(1), 71–86.

Schneidre, J. W. (1988). Disability as Moral Experience: Epilepsy and Self in Routine Relationships. *Journal of Social Issues*, **44**(1), 63–78. https://doi.org/10.1111/j.1540-4560.1988.tb02049.x

Simmonds, M. (Director). (2021). *Autism and the Black community*. https://www.youtube.com/watch?v = LW-C_MVxNEU

Singer, A., Lutz, A., Escher, J., & Halladay, A. (2023). A full semantic toolbox is essential for autism research and practice to thrive. *Autism Research*, **16**(3), 497–501. https://doi.org/10.1002/aur.2876

Singletary, A. D. (2020). *Navigating Success: The Experiences of Black Teachers Code-switching in Predominately White Schools* [University of Kansas]. https://kuscholarworks.ku.edu/bitstream/handle/1808/31836/Singletary_ku_0099D_17012_DATA_1.pdf?sequence = 1&isAllowed = y

Someki, F., Torii, M., Brooks, P. J., Koeda, T., & Gillespie-Lynch, K. (2018). Stigma associated with autism among college students in Japan and the United States: An online training study. *Research in Developmental Disabilities*, **76**, 88–98. https://doi.org/10.1016/j.ridd.2018.02.016

Strang, J. F., Powers, M. D., Knauss, M., Sibarium, E., Leibowitz, S. F., Kenworthy, L., Sadikova, E., Wyss, S., Willing, L., Caplan, R., Pervez, N., Nowak, J., Gohari, D., Gomez-Lobo, V., Call, D., & Anthony, L. G. (2018). "They Thought It Was an Obsession": Trajectories and Perspectives of Autistic Transgender and Gender-Diverse Adolescents. *Journal of Autism and Developmental Disorders*, **48**(12), 4039–4055. https://doi.org/10.1007/s10803-018-3723-6

Tei, S., Fujino, J., Itahashi, T., Aoki, Y., Ohta, H., Kubota, M., Hashimoto, R., Nakamura, M., Kato, N., & Takahashi, H. (2019). Egocentric biases and atypical generosity in autistic individuals. *Autism Research*, **12**(11), 1598–1608. https://doi.org/10.1002/aur.2130

Treweek, C., Wood, C., Martin, J., & Freeth, M. (2019). Autistic people's perspectives on stereotypes: An interpretative phenomenological analysis. *Autism*, **23**(3), 759–769. https://doi.org/10.1177/1362361318778286

Turnock, A., Langley, K., & Jones, C. R. G. (2022). Understanding Stigma in Autism: A Narrative Review and Theoretical Model. *Autism in Adulthood*, **4**(1), 76–91. https://doi.org/10.1089/aut.2021.0005

Ventour-Williams, T. (2022). Autistic While Black in the UK: Masking, Codeswitching, and Other (Non)fictions. *NeuroClastic*. https://neuroclastic.com/long-read-autistic-while-black-in-the-uk-masking-codeswitching-and-other-nonfictions/

Vogel, D. L., Bitman, R. L., Hammer, J. H., & Wade, N. G. (2013). Is stigma internalized? The longitudinal impact of public stigma on self-stigma. *Journal of Counseling Psychology*, **60**(2), 311–316. https://doi.org/10.1037/a0031889

Walker, N. (2021). *Neuroqueer Heresies*. Autonomous Press.

Walker, N., & Raymaker, D. M. (2021). Toward a Neuroqueer Future: An Interview with Nick Walker. *Autism in Adulthood*, **3**(1), 5–10. https://doi.org/10.1089/AUT.2020.29014.NJW

Weiss, J. A., & Fardella, M. A. (2018). Victimization and perpetration experiences of adults with autism. *Frontiers in Psychiatry*. https://doi.org/10.3389/fpsyt.2018.00203

Welang, N. (2018). Triple Consciousness: The Reimagination of Black Female Identities in Contemporary American Culture. *Open Cultural Studies*, **2**(1), 296–306. https://doi.org/10.1515/culture-2018-0027

Welch, C., Senman, L., Loftin, R., Picciolini, C., Robison, J., Westphal, A., Perry, B., Nguyen, J., Jachyra, P., Stevenson, S., Aggarwal, J., Wijekoon, S., Baron-Cohen, S., & Penner, M. (2022). Understanding the Use of the Term "Weaponized Autism" in An Alt-Right Social Media Platform. *Journal of Autism and Developmental Disorders*. https://doi.org/10.1007/s10803-022-05701-0

Wolfensberger, W., & Tullman, S. (1982). A brief outline of the principle of normalization. *Rehabilitation Psychology*, **27**, 131–145. https://doi.org/10.1037/h0090973

Wood, C., & Freeth, M. (2016). Students' Stereotypes of Autism. *Journal of Educational Issues*, **2**(2), 131–140.

Yergeau, M. (2013). Clinically significant disturbance: On theorists who theorize theory of mind. *Disability Studies Quarterly*, **33**(4).

Young, I. M. (1990). *Justice and the Politics of Difference*. https://books.google.co.uk/books?hl=en&lr=&id=Q6keKguPrsAC&oi=fnd&pg=PP11&dq=Young,+M.+Justice+and+the+Politics+of+Difference.+Princeton:+Princeton+University+Press%3B+1990.+&ots=F_344vtdzk&sig=2FFcGh4h7wtgugHnl9dqOuE1hXA

Yu, L., Stronach, S., & Harrison, A. J. (2020). Public knowledge and stigma of autism spectrum disorder: Comparing China with the United States. *Autism*, **24**(6), 1531–1545. https://doi.org/10.1177/1362361319900839

# Chapter 8

Alkhaldi, R. S., Sheppard, E., & Mitchell, P. (2019). Is There a Link Between Autistic People Being Perceived Unfavorably and Having a Mind That Is Difficult to Read? *Journal of Autism and Developmental Disorders*, **49**(10), 3973–3982. https://doi.org/10.1007/s10803-019-04101-1

American Psychiatric Association. (2013). *Diagnostic and statistical manual of mental disorders (DSM-5®)*. American Psychiatric Pub.

ASAN. (2023). #StopTheShock: The Judge Rotenberg Center, Torture, and How We can Stop It. *Autistic Self Advocacy Network*. https://autisticadvocacy.org/actioncenter/issues/school/climate/jrc/

Baron-Cohen, S. (1997). *Mindblindness: An essay on autism and theory of mind*. MIT press.

Baron-Cohen, S., Leslie, A. M., & Frith, U. (1985). Does the autistic child have a "theory of mind"? *Cognition*, **21**(1), 37–46. https://doi.org/10.1016/0010-0277(85)90022-8

Bascombe, J. (2011). *Quiet Hands*.

Beardon, L. (2008). Is Autism really a disorder part 2: Theory of Mind? Rethink how we think. *The Journal of Inclusive Practice in Further and Higher Education*, **1**(1), 19–21.

Bergenmar, J., Rosqvist, H. B., & Lönngren, A.-S. (2015). Autism and the Question of the Human. *Literature and Medicine*, **33**(1), 202–221. https://doi.org/10.1353/lm.2015.0009

Birkett, L., McGrath, L., & Tucker, I. (2022). Muting, filtering and transforming space: Autistic children's sensory 'tactics' for navigating mainstream school space following transition to secondary school. *Emotion, Space and Society*, **42**, 100872. https://doi.org/10.1016/j.emospa.2022.100872

Bolis, D., Balsters, J., Wenderoth, N., Becchio, C., & Schilbach, L. (2017). Beyond Autism: Introducing the Dialectical Misattunement Hypothesis and a Bayesian Account of Intersubjectivity. *Psychopathology*, **50**(6), 355–372. https://doi.org/10.1159/000484353

Bronfenbrenner, U. (1977). Toward an experimental ecology of human development. *American Psychologist*, **32**(7), 513.

Brown, N. M., Brown, S. N., Briggs, R. D., Germán, M., Belamarich, P. F., & Oyeku, S. O. (2017). Associations Between Adverse Childhood Experiences and ADHD Diagnosis and Severity. *Academic Pediatrics*, **17**(4), 349–355. https://doi.org/10.1016/j.acap.2016.08.013

Carrington, S., & Graham, L. (2001). Perceptions of School by Two Teenage Boys with Asperger Syndrome and their Mothers: A Qualitative Study. *Autism*, **5**(1), 37–48. https://doi.org/10.1177/1362361301005001004

Chapman, L., Rose, K., Hull, L., & Mandy, W. (2022). "I want to fit in… but I don't want to change myself fundamentally": A qualitative exploration of the relationship between masking and mental health for autistic teenagers. *Research in Autism Spectrum Disorders*, **99**, 102069. https://doi.org/10.1016/j.rasd.2022.102069

Conn, C. (2015). 'Sensory highs', 'vivid rememberings' and 'interactive stimming': Children's play cultures and experiences of friendship in autistic autobiographies. *Disability & Society*, **30**(8), 1192–1206. https://doi.org/10.1080/09687599.2015.1081094

Conn, C. (2019). *Autism, Pedagogy and Education: Critical Issues for Value-based Teaching*. Springer International Publishing. https://doi.org/10.1007/978-3-030-32560-2

Conway, J. R., Catmur, C., & Bird, G. (2019). Understanding individual differences in theory of mind via representation of minds, not mental states. *Psychonomic Bulletin & Review*, **26**(3), 798–812. https://doi.org/10.3758/s13423-018-1559-x

Crompton, C. J., Ropar, D., Evans-Williams, C. V. M., Flynn, E. G., & Fletcher-Watson, S. (2020). Autistic peer-to-peer information transfer is highly effective. *Autism*. https://doi.org/10.1177/1362361320919286

Cunningham, M. (2022). 'This school is 100% not autistic friendly!' Listening to the voices of primary-aged autistic children to understand what an autistic friendly primary school should be like. *International Journal of Inclusive Education*, **26**(12), 1211–1225. https://doi.org/10.1080/13603116.2020.1789767

Dekel, R., & Goldblatt, H. (2008). Is there intergenerational transmission of trauma? The case of combat veterans' children. *American Journal of Orthopsychiatry*, **78**(3), 281–289. https://doi.org/10.1037/a0013955

Doherty-Sneddon, G., Riby, D. M., & Whittle, L. (2012). Gaze aversion as a cognitive load management strategy in autism spectrum disorder and Williams syndrome: Gaze behaviour in WS and ASD. *Journal of Child Psychology and Psychiatry*, **53**(4), 420–430. https://doi.org/10.1111/j.1469-7610.2011.02481.x

Fataar, A., Motala, S., Keet, A., Lalu, P., Nuttall, S., Menon, K., & Staphorst, L. (2022). The university in techno-rational times: Critical universities studies, South Africa. *Educational Philosophy and Theory*, 1–9. https://doi.org/10.1080/00131857.2022.2142555

Fisher, S. (2021). The Coke Bottle Effect. *Connective Family*. https://connectivefamily.com/the-coke-bottle-effect/

Fletcher-Watson, S., & Bird, G. (2020). Autism and empathy: What are the real links? In *Autism* (Vol. 24, Issue 1, pp. 3–6). SAGE Publications Sage UK: London, England.

Forster, S., & Pearson, A. (2020). "Bullies tend to be obvious": Autistic adults perceptions of friendship and the concept of 'mate crime'. *Disability and Society*. https://doi.org/10.1080/0968759 9.2019.1680347

Frith, U. (2001). Mind Blindness and the Brain in Autism. *Neuron*, **32**(6), 969–979. https://doi.org/10.1016/S0896-6273(01)00552-9

Frost, D. M. (2011). Social stigma and its consequences for the socially stigmatized. *Social and Personality Psychology Compass*, **5**(11), 824–839.

Fulton, R., Reardon, E., Kate, R., & Jones, R. (2020). *Sensory Trauma: Autism, sensory difference and the daily experience of fear*. Autism Wellbeing CIC.

Gernsbacher, M. A., Stevenson, J. L., Khandakar, S., & Goldsmith, H. H. (2008). Why Does Joint Attention Look Atypical in Autism? *Child Development Perspectives*, **2**(1), 38–45. https://doi.org/10.1111/j.1750-8606.2008.00039.x

Gibbs, V., Hudson, J., & Pellicano, E. (2022). The Extent and Nature of Autistic People's Violence Experiences During Adulthood: A Cross-sectional Study of Victimisation. *Journal of Autism and Developmental Disorders*. https://doi.org/10.1007/s10803-022-05647-3

Gibbs, V., & Pellicano, E. (2023). 'Maybe we just seem like easy targets': A qualitative analysis of autistic adults' experiences of interpersonal violence. *Autism*, 136236132211503. https://doi.org/10.1177/13623613221150375

Goodall, C. (2018). 'I felt closed in and like I couldn't breathe': A qualitative study exploring the mainstream educational experiences of autistic young people. *Autism & Developmental Language Impairments*, **3**, 239694151880440. https://doi.org/10.1177/2396941518804407

Gray-Hammond, D., & Adkin, T. (2021). Creating Autistic suffering: In the beginning there was trauma. *Emergent Divergence*. https://emergentdivergence.com/2021/09/29/creating-autistic-suffering-in-the-beginning-there-was-trauma/

Grey, B., Dallos, R., & Stancer, R. (2021). Feeling 'like you're on … a prison ship' – Understanding the caregiving and attachment narratives of parents of autistic children. *Human Systems: Therapy, Culture and Attachments*, **1**(1), 96–114. https://doi.org/10.1177/26344041211000202

Griffiths, S., Allison, C., Kenny, R., Holt, R., Smith, P., & Baron-Cohen, S. (2019). The vulnerability experiences quotient (VEQ): A study of vulnerability, mental health and life satisfaction in autistic adults. *Autism Research*, **12**(10), 1516–1528.

Haruvi-Lamdan, N., Horesh, D., Zohar, S., Kraus, M., & Golan, O. (2020). Autism Spectrum Disorder and Post-Traumatic Stress Disorder: An unexplored co-occurrence of conditions. *Autism*, **24**(4), 884–898. https://doi.org/10.1177/1362361320912143

Heyworth, M., Chan, T., & Lawson, W. (2022). Perspective: Presuming Autistic Communication Competence and Reframing Facilitated Communication. *Frontiers in Psychology*, 13. https://www.frontiersin.org/articles/10.3389/fpsyg.2022.864991

Howe, F. E. J., & Stagg, S. D. (2016). How Sensory Experiences Affect Adolescents with an Autistic Spectrum Condition within the Classroom. *Journal of Autism and Developmental Disorders*, **46**(5), 1656–1668. https://doi.org/10.1007/s10803-015-2693-1

Hume, R., & Burgess, H. (2021). "I'm Human After All": Autism, Trauma, and Affective Empathy. *Autism in Adulthood*, 2(3), 221–229. https://doi.org/10.1089/aut.2020.0013

Hummerstone, H., & Parsons, S. (2023). Co-designing methods with autistic students to facilitate discussions of sensory preferences with school staff: Exploring the double empathy problem. *International Journal of Research & Method in Education*, **46**(1), 70–82. https://doi.org/10.1080/174 3727X.2022.2071864

ICARS. (2023). *The ICARS Report England.* International Coalition Against Restraint and Seclusion. https://againstrestraint.com/wp-content/uploads/2023/04/icars_report_23.pdf

Jones, E. K., Hanley, M., & Riby, D. M. (2020). Distraction, distress and diversity: Exploring the impact of sensory processing differences on learning and school life for pupils with autism spectrum disorders. *Research in Autism Spectrum Disorders*, **72**, 101515. https://doi.org/10.1016/j.rasd.2020.101515

Jones, E., & Wessely, S. (2006). Psychological trauma: A historical perspective. *Psychiatry*, **5**(7), 217–220. https://doi.org/10.1053/j.mppsy.2006.04.011

Jordan, R. (1999). *Autistic spectrum disorders: An introductory handbook for practitioners.* David Fulton Publishers.

Kapp, S. K., Steward, R., Crane, L., Elliott, D., Elphick, C., Pellicano, E., & Russell, G. (2019). 'People should be allowed to do what they like': Autistic adults' views and experiences of stimming. *Autism*, **23**(7), 1782–1792.

Kennedy, A. C., Bybee, D., & Greeson, M. R. (2014). Examining cumulative victimization, community violence exposure, and stigma as contributors to PTSD symptoms among high-risk young women. *American Journal of Orthopsychiatry*, **84**(3), 284–294. https://doi.org/10.1037/ort0000001

Kerns, C. M., Lankenau, S., Shattuck, P. T., Robins, D. L., Newschaffer, C. J., & Berkowitz, S. J. (2022). Exploring potential sources of childhood trauma: A qualitative study with autistic adults and caregivers. *Autism*, **26**(8), 1987–1998. https://doi.org/10.1177/13623613211070637

Kildahl, A. N., Bakken, T. L., Iversen, T. E., & Helverschou, S. B. (2019). Identification of Post-Traumatic Stress Disorder in Individuals with Autism Spectrum Disorder and Intellectual Disability: A Systematic Review. *Journal of Mental Health Research in Intellectual Disabilities*, **12**(1–2), 1–25. https://doi.org/10.1080/19315864.2019.1595233

Kildahl, A. N., Helverschou, S. B., Bakken, T. L., & Oddli, H. W. (2020). "If we do not look for it, we do not see it": Clinicians' experiences and understanding of identifying post-traumatic stress disorder in adults with autism and intellectual disability. *Journal of Applied Research in Intellectual Disabilities*, **33**(5), 1119–1132. https://doi.org/10.1111/jar.12734

Kinnaird, E., Stewart, C., & Tchanturia, K. (2019). Investigating alexithymia in autism: A systematic review and meta-analysis. *European Psychiatry*, **55**, 80–89.

Kira, I. A. (2001). Taxonomy of trauma and trauma assessment. *Traumatology*, **7**(2), 73–86. https://doi.org/10.1177/153476560100700202

Kraemer, I. (2021). Why ABA Therapy is Harmful to Autistic People. *Autistic Science Person.* https://autisticscienceperson.com/why-aba-therapy-is-harmful-to-autistic-people/#autistic-peoples-experiences%20)

Lawson, W. B. (2020). Adaptive Morphing and Coping with Social Threat in Autism: An Autistic Perspective. *Journal of Intellectual Disability-Diagnosis and Treatment*, **8**, 519–526.

Leadbitter, K., Buckle, K. L., Ellis, C., & Dekker, M. (2021). Autistic Self-Advocacy and the Neurodiversity Movement: Implications for Autism Early Intervention Research and Practice. *Frontiers in Psychology*, **12**, 635690. https://doi.org/10.3389/fpsyg.2021.635690

Levine, H. B. (2021). Trauma, process and representation. *The International Journal of Psychoanalysis*, **102**(4), 794–807. https://doi.org/10.1080/00207578.2020.1841923

Lilley, R., Lawson, W., Hall, G., Mahony, J., Clapham, H., Heyworth, M., Arnold, S., Trollor, J., Yudell, M., & Pellicano, E. (2023). "Peas in a pod": Oral History Reflections on Autistic Identity in Family and Community by Late-Diagnosed Adults. *Journal of Autism and Developmental Disorders*, **53**(3), 1146–1161. https://doi.org/10.1007/s10803-022-05667-z

Macdonald, S. J., Donovan, C., & Clayton, J. (2021). 'I may be left with no choice but to end my torment': Disability and intersectionalities of hate crime. *Disability & Society*, 1–21.

MacLennan, K., O'Brien, S., & Tavassoli, T. (2022). In Our Own Words: The Complex Sensory Experiences of Autistic Adults. *Journal of Autism and Developmental Disorders*, **52**(7), 3061–3075. https://doi.org/10.1007/s10803-021-05186-3

McDougal, E., Riby, D. M., & Hanley, M. (2020). Teacher insights into the barriers and facilitators of learning in autism. *Research in Autism Spectrum Disorders*, **79**, 101674. https://doi.org/10.1016/j.rasd.2020.101674

McGill, O., & Robinson, A. (2021). "Recalling hidden harms": Autistic experiences of childhood applied behavioural analysis (ABA). *Advances in Autism*, **7**(4), 269–282. https://doi.org/10.1108/AIA-04-2020-0025

McKinnon, I., Wigham, S., Reid, K., Milton, D., Lingham, R., & Rodgers, J. (2021). *Utility of Complex Trauma Questionnaires for Adults on the Autism Spectrum with Mild Intellectual Disability: A Systematic Review*. International Society for Autism Research Annual Meeting (INSAR). https://eprints.ncl.ac.uk/273710

McShane, J. (2020). We know off-rolling happens. Why are we still doing nothing? *Support for Learning*, **35**(3), 259–275. https://doi.org/10.1111/1467-9604.12309

Miller, D., Rees, J., & Pearson, A. (2021). "Masking Is Life": Experiences of Masking in Autistic and Nonautistic Adults. *Autism in Adulthood*, **3**(4), 330–338. https://doi.org/10.1089/aut.2020.0083

Milosavljevic, B., Carter Leno, V., Simonoff, E., Baird, G., Pickles, A., Jones, C. R. G., Erskine, C., Charman, T., & Happé, F. (2016). Alexithymia in Adolescents with Autism Spectrum Disorder: Its Relationship to Internalising Difficulties, Sensory Modulation and Social Cognition. *Journal of Autism and Developmental Disorders*, **46**(4), 1354–1367. https://doi.org/10.1007/s10803-015-2670-8

Milton, D. (2018). Autistic Development, Trauma and Personhood: Beyond the Frame of the Neoliberal Individual. In K. Runswick-Cole, T. Curran, & K. Liddiard (Eds.), *The Palgrave Handbook of Disabled Children's Childhood Studies* (pp. 461–476). Palgrave Macmillan UK. https://doi.org/10.1057/978-1-137-54446-9_29

Milton, D. E. M. (2012). On the ontological status of autism: The 'double empathy problem'. *Disability & Society*, **27**(6), 883–887.

Morton, H. E. (2021). Assessment of Bullying in Autism Spectrum Disorder: Systematic Review of Methodologies and Participant Characteristics. *Review Journal of Autism and Developmental Disorders*, **8**(4), 482–497. https://doi.org/10.1007/s40489-020-00232-9

Moyse, Ruth. (2021). *Missing: The autistic girls absent from mainstream secondary schools*. https://doi.org/10.48683/1926.00097405

Nadal, K. L. (2018). Microaggressions and traumatic stress: Theory, research, and clinical treatment. *American Psychological Association*.

Nadal, K. L., Erazo, T., & King, R. (2019). Challenging Definitions of Psychological Trauma: Connecting Racial Microaggressions and Traumatic Stress. *Journal for Social Action in Counseling & Psychology*, **11**(2), 2–16. https://doi.org/10.33043/JSACP.11.2.2-16

Neumeier, S. M., & Brown, L. X. Z. (2020). Torture in the name of Treatment: The Mission to Stop the Shocks in the Age of Deinstitutionalisation. In S. K. Kapp (Ed.), *Autistic Community and the Neurodiversity Movement: Stories from the Frontline* (pp. 195–209). Springer Singapore. https://doi.org/10.1007/978-981-13-8437-0

NHS. (2023). *Trauma: Information about the role of trauma in mental health*. https://www.tewv.nhs.uk/about-your-care/conditions/trauma/

Nicolaidis, C., Milton, D., Sasson, N. J., Sheppard, E. (Lizzy), & Yergeau, M. (2019). An Expert Discussion on Autism and Empathy. *Autism in Adulthood*, **1**(1), 4–11. https://doi.org/10.1089/aut.2018.29000.cjn

Nuske, H. J., Vivanti, G., & Dissanayake, C. (2013). Are emotion impairments unique to, universal, or specific in autism spectrum disorder? A comprehensive review. *Cognition & Emotion*, **27**(6), 1042–1061. https://doi.org/10.1080/02699931.2012.762900

Olweus, D. (1997). Bully/victim problems in school: Facts and intervention. *European Journal of Psychology of Education*, **12**(4), 495–510. https://doi.org/10.1007/BF03172807

Oprea, C., & Stan, A. (2012). Mothers of Autistic Children. How do They Feel? *Procedia - Social and Behavioral Sciences*, **46**, 4191–4194. https://doi.org/10.1016/j.sbspro.2012.06.224

Papadopoulos, C. (2016). Autism stigma and the role of ethnicity and culture. *Network Autism*.

Pearson, A., Rees, J., & Forster, S. (2022). "This Was Just How This Friendship Worked": Experiences of Interpersonal Victimization Among Autistic Adults. *Autism in Adulthood*, **4**(2), 141–150. https://doi.org/10.1089/aut.2021.0035

Pearson, A., & Rose, K. (2021). A Conceptual Analysis of Autistic Masking: Understanding the Narrative of Stigma and the Illusion of Choice. *Autism in Adulthood*. https://doi.org/10.1089/aut.2020.0043

Pearson, A., Rose, K., & Rees, J. (2023). 'I felt like I deserved it because I was autistic': Understanding the impact of interpersonal victimisation in the lives of autistic people. *Autism*, **27**(2), 500–511. https://doi.org/10.1177/13623613221104546

Phung, J., Penner, M., Pirlot, C., & Welch, C. (2021). What I Wish You Knew: Insights on Burnout, Inertia, Meltdown, and Shutdown From Autistic Youth. *Frontiers in Psychology*, **12**, 741421. https://doi.org/10.3389/fpsyg.2021.741421

Pukki, H., Bettin, J., Outlaw, A. G., Hennessy, J., Brook, K., Dekker, M., Doherty, M., Shaw, S. C. K., Bervoets, J., Rudolph, S., Corneloup, T., Derwent, K., Lee, O., Rojas, Y. G., Lawson, W., Gutierrez, M. V., Petek, K., Tsiakkirou, M., Suoninen, A., … Yoon, W.-H. (2022). Autistic Perspectives on the Future of Clinical Autism Research. *Autism in Adulthood*, **4**(2), 93–101. https://doi.org/10.1089/aut.2022.0017

Pyne, J. (2020). "Building a Person": Legal and Clinical Personhood for Autistic and Trans Children in Ontario. *Canadian Journal of Law and Society / Revue Canadienne Droit et Société*, **35**(2), 341–365. https://doi.org/10.1017/cls.2020.8

Quarmby, K. (2011). *Scapegoat: How we are failing disabled people*. Portobello.

Quinn, A. (2018). *Unbroken: Learning to live beyond diagnosis*. Welbeck Publishing Group.

Ramo-Fernández, L., Schneider, A., Wilker, S., & Kolassa, I.-T. (2015). Epigenetic Alterations Associated with War Trauma and Childhood Maltreatment: Epigenetics of trauma and violence. *Behavioral Sciences & the Law*, **33**(5), 701–721. https://doi.org/10.1002/bsl.2200

Reuben, K. E., Stanzione, C. M., & Singleton, J. L. (2021). Interpersonal Trauma and Posttraumatic Stress in Autistic Adults. *Autism in Adulthood*.

Ringel, S., & Brandell, J. R. (2011). *Trauma: Contemporary directions in theory, practice, and research*. Sage.

Rose, K., & Vivian, S. (2020). *Regarding the use of Dehumanising Rhetoric*. https://theautisticadvocate.com/2020/02/regarding-the-use-of-dehumanising-rhetoric/

Rumball, F., Brook, L., Happé, F., & Karl, A. (2021). Heightened risk of posttraumatic stress disorder in adults with autism spectrum disorder: The role of cumulative trauma and memory deficits. *Research in Developmental Disabilities*, **110**, 103848. https://doi.org/10.1016/j.ridd.2020.103848

Rumball, F., Happé, F., & Grey, N. (2020). Experience of Trauma and PTSD Symptoms in Autistic Adults: Risk of PTSD Development Following DSM-5 and Non-DSM-5 Traumatic Life Events. *Autism Research*.

Sandoval-Norton, A. H., Shkedy, G., & Shkedy, D. (2019). How much compliance is too much compliance: Is long-term ABA therapy abuse? *Cogent Psychology*, **6**(1), 1641258. https://doi.org/10.1080/23311908.2019.1641258

Sassu, K. A., & Volkmar, F. R. (2023). Autism and intersectionality: Considerations for school-based practitioners. *Psychology in the Schools*, **60**(2), 408–418. https://doi.org/10.1002/pits.22757

Shakespeare, T. (2012). Blaming the victim: Disability hate crime. *The Lancet*. https://doi.org/10.1016/s0140-6736(12)61492-5

Smitten, J. (2022). *Masking in Autistic Children: The Child's Voice* [Sheffield Hallam University]. https://www.jodiesmitten.co.uk/2023/03/22/masking-in-autistic-children-the-childs-voice/?fbclid=IwAR1iZC0ME6VuUusnUsp0XK6R-7hz-SjIsjvyex0tCoa3gL06Ml4T9pAH0sw

Spaeth, E., & Pearson, A. (2021). *A Reflective Analysis on Neurodiversity and Student Wellbeing: Conceptualising Practical Strategies for Inclusive Practice* [Preprint]. PsyArXiv. https://doi.org/10.31234/osf.io/dc3gw

Teague, S. J., Gray, K. M., Tonge, B. J., & Newman, L. K. (2017). Attachment in children with autism spectrum disorder: A systematic review. *Research in Autism Spectrum Disorders*, **35**, 35–50. https://doi.org/10.1016/j.rasd.2016.12.002

Tomasello, M., & Camaioni, L. (1997). A Comparison of the Gestural Communication of Apes and Human Infants. *Human Development*, **40**(1), 7–24. https://doi.org/10.1159/000278540

Verhoeven, M., Poorthuis, A. M. G., & Volman, M. (2019). The Role of School in Adolescents' Identity Development. A Literature Review. *Educational Psychology Review*, **31**(1), 35–63. https://doi.org/10.1007/s10648-018-9457-3

Walker, N. (2021). *Neuroqueer Heresies*. Autonomous Press.

Warrier, V., & Baron-Cohen, S. (2021). Childhood trauma, life-time self-harm, and suicidal behaviour and ideation are associated with polygenic scores for autism. *Molecular Psychiatry*, **26**(5), 1670–1684. https://doi.org/10.1038/s41380-019-0550-x

Watermeyer, B., & Swartz, L. (2016). Disablism, Identity and Self: Discrimination as a Traumatic Assault on Subjectivity: Disablism as a traumatic assault. *Journal of Community & Applied Social Psychology*, **26**(3), 268–276. https://doi.org/10.1002/casp.2266

Weiss, J. A., & Fardella, M. A. (2018). Victimization and perpetration experiences of adults with autism. *Frontiers in Psychiatry*. https://doi.org/10.3389/fpsyt.2018.00203

Wigham, S., McKinnon, I., Reid, K., Milton, D., Lingam, R., & Rodgers, J. (2021). Questionnaires used in complex trauma intervention evaluations and consideration of their utility for autistic adults with mild intellectual disability: A systematic review. *Research in Developmental Disabilities*, **117**, 104039. https://doi.org/10.1016/j.ridd.2021.104039

Williams, E. I., Gleeson, K., & Jones, B. E. (2019). How pupils on the autism spectrum make sense of themselves in the context of their experiences in a mainstream school setting: A qualitative metasynthesis. *Autism*, **23**(1), 8–28. https://doi.org/10.1177/1362361317723836

Wood, R., & Lawson, W. B. (2019). *Inclusive education for autistic children: Helping children and young people to learn and flourish in the classroom*. Jessica Kingsley Publishers.

Woodlock, D. (2020). The history and politics of trauma theory. *DVSA Supervision and Research*. https://www.dvsa.net.au/post/the-history-and-politics-of-trauma-theory

Yergeau, M. (2013). Clinically significant disturbance: On theorists who theorize theory of mind. *Disability Studies Quarterly*, **33**(4).

Zimmerman, J. (2022). Jordyn Zimmerman's Remarks to the Interagency Autism Coordinating Committee. *Communication FIRST*. https://communicationfirst.org/jordyn-zimmermans-remarks-to-the-interagency-autism-coordinating-committee/

# Chapter 9

Achenbach, T. M. (2011). Child Behavior Checklist. In J. S. Kreutzer, J. DeLuca, & B. Caplan (Eds.), *Encyclopedia of Clinical Neuropsychology* (pp. 546–552). Springer New York. https://doi.org/10.1007/978-0-387-79948-3_1529

Atherton, G., Edisbury, E., Piovesan, A., & Cross, L. (2022). Autism Through the Ages: A Mixed Methods Approach to Understanding How Age and Age of Diagnosis Affect Quality of Life. *Journal of Autism and Developmental Disorders*, **52**(8), 3639–3654. https://doi.org/10.1007/s10803-021-05235-x

Bargiela, S., Steward, R., & Mandy, W. (2016). The Experiences of Late-diagnosed Women with Autism Spectrum Conditions: An Investigation of the Female Autism Phenotype. *Journal of Autism and Developmental Disorders*. https://doi.org/10.1007/s10803-016-2872-8

Baron-Cohen, S., Wheelwright, S., Hill, J., Raste, Y., & Plumb, I. (2001). The "Reading the Mind in the Eyes" Test Revised Version: A Study with Normal Adults, and Adults with Asperger Syndrome or High-functioning Autism. *Journal of Child Psychology and Psychiatry*, **42**(2), 241–251. https://doi.org/10.1111/1469-7610.00715

Butler, J. (1988). Performative Acts and Gender Constitution: An Essay in Phenomenology and Feminist Theory. *Theatre Journal*, **40**(4), 519. https://doi.org/10.2307/3207893

Cage, E., & Troxell-Whitman, Z. (2019). Understanding the Reasons, Contexts and Costs of Camouflaging for Autistic Adults. *Journal of Autism and Developmental Disorders*. https://doi.org/10.1007/s10803-018-03878-x

Chapman, L., Rose, K., Hull, L., & Mandy, W. (2022). "I want to fit in… but I don't want to change myself fundamentally": A qualitative exploration of the relationship between masking and mental health for autistic teenagers. *Research in Autism Spectrum Disorders*, **99**, 102069. https://doi.org/10.1016/j.rasd.2022.102069

Cook, A., Ogden, J., & Winstone, N. (2018). Friendship motivations, challenges and the role of masking for girls with autism in contrasting school settings. *European Journal of Special Needs Education*, **33**(3), 302–315. https://doi.org/10.1080/08856257.2017.1312797

Cook, J., Crane, L., Bourne, L., Hull, L., & Mandy, W. (2021). Camouflaging in an everyday social context: An interpersonal recall study. *Autism*, 1362361321992641. https://doi.org/10.1177/1362361321992641

Cook, J., Crane, L., Hull, L., Bourne, L., & Mandy, W. (2022). Self-reported camouflaging behaviours used by autistic adults during everyday social interactions. *Autism*, **26**(2), 406–421. https://doi.org/10.1177/13623613211026754

Cook, J., Hull, L., Crane, L., & Mandy, W. (2021). Camouflaging in autism: A systematic review. *Clinical Psychology Review*, **89**, 102080. https://doi.org/10.1016/j.cpr.2021.102080

Corbett, B. A., Schwartzman, J. M., Libsack, E. J., Muscatello, R. A., Lerner, M. D., Simmons, G. L., & White, S. W. (2021). Camouflaging in Autism: Examining Sex-Based and Compensatory Models in Social Cognition and Communication. *Autism Research*, **14**(1), 127–142. https://doi.org/10.1002/aur.2440

Dean, M., Harwood, R., & Kasari, C. (2017). The art of camouflage: Gender differences in the social behaviors of girls and boys with autism spectrum disorder. *Autism*, **21**(6), 678–689. https://doi.org/10.1177/1362361316671845

Evans, B. (2014). The Foundations of Autism: The Law Concerning Psychotic, Schizophrenic, and Autistic Children in 1950s and 1960s Britain. *Bulletin of the History of Medicine*, **88**(2), 253–285. https://doi.org/10.1353/bhm.2014.0033

Gould, J. (2017). Towards understanding the under-recognition of girls and women on the autism spectrum. *Autism*. https://doi.org/10.1177/1362361317706174

Hannon, B., Mandy, W., & Hull, L. (2023). A comparison of methods for measuring camouflaging in autism. *Autism Research*, **16**(1), 12–29. https://doi.org/10.1002/aur.2850

Hull, L., Mandy, W., Lai, M. C., Baron-Cohen, S., Allison, C., Smith, P., & Petrides, K. V. (2019). Development and Validation of the Camouflaging Autistic Traits Questionnaire (CAT-Q). *Journal of Autism and Developmental Disorders*. https://doi.org/10.1007/s10803-018-3792-6

Hull, L., Petrides, K. V., & Mandy, W. (2020a). Cognitive Predictors of Self-Reported Camouflaging in Autistic Adolescents. *Autism Research*.

Hull, L., Petrides, K. V., & Mandy, W. (2020b). The Female Autism Phenotype and Camouflaging: A Narrative Review. *Review Journal of Autism and Developmental Disorders*. https://doi.org/10.1007/s40489-020-00197-9

Jorgenson, C., Lewis, T., Rose, C., & Kanne, S. (2020). Social Camouflaging in Autistic and Neurotypical Adolescents: A Pilot Study of Differences by Sex and Diagnosis. *Journal of Autism and Developmental Disorders*, 1–12.

Jurgens, A. (2020). Neurodiversity in a neurotypical world. In *Neurodiversity Studies: A new critical paradigm* (pp. 73–88). Routledge.

Lai, M. C., Lombardo, M. V., Chakrabarti, B., Ruigrok, A. N. V., Bullmore, E. T., Suckling, J., Auyeung, B., Happé, F., Szatmari, P., Baron-Cohen, S., Bailey, A. J., Bolton, P. F., Carrington, S., Catani, M., Craig, M. C., Daly, E. M., Deoni, S. C. L., Ecker, C., Henty, J., … Williams, S. C. (2019). Neural self-representation in autistic women and association with 'compensatory camouflaging'. *Autism*. https://doi.org/10.1177/1362361318807159

Lai, M. C., Lombardo, M. V., Ruigrok, A. N. V., Chakrabarti, B., Auyeung, B., Szatmari, P., Happé, F., & Baron-Cohen, S. (2017). Quantifying and exploring camouflaging in men and women with autism. *Autism*. https://doi.org/10.1177/1362361316671012

Loomes, R., Hull, L., & Mandy, W. P. L. (2017). What Is the Male-to-Female Ratio in Autism Spectrum Disorder? A Systematic Review and Meta-Analysis. *Journal of the American Academy of Child & Adolescent Psychiatry*, **56**(6), 466–474. https://doi.org/10.1016/j.jaac.2017.03.013

Lord, C., Brugha, T. S., Charman, T., Cusack, J., Dumas, G., Frazier, T., Jones, E. J. H., Jones, R. M., Pickles, A., & State, M. W. (2020). Autism spectrum disorder. *Nature Reviews Disease Primers*, **6**(1), 1–23.

Lundin Remnélius, K., & Bölte, S. (2023). Camouflaging in Autism: Age Effects and Cross-Cultural Validation of the Camouflaging Autistic Traits Questionnaire (CAT-Q). *Journal of Autism and Developmental Disorders*. https://doi.org/10.1007/s10803-023-05909-8

Mandy, W., Pellicano, L., St Pourcain, B., Skuse, D., & Heron, J. (2018). The development of autistic social traits across childhood and adolescence in males and females. *Journal of Child Psychology and Psychiatry*, **59**(11), 1143–1151.

Mattern, H., Cola, M., Tena, K. G., Knox, A., Russell, A., Pelella, M. R., Hauptmann, A., Covello, M., Parish-Morris, J., & McCleery, J. P. (2023). Sex differences in social and emotional insight in youth with and without autism. *Molecular Autism*, **14**(1), 10. https://doi.org/10.1186/s13229-023-00541-w

Miller, D., Rees, J., & Pearson, A. (2021). "Masking Is Life": Experiences of Masking in Autistic and Nonautistic Adults. *Autism in Adulthood*, 2(4), 330–338. https://doi.org/10.1089/aut.2020.0083

Milner, V., Colvert, E., Mandy, W., & Happé, F. (2023). A comparison of self-report and discrepancy measures of camouflaging: Exploring sex differences in diagnosed autistic versus high autistic trait young adults. *Autism Research*, **16**(3), 580–590. https://doi.org/10.1002/aur.2873

Milner, V., Mandy, W., Happé, F., & Colvert, E. (2023). Sex differences in predictors and outcomes of camouflaging: Comparing diagnosed autistic, high autistic trait and low autistic trait young adults. *Autism*, **27**(2), 402–414. https://doi.org/10.1177/13623613221098240

Milton, D., & Sims, T. (2016). How is a sense of well-being and belonging constructed in the accounts of autistic adults? Disability & Society, 31(4), 520–534.

Pearson, A., & Rose, K. (2021). A Conceptual Analysis of Autistic Masking: Understanding the Narrative of Stigma and the Illusion of Choice. *Autism in Adulthood*. https://doi.org/10.1089/aut.2020.0043

Pearson, A., Rose, K., & Rees, J. (2023). 'I felt like I deserved it because I was autistic': Understanding the impact of interpersonal victimisation in the lives of autistic people. *Autism*, **27**(2), 500–511. https://doi.org/10.1177/13623613221104546

Perry, E., Mandy, W., Hull, L., & Cage, E. (2021). Understanding camouflaging as a response to autism-related stigma: A Social Identity Theory approach. *Journal of Autism and Developmental Disorders*, 1–11.

Ratto, A. B., Kenworthy, L., Yerys, B. E., Bascom, J., Wieckowski, A. T., White, S. W., Wallace, G. L., Pugliese, C., Schultz, R. T., Ollendick, T. H., Scarpa, A., Seese, S., Register-Brown, K., Martin, A., & Anthony, L. G. (2018). What About the Girls? Sex-Based Differences in Autistic Traits and Adaptive Skills. *Journal of Autism and Developmental Disorders*, **48**(5), 1698–1711. https://doi.org/10.1007/s10803-017-3413-9

Ross, A., Grove, R., & McAloon, J. (2023). The relationship between camouflaging and mental health in autistic children and adolescents. *Autism Research*, **16**(1), 190–199. https://doi.org/10.1002/aur.2859

Rynkiewicz, A., Schuller, B., Marchi, E., Piana, S., Camurri, A., Lassalle, A., & Baron-Cohen, S. (2016). An investigation of the 'female camouflage effect' in autism using a computerized ADOS-2 and a test of sex/gender differences. *Molecular Autism*, **7**(1), 10. https://doi.org/10.1186/s13229-016-0073-0

Sasson, N. J., Morrison, K. E., Kelsven, S., & Pinkham, A. E. (2020). Social cognition as a predictor of functional and social skills in autistic adults without intellectual disability. *Autism Research*, **13**(2), 259–270.

Schneid, I., & Raz, A. E. (2020). The mask of autism: Social camouflaging and impression management as coping/normalization from the perspectives of autistic adults. *Social Science & Medicine*, **248**, 112826.

Schuck, R. K., Flores, R. E., & Fung, L. K. (2019). Brief Report: Sex/Gender Differences in Symptomology and Camouflaging in Adults with Autism Spectrum Disorder. *Journal of Autism and Developmental Disorders*, **49**(6), 2597–2604. https://doi.org/10.1007/s10803-019-03998-y

Sedgewick, F., Hill, V., & Pellicano, E. (2018). 'It's different for girls': Gender differences in the friendships and conflict of autistic and neurotypical adolescents. *Autism*, **23**(5), 1119–1132. https://doi.org/10.1177/1362361318794930

Skuse, D. H., Mandy, W. P. L., & Scourfield, J. (2005). Measuring autistic traits: Heritability, reliability and validity of the Social and Communication Disorders Checklist. *British Journal of Psychiatry*, **187**(6), 568–572. https://doi.org/10.1192/bjp.187.6.568

Smitten, J. (2022). *Masking in Autistic Children: The Child's Voice* [Sheffield Hallam University]. https://www.jodiesmitten.co.uk/2023/03/22/masking-in-autistic-children-the-childs-voice/?fbclid = IwAR1iZC0ME6VuUusnUsp0XK6R-7hz-SjIsjvyex0tCoa3gL06Ml4T9pAH0sw

Timimi, S., Milton, D., Bovell, V., Kapp, S., & Russell, G. (2019). Deconstructing Diagnosis: Four Commentaries on a Diagnostic Tool to Assess Individuals for Autism Spectrum Disorders. *Autonomy* (Birmingham, England), **1**(6), AR26.

Wharmby, P. (2022). *Un-typical: How the world isn't built for autistic people and what we should do about it*. Harper Collins.

Willey, L. H. (2014). *Pretending to be normal: Living with asperger's syndrome (autism spectrum disorder) expanded edition*. Jessica Kingsley Publishers.

Williams, Z. J. (2022). Commentary: The construct validity of 'camouflaging' in autism: psychometric considerations and recommendations for future research - reflection on Lai et al. (2020). *Journal of Child Psychology and Psychiatry*, **63**(1), 118–121. https://doi.org/10.1111/jcpp.13468

Wood-Downie, H., Wong, B., Kovshoff, H., Mandy, W., Hull, L., & Hadwin, J. A. (2020). Sex/gender differences in camouflaging in children and adolescents with autism. *Journal of Autism and Developmental Disorders*, 1–12.

Zeidan, J., Fombonne, E., Scorah, J., Ibrahim, A., Durkin, M. S., Saxena, S., Yusuf, A., Shih, A., & Elsabbagh, M. (2022). Global prevalence of autism: A systematic review update. *Autism Research*, **15**(5), 778–790. https://doi.org/10.1002/aur.2696

# Chapter 10

Arnold, S. R., Higgins, J. M., Weise, J., Desai, A., Pellicano, E., & Trollor, J. N. (2023a). Confirming the nature of autistic burnout. *Autism*, 13623613221147410.

Arnold, S. R., Higgins, J. M., Weise, J., Desai, A., Pellicano, E., & Trollor, J. N. (2023b). Towards the measurement of autistic burnout. *Autism*, 13623613221147400.

Bakker, A. B., Demerouti, E., & Verbeke, W. (2004). Using the job demands-resources model to predict burnout and performance. *Human Resource Management*, **43**(1), 83–104. https://doi.org/10.1002/hrm.20004

Beck, J. S., Lundwall, R. A., Gabrielsen, T., Cox, J. C., & South, M. (2020). Looking good but feeling bad: "Camouflaging" behaviors and mental health in women with autistic traits. *Autism*. https://doi.org/10.1177/1362361320912147

Belcher, H. L., Morein-Zamir, S., Stagg, S. D., & Ford, R. M. (2022). Shining a Light on a Hidden Population: Social Functioning and Mental Health in Women Reporting Autistic Traits But Lacking Diagnosis. *Journal of Autism and Developmental Disorders*. https://doi.org/10.1007/s10803-022-05583-2

Botha, M., & Frost, D. M. (2020). Extending the Minority Stress Model to Understand Mental Health Problems Experienced by the Autistic Population. *Society and Mental Health*, **10**(1), 20–34. https://doi.org/10.1177/2156869318804297

Bowri, M., Hull, L., Allison, C., Smith, P., Baron-Cohen, S., Lai, M.-C., & Mandy, W. (2021). Demographic and psychological predictors of alcohol use and misuse in autistic adults. *Autism*, **25**(5), 1469–1480. https://doi.org/10.1177/1362361321992668

Bradley, L., Shaw, R., Baron-Cohen, S., & Cassidy, S. (2021). Autistic Adults' Experiences of Camouflaging and Its Perceived Impact on Mental Health. *Autism in Adulthood*, **3**(4), 320–329. https://doi.org/10.1089/aut.2020.0071

Cage, E., Botha, M., McDevitt, L., King, K. N., Biscoe, L., Tucker, K., & Pearson, A. (2022). *Diagnosis as a new beginning not an end: A participatory photovoice study on navigating an autism diagnosis in adulthood* [Preprint]. PsyArXiv. https://doi.org/10.31234/osf.io/qg9bt

Cage, E., Di Monaco, J., & Newell, V. (2018). Experiences of autism acceptance and mental health in autistic adults. *Journal of Autism and Developmental Disorders*, **48**(2), 473–484.

Cassidy, S. A., Gould, K., Townsend, E., Pelton, M., Robertson, A. E., & Rodgers, J. (2019). Is Camouflaging Autistic Traits Associated with Suicidal Thoughts and Behaviours? Expanding the Interpersonal Psychological Theory of Suicide in an Undergraduate Student Sample. *Journal of Autism and Developmental Disorders*. https://doi.org/10.1007/s10803-019-04323-3

Cassidy, S., Bradley, L., Shaw, R., & Baron-Cohen, S. (2018). Risk markers for suicidality in autistic adults. *Molecular Autism*. https://doi.org/10.1186/s13229-018-0226-4

Chapman, L., Rose, K., Hull, L., & Mandy, W. (2022). "I want to fit in… but I don't want to change myself fundamentally": A qualitative exploration of the relationship between masking and mental health for autistic teenagers. *Research in Autism Spectrum Disorders*, **99**, 102069. https://doi.org/10.1016/j.rasd.2022.102069

Cremone, I. M., Carpita, B., Nardi, B., Casagrande, D., Stagnari, R., Amatori, G., & Dell'Osso, L. (2023). Measuring Social Camouflaging in Individuals with High Functioning Autism: A Literature Review. *Brain Sciences*, **13**(3), 469. https://doi.org/10.3390/brainsci13030469

Dababnah, S., Kim, I., & Shaia, W. E. (2022). 'I am so fearful for him': A mixed-methods exploration of stress among caregivers of Black children with autism. *International Journal of Developmental Disabilities*, **68**(5), 658–670. https://doi.org/10.1080/20473869.2020.1870418

de Broize, M., Evans, K., Whitehouse, A. J. O., Wray, J., Eapen, V., & Urbanowicz, A. (2022). Exploring the Experience of Seeking an Autism Diagnosis as an Adult. *Autism in Adulthood*, **4**(2), 130–140. https://doi.org/10.1089/aut.2021.0028

Dwyer, P. (2019). BURNOUT AND EXPECTATIONS. *AUTISTIC SCHOLAR Thoughts On Autism, Neurodiversity, And More.* https://www.autisticscholar.com/burnout-and-expectations/

Epstein, R., Blake, J. J., & González, T. (2017). *Girlhood Interrupted: The Erasure of Black Girls' Childhood.* Georgetown Law Center on Poverty and Inequality. https://genderjusticeandopportunity.georgetown.edu/wp-content/uploads/2020/06/girlhood-interrupted.pdf

Flood, C. (2023). 'I drank because I was socially awkward, then I got sober and discovered I'm autistic' Lesser-known reasons why some people become dependent on alcohol. *Society for the Study of Addiction.* https://www.addiction-ssa.org/i-drank-because-i-was-socially-awkward-then-i-got-sober-and-discovered-im-autistic/

Forbes, K. (2020). Autism is my Identity and my Culture. *Intune Pathways.* https://www.kristyforbes.com.au/blog/autism-is-my-identity-and-my-culture

Fusar-Poli, L., Brondino, N., Politi, P., & Aguglia, E. (2022). Missed diagnoses and misdiagnoses of adults with autism spectrum disorder. *European Archives of Psychiatry and Clinical Neuroscience*, **272**(2), 187–198. https://doi.org/10.1007/s00406-020-01189-w

Gould, J. (2017). Towards understanding the under-recognition of girls and women on the autism spectrum. *Autism.* https://doi.org/10.1177/1362361317706174

Gray-Hammond, D. (2023). Drug use, addiction, and neuroqueering. *Emergent Divergence.* https://emergentdivergence.com/2023/02/10/drug-use-addiction-and-neuroqueering/

Gulley, K., & Hammond, T. (2022). *Autistic Voices: This Was Never About ABA.* The Kisha Project. https://thekishaproject.com/aba/

Higgins, J. M., Arnold, S. R., Weise, J., Pellicano, E., & Trollor, J. N. (2021). Defining autistic burnout through experts by lived experience: Grounded Delphi method investigating# AutisticBurnout. *Autism*, **25**(8), 2356–2369.

Hobfoll, S. E. (1989). Conservation of resources: A new attempt at conceptualizing stress. *American Psychologist*, **44**, 513–524. https://doi.org/10.1037/0003-066X.44.3.513

Hull, L., Levy, L., Lai, M.-C., Petrides, K. V., Baron-Cohen, S., Allison, C., Smith, P., & Mandy, W. (2021). Is social camouflaging associated with anxiety and depression in autistic adults? *Molecular Autism*, **12**(1), 13. https://doi.org/10.1186/s13229-021-00421-1

Hull, L., Petrides, K. V., Allison, C., Smith, P., Baron-Cohen, S., Lai, M. C., & Mandy, W. (2017). "Putting on My Best Normal": Social Camouflaging in Adults with Autism Spectrum Conditions. *Journal of Autism and Developmental Disorders*. https://doi.org/10.1007/s10803-017-3166-5

Hutson, T. M., McGhee Hassrick, E., Fernandes, S., Walton, J., Bouvier-Weinberg, K., Radcliffe, A., & Allen-Handy, A. (2022). "I'm just different–that's all–I'm so sorry … ": Black men, ASD and the urgent need for DisCrit Theory in police encounters. *Policing: An International Journal*, **45**(3), 524–537. https://doi.org/10.1108/PIJPSM-10-2021-0149

Jeffrey-Wilensky, J. (2020). How autism researchers can better reach Black families. *Spectrum News*. https://www.spectrumnews.org/opinion/q-and-a/how-autism-researchers-can-better-reach-black-families/

Lai, M. C., Lombardo, M. V., Ruigrok, A. N. V., Chakrabarti, B., Auyeung, B., Szatmari, P., Happé, F., & Baron-Cohen, S. (2017). Quantifying and exploring camouflaging in men and women with autism. *Autism*. https://doi.org/10.1177/1362361316671012

Leedham, A., Thompson, A. R., Smith, R., & Freeth, M. (2020). 'I was exhausted trying to figure it out': The experiences of females receiving an autism diagnosis in middle to late adulthood. *Autism*, **24**(1), 135–146.

Levy, S. (2022). *Autistic Traits, Substance Use, and Social Anxiety* [University of Alabama]. https://ir.ua.edu/handle/123456789/8521

Lilley, R., Lawson, W., Hall, G., Mahony, J., Clapham, H., Heyworth, M., Arnold, S. R., Trollor, J. N., Yudell, M., & Pellicano, E. (2022). 'A way to be me': Autobiographical reflections of autistic adults diagnosed in mid-to-late adulthood. *Autism*, **26**(6), 1395–1408. https://doi.org/10.1177/13623613211050694

Linden, A., Best, L., Elise, F., Roberts, D., Branagan, A., Tay, Y. B. E., Crane, L., Cusack, J., Davidson, B., Davidson, I., Hearst, C., Mandy, W., Rai, D., Smith, E., & Gurusamy, K. (2023). Benefits and harms of interventions to improve anxiety, depression, and other mental health outcomes for autistic people: A systematic review and network meta-analysis of randomised controlled trials. *Autism*, **27**(1), 7–30. https://doi.org/10.1177/13623613221117931

Livingston, L. A. (2021). Substance use, coping, and compensation in autism. *The Lancet Psychiatry*, **8**(8), 641–642. https://doi.org/10.1016/S2215-0366(21)00205-4

Lovelace, T. S., Comis, M. P., Tabb, J. M., & Oshokoya, O. E. (2022). Missing from the Narrative: A Seven-Decade Scoping Review of the Inclusion of Black Autistic Women and Girls in Autism Research. *Behavior Analysis in Practice*, **15**(4), 1093–1105. https://doi.org/10.1007/s40617-021-00654-9

Mantzalas, J., Richdale, A. L., Adikari, A., Lowe, J., & Dissanayake, C. (2022). What is autistic burnout? A thematic analysis of posts on two online platforms. *Autism in Adulthood*, **4**(1), 52–65.

Mantzalas, J., Richdale, A. L., & Dissanayake, C. (2022). A conceptual model of risk and protective factors for autistic burnout. *Autism Research*, **15**(6), 976–987.

McQuaid, G., Strang, J., & Jack, A. (2022). *Borderline personality and late, missed, and mis-diagnosis in female autism: A review of the literature* [Preprint]. PsyArXiv. https://doi.org/10.31234/osf.io/t37vj

Miller, D., Rees, J., & Pearson, A. (2021). "Masking Is Life": Experiences of Masking in Autistic and Nonautistic Adults. *Autism in Adulthood*, **3**(4), 330–338. https://doi.org/10.1089/aut.2020.0083

Pearson, A., & Rose, K. (2021). A Conceptual Analysis of Autistic Masking: Understanding the Narrative of Stigma and the Illusion of Choice. *Autism in Adulthood*. https://doi.org/10.1089/aut.2020.0043

Pearson, A., Rose, K., & Rees, J. (2023). 'I felt like I deserved it because I was autistic': Understanding the impact of interpersonal victimisation in the lives of autistic people. *Autism*, **27**(2), 500–511. https://doi.org/10.1177/13623613221104546

Raymaker, D. M., Teo, A. R., Steckler, N. A., Lentz, B., Scharer, M., Delos Santos, A., Kapp, S. K., Hunter, M., Joyce, A., & Nicolaidis, C. (2020). "Having all of your internal resources exhausted beyond measure and being left with no clean-up crew": Defining autistic burnout. *Autism in Adulthood*, **2**:2, 132–143. https://doi.org/10.1089/aut.2019.0079

Rebarbar, E. (2021). The Unexplored Link Between Autism and Substance Abuse. *NeuroClastic*. https://neuroclastic.com/the-unexplored-link-between-autism-and-substance-abuse/

Rose, K. (2018a). An Autistic Burnout. *The Autistic Advocate*. https://theautisticadvocate.com/2018/05/an-autistic-burnout/

Rose, K. (2018b). *Masking: I am not OK*. https://theautisticadvocate.com/2018/07/masking-i-am-not-ok/

Rose, K. (2018c). We are not ok. *The Autistic Advocate*. https://theautisticadvocate.com/2018/08/we-are-not-ok/

Ross, A., Grove, R., & McAloon, J. (2023). The relationship between camouflaging and mental health in autistic children and adolescents. *Autism Research*, **16**(1), 190–199. https://doi.org/10.1002/aur.2859

Royal College of Psychiatrists. (2020). *The psychiatric management of autism in adults* (No. CR228). https://www.rcpsych.ac.uk/docs/default-source/improving-care/better-mh-policy/college-reports/college-report-cr228.pdf?sfvrsn = c64e10e3_2

Spence, O. (2020). "Zero Tolerance" of Black Autistic Boys: Are schools failing to recognise the needs of African Caribbean Boys with a diagnosis of autism? In The Neurodiversity Reader: *Exploring Concepts, Lived Experience and Implications* for Practice (pp. 41–47). Pavilion.

Sykes, M. (2023). *Illuminated: Autism & all the things I've left unsaid*. HarperNorth.

Thornton, C. (2021). ABA for Creating Masking Black Autistics. *NeuroClastic*. https://neuroclastic.com/aba-for-creating-masking-black-autistics/

Ventour-Williams, T. (2022). Autistic While Black in the UK: Masking, Codeswitching, and Other (Non)fictions. *NeuroClastic*. https://neuroclastic.com/long-read-autistic-while-black-in-the-uk-masking-codeswitching-and-other-nonfictions/

Weir, E., Allison, C., & Baron-Cohen, S. (2021). Understanding the substance use of autistic adolescents and adults: A mixed-methods approach. *The Lancet Psychiatry*, **8**(8), 673–685. https://doi.org/10.1016/S2215-0366(21)00160-7

# Chapter 11

Ai, W., Cunningham, W. A., & Lai, M.-C. (2022). Reconsidering autistic 'camouflaging'as transactional impression management. *Trends in Cognitive Sciences*.

Baggs, M. (2020). Losing. In S. K. Kapp (Ed.), *Autistic Community and the Neurodiversity Movement: Stories from the Frontline*. Springer Singapore. https://doi.org/10.1007/978-981-13-8437-0

Baron-Cohen, S. (1997). *Mindblindness: An essay on autism and theory of mind*. MIT press.

Bervoets, J., Milton, D., & Van De Cruys, S. (2021). Autism and intolerance of uncertainty: An ill-fitting pair. *Trends in Cognitive Sciences*, **25**(12), 1009–1010. https://doi.org/10.1016/j.tics.2021.08.006

Boorse, J., Cola, M., Plate, S., Yankowitz, L., Pandey, J., Schultz, R. T., & Parish-Morris, J. (2019). Linguistic markers of autism in girls: Evidence of a "blended phenotype" during storytelling. *Molecular Autism*, **10**(1), 14. https://doi.org/10.1186/s13229-019-0268-2

Botha, M., Dibb, B., & Frost, D. M. (2022). 'Autism is me': An investigation of how autistic individuals make sense of autism and stigma. *Disability & Society*, **37**(3), 427–453. https://doi.org/10.1080/09687599.2020.1822782

Chandler, R. J., Russell, A., & Maras, K. L. (2019). Compliance in autism: Self-report in action. *Autism*, **23**(4), 1005–1017.

Chapman, L., Rose, K., Hull, L., & Mandy, W. (2022). "I want to fit in... but I don't want to change myself fundamentally": A qualitative exploration of the relationship between masking and mental health for autistic teenagers. *Research in Autism Spectrum Disorders*, **99**, 102069. https://doi.org/10.1016/j.rasd.2022.102069

Chapman, R., & Carel, H. (2022). Neurodiversity, epistemic injustice, and the good human life. *Journal of Social Philosophy*, **53**(4), 614–631. https://doi.org/10.1111/josp.12456

Chevallier, C., Kohls, G., Troiani, V., Brodkin, E. S., & Schultz, R. T. (2012). The social motivation theory of autism. *Trends in Cognitive Sciences*, **16**(4), 231–239.

Friston, K. J., Lawson, R., & Frith, C. D. (2013). On hyperpriors and hypopriors: Comment on Pellicano and Burr. *Trends in Cognitive Sciences*, **17**(1), 1. https://doi.org/10.1016/j.tics.2012.11.003

Fulton, R., Reardon, E., Kate, R., & Jones, R. (2020). *Sensory Trauma: Autism, sensory difference and the daily experience of fear*. Autism Wellbeing CIC.

Goffman, E. (1959). *The presentation of self in everyday life*. (Vol. 259). Garden City.

Hopkins, Z., Yuill, N., & Keller, B. (2016). Children with autism align syntax in natural conversation. *Applied Psycholinguistics*, **37**(2), 347–370. https://doi.org/10.1017/S0142716414000599

Hull, L., Petrides, K. V., Allison, C., Smith, P., Baron-Cohen, S., Lai, M. C., & Mandy, W. (2017). "Putting on My Best Normal": Social Camouflaging in Adults with Autism Spectrum Conditions. *Journal of Autism and Developmental Disorders*. https://doi.org/10.1007/s10803-017-3166-5

Jenkinson, R., Milne, E., & Thompson, A. (2020). The relationship between intolerance of uncertainty and anxiety in autism: A systematic literature review and meta-analysis. *Autism*, **24**(8), 1933–1944. https://doi.org/10.1177/1362361320932437

Lawson, W. B. (2020). Adaptive Morphing and Coping with Social Threat in Autism: An Autistic Perspective. *Journal of Intellectual Disability-Diagnosis and Treatment*, **8**, 519–526.

Livingston, L. A., Shah, P., Milner, V., & Happé, F. (2020). Quantifying compensatory strategies in adults with and without diagnosed autism. *Molecular Autism*. https://doi.org/10.1186/s13229-019-0308-y

Miller, D., Rees, J., & Pearson, A. (2021). "Masking Is Life": Experiences of Masking in Autistic and Nonautistic Adults. *Autism in Adulthood*, **3**(4), 330–338. https://doi.org/10.1089/aut.2020.0083

Pearson, A., & Rose, K. (2021). A Conceptual Analysis of Autistic Masking: Understanding the Narrative of Stigma and the Illusion of Choice. *Autism in Adulthood*. https://doi.org/10.1089/aut.2020.0043

Pellicano, E., & Burr, D. (2012). When the world becomes 'too real': A Bayesian explanation of autistic perception. *Trends in Cognitive Sciences*, **16**(10), 504–510. https://doi.org/10.1016/j.tics.2012.08.009

Petrolini, V., Rodríguez-Armendariz, E., & Vicente, A. (2023). Autistic camouflaging across the spectrum. *New Ideas in Psychology*, **68**, 100992. https://doi.org/10.1016/j.newideapsych.2022.100992

Radulski, E. M. (2022). Conceptualising Autistic Masking, Camouflaging, and Neurotypical Privilege: Towards a Minority Group Model of Neurodiversity. *Human Development*, **66**(2), 113–127. https://doi.org/10.1159/000524122

Rifai, O. M., Fletcher-Watson, S., Jiménez-Sánchez, L., & Crompton, C. J. (2022). Investigating Markers of Rapport in Autistic and Nonautistic Interactions. *Autism in Adulthood*, **4**(1), 3–11. https://doi.org/10.1089/aut.2021.0017

Rose, K. (2023). Autistic Masking and Autistic Burnout. *The Autistic Advocate*. https://theautisticadvocate.com/autistic-masking/

Rowland, S. (2020). *S.E.N.D. In The Clowns: Essential Autism / ADHD Family Guide*. Hashtag Press.

Snyder, M. (1987). *Public appearances, Private realities: The psychology of self-monitoring*. WH Freeman/Times Books/Henry Holt & Co.

Solazzo, S., Kojovic, N., Robain, F., & Schaer, M. (2021). Measuring the Emergence of Specific Abilities in Young Children with Autism Spectrum Disorders: The Example of Early Hyperlexic Traits. *Brain Sciences*, **11**(6), 692. https://doi.org/10.3390/brainsci11060692

Spaeth, E., & Pearson, A. (2021). *A Reflective Analysis on Neurodiversity and Student Wellbeing: Conceptualising Practical Strategies for Inclusive Practice* [Preprint]. PsyArXiv. https://doi.org/10.31234/osf.io/dc3gw

Stark, E., Stacey, J., Mandy, W., Kringelbach, M. L., & Happé, F. (2021a). Autistic Cognition: Charting Routes to Anxiety. *Trends in Cognitive Sciences*, **25**(7), 571–581. https://doi.org/10.1016/j.tics.2021.03.014

Stark, E., Stacey, J., Mandy, W., Kringelbach, M. L., & Happé, F. (2021b). 'Uncertainty attunement' has explanatory value in understanding autistic anxiety. *Trends in Cognitive Sciences*, **25**(12), 1011–1012. https://doi.org/10.1016/j.tics.2021.09.006

Williams, G. L., Wharton, T., & Jagoe, C. (2021). Mutual (Mis)understanding: Reframing Autistic Pragmatic "Impairments" Using Relevance Theory. *Frontiers in Psychology*, **12**. https://www.frontiersin.org/articles/10.3389/fpsyg.2021.616664

# Chapter 12

Adkin, T. (2023). Mask on, Mask off: How the common understanding of Autistic masking is creating another mask. *Emergent Divergence*. https://emergentdivergence.com/2023/05/08/mask-on-mask-off-how-the-common-understanding-of-autistic-masking-is-creating-another-mask/?fbclid=IwAR3z6SxYtoD9OYy3Ldedo2OXFHXfHv69WMmjTQ-rZoBCwUwp4I8161rBWkc

Beardon, L. (2022). 'Autopia': A vision for autistic acceptance and belonging. *In The Routledge International Handbook of Critical Autism Studies*. Routledge.

Botha, M. (2020). *Autistic community connectedness as a buffer against the effects of minority stress*. University of Surrey.

Botha, M., Hanlon, J., & Williams, G. (2020). *Does language matter? Identity-first versus person-first language use in autism research: A response to Vivanti*.

Bottema-Beutel, K., Kapp, S. K., Lester, J. N., Sasson, N. J., & Hand, B. N. (2020). Avoiding ableist language: Suggestions for autism researchers. *Autism in Adulthood*.

Brach, T. (2000). *Radical self-acceptance* (Unabridged). Sounds True.

Bronfenbrenner, U. (1977). Toward an experimental ecology of human development. *American Psychologist*, **32**(7), 513.

Chapman, L., Rose, K., Hull, L., & Mandy, W. (2022). "I want to fit in… but I don't want to change myself fundamentally": A qualitative exploration of the relationship between masking and mental health for autistic teenagers. *Research in Autism Spectrum Disorders*, **99**, 102069. https://doi.org/10.1016/j.rasd.2022.102069

Cook, J., Crane, L., Bourne, L., Hull, L., & Mandy, W. (2021). Camouflaging in an everyday social context: An interpersonal recall study. *Autism*, 1362361321992641. https://doi.org/10.1177/1362361321992641

Cook, J., Crane, L., Hull, L., Bourne, L., & Mandy, W. (2022). Self-reported camouflaging behaviours used by autistic adults during everyday social interactions. *Autism*, **26**(2), 406–421. https://doi.org/10.1177/13623613211026754

Fricker, M. (2007). Epistemic injustice: Power and the ethics of knowing. https://books.google.co.uk/books?hl=en&lr=&id=lncSDAAAQBAJ&oi=fnd&pg=PR9&dq=Fricker,+M.+Epistemic+injustice+:+power+and+the+ethics+of+knowing.+Oxford:+Oxford+University+Press%3B+2007.+&ots=3fJeUPHdO-&sig=YfmkI6737W45ABxUXAy-3tVYRuc

Gulley, K., & Hammond, T. (2022). Autistic Voices: This Was Never About ABA. *The Kisha Project*. https://thekishaproject.com/aba/

Higgins, J. M., Arnold, S. R., Weise, J., Pellicano, E., & Trollor, J. N. (2021). Defining autistic burnout through experts by lived experience: Grounded Delphi method investigating# AutisticBurnout. *Autism*, **25**(8), 2356–2369.

Hull, L., Petrides, K. V., Allison, C., Smith, P., Baron-Cohen, S., Lai, M. C., & Mandy, W. (2017). "Putting on My Best Normal": Social Camouflaging in Adults with Autism Spectrum Conditions. *Journal of Autism and Developmental Disorders*. https://doi.org/10.1007/s10803-017-3166-5

Hull, L., Petrides, K. V., & Mandy, W. (2020). Cognitive Predictors of Self-Reported Camouflaging in Autistic Adolescents. Autism Research.

Jellett, R., & Flower, R. L. (2023). How can psychologists meet the needs of autistic adults? *Autism*. https://doi.org/10.1177/13623613221147346

Lam, G. Y. H., Sabnis, S., Migueliz Valcarlos, M., & Wolgemuth, J. R. (2021). A Critical Review of Academic Literature Constructing Well-Being in Autistic Adults. *Autism in Adulthood*, **3**(1), 61–71. https://doi.org/10.1089/aut.2020.0053

Lilley, R., Lawson, W., Hall, G., Mahony, J., Clapham, H., Heyworth, M., Arnold, S. R., Trollor, J. N., Yudell, M., & Pellicano, E. (2022). 'A way to be me': Autobiographical reflections of autistic adults diagnosed in mid-to-late adulthood. *Autism*, **26**(6), 1395–1408. https://doi.org/10.1177/13623613211050694

Miller, D., Rees, J., & Pearson, A. (2021). "Masking Is Life": Experiences of Masking in Autistic and Nonautistic Adults. *Autism in Adulthood*, **3**(4), 330–338. https://doi.org/10.1089/aut.2020.0083

Milton, D., & Sims, T. (2016). How is a sense of well-being and belonging constructed in the accounts of autistic adults? *Disability & Society*, **31**(4), 520–534.

Montgomery, C. (2021). Wolfensberger at the Door. *Cal's Blog: A Blog about Disability*. https://montgomerycal.wordpress.com

Natri, H. M., Abubakare, O., Asasumasu, K., Basargekar, A., Beaud, F., Botha, M., Bottema-Beutel, K., Brea, M. R., Brown, L. X. Z., Burr, D. A., Cobbaert, L., Dabbs, C., Denome, D., Rosa, S. D. R., Doherty, M., Edwards, B., Edwards, C., Liszk, S. E., Elise, F., … Zisk, A. H. (2023). Anti-ableist language is fully compatible with high-quality autism research: Response to S inger et al. (2023). *Autism Research*, **16**(4), 673–676. https://doi.org/10.1002/aur.2928

Pavlopoulou, G. (2020). A Good Night's Sleep: Learning About Sleep From Autistic Adolescents' Personal Accounts. *Frontiers in Psychology*, **11**, 583868. https://doi.org/10.3389/fpsyg.2020.583868

Pearson, A., & Rose, K. (2021). A Conceptual Analysis of Autistic Masking: Understanding the Narrative of Stigma and the Illusion of Choice. *Autism in Adulthood*. https://doi.org/10.1089/aut.2020.0043

Pearson, A., Rose, K., & Rees, J. (2023). 'I felt like I deserved it because I was autistic': Understanding the impact of interpersonal victimisation in the lives of autistic people. *Autism*, **27**(2), 500–511. https://doi.org/10.1177/13623613221104546

Raymaker, D. M., Teo, A. R., Steckler, N. A., Lentz, B., Scharer, M., Delos Santos, A., Kapp, S. K., Hunter, M., Joyce, A., & Nicolaidis, C. (2020). "Having all of your internal resources exhausted beyond measure and being left with no clean-up crew": Defining autistic burnout. *Autism in Adulthood*, **2**:2, 132–143. https://doi.org/10.1089/aut.2019.0079

Riccio, A., Kapp, S. K., Jordan, A., Dorelien, A. M., & Gillespie-Lynch, K. (2021). How is autistic identity in adolescence influenced by parental disclosure decisions and perceptions of autism? *Autism*, **25**(2), 374–388. https://doi.org/10.1177/1362361320958214

Simmonds, M. (Director). (2021). *Autism and the Black community*. https://www.youtube.com/watch?v=LW-C_MVxNEU

Singer, A., Lutz, A., Escher, J., & Halladay, A. (2023). A full semantic toolbox is essential for autism research and practice to thrive. *Autism Research*, **16**(3), 497–501. https://doi.org/10.1002/aur.2876

Todres, L. (2005). Clarifying the life-world: Descriptive phenomenology. *Qualitative Research in Health Care*, 104–124.

Waisman, T. T. (2020). *How Higher Education Leaders, Faculty Members, and Professional Staff Can Enhance Services and Outcomes for Autistic Students*.

Walker, N., & Raymaker, D. M. (2021). Toward a Neuroqueer Future: An Interview with Nick Walker. *Autism in Adulthood*, **3**(1), 5–10. https://doi.org/10.1089/AUT.2020.29014.NJW

Zimmerman, J. (2022). Jordyn Zimmerman's Remarks to the Interagency Autism Coordinating Committee. *Communication FIRST*. https://communicationfirst.org/jordyn-zimmermans-remarks-to-the-interagency-autism-coordinating-committee/

# Chapter 13

Ai, W., Cunningham, W. A., & Lai, M.-C. (2022). Reconsidering autistic 'camouflaging'as transactional impression management. *Trends in Cognitive Sciences*.

Alcorn, A., McGeown, S., Aitken, D., Mandy, W., Murray, F., & Fletcher-Watson, S. (2023). *Learning About Neurodiversity at School: Key concepts for communicating neurodiversity to primary school children, from the LEANS project participatory design process*. International Society for Autism Research, Stockholm. https://www.research.ed.ac.uk/en/publications/learning-about-neurodiversity-at-school-key-concepts-for-communic

ASAN. (2009). Horrific Autism Speaks "I am Autism" ad transcript. *Autistic Self Advocacy Network*. https://autisticadvocacy.org/2009/09/horrific-autism-speaks-i-am-autism-ad-transcript/

Belcher, H. L., Morein-Zamir, S., Mandy, W., & Ford, R. M. (2022). Camouflaging Intent, First Impressions, and Age of ASC Diagnosis in Autistic Men and Women. *Journal of Autism and Developmental Disorders*, **52**(8), 3413–3426. https://doi.org/10.1007/s10803-021-05221-3

Botha, M., & Cage, E. (2022). "Autism research is in crisis": A mixed method study of researcher's constructions of autistic people and autism research. *Frontiers in Psychology*, **13**, 1050897. https://doi.org/10.3389/fpsyg.2022.1050897

Brownlow, C., Lawson, W., Pillay, Y., Mahony, J., & Abawi, D. (2021). "Just Ask Me": The Importance of Respectful Relationships Within Schools. *Frontiers in Psychology*, **12**, 678264. https://doi.org/10.3389/fpsyg.2021.678264

Chambers, B. (2021). *A psalm for the wild-built (First Edition)*. Tordotcom, a Tom Doherty Associates Book.

Lai, M.-C., Hull, L., Mandy, W., Chakrabarti, B., Nordahl, C. W., Lombardo, M. V., Ameis, S. H., Szatmari, P., Baron-Cohen, S., Happé, F., & Livingston, L. A. (2020). Commentary: 'Camouflaging' in autistic people – reflection on Fombonne (2020). *Journal of Child Psychology and Psychiatry*, n/a(n/a). https://doi.org/10.1111/jcpp.13344

Livingston, L. A., & Happé, F. (2017). Conceptualising compensation in neurodevelopmental disorders: Reflections from autism spectrum disorder. *Neuroscience and Biobehavioral Reviews*. https://doi.org/10.1016/j.neubiorev.2017.06.005

Michael, C. (2021). Is Being Othered a Co-Occurring Condition of Autism? *Autism in Adulthood*. https://doi.org/10.1089/aut.2021.0019

Milton, D. E. M. (2012). On the ontological status of autism: The 'double empathy problem'. *Disability & Society*, **27**(6), 883–887.

Pearson, A., & Rose, K. (2021). A Conceptual Analysis of Autistic Masking: Understanding the Narrative of Stigma and the Illusion of Choice. *Autism in Adulthood*. https://doi.org/10.1089/aut.2020.0043

Pearson, A., Surtees, A., Crompton, C. J., Goodall, C., Pillai, D., Sedgewick, F., & Au-Yeung, S. K. (2022). Editorial: Addressing community priorities in autism research. *Frontiers in Psychology*, **13**, 1040446. https://doi.org/10.3389/fpsyg.2022.1040446

Pellicano, E., Dinsmore, A., & Charman, T. (2014). What should autism research focus upon? Community views and priorities from the United Kingdom. *Autism*, **18**(7), 756–770. https://doi.org/10.1177/1362361314529627

Petrolini, V., Rodríguez-Armendariz, E., & Vicente, A. (2023). Autistic camouflaging across the spectrum. *New Ideas in Psychology*, **68**, 100992. https://doi.org/10.1016/j.newideapsych.2022.100992

Rose, K., & Vivian, S. (2020). *Regarding the use of Dehumanising Rhetoric*. https://theautisticadvocate.com/2020/02/regarding-the-use-of-dehumanising-rhetoric/

# Glossary

| | |
|---|---|
| **AAB** | African American / Black |
| **AAC** | Augmented and Alternative Communication<br>▪ A variety of methods/devices that enable a non/semi speaker to communicate through means alternative to mouth words |
| **ABA** | Applied Behaviour Analysis<br>▪ A controversial yet widely used form of behavioural intervention with a minimal evidence base |
| **Ableism** | Discrimination in favour of people described as able-bodied |
| **ACC** | Autistic Community Connectedness |
| **Acceptance** | In relation to the advoc8 framework: to understand the self and to be understood by others - inducing a level of internal and external acceptance |
| **ACEs** | Adverse Childhood Experiences |
| **Adaptive Morphing** | Describes the process of identity monitoring in autistic people as a non-intentional, safety-driven adaptation<br>▪ Coined by Wenn Lawson (2020) |
| **ADHD** | Attention Deficit and Hyperactivity Disorder |
| **ADI-R** | Autism Diagnostic Interview Revised Version |
| **ADOS** | Autistic Diagnostic Observation Schedule II |
| **Advoc8 Framework Objectives** | The Four As: acceptance, agency, autonomy and authenticity<br>▪ Rose (2020) |
| **Affordances** | A way of describing the relationship between autistic sensory processing and the outside world which acknowledges and validates differences in these interactions |
| **Agency** | The capacity for someone to understand their choices |

| | |
|---|---|
| **Alexithymia** | A disconnect or delay between the brain and emotions/an emotional experience |
| **Androgens** | Natural or synthetic hormones which regulate development and maintenance of male characteristics e.g Testosterone |
| **Anthropomorphism** | Assigning human characteristics, motivations, or behaviours to non-humans, inanimate objects or natural phenomena |
| **Anti Semitism** | Hostility, prejudice or discrimination against Jews |
| **AQ** | Autism Quotient |
| **AS** | Asperger Syndrome<br>■ A differential diagnosis within the same broad category of autism which was removed from the DSM in 2013 |
| **Assimilation** | The act or process of blending in with others in order to avoid negative social consequences, and become part of a group, country, society etc |
| **Autgender** | A concept used to describe how gender can be inherently intertwined with the experience of being autistic |
| **Autistic Culture** | The shared experiences, beliefs and values of autistic people, largely rooted in a shared understanding of the neurodiversity paradigm |
| **Autistic Embodiment** | The feeling and experience of being Autistic |
| **Bullying** | Repeated and intentional actions which harm another individual or group |
| **c-PTSD** | Complex PTSD an response to an accumulation of traumatic experiences<br>■ Additionally defined through the presence of emotional and interpersonal difficulties ie. internalised shame, worthlessness, difficulties connecting to others |
| **Camouflaging** | Autistic self-monitoring and the attempt to 'hide' or 'fit in' within social situations<br>■ Preferred term: masking |

| | |
|---|---|
| **CASS** | Contextual Assessment of Social Skills |
| **CAT-Q** | Camouflaging Autistic traits Questionnaire<br>■ Designed to examine self-reported features of masking in autistic people |
| **Challenging Behaviour** | A term used to describe behaviours which are commonly the expressions of autistic distress |
| **Chromonormativity** | The expectation that people will progress through a set of life stages at a particular time, following a particular set of expectations |
| **Cisgender** | Someone who identifies with the gender assigned to them at birth |
| **CMNAB** | Conceptual Model of Autistic Burnout<br>■ Coined by Mantazala and colleagues (2022), CMAB suggests a relationship between personal demands and resources, mental strain, wellbeing and additional variables. |
| **Code Switching** | Actively altering how you present to the world in order to 'fit in'. |
| **Cognitive** | Connected with thinking or conscious mental processes |
| **Coke Bottle Effect** | A term used to describe the release of suppressed distress and anxiety experienced by a child transitioning from an unsafe environment (such as school) to a 'safe' environment (such as home). Analogous to shaking a bottle of cola and releasing the lid. |
| **Complex Trauma** | Traumatic experiences involving the accumulation of multiple events throughout a lifetime |
| **Computational Impression Management** | Impression management underpinned by socio-cognitive predictive processes |
| **Confirmation bias** | The tendency to interpret or look for information which supports your current beliefs or ideals, and ignore information which might support alternative views |

| | |
|---|---|
| **Conservation of Resources theory** | A theory that describes the motivation that drives humans to maintain their current resources and also seek new resources<br><br>   ■ Hobfall 1989 |
| **Critical Race Theory** | A theory and social movement which views race not as a biological feature, but as a result of social constructs used to differentiate human beings<br><br>   ■ Coined by Kimberlé Crenshaw. |
| **Cross-Neurotype Theory of Mind** | A theory which acknowledges the differences between ND and NT communication, and therefore states that communication 'impairment' is irrelevant, as both groups are equally 'impaired' and equally to blame for any communication issues, so therefore neither is 'wrong' but methods of communication are simply different<br><br>   ■ Beardon |
| **Cultural Competency** | Knowledge of another culture's conventions and experiences<br><br>   ■ Jellett |
| **CYP** | Children and Young People |
| **Dehumanisation** | The process of depriving a person or group of human qualities |
| **Demarcation** | The setting of boundaries or limits to provide separation and/or distinction |
| **DEP** | The Double Empathy Problem<br><br>   ■ The concept that humans are very bad at seeing things from others perspectives, when experiences are very different<br><br>   ■ Milton |
| **Depersonalisation** | When an individual who is part of a larger collective, becomes somewhat interchangeable with another, based on modelling of certain features |

| | |
|---|---|
| **Dialectical Attunement** | The concept that 'I', the self, is a dynamic construction made of subjective and objective factors both related to internal processes and the bi-directional interactions you have externally with multiple different elements. |
| **Dialectical attunement** | is the awareness of those elements and the attempt to harmonise them into one consolidated persona<br>■ Bolis |
| **DISCO** | Diagnostic Interview for Social and Communication Disorders<br>■ Developed by Wing and Gould |
| **Disconnect Theory** | The concept that individuals use context-specific information to inform the way they will act in that context, rather than engaging with all contexts in the same way.<br>■ Ragins 2008 |
| **DMH** | Dialectical Misattunement Hypothesis<br>■ A concept which acknowledges communication difficulties can occur due to misalignment of both parties |
| **Double Consciousness** | The experience of experiencing being racially othered, leading to heightened self-monitoring and the projection of a more acceptable version of yourself to white people, across multiple contexts<br>■ Coined by DuBois |
| **Dramaturgy** | Concept which describes our interactions with others as featuring a 'front' and 'back' element, which would impact on the 'performance' created for both the actor and the observer<br>■ Coined by Goffman. |
| **DSM** | Diagnostic and Statistical Manual |
| **Dysregulation** | The inability to control or regulate emotional responses |

| | |
|---|---|
| **Ecological Systems Approach** | A theory which views child development as a complex system of relationships, all interacting on multiple levels, and affected by cultural values, laws and customs. Brofenbrenner proposed that an individual's environment was composed of five systems; the microsystem, the mesosystem, the exosystem, the macrosystem and the chronosystem<br><br>■ Brofenbrenner (1974). N.B This theory was later redefined by Brofenbrenner (1994) as the Bioecological Model. |
| **Egocentrism** | Extreme self-bias, often at the expense of or in disregard of others |
| **Eight Dimensions** | Eight aspects of need identified as part of an experience sensitive approach for Autistic people, developed from Todres' 'life world' work<br><br>■ Pavlopoulou, 2020 |
| **Emancipation** | The act of freeing or being freed |
| **EMB** | Extreme Male Brain theory<br><br>■ Coined by Professor Simon Baron-Cohen, this theory suggests that the features used to identify autistic people are extreme manifestations of traits associated with a 'male brain type'. |
| **Enactivist Approach** | Acknowledges the interaction between the social world and our biology, in shaping who we are and how we think |
| **Endemic** | Something which is only found in a certain locality or area, or is common to a certain situation |
| **Epistemic Injustice** | Refers to the creation of knowledge about a particular group or individual that marginalises and misrepresents their experiences |
| **Epistemic Struggle** | The struggle faced by autistic people as they attempt to establish their own understanding of their experiences, in the face of outsider conceptualisations<br><br>■ Bertilssdotter Rosqvist and Jackson-Perry |

| | |
|---|---|
| **Essentialist Approach** | A view that any entity has innate and universal qualities<br><br>■ ie. Assumes that disability must have a biological cause, so therefore all the problems a disabled person faces can be attributed to the disability, and they are a victim of it. |
| **Eugenics** | The study or practice of attempting to improve the human gene pool through encouraging reproduction in those who have 'desirable' traits, and discouraging or actively preventing reproduction in those with 'undesirable' traits |
| **Executive Function** | The ability to multitask, focus attention, plan and execute tasks<br><br>■ Usually considered through a normative lens without accounting for mitigating factors |
| **Existentialism** | A philosophical view which identifies people as having free will, and the responsibility to make meaningful, authentic choices in their lives |
| **Exosystem** | The Exosystem consists of any environment which indirectly impacts an individual's life. For example governing agencies<br><br>■ See Bronfenbrenner's Ecological Systems model. |
| **FAP\*** | Female Autism Phenotype<br><br>■ A problematic theory which states that women are likely to be underrepresented in autism diagnostics due to a lack of recognition in the way in which expression of autistic traits<br>*Also a slang term for masturbation |
| **Fawning** | An aspect of masking whereby an individual suppresses their own need/identity, instead presenting a compliant and pliable demeanour |
| **Flow** | A neurodiversity affirming term defining Autistic people's deep attention states<br><br>■ Unpreferred term: Hyperfocus |

| | |
|---|---|
| **FPE** | Female Protective Effect<br>■ This theory suggests that genetic expression may account for differences seen in males and females in regard to autism diagnosis |
| **Gatekeeping** | To limit or control access to something<br>■ For example, self-identified autistics not gaining access to support due to lack of a formal diagnosis |
| **Generational Trauma** | The transmission of traumatic processes, and their effects, through multiple generations of a family<br>■ e.g cycles of abuse and the associated normalisation |
| **Genetic** | Relating to your genetic code or genes |
| **Genetic Predisposition** | Refers to an increased chance that you will develop a certain trait or disease, based on your genetic code |
| **Hate Relationships** | Violence and abuse from people known to the victim, but not well enough to be classified as a close interpersonal relationship i.e. neighbour |
| **Hermeneutical injustice** | The experience of being excluded from a significant area of your social experience and/or understanding, due to prejudice preventing shared resources for social interpretation<br>■ e.g. autism being framed as a deficit defined by perceived impairments in social communication, social imagination, and stereotypy compared to the non-autistic population |
| **Hermeneutics** | The theory and methodology of interpretation, especially within biblical texts, wisdom literature and philosophical texts |
| **Heterogeneous** | Consisting of different qualities |
| **Homogenous** | Consisting of the same qualities |
| **Homophobia** | The fear or dislike of someone based on prejudice and negative beliefs about lesbian, gay or bi people, or those who are perceived to be. |
| **Hyper-Empathy** | Intensely feeling the emotional states of others |

| | |
|---|---|
| **Hypersensitivity** | Being more sensitive to aspects of your sensory environment, either internally or externally. |
| **Hyposensitivity** | Being less sensitive to aspects of your sensory environment, either internally or externally. |
| **Identify First** | The preferred usage of terms referring to an individual regarding their disability: Autistic person |
| **IDT** | Interactive Drawing Test |
| **Implicit Bias** | Refers to unconscious attitudes or stereotypes which affect the way we see and interact with the world<br>■ Also known as unconscious bias. For example, seeing a Black man walking in your direction and crossing the street because you unconsciously associate Black individuals as violent |
| **Impression Management (IM)** | A term used to refer to the process of attempting to control the way that other people perceive us through the way we present ourselves to them |
| **Interlocutor** | Someone who is taking part in a conversation |
| **Intersectionality** | The interconnected/overlapping social characteristics such as disability, ethnicity, race, sex, gender, sexual preference |
| **Invisible Stigma** | Those which can easily be concealed resulting in the ability to 'pass for normal' and avoid negative outcomes associated with stigmatisation |
| **IPV** | Interpersonal Victimisation<br>■ Violence and abuse which occurs within a close personal relationship i.e. friends, family members and partners, colleagues, carers or teachers |
| **IQ** | Intelligence Quota |
| **Job Demands-Resources Model** | A model which states that when job demands are high, and job resources/positives are low; stress and burnout will increase.<br>■ Bakker et al, 2007 |

| | |
|---|---|
| **Kinematics** | A subfield of physics which describes the motion of points, bodies, and body systems, without reference to the causes of motion (i.e forces). Often referred to as the "geometry of motion" |
| **LD / Learning Disability** | A difficulty with learning or understanding certain kinds of information, learning particular skills, or needing help with various aspects of daily living<br><br>▪ Also referred to as intellectual disability. Measured by an IQ score lower than 70, though this is not always tested when people are labelled as such. |
| **LGBTQIA+** | Lesbian, Gay, Bisexual, Transgender, Queer, Questioning, Intersex, Asexual, Plus (to encompass all gender identities and sexual orientations which letters and words cannot yet fully describe) |
| **Macrosystem** | The macrosystem encompasses all cultural and societal elements which can impact an individual. At this level, the macrosystem can have direct or indirect impact on the individual, but the individual is unlikely to be able to impact the macrosystem.<br><br>▪ See Bronfenbrenner's Ecological Systems model. |
| **Marginalisation** | The treatment of a person, group, or concept as insignificant or peripheral, that leads to them being excluded from society |
| **Masking** | A developmental response to stigma and trauma involving suppressing and projecting aspects of identity in order to maintain safety<br><br>▪ Unpreferred term: Camouflaging |
| **Medical Model of Disability** | A focus on disability that looks at disability as a 'problem' that needs to be fixed |
| **Meltdown** | The experience of significant distress or overwhelm manifesting in an involuntary response characterised by an outpouring of anxiety and externally directed energy |

| Mesosystem | The Mesosystem encompasses all interactions between an individual's microsystems. For example, interactions between parents and teachers. |
|---|---|
| | ▪ See Bronfenbrenner's Ecological Systems model. |
| Meta-Synthesis | A methodology which brings together a large quantity of (qualitative) research, in order to form new interpretations within a specific field of study |
| Microaggressions | A form of prejudice which where everyday actions or behaviours reflect our internal biases, and cause harm to marginalised groups |
| | ▪ Ie. Asking a Black person where they are "really from", or documentation which only refers to the gender binary at the exclusion of others |
| Microsystem | The Microsystem is the immediate environment around an individual, which also makes it the most influential. For example, family and school. |
| | ▪ See Bronfenbrenner's Ecological Systems model. |
| Mimicry | The action of copying behaviour, actions or sounds of another person. |
| Minority Stress | Excess stress experienced by marginalised people as a result of a mismatch between the world which exists, and their experiences within it |
| | ▪ Proposed by Myer (2003) |
| Monotropism | An Autistic theory of the Autistic experience framed around the use of attention and sensory processing, describing the difficulties Autistic people have transitioning between deep states of attention |
| | ▪ See: Polytropism |
| Moratorium | A period of time where activity is suspended |
| Motor Resonance | Activation in the motor system in response to watching another person perform a movement |

| Neoliberal | A capitalist political ideal which has a strong focus on economic growth and 'free' market, as a means to achieve progress, and a reduction of government to shift from public to private sector control<br><br>   ■ Neoliberalism encourages individual responsibility often to the cost of individual health |
|---|---|
| **Neural Processes** | The biological processes which occur throughout out nervous system |
| **Neurobiology** | The interactions between and interconnectivity of neurological processes and biological processes in the human body |
| **Neurocosmopolitan** | An ideal whereby we not only accept the neurodiversity paradigm, but seek to actively embrace, honour and preserve neurodiversity<br><br>   ■ Coined by Nick Walker and Ralph Savarese |
| **Neurodivergence** | Groups of people whose communication, processing, perception and interaction permanently diverges from what would be considered 'typical' in a multitude of ways, but similarly enough collectively for them to be considered an identifiable group |
| **Neurominority** | Groups which share a similar form of neurodivergence, which is immutable and shapes who they are, and is responded to by the outside world with stigma and othering |
| **Neuronormative** | A focus on the needs of people that might be considered neurotypical |
| **Neuroqueering** | The practice of queering (subverting, defying, disrupting, liberating oneself from) neuronormativity and heteronormativity simultaneously.<br><br>   ■ Coined by Nick Walker |
| **Non-Binary** | An umbrella term to describe people whose gender identity does not sit comfortably within the gender binary of 'man' or 'woman'. |
| **Normative** | Something which relates to the 'norm' or standard. |

| | |
|---|---|
| **Oestrogens** | Natural or synthetic hormones which regulate development and maintenance of female characteristics e.g Oestrogen |
| **Othering** | Being treated differently on the basis of perceived differences ie. social style and neurocognitive functioning |
| **Pathology** | To regard or treat as psychologically abnormal and/ or represent something as a disease. |
| **PECs** | Picture Exchange Communication System<br>  ■ A reductive Applied Behavioural Analysis communication tool that mostly limits communication to a series of requests decided by the PECs facilitator. |
| **Person First Language** | The current professional usage of terms referring to an individual regarding their disability: Person with Autism |
| **Phenomenology** | The philosophical study of human consciousness and self-awareness |
| **Polygenic** | Poly' meaning many and 'genic' involving genes - many diseases are polygenic or complex |
| **Polygenic Risk Score** | An estimation of how an individual's genetics will affect their relative risk for a certain disease |
| **Polytropism** | The concept that Neurotypical brains transition more easily between states of attention, but are less able than Autistic to focus at depth<br>  ■ See: Monotropism |
| **Polyvictimisation** | The experience of multiple types of victimisation |
| **Positive Behavioural Support** | A framework which was developed to reduce 'challenging behaviour' through reinforcement of normative behaviour |
| **Projection of Acceptability** | A self-preservation tool grounded in attempting to predict and meet the expectations of others, and how autistic people, in order to avoid being further stigmatised, may unconsciously and consciously play into those expectations<br>  ■ Developed by Kieran Rose (2020) |

| Proprioception | The sense that lets a person know where their body is in space and time and in relation to objects |
| --- | --- |
| | ■ One of the three commonly unrecognised sensory processes |
| Prototypical | Something which represents an original on which others are modelled or derived from |
| Psycho-Emotional Disablement | Focuses on the relationship between disabled people and others or with themselves, where the environment, societal norms, and invalidation, have a destructive impact on autistic lives |
| | ■ Milton and Sims |
| Psychoanalysis | A set of theories and therapeutic techniques which focus on the unconscious mind. |
| | ■ Developed by Sigmund Freud |
| Psychogenic | Something which originates in the mind through mental or emotional processing |
| Psychosocial Development | A theory which describes the development of self and identity through 8 specific stages |
| | ■ Developed by Erik Erikson |
| PTSD | Post-Traumatic Stress Disorder |
| Public Stigma | Where the direct consequences of stigma result in the discrimination against stigmatised people and groups |
| Qualitative | Relating to information which cannot be easily measured in a numerical way |
| Quantitative | Relating to number or quantity |
| RAADS | Ritvo Autism Asperger Diagnostic Scale |
| Racialisation | The process through which racial identities / groups are formed |
| Racism | A form of discrimination or prejudice based on race |
| Radical Self-Acceptance | The concept of radical self-acceptance is based in Buddhist philosophy, and focuses on developing an embodied awareness of Self, and by doing so, freeing ourselves from shame and suffering |
| Reciprocity | An exchange with others for mutual benefit |

| | |
|---|---|
| **Refrigerator Mother Theory** | The belief that "the precipitating factor in infantile autism is the parents wish that the child should not exist" given the "burden" of caring for an autistic child due to their behavioural demands |
| **RMET** | Reading the Mind in the Eyes test |
| **RMET-C** | Reading the Mind in the Eyes test - Child Version |
| **RRBs** | Repetitive behaviours |
| **SCDC** | Social and Communication Disorders Checklist |
| **Schemas** | A representation used to support the explanation of an experience or reality |
| **Schizophrenia** | One of a number of related 'Spectrum conditions', Schizophrenia describes the perception of different realities via a fragmented sense of self, which may cause distress exacerbated by societal barriers. |
| **SCQ** | Social Communication Questionnaire |
| **Scripting** | Creating scripts and rehearsing interactions in order to minimise perceptions of awkwardness or social-misalignment |
| **SCT** | Social Categorisation Theory <br> ■ Explains how we categorise people around us in order to identify and understand them, and in doing so we have a reference point to understand our own place in the world |
| **Self-Stigma** | Where the stigmatised person internalises negative perceptions into their own self-concept, leading to the acceptance of lower status, and the belief that it is deserved |
| **Self-Concept** | The emergence of the ability to recognise yourself as an individual being |
| **Self-medication** | The use of mediation as a way to manage the effects of masking |
| **Self-Monitoring (SM)** | A term used to refer to the process of attempting to control the way that other people perceive us through the way we present ourselves to them |

| | |
|---|---|
| **Self-Perception Theory** | A theory that suggests that we learn about ourselves, and the beliefs and attitudes, through observing our own behaviour in the context in which it occurs, whether this be in private or in interaction with others<br><br>■ Developed by Bem (1972) |
| **Self-Regulation** | The ability to control your own behaviour, emotions and thoughts without external support |
| **Self-Regulatory Focus** | A term used to describe the balance between our actual self, and the self we feel we should appear to others<br><br>■ Higgins (1987) |
| **Sensory Trauma** | The experience of sensory bombardment and overwhelm due to the inability to escape a chronic stressor, as well as the invalidation of this experience |
| **Sexually dimorphism** | When individuals of different sexes with the same species are very different from one another |
| **SIT** | Social Identity Theory<br><br>■ Proposes that during our lifetime, we adopt the identity of the groups to which we belong |
| **Social Model of Disability** | A focus on disability that recognises natural variations in human existence and looks to resolve external barriers to disabled people |
| **Socio-Cognitive** | The way in which learning occurs within a social context |
| **Socio-Ecological** | The interactions between society and the environment around us |
| **SRS** | Social Responsiveness Scale |
| **Sterilisation** | The act of making a living being unable to reproduce |
| **Stigma** | A set of negative and often unfair beliefs that a society or group of people have about something |
| **Stimming** | A form of autistic expression and self-regulation which may be observed as repetitive actions and/or sounds.<br><br>■ Also referred to as Self-Stimulating behaviours |

| | |
|---|---|
| **Strategic Essentialism** | A strategy used by minority groups, to create a coalition, which enables belonging and solidarity for the benefit of social action.<br>■ Spivak |
| **Suicidal ideation** | A broad term used to describe a wide range of contemplations and preoccupations with death and suicide |
| **Supercrip** | A stereotype of a disabled person who is able to 'overcome' their disability and accomplish an impressive task. Rooted in capitalist ideas of worth<br>■ i.e. Autism as a 'superpower' or a disabled person being 'inspirational' |
| **Suppression** | Suppressing aspects of self as part of the core aspects of masking<br>■ i.e. Redirecting or suppressing stims, emotional responses and sensory experiences, as well as suppression personal identity and expression |
| **Systemic racism** | Forms of racism which are pervasive and deeply embedded throughout systems, laws, policies and practices, established beliefs and attitudes, which perpetuates discrimination and harm to people of colour |
| **Testimonial Injustice** | The dismissal or discrediting of a person's experience due to their status<br>■ i.e. Believing that autistic people would not be able to reflect on their own experiences because of the difficulties we face relating to non-autistic people |
| **The Neurodiversity (ND) Paradigm** | A principle which acknowledges that neurodiversity is a natural form of human diversity. |
| **Theory of Symbolic Interaction** | A theory which views selfhood and identity as a relational process.<br>■ Coined by Mead & Bulmer |
| **TNB+** | Transgender, Non-Binary, Plus (to encompass all gender identities and sexual orientations which letters and words cannot yet fully describe) |

| | |
|---|---|
| **ToM** | Theory-of-Mind<br><br>&#9632; Coined by Baron-Cohen, ToM is described as the ability to think about mental states both our own and those of others. It encompasses the ability to attribute mental states (including emotions, beliefs, knowledge and desires) and recognise that others may have differing thoughts and beliefs. |
| **Transactional Impression Management** | The notion that impression management involves a relational component that may be impacted by differences between interlocutors<br><br>&#9632; Developed by Ai and colleagues |
| **Transdiagnostic Approach** | A approach by which a specific diagnostic label becomes less important, and we focus more on identifying and supporting specific needs |
| **Transgender** | An umbrella term to describe people whose gender is not the same as the sex they were assigned at birth |
| **Transphobia** | The fear or dislike of a person based on them being transgender or perceived as transgender |
| **Trauma** | A deeply disturbing, distressing, and/or harmful experience which causes long lasting emotional and psychological effects |
| **Triad of Impairments** | Three areas noted as 'impairments' by Wing and Gould in a seminal study of autistic characteristics: social interaction, language and stereotyped behaviour |
| **Tripartite Model of Masking** | A theory of camouflaging which explored experiences of self-suppression within social interactions, and proposed that camouflaging consisted of three key features: masking, assimilation and compensation |
| **Triple Consciousness** | A term used by some autistic scholars to explain the multi-layered IM processes that they engage in in navigating different identity relevant spaces.<br><br>&#9632; Used by Simmonds to describe the experience of being a Black autistic woman. |

| | |
|---|---|
| **Triple- A Intervention** | An intervention strategy developed for educators to increase understanding and support a more inclusive classroom environment, focusing on the 'Triple-A' of attention differences, sensory arousal differences and anxiety<br><br>   ■ Developed by Hanley et. al |
| **Uncertainty Attunement** | A re-framing of the term 'intolerance of uncertainty' which acknowledges the increased anxiety autistic people experience over unpredictable outcomes |
| **Utilitarian** | An ethical theory which determines right or wrong based on outcomes, focusing on the idea that the best ethical choice is the one which will produce the greatest good for the majority |
| **Visible Stigma** | Those which cannot (easily) be concealed e.g race or 'visible' disabilities |
| **White Supremacy** | The belief that white people are superior to those of other races |
| **WEIRD** | Western, educated, industrialised, rich and democratic |